A Final Promise

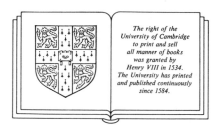

The right of the
University of Cambridge
to print and sell
all manner of books
was granted by
Henry VIII in 1534.
The University has printed
and published continuously
since 1584.

Cambridge University Press

Cambridge

New York   New Rochelle

Melbourne   Sydney

Frederick E. Hoxie

A Final Promise:
The Campaign
to Assimilate
the Indians,
    1880–1920

Published by the Press Syndicate of the University of Cambridge
The Pitt Building, Trumpington Street, Cambridge CB2 1RP
32 East 57th Street, New York, NY 10022, USA
10 Stamford Road, Oakleigh, Melbourne 3166, Australia

First published 1984 by the University of Nebraska Press
First paperback edition published by Cambridge University Press 1989

Printed in the United States of America

Library of Congress Cataloging in Publication Data
Hoxie, Frederick E., 1947–
A final promise.
Bibliography: p.
Includes index.
I. Indians of North America – Cultural assimilation.
2. Indians of North America – Government relations –
1869–1934.   I. Title.
E98.C89H68   1989   973'.0497   88-043432

ISBN 0-521-37987-3 (pbk)

Contents

For Elizabeth

Preface to
the Paperback Edition

Like many books, this one began with what seemed a simple question. I was curious to know what drove American leaders in the nineteenth century to design and implement laws that were so obviously flawed and so clearly damaging to the people they were supposed to help.

A Final Promise rests on the supposition that Indian–white relations are guided in part by the values and preoccupations of EuroAmerican culture. As they set about answering the "Indian Question," nineteenth century Congressmen, missionaries, and schoolmasters believed themselves to be engaged in both the tactics of Indian "uplift," and the strategy of cultural expansion. Their short term motivations may have been venal, benign, or humanitarian, but they were always mixed with long term ideas about the nature and future of American society. Old Lodge Skins, the Cheyenne elder in Thomas Berger's *Little Big Man* put it more simply: "White people," he declared, referring to soldiers, traders, missionaries and government agents, "are crazy."

In addition to exploring the broad concerns that made white people "crazy," this book argues that the nature of that craziness changed over time. In the late nineteenth century politicians and intellectuals spent a great deal of time thinking about how to incorporate previously alien peoples into what they thought of as a homogeneous society. As they engaged in this inquiry, their ideas changed. In general, they moved away from a faith in universal citizenship and general equality, and towards a more hierarchical view. White leaders were more pessimistic about social and political equality in 1920 than they were in 1880. Not surprisingly, during this same period reformers and politicians revised their thinking about assimilation in general and even redefined the term. This redefinition of terms both affected – and was affected by – shifts in federal programs for American Indians.

The joke in Old Lodge Skins's declaration that white people "are crazy," is the fact that government agents and schoolmasters regularly reported to their superiors that the *Indians* were crazy. Native people would not live by the clock or the calendar, they would not farm, they would not pray as Christians wanted them to, they would not cut their hair or wear pants. At most agencies there was a great chasm separating the values and aspirations of tribal people and those who attempted to "civilize" them. It is not too much of an exaggeration to say that each group thought the other was crazy.

But the "agents of civilization" had the upper hand and were willing to use force to set the terms for cross-cultural interaction. *A Final Promise* opens with the end of large-scale Plains warfare and the beginning of the federal government's effort to administer Indian communities according to a uniform set of principles. By 1920, this government effort had created the social, political and economic context for modern Indian life. *A Final Promise* traces the evolution of ideas and policy by focusing primarily on the non-Indians who wielded official power during this period. While this approach does not explore the many native stories of the era, it should assist us in understanding the environment Indian people were forced to inhabit.

Finally, both the origins of *A Final Promise* and Cambridge University Press's decision to publish a paperback edition of it suggest that American Indian history is not an exotic subfield or regional preoccupation. Despite their wrongheaded analyses, nineteenth century policymakers grappled with serious issues: the nature of American democracy and the meaning of equality. Their errors – and their conviction that they were correct – are profoundly instructive to anyone interested in the past. They teach us to be skeptical, they warn us to be humble, and above all they demonstrate that democracy is endangered when those affected by policy decisions have no opportunity to participate in the political process.

As in the original edition of *A Final Promise*, I am grateful to all who assisted me during the preparation of the manuscript and I remain pleased to acknowledge responsibility for any errors that may lie herein. In addition I wish to thank several people who encouraged the preparation of a paperback edition. Frank Smith of Cambridge University Press invited a proposal from me; I deeply appreciate his interest in my work. Also encouraging were William R. Swagerty, Michael D. Green, Mary Ryan, R. David Edmunds, Melissa Meyer, Harry Kersey, and Robert Williams, the last a man whom I have never met but whose support has been more than gracious. Finally, I must add my gratitude to Holly Hoxie whose support and unflagging commitment to the truth inspire me daily.

Frederick E. Hoxie
The Newberry Library

The conviction that everything that happens on earth must be comprehensible to man can lead to interpreting history by commonplaces. Comprehension does not mean denying the outrageous, deducing the unprecedented from precedents, or explaining phenomena by such analogies and generalities that the impact of reality and the shock of experience are no longer felt. It means, rather, examining and bearing consciously the burden which our century has placed on us—neither denying its existence nor submitting meekly to its weight. Comprehension, in short, means the unpremeditated, attentive facing up to, and resisting of, reality—whatever it may be.

Hannah Arendt, *The Origins of Totalitarianism*

Preface

From the time of the nation's founding, American politicians, missionaries, and reformers protested to their critics that warfare with the country's native inhabitants was only the regrettable first step in a process of assimilation. While others gloried in the annihilation of tribal peoples, pious leaders from Thomas Jefferson to William Lloyd Garrison asserted that the Indians, once "freed" from their "savage" heritage, would participate fully in the nation's institutions. This final promise rested on two assumptions. The first was clear: natives were savages. Whether "noble" or "godless," Native Americans existed outside the white man's world and were by definition ineligible for automatic membership in "civilized" society. Second, national leaders expected that the destruction of "savagery" and the expansion of Christian "civilization" would convert individual natives into docile believers in American progress. With these ideas in hand, the future appeared predictable. On some future day, the Indians would be surrounded, defeated, and somehow rendered eager to join the dominant culture.

Between 1860 and 1880, it became obvious that this old assimilationist commitment was about to be tested for the last time. With shocking speed, the Indians who had previously avoided American domination suffered complete military defeat. Every tribe and band was now encircled by a rising tide of farmers, miners, and entrepreneurs. That "future day" when "savagery" would meet its end was at hand.

What follows is an investigation of the effort to fulfill the Americans' final promise to the Indians. I will describe the process by which political leaders and their constituents adjusted to the reality that all natives would now live within the borders of the nation. This period of adjustment—during which Indians became an internal American minority group—is usually presented as an era of assimilation. According to the traditional view, the government in the late nineteenth century embarked on a wrong-headed but persistent campaign to push Native Americans into American citizenship and force them to adopt Anglo-American standards of landownership, dress, and behavior. Such an interpretation fails to recognize that the assimilation campaign consisted of two distinct phases.

In the first phase there was widespread interest in transforming Indians into "civilized" citizens. Fueled by the memory of the Civil War and a self-serving desire to dismantle the tribal domains, politicians and reformers fashioned an elaborate program to incorporate Native Americans into the nation. In the second phase, Americans altered much of that original program. Reacting to new, more pessimistic assessments of Indian abilities, as well as to the rising power of western politicians, policy makers redefined their objectives and altered the federal effort. They continued to work for the incorporation of Native Americans into the majority society, but they no longer sought to transform the Indians or to guarantee their equality. By 1920 a new, more pessimistic spirit governed federal action.

Understanding that the assimilation campaign passed through two stages—each marked by its own set of assumptions, expectations, and programmatic emphases—helps clarify the last century of the Native American experience. In the eighteenth and nineteenth centuries, those who conquered tribal lands and fought native peoples defended their actions with a promise to compensate their victims with full membership in a "civilized" nation. But as the assimilation program got underway, it became apparent that such compensation would be impossible. Not only did Indians resist the process, but complete acceptance of them demanded more of the nation's institutions, social values, and cultural life than the citizenry was willing to grant.

And so American leaders altered the terms of their pledge. As a consequence, modern Indians found themselves defined and treated as peripheral people—partial members of the commonwealth—and a web of attitudes, beliefs, and practices soon appeared to bind them in a state of economic dependence and political powerlessness. To be sure, Native Americans were incorporated into the nation, but their new status bore a greater resemblance to the position of the United States' other nonwhite peoples than it did to the "full membership" envisioned by nineteenth-century reformers. By 1920 they had become an American minority group, experiencing life on the fringes of what had come to be regarded as a "white man's land." The assimilation campaign was complete.

Today the dependence and powerlessness cultivated by the assimilation campaign continues to be a major theme in the life of Native American communities. Despite the reforms of the New Deal era and the legal victories of recent decades, federal actions continue to betray an ambivalence toward Indian equality. Educational programs regularly join poor curricula with low expectations, while legal protection and resource management occur in an atmosphere highly charged by economic pressure and fears of political backlash. Doubts concerning the abilities of native people and resistance from state and local governments undermine federal efforts. Policy goals are rarely clear or long-lasting. In this sense, the assimilation campaign has produced a legacy of racial distrust and exploitation we have thus far been unable to set aside.

There are two ways to illuminate the shifting history of the government's assimilation campaign in the late nineteenth and early twentieth centuries. The first is to concentrate on the administration of government policies. Native resistance, economic development, political realignment, and shifts in cultural perception affected the implementation of specific programs; these particular events deserve description and analysis.

But one must also take into account important changes that were occurring in the nation's larger political culture. In the early nineteenth century, most Americans envisioned their society as homogeneous. People were either "citizens" (members of society) or "savages" (those ineligible for citizenship). Although the United States was relatively open to immigration from overseas, the country's leaders usually insisted that newcomers adhere to Protestant, Anglo-Saxon standards of conduct. Blacks and Asians, like Indians, were for the most part barred from this society while most European immigrants were admitted.

In the 1880s and 1890s, as the nation was evolving into an industrial state and the stream of immigrants was growing in diversity, the old model of society seemed inappropriate. Policy makers began to imagine a new category of membership. They modified the old division between external "savages" and domestic citizens, for in their eyes homogeneity was no longer possible and groups of people could no longer be wholly included or wholly excluded from the country's institutions. In place of the old ideas, politicians and intellectuals began thinking that nonwhite minorities could be granted *partial* membership in the nation. In a complex, modern country, with its hierarchy of experts, managers, and workers, "aliens" could most easily and efficiently be incorporated into society's bottom ranks. In this way minorities could serve the dominant culture without qualifying for social and political equality. Not surprisingly, the new, more limited interpretation of Indian assimilation gained popularity during the first two decades of the new century, at the same time that the thoroughgoing segregation of blacks, the exclusion of Japanese immigrants, and the virtual suspension of immigration from southern and eastern Europe were winning popular approval. Clearly, a study of the Indian assimilation campaign should look beyond specific government programs and the problem of their administration to consider their relationship to broader changes in the United States' political culture.

My objective, then, is dual. First, I will describe the sources and effects of the campaign to bring all Indians inside the boundaries of the United States. That campaign produced the social and economic suffering that has been a central feature of Native American life in this century. Second, I will explain how the assimilation campaign was itself a reflection of America's move beyond a preoccupation with the Indians' "savagery" and toward the more complex outlook of our own time. When intellectuals and policy makers searched beyond the old certainty that Indians were savages, they initiated a lengthy process of reexamination and adjustment that is still underway.

Before proceeding, three disclaimers are in order. First, because I have focused on the behavior of white leaders, I have followed their interests and prejudices. Most thinkers and policy makers of the late nineteenth and early twentieth centuries assumed that the "Indian question" involved the trans-Mississippi West, and I have accepted this tendency to define national policy in terms of that region. I have therefore paid little attention to the many eastern tribes that my subjects ignored, and—like them—have treated Oklahoma as a special case with limited significance for national policy formulation.

Second, more than two-thirds of the text is devoted to the years after 1900. This is a function of the extensive secondary literature that already exists on the earlier period as well as a measure of the importance of the early twentieth century In the years after 1900 the assimilation campaign of the 1880s was fundamentally altered. During that process relationships between Indians and whites became fixed in ways that have persisted down to the present.

And third, I should make clear what this book is and is not. Native American history has traditionally been the province of two groups of scholars. Ethnohistorians have produced studies of tribal groups. Many of the best of these detail the impact of European cultures on Native American cultures. Such work has done a great deal to make native behavior understandable in non-Indian terms. Recently these efforts have gone further, to reveal the tribes' positive influence on white society. Nevertheless, such studies often fail to view the Indians' relations with whites as a clash of two complex cultures. Rather, their chief concern is with the process of native action in the face of a relentless and impersonal American expansion.

To understand the motives of non-Indians, one must look to a second body of historians, who describe the government's policies in a particular region or period. The fundamental concern of this group is usually the guilt or innocence of their subjects in the annihilation of Native American communities. The literature is filled with good and evil actors alternately winning and losing the day for the Indians, bringing on either the "final defeat" or a "new dawn." Very few students of white society have gone beyond this scenario to attempt to view Indian affairs in a broader, national context, and to ask, How did *this society*, at *this time*, produce *these ideas* and *these actions*?

It is as much a comment on the historical profession as on Native American historiography itself to point out that it is time for non-Indian historians to do for their own society what the anthropologists and ethnohistorians have been so eager to do for tribal peoples: to attempt to see attitudes and actions as expressions of a complex culture confronting an alien people in a rapidly changing environment. This effort carries my study beyond the sources typically employed in policy analysis—to popular literature, anthropological theory, and the history of education. Although the connections between these topics and specific programs might appear obscure, they are crucial to an understanding of the assimilation campaign. They indicate the nature of the environment politicians and bureaucrats inhabited and reveal the extent to which that environment shaped both the formulation and the administration of federal policy.

Because my primary focus is federal policy as a reflection of changes in white society, much of the influence of Native Americans has been slighted. The effect of Indian communities on policy formulation during these years must await other much-needed studies. Until those studies appear, every history—including this one—will be incomplete.

The assimilation campaign was a product of specific ideas and programs as well as of the United States' political culture. Thus, my study is a work of history: I discuss individual events, particular ideas, certain pieces of legislation, and important actors. But the point of the discussion is to place the assimilation campaign in the context of a national experience. This is political history, but only if politics is broadly defined as the interplay of ideas and interests with changing perceptions of both the problems and the solutions in Indian affairs. With this work we should be able to move away from accusations of guilt and professions of innocence and begin to understand better both the actions of the inscrutable white man and the responses of Native Americans.

One of the most pleasant aspects of completing this project is the opportunity it provides to thank publicly the many people and institutions that had a hand in its preparation. I first heard the expression "community of scholars" long ago, but it was not until I wrote this book that I understood what it could mean.

The staffs of the Boston Public Library, Harvard University's Widener and Langdell Libraries, the Goldfarb Library at Brandeis University, the Newberry Library in Chicago, Illinois, and the Library of Congress assisted me regularly and reliably during the research. Moreover, I have enjoyed the aid and hospitality of archivists at the Beinecke Rare Book and Manuscript Library at Yale, the Houghton Library at Harvard, the Harvard University Archives, the Manuscripts Division of the Library of Congress, the National Archives, the National Anthropological Archives, and the Wisconsin State Historical Society. And my friends at Antioch's Olive Kettering Library always responded promptly to my requests for books and citations; their enclave of quiet efficiency requires a special acknowledgment.

I am grateful for the financial support of the Irving and Rose Crown Fellowship in American Studies at Brandeis University, a predoctoral fellowship at the Newberry Library Center for the History of the American Indian, and a grant from the Antioch College Faculty Fund.

The list of friends and colleagues who have helped enliven my prose, verify my conclusions, and keep me out of the briar patch should include Robert Bieder, Hugh Donahue, Robert Fogarty, David Gould, Michael Grossberg, Dirk Hartog, Mark Higbee, Curtis Hinsley, Joan Mark, and David Reed. In addition, I have received both advice and encouragement from a number of persons whose openness and generosity are a measure of what is right with American academic life. These include Robert Berkhofer, Helen Codere, John

Demos, Lawrence Kelly, Howard Lamar, Richard Metcalf, Marvin Meyers, Paul Prucha, and Helen Tanner. It is not difficult for one who is a teacher to thank *his* teachers, for he knows how much goes into the job and how uncertain are its consequences. N. Gordon Levin's ideas and enthusiasm propelled me into the project, while the wit, curiosity, and matchless energy of Morton Keller got me out. While everyone mentioned should share whatever credit accrues to this project, I alone am responsible for what I have written.

Parents and spouse come last—not because of sentimentality, but because at the end one wonders, "Why did I do this?" Catherine, John, and Elizabeth Hoxie convinced me that it mattered.

Chapter 1

The Appeal of Assimilation

On the morning of January 15, 1879, a front-page story in the *Boston Post* carried its readers far from their New England homes. An exclusive dispatch reported that a group of Cheyenne Indians had escaped from Fort Robinson, Nebraska: "Out into the night and frozen snow [the Indians] leaped and on the discovery of their escape they were pursued and slaughtered." The article evoked scenes of warriors plunging through deep snow, pursued by soldiers who fired into the night. For a few days newspapers from California to Georgia covered the story with similar enthusiasm. A headline in St. Louis, despite its ignorance of winter conditions in western Nebraska, was typical: "Several Soldiers Killed and Many Indians Made to Bite the Dust."[1]

The excitement following the Cheyenne outbreak did not continue. The incident was confined to a small area; and as more details of the fighting became known, pride in the cavalry's skill turned to disgust. The conflict had pitted mounted troops against 150 men, women, and children. The Indians—members of Dull Knife's band of Northern Cheyenne—had been confined to Fort Robinson after they refused to return to their bleak reservation in Indian Territory (present-day Oklahoma). The camp commander cut off the group's food and water. On the fifth night of their confinement the Indians gathered weapons they had hidden under the floorboards of the bar- racks and staged their pitiful breakout. This was not Kit Carson opening the southern plains or Custer battling for the inland empire. It was a shabby police action carried out by a well-equipped garrison force against a starving band of refugees. "The affair was a brutal and inhuman massacre," proclaimed the *Atlanta Constitution*, "a das- tardly outrage upon humanity and a lasting disgrace to our boasted civilization."[2]

But the cruelty of the Fort Robinson incident was only partially responsible for the public outrage. The fighting in Nebraska seemed to be the harbinger of a new, repugnant form of Indian warfare. The Cheyennes were wards of the government, a people long since de- feated in battle. Their purpose in leaving Indian Territory—and escaping from the army post—was similar to that of other racial groups in the late nineteenth century. Like their black and Asian contemporaries in the South and Far West, they were seeking a place for themselves in a changing and unsettled society. The confronta- tion with the cavalry suggested that their search was doomed.

Before the Civil War it had been possible to imagine that Indians and whites could remain permanently separate from one another. A series of policies, beginning in the eighteenth century with the adop- tion of the first Trade and Intercourse Acts and continuing through the removal and early reservation eras, were aimed at keeping the two races apart. That goal satisfied a number of interests. Humani- tarians believed that separation would reduce the level of violence on the frontier and provide Indians with enough time to become "civilized." Expansionists thought that designating specific areas as "Indian country" allowed remaining lands to be settled more rapidly. And for many tribes, reservations were the only way to retain a por- tion of their national autonomy.

After 1865, the Grant and Hayes administrations tried to revitalize this separation strategy with their celebrated peace policy. For a decade the Indian Office endeavored to consolidate agencies, end corruption in the federal bureaucracy, and replace tribal agents with men approved by the nation's religious leaders. Government officials hoped that an efficient evangelical Indian service could successfully "civilize" the Native American population before it was completely overrun by white settlement.

The peace policy was a praiseworthy effort. A product of the idealism of the reconstruction era, it won enthusiastic backing from both politicians and reformers. Unfortunately, like so many ambitious schemes of the postwar period, it did not work. President Grant assigned most of the agency openings to Protestants, thereby alienating the one group—the Catholics—with the most experience in the West. Many of his appointees were Methodists and Quakers who were ill prepared for the responsibility. Appropriations for schools and farming implements were almost nonexistent. Because administrators had difficulty deciding on the location of the new consolidated agencies, tribes were repeatedly moved or asked to accommodate themselves to white encroachment. And an extended struggle over whether to locate the Indian Office in the War or the Interior Department undermined the government's efforts.[3]

For many, the Northern Cheyenne incident typified the failure of the peace policy. That tribe had been moved from its traditional home in the northern plains to a "consolidated" reservation in Indian Territory. The Indians hated the relocation; there they found food supplies low and medical care unavailable. And so they escaped, forcing the army to hunt them down and return them to their reservation. After a decade of effort, the government seemed incapable of producing anything but more bloody headlines.

The outcry surrounding the Fort Robinson tragedy subsided in a few weeks. After all, Indian affairs were a relatively minor feature of national life and the natives themselves represented only a tiny percentage of the American population. But the issues raised by the fighting did not disappear, for the Cheyenne escape proved to be only the first in a year-long succession of disastrous encounters between the government and Native Americans. Additional incidents captured public attention and brought the failure of both the peace policy and the entire separation strategy home to the American people.

The first of these incidents began to unfold in late January 1879, when the Cheyennes were burying their dead outside Fort Robinson. Standing Bear and a small band of his fellow Poncas escaped from Indian Territory. Following the same general trail that Dull Knife had used the previous fall, the group headed north toward their homes along the Niobrara River. In March, army units detained the chief and ordered him to return to his agency. While the Indian Office prepared transportation, he was confined at Fort Omaha, Nebraska.

Despite their similar predicaments, the Poncas did not share the fate of the Northern Cheyennes. Standing Bear's arrest came less than two months after the January massacre, and the memory of that night was not far from the minds of the public or the officials handling the new case. What is more, the Poncas were an agricultural people who had never warred on the United States. Before long a committee of local ministers had formed to petition for the chief's release. Even the military wanted to set him free. General George Crook, the local commander who would later distinguish himself as the captor of Geronimo, cooperated in this effort by encouraging a habeas corpus suit to test the legality of Standing Bear's imprisonment. Crook had no special love for Native Americans—he called the Apaches the "tiger of the human species"—but he saw no reason to damage the army's reputation further by repeating the heavy-handed tactics used at Fort Robinson.[4]

Two Omaha attorneys (one of whom normally served the Union Pacific Railroad) volunteered to handle Standing Bear's case. They based their brief on the old man's constitutional rights, arguing, "In time of peace, no authority, civil or military, exists for transporting Indians from one section of the country to another . . . nor to confine them to any particular reservation against their will." Thomas Henry Tibbles, an editor for the *Omaha Herald*, offered to publicize the case and together with the ministers' committee he soon succeeded in turning the prisoner of Fort Omaha into the "celebrated Chief Standing Bear." By April 30, when U.S. District Court Judge

Elmer Dundy heard oral arguments in *Standing Bear* v. *Crook*, the plight of the Poncas had become familiar to newspaper readers across the country.[5]

Dundy announced his decision to release the chief on May 12, and editorial writers greeted the news with uniform enthusiasm. San Francisco's *Alta California* referred to the ruling as the "only case now recollected where a court of this country [had] rendered justice to the Indian as if he were a human being." The *Chicago Tribune* agreed, pointing out that the court's action foretold a new era in Indian affairs: "Means should be devised by which an Indian, when he has attained the necessary degree of civilization, shall be released from the arbitrary control of the Indian Bureau and allowed all the rights and immunities of a free man." Standing Bear's release encouraged critics of the government's programs. The decision effectively removed the legal basis for the entire separation strategy. It appeared that the Indian Office was no longer able to confine tribes to reservations and force "civilization" on them.[6]

The *Standing Bear* decision was a blow to the government's power to create reservations; the "Ute War" that broke out four months later raised fundamental questions about the reasons for maintaining such enclaves. Nathan C. Meeker, an honest, humanitarian Indian agent, was killed by members of the tribe entrusted to his care. The Utes resented Meeker's insistence that they forsake their old ways and become farmers. And they mistrusted him for suggesting that they give up their mountain hunting grounds and content themselves with small homesteads.[7]

Despite his inexperience, Meeker had struck his superiors as the perfect peace policy agent. He was an ardent Christian and an agricultural expert who had long been interested in social reform. He helped found the farming community of Greeley, Colorado, and had served for years as the agricultural editor of the *New York Tribune*. Responding to his editor's famous admonition, he had indeed gone west to grow up with the country, and had devoted himself to making the frontier a more humane and prosperous place. But Meeker had no diplomatic skill. He did not understand the Utes' fear of Colorado's booming white population. Prospectors and other adventurers were appearing on the tribe's lands in growing numbers, and the agent made little attempt to remove them. He concentrated instead on farming instruction. In early September 1879, after a heated argument with some headmen, Meeker became nervous and called for the cavalry. The Utes grew fearful and tensions rose. As the troops drew near, fighting broke out and Meeker was killed. On October 2 the *Chicago Tribune* announced its view of the tragedy in a dramatic headline: "Massacred By Utes!"[8]

The officer in charge of the cavalry detachment was also killed, along with twelve soldiers, several agency employees, and thirty-seven members of the tribe. The nation's press was uniform in its sympathy for Meeker and the other white victims, but (as had been the case in January) descriptions of the fighting were soon buried under an avalanche of editorials condemning the reservation system. Within two days of its initial headline, the *Chicago Tribune* observed, "There are two sides to every question, even an Indian question." The editorial went on to list the problems that had plagued the Ute agency and to conclude that the tribe had turned to violence because it had been so "exasperated" by the agent's stubbornness. Even western papers shared this view. The *Virginia City* (Nev.) *Territorial Enterprise* noted on October 30, "It is daily growing more and more certain that there was no occasion for trouble with the Utes; that, if justice had been done them, there would have been no outbreak." The *Alta California* made this argument even more forcefully. It denounced the reservation policy as a "murderous system": "[It] is starvation for the savage, it is oppression by the lawless white pioneer; it is death to our gallant officers and men." Meeker's honesty and good intentions were irrelevant. "One thing is certain," the San Francisco editors observed, "and that is that our whole Indian policy is a miserable one and a failure."[9]

Two events at the end of 1879 amplified the papers' criticisms. First, Standing Bear made an extensive tour of the East Coast. Appearing before large audiences in Chicago, Boston, New York, Philadelphia, and Washington, the newly freed Ponca chief condemned the reservation system and called for the extension of constitutional guarantees to Indians. Second, in December a well-publicized dispute arose between the secretary of the interior and critics of the government's Indian policy. This controversy reached its climax in late January 1880, when the commissioner of Indian affairs resigned after being charged with corruption. Both the Standing Bear tour and the mounting attacks on the Indian Office galvanized criticism of the government's programs. Indian policy reform became a national issue, and groups emerged to lead the critics and lobby the politicians.

Standing Bear was not the first Native American leader to argue his case before crowds of eastern sympathizers, nor would he be the last. John Ross, Black Hawk, and Red Cloud had preceded him, and Geronimo and Sitting Bull would follow. Officials often brought chiefs and headmen to Washington to be cowed by the splendor of the Great White Father's dusty city, interviewed by his scientists, and cooed over by the press. But the Ponca's tour was unique. His visit was not official—it was organized as a political campaign rather than as a state visit. The reason for this difference (and the primary cause of the trip's dramatic success) was the work and showmanship of Thomas Tibbles.

Tibbles was an experienced agitator. Born in Ohio in 1840, he had moved west as a young man, first to Illinois with his parents, and then (at the age of sixteen) to Kansas to ride with John Brown. Tibbles served briefly in the Civil War, but soon returned to the Middle Border, where he spent the Reconstruction era promoting evangelical Methodism and greenback reform. During the depression of the 1870s he moved to Omaha and began a career in journalism. Following the Ponca crusade Tibbles married an Indian woman and lived for a time on her reservation. Later, he would turn to homesteading, fiction writing, and, finally, politics. He ended his public career as Tom Watson's running mate on the Populist ticket in the 1904 presidential election.[10]

In the spring of 1879 Tibbles found himself at the center of a cause with national appeal. The Standing Bear case promised to raise the eccentric journalist from frontier obscurity, and Tibbles was determined to make the most of the opportunity. Within a few days of his first interviews with General Crook and the chief, the newspaperman was sending stories over the wire to Chicago and New York. In July, after Standing Bear was released, Tibbles traveled east to ar-range a fall tour. The purpose of the trip would be to publicize the evils of the reservation system and raise money for future court action.

Standing Bear made his Chicago debut in October. Each of the chief's appearances was carefully orchestrated. Tibbles selected two young, well-educated Omaha Indians to accompany the elderly Ponca: Susette LaFlesche and her brother Joseph. While on stage Susette obscured the memory of her French and English grandfathers and bore an English version of her tribal name: Bright Eyes. She appeared in buckskin, translated the chief's speech, and delivered a brief appeal of her own. The effect of her mannered Indianness was electric. "This," exclaimed Longfellow upon meeting her, "is Minnehaha." Susette's brother Joe appeared on the platform in "civilized" attire and acted as the chief's interpreter. Tibbles also chose his audiences carefully. In Chicago, where the newspapers were filled with stories about "murderous Utes," the group's stay was brief. In cities like Boston, where they found allies among both press and public, they settled in for several weeks.[11]

But showmanship alone was not responsible for the success of the tour. Tibbles cast the chief's appeal in constitutional terms. He began each appearance with a description of the government's hated programs. The reservation, he declared, created "a horde of minor but absolute monarchs over a helpless race." Standing Bear and Bright Eyes would repeat these charges. The Indian woman would tell of corruption and plead for support, saying that her people "ask you for their liberty." And the famous Ponca would bring the message home: "We are bound, we ask you to set us free." Indian citizenship, education, and the abolition of the reservation system were all identified as solutions for the present injustice.[12]

The audiences who flocked to hear Standing Bear found him irresistible. While political expediency had long since emasculated the ambitious programs of the immediate postwar era, the antislavery crusade still evoked pleasant memories. The Union's great victory was trotted out each election eve, praised at every patriotic celebration, and preserved by all the Republican hacks who could commandeer platforms large enough to accommodate a delegation of veterans. Tibbles's tour played on this nostalgia by giving people an opportunity to reaffirm their symbolic attachment to constitutional principles. "I think I feel as you must have in the old abolition days," wrote one such person to Thomas Wentworth Higginson a few days after she had heard Standing Bear. Helen Hunt Jackson continued those sentiments: "I cannot think of anything else from morning to night."[13]

By mid-November it was clear that the tour was a triumph. Five hundred Bostonians representing the city's business and political establishment attended a noon meeting at the Mercantile Exchange a few days before Thanksgiving. By a voice vote they approved a resolution calling for Indian citizenship, and they created an executive body to investigate the plight of the Poncas. This group, later named the Boston Indian Citizenship Committee, sponsored the remainder of Standing Bear's trip. December and January were spent in New York, and the following three months in Philadelphia, Washington, and Baltimore. Everywhere the chief and his entourage appeared before friendly audiences and won the support of local Republicans and Protestant ministers.[14]

The final crisis of 1879 occurred while Standing Bear was filling lecture halls in New York and Brooklyn. In mid-December Commissioner of Indian Affairs Ezra A. Hayt was accused of covering up wrongdoing on an Arizona reservation so as to protect the business interests of his friends; six weeks later he resigned. Before his departure, the commissioner was defended by the man who appointed him, Interior Secretary Carl Schurz. The sudden resignation attracted the attention of the government's critics and confirmed again their belief in the evils of the reservation system.

Though he was an efficient administrator, Schurz had done little during his two years in office to please those who had a stake in the operations of his department. White westerners were angered by his attacks on agency corruption as well as his reluctance to use force to subdue unruly tribes. The army resented his opposition to their proposal to transfer the Indian Office to the War Department. And the churches felt betrayed by his decision to suspend their control over agency appointments. At the end of 1879 all of these groups—now joined by Standing Bear's excited supporters—trained their fire on the secretary.

Schurz's most outspoken critic was Helen Hunt Jackson. A popular author of children's books who first discovered the plight of the
Indians at one of Standing Bear's Boston appearances, Jackson lev-
eled both barrels at the secretary on December 15. In columns appearing first in the *New York Tribune* and later reprinted across the
country, she attacked Schurz for his actions in the Northern Cheyenne and Ponca cases and called on him to end the "tyranny" of the
reservations. Surprised and hurt by these appeals, the secretary gave
way to anger, writing that his critics' efforts were "in danger of being
wasted on the unattainable." Horace Greeley at the *Tribune* responded for the critics and raised the verbal stakes. The "despotic
power" of the agents, he wrote, was "a more direct denial of human
rights than was slavery." [15]

When Commissioner Hayt resigned and left Washington at the
end of January, Jackson and her fellow critics felt vindicated. One
editor hooted that the secretary had "no more conception of his
duties than a wild Zulu has of the magnetic telegraph." But even
Schurz's supporters saw more than a grain of truth in a Chicago editorial: "The temptation to steal is so great and the opportunities so
abundant that no Secretary of the Interior, no matter how competent
and honest he may be himself, . . . will be able to put a stop to corrupt practices. . . . The only remedy for abuses in the management of
Indian affairs is to abandon the present system of supporting and
coddling the Indians." [16]

In the past the impact of disasters like those of 1879 had quickly
dissipated. Massacres or revelations of corruption had shocked, then
bored the public. But as the 1880s began, a central truth was becoming self-evident: the government's policy was unworkable. The crisis of 1879 was conceptual as well as political. Not only were the
Indian Office's specific actions unpopular, but each misstep called
forth attacks on an entire approach to policy making. Critics everywhere demanded an end to the "despotic" and "corrupt" reservation
system.

What was the alternative? The angry public and the activists mo-
bilized by the Ponca tour were beginning to agree on an answer: total
assimilation. They promised that dismantling the reservation system (and the separation strategy that lay behind it) would end fron-

tier violence, stop agency corruption, and "civilize" the Indians while demonstrating the power and vitality of America's institutions. Such expectations were most common among the eastern Protestants and Republicans who had flocked to hear Standing Bear and Bright Eyes. These groups most clearly articulated the assimilation argument and formed the core of the organizations that began to lobby for its adoption.

Three reform associations emerged in the 1880s to tap the growing public interest in Indian assimilation. The first, the Boston Indian Citizenship Committee, was organized in the aftermath of the Standing Bear tour. The committee exploited its connections with the state's prominent Republican politicians and helped publicize the attacks on Schurz. It included Governor John Davis Long; Boston mayor Frederick Prince (a Democrat); Protestant minister Rufus Ellis; old abolitionists Dr. Oliver Wendell Holmes and Wendell Phillips; and—significantly—the city's postmaster, Edward S. Tobey, whose political patron was the state's senior U.S. senator, Henry L. Dawes.[17]

Efforts to organize what was to become the Women's National Indian Association began in 1879. Reviving the old abolitionist tactic of presenting petitions to Congress, Amelia Stone Quinton and Mary Bonney of Philadelphia began circulating statements urging the government to "keep faith" with the tribes." The first of these was submitted during Standing Bear's visit to Washington in early 1880. The group soon established branches in a number of eastern cities, urging each of them to call for the "civilization, Christianization and enfranchisement" of the tribes. Separate branches also undertook individual acts of charity such as supporting schools, providing funds for farm equipment, and marketing Indian handicrafts.[18]

For three years the Women's National Indian Association and the Boston Committee were the only voices advocating total assimilation as a remedy for the failures of the reservation system. They were amply reinforced, however, in 1882, when Herbert Welsh organized the Indian Rights Association following a trip to Sioux country. A member of a prominent Philadelphia family, Welsh was a nephew of one of the principal architects of Grant's peace policy. But his energies were devoted to abolishing the older program. The reservations, he wrote, "are islands, and about them a sea of civilization, vast and irresistible, surges." The leader of the new association argued that the government should "educate the Indian race and so prepare it for gradual absorption into ours." Welsh's association pursued these goals by maintaining a permanent lobbyist in Washington, conducting its own investigations of Indian affairs, and publishing a long list of reports and pamphlets.[19]

Each new reform organization bore a surface similarity to the antislavery groups of the 1840s and 1850s and to the previous decade's peace policy advocates. Like their predecessors they campaigned for "equal rights" for Native Americans and declared that they were driven by a sense of Christian mission. But the reformers of the 1880s also wanted to dismantle the reservations. Muting their sectarian differences, they acted with greater political sophistication. Their annual conferences at Lake Mohonk, New York, bespoke a more modern approach. Begun in 1883, the meetings attracted dozens of religious leaders, politicians, and reformers to an upstate resort for a weekend of speeches, reports on legislation, and debate. Each year the Mohonk delegates would fashion a platform to guide the next year's efforts. While Catholics were not welcome, and the number of participating politicians soon declined, the Lake Mohonk Conferences of the Friends of the Indian were marked by a minimum of factionalism and a general willingness to shape contrasting interests into common proposals.

But organization alone could not create support for the assimilation remedy. Like all agitators, the reformers became successful only when they linked their agenda to the wider concerns and aspirations of the American public. The late nineteenth century was a time when growing social diversity and shrinking social space threatened many Americans' sense of national identity. In the past, the country's communities had been intensely local and homogeneous. Cultural differences were tolerated, but the white Protestant majority continued to imagine that its values and the nation's were identical. Suddenly, amid unprecedented industrial expansion and dramatic increases in the rate of immigration, this majority found itself surrounded by people who did not share their cultural heritage or their definition of Americanism. At the same time, tremendous technological changes brought social groups closer together. The city became a metropolis, towns entered the orbit of industrial centers, and villages became crossroads for rail lines stretching across the continent. Even isolated farmers were drawn into an expanding web of commercial exchange. The Indian reformers of the 1880s responded to those conditions as well as to the specific suffering of Native Americans.

Before the Civil War, American social life had followed a pattern reminiscent of the Indian Office's separation strategy. The majority believed that minority ethnic groups were deviants from the national norm who should maintain a separate existence. Separation was more attractive than group conflict. Just as the government maintained tribes in cultural enclaves, so the white Protestant majority found it easier to deal with blacks or Irishmen as discrete units. Slavery was the most obvious example of this tendency, but the pattern was apparent in other areas. Farming communities and small towns often had distinct ethnic identities. Cities divided themselves into neighborhoods that functioned independently from the whole. In this compartmentalized society, minority groups welcomed the opportunity to be socially isolated and culturally autonomous. But the decades following the Civil War demonstrated that most Americans—like the Indians—would soon have to live nearer than ever before to people quite different from themselves. The new environment would require a new pattern of social relationships and a new set of social values. The Indian reformers provided an attractive model for those new relationships.

The political and economic expansion of the postwar era undermined America's "island communities." Americans—especially the white Protestant majority—felt the need to define more precisely the meaning of national citizenship. In this respect they shared a number of the Indian reformers' concerns. Like Herbert Welsh and Amelia Quinton they wondered how minority cultures could become integral parts of a modern nation. Like the Boston merchants they asserted that legal citizenship would promote cultural unity. And like Helen Hunt Jackson, they tried to specify the proper role of national institutions in hastening the assimilation process.

Herbert Welsh had condemned the reservations for being "islands" in the midst of civilization, but in a sense white Protestants could say the same thing about American ethnic groups who felt the "sea" of a new industrial world surging around them. And of course discomfort arose because leaders could not foresee the exact shape of that new world or the effect it would have on their way of life. By discussing the Indians' future, the white majority could also explore its own.

Newspaper editorials in 1879 provide a more precise measure of the reformers' attitudes, for they show that despite its sympathy, the public had no interest in delaying or diverting America's westward march to accommodate Native Americans. Every editor agreed that the problem was not how to keep whites away from tribal lands, but how to manage Indians so that American "progress" could continue. The *New Orleans Times-Picayune*, for example, argued that the Indian could not "any longer be permitted to usurp for the purpose of barbarism, the fertile lands, the products of mines, the broad valleys and wooded mountain slopes, which organized society regards as magazines of those forces which civilization requires for its maintenance and development." Expansionists dwelled in every camp. Even the ardent reformers on the *New York Tribune* pointed out that the destruction of reservations would provide a "powerful impetus" for the development of the nation's resources.[20]

As they condemned the Indians for failing to "develop" their lands and called for more "civilization," editors added that the nation had a special obligation to the tribes. "The sins committed by Americans upon Indians . . . are a perpetual stain upon our history," the *Virginia City Territorial Enterprise* declared, adding that these transgressions "should be continued no longer." At the same time the editors made it clear that help for Native Americans did not require white Protestants to abandon their sense of racial superiority. Journals that vilified the Chinese "rat-eaters," denounced the new immigrants as the "off-scouring of European prisons," condemned the "Roman church," or warned of the imminent arrival of "Negro paupers" in the North did not find it difficult to express sympathy for Indians.[21]

Whatever the motives of reformers like Thomas Tibbles and Helen Hunt Jackson, the campaign that began in 1879 did not threaten prevailing racial and cultural attitudes. The San Francisco *Alta California*, for example, juxtaposed attacks on Secretary Schurz with a public declaration that it had "never employed Chinese in any department." The *Atlanta Constitution* condemned the Fort Robinson massacre while it defended the "contentment" of southern blacks. And the *Boston Daily Advertiser*, edited by a member of the Boston Indian Citizenship Committee, was aggressively anti-Catholic. Clearly, the total assimilation being offered the Indians would require conformity to the standards of the white Protestant majority culture.[22]

Total assimilation was a goal that combined concern for native suffering with faith in the promise of America. Once the tribes were brought into "civilized" society, there would be no reason for them to "usurp" vast tracts of "underdeveloped" land. And membership in a booming nation would be ample compensation for the dispossession they had suffered. But most important, the extension of citizenship and other symbols of membership in American society would reaffirm the power of the nation's institutions to mold all people to a common standard. Success in assimilating Indians would reaffirm the dominance of the white Protestant majority, for such an achievement would extend the reach of the majority's cultural norms. As the *New York Tribune* put it in February 1880, "The original owner of the soil, the man from whom we have taken the country, in order that we may make of it the refuge of the world, where all men should be free if not equal, is the only man in it who is not recognized as entitled to the rights of a human being." The force of the statement was clear: extend the "rights of a human being" to the Indians, expand the American "refuge," and prove that when the pioneers had "taken the country" they had served a higher good. Moreover, the editorials' implications were quite satisfying: traditional American values continued to represent the best foundation for the nation's future.[23]

Like the sweep of a search light, the events of 1879 momentarily illuminated the weakness and unpopularity of the separation strategy. Not only were reservations the provinces of corrupt and cruel administrators, but they didn't work: they had not "civilized" anyone.

Nevertheless, it would take more than exposure and the cries of the outraged to overturn so long-standing a policy. Once the bright light of crisis had passed, legislators and bureaucrats were bound to descend into their traditional ruts. If the general desire for a new policy of rapid assimilation was to be translated into specific programs, a fresh blueprint for government action would have to be adopted by the nation's leaders. American policy makers had long viewed the strategy of racial separation as both humanitarian and practical. If they were to reject that strategy, the nation's leaders would need a new guide for their actions.

In March 1879, while Standing Bear was confined at Fort Omaha, two events occurred in Washington, D.C., that focused attention on an important source of ideas about the Indians' future. On March 3 Congress passed the annual civil appropriations bill. It authorized an appropriation of twenty thousand dollars to establish a bureau of ethnology within the Smithsonian Institution. On the following day, the recently organized Anthropological Society of Washington met to hear its first paper, "Relic Hunting," by Frank Cushing. The founding of the Bureau of Ethnology (after 1893, the Bureau of American Ethnology) and the Anthropological Society of Washington mark the emergence of professional anthropology in the United States. The Bureau was the nation's first institution committed exclusively to ethnological inquiry, and the society the first scholarly association in the field. Together they represented anthropology's passage from individual, privately financed research to large coordinated studies conducted by teams of trained experts. After 1879 the discipline was led by a group of scientists with stable institutional affiliations and a common interest in the scholarly examination of human society.[24]

The most interesting societies available for ethnological research were the Indian tribes of North America. There were several reasons for this. Indians were accessible—militarily defeated, marvelously exotic, and relatively close at hand. They were also diverse, having produced varied cultures in every section of the continent. And perhaps most significant, Native Americans were "safe" subjects for scrutiny. Unlike European immigrants, blacks, or Asians, Indians still were living outside "civilized" society; in the 1880s it was unlikely that investigations of native cultures would offend any political constituencies or disrupt a settled community. White southerners would certainly have seen research in their region as Yankee "meddling," westerners would have balked at the prospect of Washington experts arriving to study Asians, but aside from a few missionaries who wanted to erase the memory of the race's "heathen" past, few white men protested the anthropologists' preoccupation with Indians. By 1879 the bond between scientists and Native Americans was well established.[25]

But the anthropologists of the late nineteenth century had more in common than an incipient professionalism and their fascination with Indians. The men and women who staffed the new bureau and participated in the anthropological society also shared a common intellectual heritage. They came from widely different backgrounds— some had very little advanced training—but they all accepted social evolution as the general explanation of human development. Lewis Henry Morgan (1818–81) was the chief American proponent of this point of view. Even though his career (which began in 1851 with the publication of *The League of the Iroquois*) was drawing to a close in 1879, he was easily the country's most respected anthropologist. His Iroquois volume pioneered the use of field observations in tribal studies, and *Systems of Consanguinity and Affinity of the Human Family* (1871) introduced comparative kinship studies to ethnology. Morgan's most important work was *Ancient Society*, which received an enthusiastic reception when it appeared in 1877. The book traced the development of intelligence, the family, government, and the idea of property through all of human history. The historian and philosopher Henry Adams wrote that *Ancient Society* "must be the foundation of all future works in American historical science." Major John Wesley Powell, the founding director of the Bureau of Ethnology, was even more enthusiastic. After receiving his advance copy of the book he reported, "The first night I read until two o'clock. I shall take it into the field and in my leisure hours study it carefully, reading it many times."[26]

Throughout the nineteenth century scientific social theorists had described human history in terms of movement from simplicity to complexity. Building on this tradition, Morgan taught that societal development occurred in three stages—savagery, barbarism, and civilization—and that all people could be placed at one of these levels. The order and clarity of this perspective appealed to students of Indian life, but it was also attractive because it combined sympathy for the "savage" tribes with a justification for "civilization's" conquest. A century ago it seemed clear to most Americans that native people fit into a lower stage of culture. One could hope that Indians would rise to a "higher" plane, while finding comfort in the idea that cruel policies such as removal or punitive warfare were unavoidable steps along the road to progress.[27]

On one level Morgan typified the sympathy and resignation that coexisted in social evolutionary thinking. He classified most tribes as savage or barbarian, and feared that the Indians would be unable to shift to higher levels of development before they were swept away by their civilized conquerors. But the author of *Ancient Society* believed the process could produce positive results. In fact, his great work had a distinctly optimistic quality, for it attempted to turn evolutionary thinking on its head. Morgan argued that the study of cultural inequality could produce guidelines for human advancement.

Morgan grew up in central New York state in the early nineteenth century. As a young man he witnessed the displacement of the Iroquois tribes by American settlement and recognized the drastic changes that occurred whenever "civilized" societies came into contact with Indians. The Indians' habits, he reported, were "perishing daily and [had] been perishing for upwards of three centuries." Could the consequences of this upheaval be positive? For Morgan, the answer was certain. "It can now be asserted," he wrote, "that savagery preceded barbarism in all the tribes of mankind, as barbarism is known to have preceded civilization. The history of the human race is one in source, one in experience, one in progress."[28]

Since civilization was the ultimate consequence of social change, it was logical to assert that change itself was part of a universal progressive process. Morgan conceded that some groups advanced more rapidly than others, but he asserted that everyone was bound to rise. What was more, he added, progress occurred at an accelerating rate: "Human progress, from first to last, has been in a ratio not rigorously but essentially geometrical. This is plain on the face of the facts; and it could not, theoretically, have occurred in any other way. Every item of absolute knowledge gained became a factor in further acquisitions, until the present complexity of knowledge was attained. Consequently . . . progress was slowest in time in the first period, and most rapid in the last." Morgan rejected racial explanations of human differences, preferring theories of environmental influences or the working of chance. He argued, for example, that even though the "Aryan and Semitic races" represented "the main streams of human progress," they began as part "of the indistinguishable mass of barbarians." Thus, "the distinction of *normal* and abnormal races falls to the ground." While he continued to believe in distinct levels of culture, the American scientist saw potential progress in all societies.[29]

For Morgan the chief measure of a society's achievements, as well as the principal instrument for its advancement, was the private ownership of property. Actually, each stage of societal development corresponded to a particular economic system. Savages were disorganized foragers who owned nothing but tools and weapons. Barbarians (the discoverers of agriculture) owned their farms in common and had no commercial activity. Civilized people prospered through individual acquisition of land, complex machinery, and domestic animals. Their wealth produced nuclear families that were flexible yet capable of maintaining rules of inheritance. Thus private property promoted both economic prosperity and social sophistication:

Property, as it increased in variety and amount, exercised a steady and constantly augmenting influence in the direction of monogamy. It is impossible to overestimate the influence of property in the civilization of mankind. It was the power that brought Aryan and Semitic nations out of barbarism into civilization. . . . Governments and laws are instituted with primary reference to its creation, protection and enjoyment. . . . With the establishment of the inheritance of property in the children of its owner, came the first possibility of the strict monogamian family.[30]

Morgan's emphasis on private property suggested that economic arrangements were more than badges of cultural development. The impact of a particular system could be far-reaching. Logically, the introduction of a more "advanced" method of landownership could inspire progress in an entire society.

By emphasizing the uniformity of progress and the accelerating speed with which it occurred, Morgan called attention to the dynamic potential of social evolutionism. Cultures were not prisoners of their stage of development. They could expect change to occur in a "positive" direction, and the principal source of these changes would be a new economic system. Shifting property relationships were the engines that produced improvements in other areas of life.

Morgan's position was ambiguous on a number of crucial points. How quickly could a people move from one stage to another? How wide was the gap between the "civilized" and "uncivilized" world? How long would it take for "barbarians" to adopt private property? Could the "civilization" process be accelerated? In a world beset by racial animosity, economic uncertainty, and national chauvinism, the idea of social evolution could become a tool for defending "advanced" peoples and exploiting those considered "backward." Morgan's predecessors—and his successors—argued that "uncivilized" peoples were destined to remain where they were. But that was not Morgan's world. He published *Ancient Society* amid a growing demand that the United States' "uncivilized" natives be "improved" and incorporated into the nation. In this environment Morgan could become an apostle of progress and hope. He rejected racial determinism and taught that social change inevitably wrought improvements in human society. Moreover, he identified one factor, private property, as the key to movement from one stage to another. Societies were not fixed; they could advance up the evolutionary scale in response to human effort.

Lewis Henry Morgan's dynamic vision influenced all the professional anthropologists of the late nineteenth century, but his impact was most striking on two who became directly involved in the formulation of Indian policy. Both John Wesley Powell (1834–1902) and Alice Cunningham Fletcher (1838–1923) applied *Ancient Society* to contemporary problems. Powell, the director of the nonpartisan Bureau of Ethnology, was quite circumspect. His efforts were largely confined to written comments and private lobbying. Fletcher was an activist. She advocated specific legislation, maintained ties to prominent reformers, and worked as a special agent for the Indian Office. Together they succeeded in fashioning a scientific defense of Indian assimilation. Their contributions were crucial, for they established the context within which politicians and reformers would act.

Soon after Morgan's death in 1881, his student and protégé Adolph Bandelier wrote that John Wesley Powell was the "direct successor to Mr. Morgan in the study of Indian life."[31] This was no exaggeration. For the next two decades Powell dominated anthropological thinking in the United States. Equally important, the Bureau of Ethnology expanded under his direction to become the chief sponsor of scholarly research in the discipline.

Powell was a unique and engaging character. Ever the eclectic and the organizer, the major never shrank from bold new theories or dramatic actions. He was a one-armed veteran of Shiloh who, before assuming control of the ethnology bureau, had already dug for fossils in the trenches before Vicksburg, taught at Illinois Normal University, made the first recorded descent of the Colorado River, organized and led the Rocky Mountain Survey, and written a pioneering study of western land management. And all the while—as he mingled with the spoilsmen and politicos of Chester Arthur's Washington— he maintained his native curiosity and optimism. While the tragic events of 1879 were unfolding in the West, he predicted confidently, "When society shall have passed to complete integration in the unification of all nations, and differentiation is perfected in universal liberty, then the sole philosophy will be science."[32]

For Powell the teachings of "that sole philosophy" were unambiguous: "In all the succession of phenomena with which anthropologists deal, . . . there is always some observable change in the direction of progress." In fact, he believed so firmly in this axiom that he set about "improving" Morgan's scheme by reducing its ambiguities and emphasizing its optimism. He added a fourth stage of cultural development—enlightenment—to account for modern industrialization. Modern nation states contained large bureaucracies and giant corporations. He argued that these institutions made people interdependent. They raised people above competition and hastened the age of enlightenment. "To the extent that culture has progressed beyond the plane occupied by the brute," the major argued, "man has ceased to work directly for himself." Powell dwelled on the positive consequences of progress. He was confident that the extension of modernity would produce a single world language, international peace, and the rule of benevolent associations.[33]

When it came to Indian assimilation, the major spoke from first-hand experience. He had traveled throughout the West and was familiar with a number of native culture areas. His most direct encounter had come in 1873, when he visited several Great Basin tribes, recording their languages and observing their customs. These contacts only confirmed Powell's belief in social evolution. He argued that the process would be neither simple nor quick, but, like many social scientists, he had great faith in his assumptions. He reported in 1874 that the Numic peoples were nomads who should be forced to a higher stage of culture. "The sooner this country is entered by white people and the game destroyed so that the Indians will be compelled to gain a subsistence by some other means than hunting," he told the House Indian Affairs Committee, "the better it will be for them." He closed with an invitation: "Let the influx of population and the slow progress of civilization . . . settle the question."[34]

According to Powell, the Bureau of Ethnology would "organize anthropological research in America." Its projects would follow Morgan's teachings. "Primitive" Indians would be their subject. The scientists hoped to record the habits and ideas of people before the forces of progress raised them to civilization and forever changed their ways of life. Powell assumed this change would come quickly and that the Bureau should therefore be prompt. At the end of its first year, he asked Congress for a 100 percent increase in the bureau's budget, warning, "If the ethnology of our Indians is ever to receive proper scientific study and treatment the work must be done at once."[35]

Social evolutionary theories also influenced Powell's view of specific findings. For example, an extensive study of the eastern mound builders proved to him that these people were at "about the same culture-status" as historic tribes and not the remnants of some lost golden civilization. The bureau's first project in South America in 1894 revealed "that the aborigines [there] like those of the North American continent, [were] partly in the higher stages of savagery and the lower stages of barbarism." The most striking example of the major's insistence on conceptual purity came in 1896, when he criticized the young ethnologist James Mooney for comparing the ghost dance religion to Christian revivalism. "The movements are not homologous," the Methodist major wrote, for the gap between civilized and uncivilized peoples was "so broad and deep that few representatives of either race [were] ever able clearly to see its further side." Progress followed a single, predictable path. The stages of culture were universal and affected every aspect of a people's way of life.[36]

Powell and the Bureau of Ethnology made two contributions to the growing interest in Indian assimilation. First, the major and his employees dominated professional anthropology. They founded the Anthropological Society of Washington and were instrumental in the organization of the American Anthropological Association in 1902. William John McGee, Powell's chief assistant, was the latter association's first president. The American Association for the Advancement of Science established a section of anthropology in 1876. Powell headed that group in 1879 and for the remainder of the century Washington scientists were the leading contributors to its survival and growth. Powell's version of social evolution—the notion of culture stages, continuous progress, and the inevitable transformation of Indian life—became dominant within the discipline. In short, he set the terms for informed discussions of Indian affairs in the 1880s.

Powell's other contribution was his direct influence on reformers and policy makers. The major was careful not to expose his new bureau to political controversy. He recognized that while powerful friends like Speaker of the House James Garfield had created his office, powerful enemies could easily destroy it. Originally Powell had hoped that the bureau would serve Congress as a source of objective information. C. C. Royce began his work on native land cessions in 1879 and the major promised that his was only the first of many projects that would illuminate "the effect of the presence of civilization upon savagery." But Congress expressed little interest in such studies and other tasks quickly forced them into the background.[37]

Powell's personal lobbying was more extensive—and more subtle. He maintained close contact with key committeemen and Interior Department officials. His published works, from the famous *Report on the Lands of the Arid Region* (1878) to the annual reports of the bureau, were liberally sprinkled with comments on the present condition of the tribes. And the major responded willingly to individual requests for advice. In 1880, for example, Senator Henry Teller asked for information concerning a Ute agreement then before Congress. Debate over the issue was being used as a sounding board for a number of new policy proposals, and Powell took the opportunity of Teller's note to write a wide-ranging essay in which he argued that three principles should guide all future government actions.

First, since a tribe's traditional lands represented "everything most sacred to Indian society," the anthropologist urged that the "removal of the Indians [was] the first step to be taken in their civilization." Second, he noted that "ownership of lands in severalty should be looked forward to as the ultimate settlement of our Indian problems." Individual land tenure would undermine both the clan system and "traditional modes of inheritance." Finally, the major recommended that citizenship and total assimilation should be the twin goals of all legislation. Enforcing treaties and maintaining reservations, he wrote, discharged "but a minor part of the debt" that the government owed the Indians: "The major portion of that debt can be paid only by giving to the Indians Anglo-Saxon civilization, that they may also have prosperity and happiness under the new civilization of this continent." Here was a chilling condensation of the social evolutionist blueprint: separate Indians from their homes and their past, divide their land into individual parcels, make them citizens, and draw them into American society. Powell's suggestions carried an air of scientific precision. Who could doubt that they were reasonable and practical?[38]

John Wesley Powell remained a firm advocate of Indian assimilation throughout the 1880s. He looked on the mounting collection of artifacts in the Smithsonian Institution not as evidence for the irreducible differences between Native Americans and "civilized" societies, but as a sure indication that the forces of assimilation were gaining the upper hand. The major believed "a new phase of Aryan civilization [was] being developed in the western half of America," and his efforts as an anthropologist were bent to the service of that vision.[39]

Alice Fletcher had none of the constraints that hampered Powell's involvement in Indian policy making. A private student of Frederick Ward Putnam at Harvard's Peabody Museum, she had concentrated most of her energy in archaeology until she heard Standing Bear and Bright Eyes in a Boston lecture hall in 1879. After that evening, she turned to ethnology. She visited Thomas Tibbles and his Omaha assistants in the West, later collaborating with Francis LaFlesche on a number of monographs. In fact, she spent most of the next forty years in field research and writing. Throughout her career, Fletcher alternated between scholarship and policy reform. She believed her work was "for the student . . . [and] for men and women who [would] be wiser and kinder by knowing their fellow countryman, the Indian as he [was] at home and in peace." As a result she was an outspoken advocate of both Indian education and the individual allotment of native lands. Perhaps more important, she served as a link between the anthropological community and the politicians who made policy.[40]

Indian education in her view did not require an elaborate justification. "The task of converting the American Indian into the Indian American," she told the commissioner of Indian affairs in 1890, "belongs to the Indian student." Not surprisingly, then, when Captain Richard Henry Pratt established the Carlisle Industrial Training School—where conversion to "civilization" was the central objective—he found in Alice Fletcher an energetic ally and supporter. She cultivated congressmen, testified in support of larger appropriations for the school, and organized VIP tours of the campus. Fletcher's activity in education reform was recognized in 1888, when Henry Dawes' Senate Indian Affairs Committee commissioned her to conduct a nationwide survey of the government's Indian school system. Her seven-hundred-page report ended with an appeal for an expansion of the program. "More . . . and better equipped schools," she wrote, were "a national need."[41]

On the question of land allotment, Fletcher rejected Powell's cautious recommendations. She urged Congress to begin assigning Indians individual tracts of land as soon as possible. The major's principal contact had been with the gathering tribes of the Great Basin. His observations of these people led him to conclude that individual landownership—while desirable—should not be forced on unwilling subjects until after they had begun to live communally. Both Fletcher's experience and her attitude were quite different. On her first trip to the West, in September 1881, she visited the Omahas and was the guest of a leading mixed-blood family. Her hosts were among the most acculturated members of an agricultural tribe that had long been in contact with white settlers. Fletcher found many Omahas upset over the recent Ponca removal and fearful that they too would be marched to Indian Territory. The local white community seemed eager for them to leave. The anthropologist was certain that the division of this tribe's lands into individual homesteads would protect the Indians from removal and dispossession while it spurred them on to "civilization." By December 1881 she was back in Washington lobbying for a special law to accomplish this goal. She supported her case with a petition (it contained signatures from 53 of the tribe's 1,121 members) and the claim that she had a special understanding of the Omahas' plight. "I have not learned from the outer, but from the inner circles," she told Massachusetts senator Henry Dawes, adding, "because I thus know them, see their needs, see their possibilities, see their limitations, I plead for them."[42]

Fletcher's Omaha proposal called for the sale of fifty thousand acres of the reservation to finance the development of individual homesteads. Not surprisingly, Nebraska's congressional delegation was quick to support her. Charles Manderson managed the bill through the Senate and the state's lone congressman, Edward Valentine, was one of its principal backers in the House. With Nebraska's representatives agreeing that "everybody [was] satisfied to have a bill of this kind passed," the Omaha Severalty Act became law on August 7, 1882.[43]

The Omaha tribe was now ready for civilization. "They are on the eve of a new life," Fletcher wrote a friend. "Soon their farms will be staked out and the beautiful lands along the Logan opened up, and the foundations of new homes laid. The future whence they must prosper or perish is at hand."⁴⁴ A few weeks after these words were written a new phase of the anthropologist's career began. The commissioner of Indian affairs appointed her a special agent charged with carrying out the survey and allotment of the Omaha lands.

The Omaha assignment was the first of three allotting projects Alice Fletcher would undertake during the next decade. Her work with the Omahas lasted until 1884. Between 1887 and 1889 she supervised the allotment of the Winnebagos, who lived on a reservation adjoining the Omahas. Finally, from 1889 to 1893, she served as the allotting agent for the Nez Perce tribe of Idaho.

Both the Omaha and Winnebago allotments involved small agricultural tribes occupying relatively productive farmland. Whether out of fear of the alternatives or a conviction that they had no choice, many of these Indians were willing to accept their allotments. Alice Fletcher reported that her charges "carefully treasure[d]" their deeds, and that groups within the tribe who opposed the new law were "steadily losing ground." She was not discouraged by opposition. After all, she told students at the Carlisle school, "severalty [meant] pioneering." Neither was she dismayed when complications arose following the end of her work. In 1887, for example, drought threatened the Omahas' crops and disputes over finances and the handling of the remaining tribal land divided the tribe. After a visit to the troubled agency Alice Fletcher reported, "Although I saw thriftlessness, yet manliness was astir; . . . the disintegration process is at work all over the reservation [and] has made the incoming of new life possible. . . . The Omaha afforded me a glimpse into the workshop into which every true Indian worker must enter and labor with a wisdom, patience, and prudence such as was never before demanded of him."⁴⁵

Alice Fletcher's career offers a clear example of the power of social evolutionary theory in late nineteenth-century America. She believed the nation's expansion and industrialization created an entirely new set of circumstances for native people. "The fact is," she wrote in 1889, "the Indian is caught in the rush of our modern life, and there is no time for him to dally with the serious questions that are upon him." Such conditions required a sharp break with the past. Thus she rejected the gradualism of the reservation system. As Morgan and Powell had taught, the forces undermining the old ways also were shaping the future. "Civilization" was sure to sweep across the West, and those who understood its impact had an obligation to minister to its victims. Fletcher argued that Native Americans should embrace individual landownership, literacy, and exclusive monogamy. She was aware of at least some of the difficulties of the task, but her studies convinced her there was no alternative. The individual Indian was "doomed to suffer and all that the best of friends [could] do [was] to give him every chance by means of education and a common sense training of his religious nature to meet the dangers that beset him."[46]

In the midst of her allotting work, Fletcher once confessed that she was "burdened with the future of this people." Nevertheless she persisted, spurred on by her convictions: change brought progress; progress ended in civilization; civilization was a singular condition that did not recognize cultural variety. The logic both of abstract principle and historical reality was compelling: one must conform to the demand of civilization—that is, assimilate—or disappear. This demand had been familiar in the removal and reservation eras, when pessimists stressed the second alternative—disappearance— but in the 1880s the emphasis had changed. Scholars now taught that assimilation was possible.[47]

The impact of anthropologists on Indian policy making was cumulative and indirect. It consisted of the influence of Morgan's dynamic social theory on discussions of progress, the weight of Powell's optimism and expertise, and the specific contributions of Alice Fletcher. By the mid-1880s, the public had a specific blueprint for interpreting and shaping events and a cadre of experts to inspire them. Powell might emphasize the positive potential of social evolution, and Fletcher could demonstrate the kind of action the new discipline required, but critics of the Indian Office did not have to rely on these anthropologists. They now had a coherent explanation of the government's failures and a practical scheme for reform. The science of man taught that the rapid incorporation of American Indians into "civilized" society was both possible and desirable. Total assimilation would exemplify and encourage the irresistible march of progress.

But the attractiveness of total assimilation rested on more than a convenient marriage of public outrage and scientific theory. The idea also drew support from politicians. Legislators and bureaucrats were attracted to the notion of bringing Indians into American society because they believed it would be both practical and popular. Total assimilation promised to refurbish the policy makers' view of themselves without alienating any constituents. Like reformers, newspapermen, and scientists, people in government believed that the successful assimilation of the nation's aboriginal population would demonstrate the United States' virtue and wisdom.

Amid the crises of 1879, it is unlikely that anyone would have predicted that Henry Dawes would soon come to dominate Indian policy making. He was not attached to a reform group, and he had shown only a passing interest in Indian affairs during his two decades in Washington, D.C. The senator had been in politics for nearly thirty years, first serving his western Massachusetts constituents in a series of local offices, then going to Washington in 1857 as one of the state's first Republican congressmen. When Charles Sumner died in 1874, party leaders chose Dawes to take his place.

In 1879 the veteran politician's chief concern was winning renomination to the Senate. This was a new experience for Dawes because he had always been a party regular. In the House he had been reluctant to challenge GOP leaders, and for his faithful service had been rewarded with patronage appointments and the chairmanship of the appropriations committee. His behavior in the Senate was similar. He cooperated with his colleagues and benefited from his amiability. Dawes had no personal ideology that overrode his loyalty to the party. And for him, the party's principles were constant: a strong central government, racial equality, sound money, and a high tariff. While his stalwart allegiances continued to serve him well, they also made Dawes increasingly vulnerable to a group of younger Republicans who became active during the 1870s. This new group (often called "halfbreeds" by their stalwart opponents) contained men from a number of ideological camps; they shared only a common antipathy to the party's aging leadership. Their chief in Massachusetts was John Davis Long, who, after being elected governor in 1879, immediately began campaigning to unseat Dawes at the following year's GOP convention.

Dawes had reason to be worried by Long's challenge. The governor was younger and more articulate. His recent campaign had involved a number of modern techniques: extensive newspaper advertising, effective organization, and concentration on the growing industrial areas around Boston. It would not be enough for Dawes to repeat the party's slogans and await the verdict of the bosses. He was sixty-two, and, despite his long career, little more than a rural loyalist. His home in Pittsfield was far from the center of power in Boston, and he seemed incapable—despite his patronage power—of overcoming the distance.

But Dawes was not defeated. He was renominated and reelected in 1880 and again in 1886. The young halfbreeds did not win their victory until 1892, when the senator retired and Henry Cabot Lodge took his place. Even more remarkable, Dawes ended his career as a kind of Victorian saint, universally acclaimed as the Indians' truest friend and therefore (however illogically) one of Massachusetts's great senators. It would seem that the senator's sudden involvement in Indian affairs in late 1879 saved his career. In the ensuing months and years, the issue provided Dawes with a platform for national leadership; it made his reputation as a lawmaker; and it bathed his political activities in the glow of a popular cause. Indian assimilation's appeal to both Dawes and his backers is a good measure of its meaning in the political life of the 1880s.

Henry Dawes never thought of himself as simply an office seeker or party reliable. Rather, he held so strongly to the stalwart wing of the GOP precisely because it seemed to represent a principled approach to government. One cannot read his speeches and letters without concluding that here was a true believer. Political contests were not competitions between interest or ethnic groups; they were confrontations between opposing philosophies. "The next election," he told a group of Republicans in 1882, "will determine not only with whom the political power shall hereafter rest, but also questions of government, grave and vital, involving the very future of the institutions under which we live." He continued:

First, and before all else in importance, it will be decided: whether under the Constitution, the Nation or the State is sovereign and whether there is power in one to maintain its life and authority in the other, with or without its consent. Whether the Nation shall protect its citizen, whoever and wherever he may be in a free and honest ballot for national officers or shall surrender him to the State. Whether or not the peace of the United States shall abide with its humble citizens, however humble and wherever he may go or dwell within the limits of the broad Union.[48]

For a man who had left the Whigs over slavery, sat in Congress during the Civil War, served as one of Lincoln's pallbearers, and joined the radical rebellion against Andrew Johnson, such talk represented more than the flapping of the bloody shirt. The supremacy of national institutions, cautious attempts at racial justice, the use of federal power—these were themes that stretched back a quarter-century for Dawes and his constituents.

Yet it was apparent that there was a great difference between the Washington of Lincoln and the capital city presided over by a succession of anonymous, bearded leaders and their battalions of placemen. For these people, the protection of national sovereignty had devolved into defending large railroads and their clients with government contracts. The defense of racial equality had been reduced to the defense of the Republican party in the South and the hope that *private* philanthropy might somehow alter the caste system there. New, divisive issues—such as the efforts to stop Chinese immigration—failed to arouse the party or its leaders to defend their principles in a new environment. Increasingly in the 1870s and 1880s, Republicans were on the defensive. They could unite on subjects of traditional concern, but they divided over the specific role of the party in shaping the nation's future.

Thus the piety of Dawes's campaign rhetoric had become something of a lie. After visiting the prim Republican White House of Rutherford B. Hayes, where, as one wag put it, "the water flowed like champagne," the senator wrote his wife: "I called on Mrs. Hayes Friday night. She 'Brother Dawes-ed' me and I 'Sister Hayes-ed' her back again, and that was pretty much all." The old Republican morality had become an uncomfortable pose, something to feel uneasy over or to joke about. In a sense, of course, this had always been the case: there had never been a time when Republican truth unhampered by interests and tensions had marched forth to do battle with its foe.[49] But by 1879 Republicans felt the need to affirm their "principled" approach to politics. This was especially true in states like Massachusetts, where the events of the 1860s had faded into mythology while the need to galvanize support and beat back young insurgents had increased.

Just as Dawes, who occupied Sumner's old desk in the Senate, took pride in showing visitors the unrepaired marks left by "Bully" Brooks's cane in 1856, so did he seek to retain his connections with the GOP's ideals. It was in this atmosphere of both nostalgia and unease that the senator first embraced the campaign for total assimilation. Indian affairs raised again the possibility that the government could "deliver" an embattled minority from tyrannical rule; it evoked an echo of the old crusade.

As a congressman Dawes had led the movement in 1870 to stop the practice of dealing with the tribes by treaty. At that time his chief concern had been government economy. Treaties enabled senators and bureaucrats to appropriate money without proper congressional review. While he occasionally commented on Indian affairs during the 1870s, he did not become a prominent public spokesman for policy reform until after Standing Bear captured Boston audiences in 1879. At the request of the Boston Indian Citizenship Committee (via its chairman, John Davis Long), Dawes joined in the attack on Secretary Schurz and his "halfbreed policies." These actions were not lost on Massachusetts Republicans, who trumpeted Dawes's statements on the Poncas and—in his son's words— overturned the "Boston prejudices" of the GOP leadership. With their backing, the senator defeated Long and won renomination in 1880.[50]

In 1881, safely reelected and impressed with the appeal of his Indian policy statements, Dawes joined the Senate Indian Affairs Committee. Despite the fact that he was a new member, he immediately became its chairman. For the next twelve years he used his position to advocate Indian assimilation. He was principally responsible for the expansion of appropriations for Indian education; the passage of the General Allotment Act that bore his name; and the approval of a number of large land cessions, among them the Crow and Blackfoot agreements and the Great Sioux agreement of 1889.

But despite its importance in Dawes's career, the wider attractiveness of Indian assimilation seems somewhat incongruous in the context of the 1880s. While Standing Bear was inciting the merchants of Boston, Southern redeemers were busily rebuilding their white supremacist state governments with the tacit approval of federal authorities. Westerners, assisted by Congress, succeeded in placing a ban on all Chinese immigration. And anti-Catholicism was a regular feature of life in most major cities. Clearly, the call for the incorporation of natives into white society ran counter to these movements. But this incongruity should not be confusing, for it illuminates the appeal of the Indian assimilation issue.

The singularity of Indian assimilation is less striking when one recalls that the goal of men like Dawes was not a blending of Indian and white societies but Anglo conformity: the alteration of native culture to fit a "civilized" model. Reformers insisted that Indians should follow the "white man's road." The expression is significant, for it indicates the kind of future being planned for Native Americans. Here was an important link between Dawes and the new anthropologists. Like them, the senator believed in a single standard of civilization and expected that Indians—like other minority groups— could be made to conform to it. Moreover, both scholars and politicians believed the incorporation process could occur quickly and contribute to the general good.[51]

A comparison of the Indians with other minorities of the period shows that Native Americans posed the smallest threat to existing social relationships. In 1879 most tribes lived in federal territories such as Washington, Arizona, the Dakotas, and what would later become Oklahoma. Most of their white neighbors had no voice in Congress. In addition, once they had been defeated militarily, the majority culture took little notice of the Indians' activities. It appeared that incorporating native people into the larger society would displace no one; it would carry few political costs. Politicians such as Dawes assumed that their programs would provoke only mild resistance from whites. Consequently they stood a good chance of succeeding.

The successful civilization of the Indians also would demonstrate the wisdom of accommodation. Native Americans might require extensive federal assistance, but that aid would simply give the Indians opportunities that were already available (at least theoretically) to other groups: jobs, schools, and citizenship. In the end Indian "advancement" would be a salutary model to hold before other minority communities. Assimilated natives would be proof positive that America was an open society, where obedience and accommodation to the wishes of the majority would be rewarded with social equality.

Thus Henry Dawes and his colleagues did not invent the appeal of total assimilation; they simply exploited it. They believed Congress could afford to take the steps necessary to introduce Native Americans to a universal process of assimilation through conformity. Positive results would advertise and encourage that process. In an essay written after his retirement, the senator emphasized these goals.

It is true that we have not yet assimilated the Indians, but it is also true that we have already absorbed the Indian. The State can only bring the Indian into the environment of civilization, and he is 'absorbed' wherever and whenever that occurs. The rest is the work of time and contact, of individual effort and social force, of education and religion. The Bohemians in Chicago, the Polish Jews in New York, are absorbed into our civilization, though they speak no English or live in squalor. Assimilation is another and a better thing, but it is the step that follows absorption.[52]

While it constituted an important acceleration of the government's assimilation efforts and produced an extraordinary degree of federal activity, the campaign to assimilate America's natives by forcing them to conform to the majority's culture was not inconsistent with contemporary attitudes toward other racial and ethnic minorities. The nation would make Native Americans the same offer it extended to other groups: membership in society in exchange for adaptation to existing cultural standards. The major difference would be

Table 1. The Dawes Loyalists, 1880–85 *

Name	Years in Senate	Mean Agreement Score
Henry W. Blair (R–N.H.)	1880–91	68
Edward Rollins (R–N.H.)	1877–83	67
William B. Allison (R–Iowa)	1872–1908	64
Benjamin Harrison (R–Ind.)	1881–87	63
Omar Conger (R–Mich.)	1881–87	60
George F. Hoar (R–Mass.)	1887–1904	59
William Windom (R–Minn.)	1871–81, 1881–83	57
William Frye (R–Maine)	1881–1911	55
Joseph Hawley (R–Conn.)	1881–1905	55
Henry Dawes (R–Mass.)	1874–1893	53
John I. Mitchell (R–Pa.)	1881–87	52
Austin Pike (R–N.H.)	1883–86	52
Elbridge Lapham (R–N.Y.)	1881–85	51

* See votes 1–19, Appendix 1. Mean agreement scores represent the average rate of agreement between Senator Dawes and his colleagues.

that federal officials would initiate and carry out this program. They could afford to do so, for the Indian assimilation campaign promised to be popular, safe, and therapeutic.

The total assimilation theme had such a wide appeal that Henry Dawes was able to rely on a substantial group of his fellow lawmakers to support his proposals. It was Dawes's legislative influence that was the key to his success. Between 1880 and 1885, for example, nineteen roll call votes affecting Indians were held in the Senate. A dozen senators who served during this period and responded to at least five of these votes can be identified as "Dawes loyalists." These men, who are listed in Table 1, followed the Massachusetts senator's lead—voting yea, nay, or abstaining—50 percent of the time or more.

In 1880 there were seventy-six people in the Senate. It would be difficult to argue that thirteen men could "dictate" policy to the entire group. Nevertheless, the Dawes faction was extremely powerful.

It was led by a committee chairman to whom people naturally deferred, and it was active in a relatively unimportant field where an average thirty-two votes were all that were needed to carry a particular measure. Thus, with Dawes's support a particular position could be assured of a substantial proportion of the votes necessary for it to prevail. As a result, when the group united it usually won. In 1880, for example, an attempt was made to cut off funds for the Board of Indian Commissioners, a group set up under the peace policy to monitor Indian Office purchasing, and provide reformers with a role in policy making. All of the Dawes loyalists opposed the proposal and it was defeated. In 1882 a motion to more than double the annual appropriation for Indian education was supported unanimously by the group; it passed, twenty-nine to eighteen. In the nineteen votes taken before 1885, a majority of the men in Table 1 voted with the winning side fourteen times.

All of the Dawes loyalists were Republicans. Two were from west of the Mississippi, but only one of these—William Windom of Minnesota—represented a state with a significant Indian population. A majority of the Dawes group was from New England. Their average age in 1880 was fifty-four. Here was the core of the Massachusetts senator's support: men who were party loyalists from traditionally Republican states who had lived through the heady victories of the Civil War and shared Dawes's proclivity for a pious, "principled" approach to politics. Only William Boyd Allison of Iowa, who became influential in the 1890s, could be called a party leader.

Dawes's opponents in the Senate came chiefly from two regions. Westerners opposed any "meddling" in their states' affairs. They saw federal programs to aid Indians as unnecessary intrusions on the domestic life of their region. The second center of opposition to Dawes and his followers was in the South. Uniformly Democratic and resentful of Republican social engineering, men like Wade Hampton of South Carolina were quick to line up against the pious reformers. Significantly, the men who represented the states surrounding Indian Territory (Kansas, Missouri, Arkansas, and Texas) were linked to both areas of opposition. They were easily Dawes's most vocal critics. Pushed by large constituencies of "sooners" eager to bypass the Indians, largely Democratic, and led by George Vest of Missouri and Richard Coke of Texas, this group called for the abolition of reservations without any concern for assimilation. Open the land to white homesteaders, they cried, and let nature take its course.

An angry exchange recorded in the House in 1884 typified the disputes between Dawes and his critics. The lower house appears to have been divided in much the same way as the Senate, with eastern Republicans leading the reform effort over the opposition of a few westerners and some southerners. In the midst of the debate over the 1885 Indian appropriations bill, James Belford (whose Colorado admirers called him the "Red Headed Rooster of the Rockies") delivered a long speech attacking the government's attempts to civilize the Indians. "If we are going to appropriate every year millions of money for the support of an idle, vagrant, malevolent, malicious race, then let us go to work and take on our hands all the paupers of the United States," he told his colleagues. "Who can tell us where a distinction should exist between the white pauper who can not obtain employment and the Indian who will not work?" Belford and his allies from the West and South opposed "paternalistic" policies of education and federal assistance. They argued that such programs were naïve and constituted unwarranted expansions of federal authority. The reforms singled out Indians for benefits they did not deserve.[53]

John Kasson, an Iowan who had begun his political career as a delegate to the Buffalo Free Soil convention in 1848, was quick to respond. Kasson argued, "A moral obligation rests upon the United States to change by proper and humane methods the system by which the Indians formerly lived, a system of which we deprived them, into the system of the white man which we are urging upon them." Like Henry Dawes, Kasson was comfortable with the use of federal power for his "moral obligation." And like the Massachusetts senator his goal was to bring the "system of the white man" to the tribes.[54]

Congressional support for Dawes's ideas was ideological; his opposition was largely sectional. Most of his supporters were men from the East who appeared motivated by the rhetoric of national action and racial uplift. They took few political risks, operating with the confidence of those who know their idealism is cheap and profitable. Critics of the reformers were relatively weak. Few states besides the ones bordering Indian Territory were directly affected by the government's policies—even unreconstructed southerners found the connections between Indian reform and their own past tenuous. In the early 1880s there was little to unite these skeptics; the appeal of assimilation overrode their objections.

In the late nineteenth century Indian assimilation represented but a small piece of a much larger issue. Every section of the country had significant numbers of the people who stood outside the majority culture. These groups were themselves quite varied. Some—most prominently the European immigrants and newly freed slaves—demanded social acceptance. Others—like the Chinese and Native Americans—held themselves aloof but were forced to accommodate themselves because of their circumstances. Nevertheless, all of these minority communities raised disturbing questions for the white Protestant majority. How would shrinking the geographic and social space that separated Americans affect the nation's social order? What kinds of new relationships would develop between minorities and the majority culture? And what would be the cost of these new relationships?

Fear of diversity was not new in America. The persistence of movements such as anti-Catholicism proved this, as did more recent events—attempts to limit immigration and the government's retreat from Reconstruction. But the 1880s produced something unique. Minority cultures confronted the majority in several areas simultaneously. And the future of one ethnic community—the Indians—was primarily in the hands of federal authorities. Thus, precisely when the issue of pluralism impressed itself with new urgency upon the nation, prominent politicians acquired an opportunity to test their solutions on a politically neutral group. Their response would measure both the country's plans for the Indians and its general attitude toward the social fact of cultural diversity.

A generation ago John Higham called the 1880s an "Age of Confidence." While historians since have refined that image by describing in greater detail the tension and cruelty of the period, the phrase remains essentially accurate. At least among the articulate leaders of the majority culture, there was a uniform conviction that economic expansion, political freedom, and the widening influence of institutions such as the home, the school, and the church would hold the country's social fabric together. Powerful white Americans reasoned that the future could be an extension of the present. Culturally homogeneous communities could distribute themselves across the landscape, and the concurrent growth of social and political institutions would ensure that uniform structures would give shape to American society. These institutions would mold the diverse—but malleable—population of the United States into a society that believed in individualism, free enterprise, the nuclear family, the common school, and the promise of prosperity.[55]

It was this deeply traditional vision that lay behind the appeal of Indian assimilation. White journalists, social scientists, and politicians believed that the "uplift" of the red man would confirm their own definition of America. In their view other groups might not be as successful as Native Americans—the Irish might be too numerous, the Chinese might be persecuted by their white neighbors, blacks might not be capable of rapid progress—but the Indians would demonstrate that a "civilized" nation could accommodate nonwhite people by encouraging them to give up their traditional lifeways. The assimilation campaign promised to destroy the Indians' ancient cultures, but that destruction would serve what reformers believed was a greater good: the expansion of "civilized" society.

Chapter 2

The Campaign Begins

Unprecedented reform activity followed the disasters of 1879. In the ensuing decade, legislators and bureaucrats worked to replace the reservation system with a program to incorporate Native Americans into the larger society. While a variety of motives—from narrow self-interest to airy idealism—lay behind this new policy, the federal government sustained a remarkable level of activity. During the 1880s federal officials became involved in the details of Indian land tenure, education, and citizenship. Appropriations expanded to support a growing bureaucracy that operated throughout the country. And a cadre of professionals emerged to operate the system. By 1890 the nation had adopted a new approach to Indian affairs and created the machinery for effecting a campaign of total assimilation.

In the wake of the Cheyenne Massacre, an exasperated Henry Dawes told his colleagues, "We appropriate from the treasury at the least $2,700,000 and . . . in the meantime the great Indian question remains unsettled; we have made no advance toward it; we have not even touched it; but we have aggravated it." Sixteen years later the senator was more sanguine. All the necessary legislation had been enacted; the task had become one of implementation. The Indian, he wrote, "is today civilized in the elemental sense of that term. He is 'surrounded everywhere by white civilization'; all his race wear civilized clothes; more than two-thirds of them cultivate the ground, live in houses, ride in Studebaker wagons, sends his children to school, drinks whiskey, may if he likes own property. What he needs is individual help." The Indian problem, he concluded, was now "no different from the Bohemian problem or the German problem."[1]

Having been exposed to the influence of "white civilization," the Indians were now expected to evolve into facsimiles of their white mentors. The "Indian problem" had not been completely solved, but the nation's lawmakers believed they had found answers to the issues that had tormented them in the 1870s. The new programs focused on three areas: Indian landholding, education, and citizenship. In each of these, divergent party and sectional interests acted together in the belief that total assimilation was both practical and possible in a relatively short time. Everyone agreed that the success of the new policies would ensure that the embarrassing incidents of 1879 would not happen again.

In 1880 the United States still recognized the existence of a substantial Indian empire. An area one and a half times the size of California lay under tribal control. Tribes maintained their own political and legal systems and for the most part were economically self-sufficient. Although scattered across the country, these pockets of native sovereignty guaranteed the Indians' continued independence. They allowed Native Americans to separate themselves from the white majority and maintain many of their traditional lifeways. Because they formed a cultural barricade, the tribes considered their reservations to be their most important possessions. For the same reason, the architects of the assimilation policy believed that any program designed to bring natives into the majority culture would require a drastic reduction in Indian landownership.

After 1879 a fundamental change in the government's Indian land policies was a certainty. The reservation system was under attack from a number of directions. The army wanted to shed its distasteful police responsibilities. Reformers who had applauded Grant's peace policies were now disenchanted. The nation's anthropologists, committed to both a version of human progress and a vision of themselves as experts, attacked the idea of permanent enclaves. And government officials, aware of the political costs of maintaining the reservation system, were ready to act.

But even without this constellation of attitudes, the tribal empire was doomed, for the nation's shrinking reservoir of "vacant" land made a new Indian land policy inescapable. West of the Mississippi the population was exploding: it rose from seven to more than eleven million in the 1870s. And much of the increase of that ten-year period took place in areas with large numbers of Indians: the population doubled in Montana and Idaho, tripled in Nebraska and Washington, and quadrupled in Arizona and Colorado. In 1870, Dakota Territory had contained almost twice as many Indians as whites. By 1880 the tribes were outnumbered by white settlers by a ratio of better than six to one. The non-Indian population in the territory had increased tenfold in a single decade.

Expansion of the nation's rail system accompanied this growth in population. In 1870 the Union Pacific was the nation's only transcontinental line. It concentrated on cross-country service and maintained few branches to western towns. But by 1880 three rival lines snaked their way to the coast and dozens of smaller regional companies were pushing into the interior, uniting the West with intersecting bands of steel.

Thus the central issue of the 1880s was not *whether* the reservation system would be changed, but *when* and *how*. Would it be nibbled to death by special interests who first attacked the choicest lands and then moved to marginal areas as these rose in value? Or would the end come swiftly, with policy makers adopting a comprehensive program aimed simultaneously at all reservations? While events never corresponded exactly to either, these two models are useful illustrations of an important aspect of the era that has often been overlooked in the historian's search for heroes and villains: laws governing Indian lands changed in the 1880s because policy makers linked the economic development of the West to the goal of total assimilation. Businessmen were often divided over the disposition of lands. What is more, Westerners were relatively weak in Congress; they were not capable of determining policy alone, no matter how vital their imagined stake in any decision. In the same way reformers could not arouse Congress with simple rhetoric. The goal of total assimilation galvanized support for a new land policy among a wide range of political interests. Consequently both ideas and interests lay behind the events of the 1880s; neither was dominant. It is no more accurate to concentrate on western venality than on the reformers' sweet promises. Self-interest meshed with idealism, for public policy makers siezed on a plan they felt would reconcile the goals of Native Americans and whites.

In the fifteen years after Standing Bear's tour nearly half of "Indian country" was opened to white settlement. Between 1880 and 1895 tribes lost 60 percent of the amount that would be taken in the next century. The Dawes Act, often cited as the principal source of land loss in this period, accounted for far less. The massive reduction in Indian landholdings that occurred in the 1880s derived primarily from seven major land cessions. These affected Ute lands in Colorado (1880), the Columbia and Colville Reservation in Washington Territory (1884 and 1892), Oklahoma (1889), the Great Sioux Reservation (1889), the Blackfoot and Crow lands in Montana (1889), and the Bannock-Shoshone reserve at Fort Hall, Idaho (1889). Some of these reservations had existed for only a few years at the time of their dissolution. Others, such as the Crow, Sioux, and Ojibwa lands, had been set aside for over twenty years. Oklahoma had been a part of Indian Territory for over a half-century when the first sections were opened to non-Indians in 1889.[2]

Business interests in the West and elsewhere played a significant role in winning approval of these land cessions. The Ute Treaty of 1880, for example, which required the White River Utes to cede all 12 million acres of their land in a mineral-rich section of Colorado, was enthusiastically supported by local businessmen and speculators. On the southern plains, the pressure to open first Oklahoma (the "unassigned lands") and then the other parts of the Indian Territory could also be traced to economic forces. The "boomers" led by

David Payne, who pestered federal authorities and helped undermine the Five Civilized Tribes, were regularly supported by railroads
and local merchants. One convention of these businessmen proclaimed, "The highest obligation of a government towards a helpless, conquered people, penned in a tract of country . . . is to teach
them the arts by which they alone can endure, and to infuse into
them the spirit of self-reliance and industry which underlies all civilization and all permanent prosperity." These people believed that
the advent of white settlers and the example of their "arts" would be
the best teachers of "self-reliance and industry." Like similar groups
throughout the West, they argued that the destruction of this tribal
preserve would be "uplifting" because it would mean "permanent
prosperity" for the region.[3]

On the northern plains railroad companies were actively involved
in the destruction of several large reservations. Three lines—the
Northern Pacific, the Chicago, Milwaukee and St. Paul, and the Great
Northern—undertook ambitious expansion programs that promised
to make them rivals of the Union Pacific. Early in their growth,
however, they each found themselves confronted with a basic fact of
railroad life: long-distance traffic cannot support a long-distance
road. As the industry's leading journal, the *Railroad Gazette*, observed in 1881, "It is one of our commonest errors to exaggerate the
amount and still more the profitableness of the through traffic of
very long lines. . . . Lines across the continent, like most other lines,
have to draw their chief support from their local traffic."[4]

When the Northern Pacific inaugurated its transcontinental service in 1883 it was already in deep trouble. The final link in its construction program had saddled the company with a huge debt; it
would take more than frontier optimism to keep its creditors at bay.
For three years, the railroad survived by selling off its land grant
in northern Dakota Territory and Montana. In 1885, for example,
freight charges earned a profit of only $91,960. With fixed interest
payments of $265,000 due on January 1, 1886, the company would
have faced a severe crisis had its land department not earned over
$1.6 million during the same period. Each of the companies might
have survived these precarious years if their supplies of land had

been unlimited and they had enjoyed a monopoly over the western trade. Instead, the amount of available land was dwindling rapidly and there was intense competition between lines.

During the 1880s, the major western railroads were faced with a financial version of Hobson's notorious choice. They were committed to expansion, but their rising fixed costs could not be met by transcontinental freight revenues or (for very long) by land sales. The single alternative available to them was spelled out by the editors of the *Railroad Gazette*. Commenting on the Northern Pacific, these observers wrote that earnings would increase only by a growth of local traffic: "This is the foundation on which the future prosperity of the company must be built." Turning to the Chicago, Milwaukee and St. Paul, which purchased and built over twenty-two hundred miles of track on the Plains between 1879 and 1881, the journal added that "nothing could justify this course but the conviction that this country was on the eve of a great growth in population and production."[5]

Thus as Senator Dawes and his colleagues began to discuss the reform of the reservation system, the most powerful businesses in the West were becoming convinced that they had a direct stake in the expansion of agricultural production. As a result they were increasingly interested in both gaining entry to and reducing the size of tribal holdings. The Northern Pacific completed its original cross-country line with rights of way through the Crow and Flathead reservations. But in the 1880s the company acquired branch lines that tapped new mines and towns and led it into the Coeur d'Alene and Nez Perce preserves. The Milwaukee road won access to the Great Sioux Reservation and the Union Pacific (through its subsidiary, the Utah and Northern) pushed north from Salt Lake after acquiring rights to Bannock and Shoshone lands near Fort Hall. It was the Great Northern, however, that was most dependent on tribal lands. The 17.5-million-acre Crow-Blackfoot cession of 1888 enabled the recently reorganized line to cross Montana and reach the Pacific. What is more, these lands also served as the basis for the company's ambitious program of attracting settlers to the northern plains. Indeed, the success of the Great Northern must be attributed in large part to the massive subsidy it received from the Indians.[6]

Of course railroad executives and businessmen did not act alone. Most settlers living near reservations saw these lands as barriers to local economic growth. In Washington Territory, for example, where the population increased nearly 500 percent during the 1880s, the demand for a reduction in the area controlled by the Colvilles was deafening. The House Indian Affairs Committee observed that there was "no room for so vast an area of unemployed land as that in the Colville Reservation and its continuance as such [was] no less an injustice to the Indians themselves than a menace to the progress of the surrounding commonwealth." The committee report was accepted without opposition and the reservation quickly opened to non-Indian settlers.[7]

In every major land cession there were specific economic interests who were bound to profit by a reduction of the reservations. Whether they were merchants, railroad executives, or simple farmers, their cry was the same: tribal lands were a barrier to prosperity. Nevertheless, the lure of profits does not in itself explain the passage of these huge land cessions. If the Kansas City merchants were strident in their declaration of 1888 it was because they had been lobbying for an opening of Indian Territory for ten years. The first "boomer" invasion of the area took place in April 1879; the land was not opened to settlement until 1889. Throughout that decade railroads with special privileges in the territory and cattlemen holding profitable leases joined the tribes in opposing the settlers' demands. One marvels not at the power of the "boomers" and their allies, but at their persistence in the face of such strong opposition.

Similarly, the railroads were neither unified nor omnipotent. Congress' failure to approve rights of way across reservations was a notorious roadblock to construction. The Utah and Northern, for example, waited seven years for lands at Pocatello to be ceded by the Indians at Fort Hall. What is more, small lines backed by individual legislators were often more successful in winning access to tribal land than were the giant transcontinentals. The result was often legalized extortion, as tiny companies with no assets other than their rights of way demanded huge sums to lease their roadbeds. And finally, companies sometimes opposed a particular reservation opening. During much of the 1880s, for example, the Northern Pacific and the Chicago, Milwaukee and St. Paul resisted settlers' demands that the Great Sioux Reservation be opened. The Northern Pacific feared a reduction in land prices that was sure to follow any increase in the number of available homesteads, while the Milwaukee felt unprepared to build on its right of way through the area. As long as the reservation remained closed, the company's exclusive rights could be protected.[8]

Settlers and railroad men were intimately involved in the great land cessions of the 1880s, but these occurred only after westerners joined forces with other political factions and succeeded in tying their self-interest to the broader goal of Indian assimilation and American progress. In Congress, the assistance of two particular groups was crucial. Southerners often lined up to vote with western railroad boomers. Attacks on tribal preserves appealed to men eager to rebuild the economy of the region and acquire their own badge of progress: a railroad to the Pacific. To apostles of the New South, fed-erally administered reservations threatened local enterprise. Indian Territory was their chief concern. It appeared to prevent railroads from connecting ports on the Gulf of Mexico to the West, and it diverted the transcontinentals north to Kansas City and Chicago rather than to New Orleans. The South was laying down hundreds of miles of track in the 1880s; delaying construction of new roads be-cause of treaty rights or past promises was, in one senator's view, "poppycock."[9]

The benefits of an alliance between westerners and southerners were first demonstrated in 1882, when Congress overrode both a half-century of tradition and numerous treaty guarantees and ap-proved a railroad right of way across Indian Territory. The measure promised to benefit not David Payne and his army of merchants and settlers, but the St. Louis and San Francisco Railroad. The Senate vote on the proposal took place in April. Nearly half the thirty-one "yea" votes recorded in the upper house came from men who repre-sented the old confederacy and Kentucky. Another eleven votes came from west of the Mississippi. More than three-quarters of the bill's opponents were easterners.[10]

When the right-of-way bill reached the House, it met with similar support and opposition. An easterner's proposal that the easement be made contingent on tribal ratification went down to defeat. And with Olin Welborn of Texas warning that the reservation threatened to stand "as a Chinese wall between the growing commerce of [the] States and Territories," a chorus of "ayes" rose to approve the measure by a voice vote. The new statute set an important precedent: Congress would now decide both the timing and the terms of reservation entries. Although treaty restrictions would still restrain most legislators, it was clear that particular issues attractive to both southerners and westerners could be approved. As one member of the upper house exclaimed in 1886 during another right-of-way debate, "The interests of these great communities on both sides [of the reservation] being vitally interested, the Territory being inhabited only by a few Indians . . . we can hardly suppose that the company would undertake to build upon any other than the usual terms." A "few Indians" could not be expected to receive more attention than the future of the "great communities" that surrounded them.[11]

Legislators interested in reforming federal land policies gladly linked their concerns to those of the reservations' enemies. By the 1880s the public had become aware of the widespread abuse of the existing homestead laws. Reformers pointed out that an enterprising settler could claim far more than the mythical 160 acres. In addition, false claims and the use of land script allowed—if they did not encourage—speculation and fraud. For this reason, angry farmers and their representatives often favored reducing the size of reservations so as to open new agricultural lands under a fresh set of rules. To them, tribal preserves were little more than land monopolies that prevented honest yeomen from acquiring their American birthright.[12]

Congressman James Weaver, later a founder of the Populist party and its first presidential nominee, was one of those who believed the destruction of the reservations would benefit the cause of agrarian reform. Keeping the reservations intact, he argued, served only to protect railroads with rights of way and cattlemen with rich leases. Weaver was an ardent supporter of the Oklahoma "boomers." To charges that Payne and his followers were simply lazy misfits, Weaver replied, "Cattle syndicates of this country are occupying that Territory." Thus, he noted, "it is no time to denounce as lawless the poor men who were trying to go in there and makes homes for their families." A few years later, William A. Peffer, a Populist senator from Kansas, put the argument more bluntly. "The time for bartering with the Indian for his land is passed," he observed, "We have come to a time when under the operation of natural laws, we need all the land in this country for homes."[13]

Westerners, southerners, and agrarian reformers formed an impressive coalition. Each member of the alliance would benefit from more land cessions. But none of these groups was interested in the future of the tribes. The attention of each was focused on a particular point or region of conflict. They lacked sufficient incentive to cast their grievances in general terms. The theme of assimilation drew these interests together, allowing them to reshape their arguments and broaden their appeal. This process occurred first in 1882, when Alice Fletcher worked with Nebraska's congressional delegation to reduce the size of the Omaha preserve. Her argument— endorsed by both reformers and scientists—was that Indians could not progress until they adopted a system of individual landownership. Her approach was vital to the passage of every major land cession of the 1880s.

Throughout the decade, Indian reform groups and their political allies in Congress were less concerned with the enforcement of existing treaties than with programs to accelerate Indian "progress" by forcing the tribes out of their traditional paths. As Henry Dawes explained in 1882, "We may cry out against the violation of treaties . . . but the fact remains the same and there will come of this outcry, however just, no practical answer to this question . . . these Indians are to be somehow absorbed into and become a part of the 50,000,000 of our people. There does not seem to be any other way to deal with them." As the author of most of the major land cession agreements of the period, Dawes acted on these principles. He believed that reductions in the size of reservations would bring the two races closer together and allow America's institutions—its schools, its political system and its expanding economy—to "raise up" the Indian.[14]

The 1888 Crow and Blackfoot cession, which provided an annual payment of $430,000 in return for nearly 30 million acres of tribal land, typified the Massachusetts senator's approach. When it emerged from the Indian Affairs Committee, the agreement's preamble noted that the reservation was "wholly out of proportion to the number of Indians occupying [it]," and that the natives should dispose of their excess property "to enable them to obtain the means to become self-supporting as a pastoral and agricultural people, and to educate their children in the paths of civilization." The document went on to stipulate that proceeds from the sale would be used for agency supplies, tools, and seed. Similar arrangements soon were pressed on the Sioux and Ojibwas.[15]

Through the efforts of people like Dawes and Fletcher, land cessions became a component of the national assimilation campaign. Many of the new statutes bore Dawes's personal stamp, but his ideas were widely shared. The House Indian Affairs Committee reported the Colville agreement with the explanation that "a lessening of the dimensions of the Colville Reservation, the planting of active, prosperous and well-ordered white communities on every side of the Indians, the building of railroads, the creation of towns and cities, the opening of mines, and the consequent establishment of markets near at hand so that the Indians can realize an income on their industry, would be the greatest blessing [the United States] could bestow upon these children of benighted savagery." These sentiments were echoed even by Westerners like Henry Teller who were eager for the tribes to give way to "progress." The Colorado senator (who corresponded with John Wesley Powell) told his colleagues, "No nation in the history of the world ever came up from savagery to civilization except it was by manual labor and no nation ever will." Teller in fact was the author of the decade's most extreme proposal for achieving rapid assimilation through a land policy. He suggested that the Great Sioux agreement, intended to reduce the size of that tribe's reservation, contain a provision requiring all Indian homesteads to be located on alternate sections of land. By mandating a "checkerboard" pattern of occupancy, the senator intended to ensure the interspersion of Indians and whites. "Isolate them as we have done and they will continue as they are," the veteran Republican cried, and he promised, "If you can put them in the midst of an intelligent community you will have them civilized in a few years."[16]

The assimilation argument was more than window-dressing. It encouraged the modification of a number of land cessions to ensure that changes in Indian lifeways would occur gradually. Congress did not simply throw natives and whites together as Teller had proposed. With the support of Dawes and his eastern allies, the Montana, Minnesota, Colville, and Sioux agreements provided that reservation openings would take place in two stages. First, tribal lands would be taken and whites would be allowed to settle in areas away from principal Indian communities. Funds from the sale of this property would be applied to teaching farming to the tribes. After a period of years, what was left of the reservation would be divided into allotments or individual homesteads. Once every family had received its land, the remaining area would be opened to settlement. Each change in the reservation's borders would have to be approved by the Indians.[17]

During the debate over the Sioux agreement of 1886 (which was intended to reduce the tribe's land base), Dawes expressed his preference for a policy of gradualism. Senator Teller represented an opposing point of view. The Indian, he declared, should be "compelled to enter our civilization whether he will or whether he wills it not." In keeping with this view, the Colorado lawmaker urged his colleagues to open all reservation lands to settlement. Dawes replied that the goal of assimilation required gentler tactics. He explained, "When the time shall come, after the white man has gone in upon this that is opened today and settled there among them . . . and the Indian himself shall have been set up in severalty . . . then negotiations with each of these tribes will be easy, and the result which the Senator says ought to come will certainly come." Aided by his legislative allies— and the general assumption that the Indians would accept his plan— Dawes won approval for this version of the Sioux agreement.[18]

Congress succeeded in reducing the native land base during the 1880s because its actions appealed to a remarkably diverse group. Settlers, railroad magnates, small merchants, Populists, southerners, apostles of western expansion, and even the Indians' new "friends" shared a desire to destroy the "Chinese wall" that separated Indians and whites. Each group had its own perspective and its own considerable stake in the land cessions, but they shared a belief that reducing the size of the reservations would promote prosperity and entice the Indians into "civilized" society.

Tribal lands were not treated like the rest of the public domain. Laws dissolving their boundaries provided for native schools and supplies for farming as well as for the gradual introduction of non-Indian settlers. Nor were the tribes perceived as simple squatters to whom the government owed nothing but the right to preempt a quarter-section of land. Amid the confusion and greed, the fraudulent negotiations and the broken promises, a new national Indian land policy was taking form. The policy reflected a belief that total assimilation would be a consequence of economic prosperity. The new program was made possible by the Indians' relative political popularity, and the promise that the government's actions would— in Senator Teller's words—"have them civilized in a few years." What to later generations seemed naïve or hypocritical appeared in the 1880s to be self-evident: the Indian of the West would grow up with the country.

Long before the Crisis of 1879 focused the public's attention on Indian assimilation, the education of Native Americans was a federal concern. During the colonial era a number of missionaries and social reformers had advocated the use of schools to "raise" the Native American to civilization. In the early nineteenth century, Congress established a "civilization fund" to support these efforts. Treaties with individual tribes often contained pledges that the "Great Father" would educate his wards. The most extravagant of these were made by the 1868 Peace Commission. It promised a schoolhouse and a teacher for every thirty children. But if these vows were ever fulfilled money usually went to missionaries; there were almost no government institutions.[19]

The year 1879 marked the beginning of a new era in federal Indian education. Over the next fifteen years congressional appropriations for native schooling rose from $75,000 to over $2 million. Twenty off-reservation government boarding schools were founded along with dozens of new agency schools. In 1882 a superintendent of Indian education was appointed to oversee the program. Perhaps most significant, instruction evolved from a haphazard affair directed by evangelical missionaries and incompetent placemen to an orderly system run by trained professionals. By the end of the 1880s federal schools operated on every reservation in the country. Native American education became the province of people devoted to applying modern techniques to the job of "civilization," and Indian schools— once an embarrassing rhetorical flourish on treaties and appropriations bills—became an integral part of the government's assimilation program.[20]

Like the supporters of new land policies, educational reformers believed that American progress would create replicas of established communities throughout the West. Each of those communities would surely have a common school. As for the Indians, they would attend institutions designed to imbue them with the habits of the majority and prepare them to participate in "civilized" society. As they prospered on the frontier, Native Americans would grow more eager for education, and more appreciative of Horace Mann's genius.

One may view the growing popularity of native education in the 1880s by tracing the career of Captain Richard Pratt. Pratt founded the Carlisle Industrial Training School in 1879, and thus began the following decade as the nation's most successful educator of Indians. Ten years later he was an embattled reactionary, defending his own brand of schooling against modern experts. His experience measures the shift from an older, evangelical style of Indian education to the reformers' approach, which was devoted to the progress and assimilation of the entire race.

Pratt was a tinsmith from Logansport, Indiana, who—like many small-town Americans—was wrenched from his quiet existence by the Civil War. The conflict gave him his first glimpse of the world beyond the Midwest. Pratt returned to his trade at the close of hostilities, but could no longer content himself with its quiet routine. In 1867 he joined the regular army and was posted immediately to the western frontier. For the next eight years the captain served as a cavalry officer and commander of Indian scouts. He was involved in the Washita River campaign, the Red River War, and a number of smaller skirmishes.

Pratt's battlefield career came to a close in April 1875, when he was ordered to escort seventy-two Kiowa, Comanche, and Southern Cheyenne warriors—the ringleaders of the recent Red River fighting—to Fort Marion, Florida, and once there to supervise their confinement. The captain watched over every aspect of his prisoners' lives. He introduced them to English, to the idea of working for wages, and to his culture's rules of behavior. He guarded them carefully, but prided himself in their increasing independence. Fort Marion was located in St. Augustine, a winter refuge for wealthy northerners. Several tourists became interested in the captain's work and soon two of them were conducting classes for the prisoners. The "civilized" warriors became a town curiosity. By chance, a few vacationers were also leaders in the Indian reform movement. One of them, Episcopal bishop Henry Whipple of Minnesota, who had been involved in missionary work among the Sioux, was deeply impressed. He wrote to Pratt in 1876, "I do not remember to have ever met a person to whom I was drawn more strongly and in whose work I have felt so deep an interest."[21] Ohio's Senator George Pendleton and Spencer Baird of the Smithsonian Institution also praised the captain and encouraged him to expand his "experiment."

As a result of these new contacts, Pratt became more confident and gained a broader view of his work. If his prisoners—some of the most recalcitrant Indians in the country—could be "tamed" by his methods, then why not the entire race? As the captain told an audience in 1878:

The mass of the Indians in our land have with few tribal exceptions remained until very recently in the enjoyment of their savage life, but now a change has come, the advance of our civilized population from the East has reached the heart of the continent. . . . The dawn of a great emergency has opened upon the Indian. . . . He is in childish ignorance of the methods and course best to pursue. We are in possession of the information and help and are able to give the help that he now so much needs.[22]

In 1877 Pratt requested permission to send his charges to Hampton Institute in Virginia. The famous school for freedmen—Booker T. Washington's alma mater—was founded in the aftermath of the Civil War by the American Missionary Association, and was directed by General Samuel Chapman Armstrong. With the general's help, Pratt's proposal was approved by the War Department in August 1878.

The alliance with Armstrong brought Pratt into contact with a still wider circle of reformers. The general had powerful supporters in Congress and easy access to the religious press. But more important, Pratt's stay at Hampton heightened his evangelical view of his work. He came to believe that his instruction not only would educate the Indian, it would transform his as well. A publicity gimmick suggested to Pratt by Armstrong symbolized this dramatic self-image. Writing in the summer of 1878, just before the captain was to leave Fort Marion for Virginia, the general instructed him, "Be sure and have them bring their wild barbarous things. . . . Good pictures of the Indians as they are will be of great use to us." Staged photographs of native children taken before and after their educational "conversions" became a staple of appeals for Indian education in the early 1880s. The viewer could not help but be struck by the contrast between the new arrivals—unkempt and blanketed—and the scrubbed and uniformed students. Only the faces, curious and bewildered, were constant.[23]

Neither Pratt nor Armstrong was satisfied with the Hampton arrangement, so in the summer of 1879 the captain requested permission to establish a boarding school of his own at an abandoned army barracks outside Carlisle, Pennsylvania. He proposed that the new institution provide both a basic common-school education and instruction in manual skills. Interior Secretary Carl Schurz agreed, and authorized an enrollment of 150 students, with more promised if the "experiment" were successful. Pratt was overjoyed. As he wrote to a reformer friend, "If Carlisle can be made a grand success then the wisdom that has existed for ages will be listened to and our poor Indian's children will . . . be trained up as they should go . . . if only we give them a chance."[24]

With Pratt's organizational talent and Armstrong's skill at public relations, the "experiment" at Carlisle was successful. By 1890 the school had nearly one thousand students. As the number of new students increased the two educators widened their appeals. Both Hampton and Carlisle had print shops that published newspapers which they distributed free to senators, congressmen, and cabinet officers. Both men were within a few hours from Washington by train. And both headmasters recognized the value of congressional inspection tours. Aided by Alice Fletcher, whom he had met in Washington, Pratt arranged for excursion trains to bring legislators to Pennsylvania to view his model school. Upon his return from one of these trips, Congressman Nathaniel Deering told his colleagues, "Here, then, is the solution of the vexed Indian problem. When we can educate the Indian children . . . other kindred questions will naturally take care of themselves."[25]

But despite the enthusiasm of their supporters in congress, Pratt and Armstrong recognized that they could not educate all forty thousand Indian children in their eastern boarding schools. They agreed that schools nearer the reservations would have to bear the responsibility of educating what the captain called the "great mass." One way of doing this—while maintaining the evangelical approach of Hampton and Carlisle—was to build duplicates of their schools in the West. Unfortunately, such a program would require substantial congressional and bureaucratic support. In 1879 that support was not in evidence—only $64,000 was allotted to the general education fund. Monies from other sources raised the total amount for Indian schools other than Hampton and Carlisle to nearly $188,000; that amount provided instruction for barely 10 percent of school-age Indian children. In addition, despite increases in the amount of money available for native schools, the Indian Office had no administrative personnel assigned to education. There was no systematic supervision of existing schools nor was there any bureaucratic machinery for identifying specific needs and planning for the future.[26]

With the successful founding of Carlisle, Indian reformers and their congressional allies began calling for an expansion of the boarding-school concept. Massachusetts' two senators, George Frisbie Hoar and Henry Dawes, led a drive to raise funds for new off-reservation institutions. Speaking of the task of civilization that stood before them, Hoar asked, "Could we not accomplish it with the present instrumentality if we had money enough?" In the House men like Michigan's Byron Cutcheson (who had recently visited Carlisle) were equally vocal. Somewhat surprisingly, however, the creation of a new group of boarding schools was primarily the achievement of a retired major general in the Colorado Militia: Secretary of the Interior Henry Teller.[27]

When Henry Teller was first mentioned as a candidate to head the Interior Department, a missionary friend of Richard Pratt noted that the choice would be "extremely absurd." The Colorado senator had opposed the reformers since 1879, when the Ute outbreak in his home state had made him a spokesman for outraged white settlers. He argued that easterners did not understand the Indian problem and should not meddle in the affairs of the frontier. Nevertheless, when President Arthur appointed him to the cabinet in 1882, Teller quickly became a champion of boarding-school education. After his first visit to Carlisle in August 1882, the new secretary wrote to Alice Fletcher, "I want to fill Pratt's school as full as it will bear." He did more than that. Not only did enrollments at Hampton and Carlisle increase during his three-year administration, but six new schools were also founded: Fort Stevenson, Dakota; Genoa, Nebraska; Fort Yuma, Arizona; Haskell Institute, Kansas; Fort Hall, Idaho; and Chilocco Training School in Indian Territory. And Indian school attendance doubled.[28]

Teller defended the new schools in coldly practical terms. In his first annual report he estimated that the expenditure of five or six million dollars for education over a fifteen-year period would make the Indian, "if not a valuable citizen, at least one from whom danger need not be apprehended." The Indian would thus "cease to be a tax on the government." Better to "civilize" the tribes than dispute with them over boundaries and property. Better also to establish new schools under a Republican administration so that contracts and jobs might be distributed for the greatest political benefit.[29]

But despite the fact that Teller had no sympathy for eastern reformers, his expansion of the boarding-school program relied on them for its support. The following list of senators shows their responses to two measures that would have expanded the government's support for Indian education.

Senators *supporting* both proposals	Senators *opposing* both proposals
William B. Allison (R–Iowa)	Francis M. Cockrell (D–Mo.)
Henry B. Anthony (R–R.I.)	Richard Coke (D–Tex.)
Henry W. Blair (R–N.H.)	James T. Farley (D–Calif.)

Senators *supporting* both proposals	Senators *opposing* both proposals
Matthew C. Butler (D–S.C.)	Augustus H. Garland (D–Ark.)
Angus Cameron (R–Wis.)	James B. Groome (D–Md.)
David Davis (D–Ill.)	Isham G. Harris (D–Tenn.)
Henry L. Dawes (R–Mass.)	Benjamin F. Jonas (D–La.)
Nathaniel P. Hill (R–Colo.)	John T. Morgan (D–Ala.)
George H. Pendleton (D–Ohio)	Preston B. Plumb (R–Kans.)
Edward H. Rollins (R–N.H.)	James L. Pugh (D–Ala.)
Alvin Saunders (R–Nebr.)	Daniel W. Voorhes (D–Ind.)
William Windom (R–Minn.)	

The first was an amendment offered in 1881 to appropriate one thousand dollars annually to supplement Richard Pratt's military salary. This amount would enable the captain to continue at Carlisle rather than return to his cavalry regiment, and the vote was seen as a referendum on the man's efforts. The second was a motion offered the following year by Massachusetts senator Hoar to raise the annual Indian education appropriation by 85 percent.[30] Three-quarters of the senators supporting both proposals were Republicans. The same percentage represented states east of the Mississippi. Nearly all the opponents of both measures were Democrats, and none came from the northeast.

The remarkable alliance between a Colorado firebrand and eastern humanitarians is vivid evidence of the extent to which Captain Pratt's evangelical view of Indian assimilation was supported by his contemporaries. Like the headmaster of Carlisle, Senator Teller believed that a period of intense "civilization" would transform the Indians into self-sufficient people. In 1884, at the end of Teller's reign at the Interior Department, Commissioner of Indian Affairs Homer Price observed that "an impartial view" of the government's recent efforts would warrant "the belief that some time in the near future . . . with the aid of such industrial, agricultural, and mechanical schools as [were] now being carried on, the Indian [would] be able to care for himself, and be no longer a burden but a help to the Government." Schools were symbols of a common faith in education's ability to convert native children to "civilization." During the re-

mainder of the decade, this evangelical vision fueled the creation of
a national Indian educational system on the model of the country's
public schools.[31]

The popularity of boarding schools as the preferred means of educating Indians was relatively short-lived. Three groups undermined
the original program. First, Democratic legislators argued that boarding schools for all forty thousand Native American children would
be prohibitively expensive. Providing such facilities would require
that congress double the entire Indian Office budget. Second, south-
eners and others hostile to the idea of federal aid for nonwhite minorities asserted that native children should not receive such elaborate training. And finally, the growing interest in Indian schools
attracted a cadre of professional educators who began to dominate
educational policy making. These people admired men like Armstrong and Pratt but were eager to introduce modern methods to the
task of "civilization."

Budgetary arguments against boarding schools made themselves
felt after the Democratic landslide of 1884. For the first time since
the Civil War the party of Calhoun and Jeff Davis controlled both the
presidency and the House of Representatives. The Democrats' election slogans had been "Retrenchment and Reform" and once in
office the party's leaders began a widespread effort to cut federal
spending. Riding what one observer called a "sweet and aromatic
wave of economy," they turned their attention to the Indian Office.
In 1885 the House took the unprecedented action of cutting the general education appropriation. But the Senate, still controlled by Republicans and the Dawes supporters on the Indian Affairs Committee, restored these cuts and provided for a 10 percent increase.[32]

Even though Captain Pratt—who had lobbied in person for the
1885 budget—celebrated this victory over the Democrats, it was obvious that a turning point had been reached. Between their inception
in 1877 and 1885, general appropriations for Indian education had
increased an average of 75 percent per year. For the ten years after
1885 the average increase was 10 percent and the largest, 35 percent,
came in 1891. "Our people," the Democratic chairman of the House
Indian Affairs Committee warned, "are growing tired of being taxed
and taxed almost out of existence to enrich a few manufacturers in

this country and to support these lazy Indians in dirt and idleness." Throughout the next two decades the budget cutters kept to this rhetorical high ground—and in the process forced their adversaries across the aisle to follow suit. Republican Henry Johnson, for example, told his House colleagues that if the Indians who met Columbus had been able to see into the future, none of the infamous events of American history would have appalled them "until they saw the apparition of the gentlemen from Indiana [Appropriations Committee chairman Richard Holman] in the noonday of the nineteenth century, standing up in the American House of Commons with his well-known face begrimed all over with the war paint of economy, holding in one hand his scalping knife and in the other that instrument of still worse torture, his contemptible, penurious Indian appropriations bill." Neither party had the congressional strength to overcome the other on this issue and both refused to moderate their positions. The result was an end to federal largesse and a corresponding modification of the Indian Office's plans for the future.[33]

For southerners and some particularly hostile westerners, these emotional budgetary arguments were often linked to doubts concerning the Native American's ability to learn. Grover Cleveland's commissioner of Indian affairs was a Tennessean who typified the attitude. John Atkins wrote that as far as he was concerned Indians should be taught the English language only. "The English language as taught in America," he added, "is good enough for all her people of all her races." Kansas senator Preston Plumb expanded on this theme. An opponent of boarding schools, Plumb declared, "It is not possible to take an Indian and by the mere process of school education put him upon the plane of the white people." Plumb's fellow Kansan John J. Ingalls was even more direct. He argued that boarding schools were "as absurd" and "futile" as going "among a herd of Texas broadhorn steers and endeavoring to turn them into Durhams and thoroughbreds by reading Alexander's herd book in their cattle-pens at Dodge City or Wichita."[34]

Despite this hostility, few politicians wanted to abandon the government's education program altogether. Everyone involved, legislators, bureaucrats, and private reformers, agreed that the "uncivilized" Indians ought somehow to be "raised" to the "plane of white people." The cruel rhetoric of Ingalls and Plumb attested to their rejection of Pratt and his new schools, but even these men assumed that the government should educate its wards. They were willing to support programs that were more closely tied to the reservations. Consequently, in the mid-1880s the Indian Office began to accommodate itself to skeptical politicians by shifting its attention away from off-reservation boarding schools and toward the creation of a more comprehensive system.

In 1881, Alfred Riggs, a Presbyterian missionary among the Sioux, sketched out his solution to the problem of Indian education for the readers of the *Journal of Education*. Writing for a professional audience, he urged the government "to organize and operate a school system for the whole Indian country which [would] do for the Indian what the public school systems of Massachusetts, or New York, or Ohio, [did] for every son and daughter of these commonwealths." Riggs's advice summarized the approach of most modern educators. They argued that the government's obligation to the now-defeated Indians required it to replace the older boarding schools with newer, more practical facilities. Their proposals were more attractive to politicians and matched the new ideas that were beginning to percolate to the surface from the Indian Office bureaucracy.[35]

J. J. Haworth became the government's first inspector of Indian education in 1882. He was responsible for overseeing school supply contracts and making personnel recommendations. The title of the position was changed in 1885 to Indian school superintendent. Now there was a bureaucratic structure charged with supervising the entire school program and making recommendations for future growth. While this "structure" first consisted of no more than an administrator and a clerk, the people involved in it were experienced educators who argued that a modern education should be the basis for the Indians' assimilation. "The position of Supervisor," wrote William Hailmann, who served from 1894 to 1898, "is not at first glance a very attractive one, [it] calls for a high degree of missionary spirit and enthusiasm in order to be successful."[36]

The meaning of the evolution from the older Pratt approach to a newer, more professional style first became clear in 1884, when Inspector Haworth spoke before the annual meeting of the National

Education Association's Department of Superintendence. With the founders of Hampton and Carlisle in the audience, Haworth attacked eastern boarding schools for their expense and their "errors in teaching." These institutions kept Indians in an artificial environment and prevented them from adapting the lessons they learned to their surroundings. Pratt responded immediately from the floor. "It is not practicable to educate them *on* the reservation," he cried, "if we desire them to be anything else than Indians." But the captain's protests found few supporters. If his experiment had been successful, and if it was politically impossible to bring all forty thousand children to the East, then was it not logical to duplicate his techniques in the West? As an editorial in the *Journal of Education* argued, "Good as is the work done at Carlisle, there is little glory in that fact if it is only a show school for the civilization of a few while the multitude remain outside pleading in vain for admittance." Pratt was not being attacked by his critics, but by followers who were seeking a politically practical way of building on his achievements.[37]

John Oberly, an Indian school superintendent (and later Indian commissioner) in the Cleveland administration, was the first to sketch out a proposal for a national educational system for Native Americans. He recommended beginning with the construction of boarding schools on each reservation. These facilities would put the lessons of Hampton and Carlisle to work for every tribe while they "reflect[ed] some of the light of civilization into the Indian camp."[38] He called also for centralizing school administration in his office. Hiring, construction, teacher training, and even the disposition of "incorrigible" students would best be handled from Washington. Finally, he suggested that Indian Office experts prepare a special series of textbooks for use in Indian schools. His immediate successors added requests for a compulsory attendance law and the delineation of grade levels in all institutions. These loyal Democrats were as interested in centralizing patronage as they were in reforming the education program, but their efforts also went a long way towards systematizing the government's attempts and placing them in the hands of specialists.

Under Benjamin Harrison such specialists moved to center stage. Between 1889 and 1893 the commissioner of Indian affairs was

Thomas Jefferson Morgan, a man whose career is best understandable to the late twentieth century only by analogy. Like modern economists and lawyers who glide silently between universities, government agencies, and private foundations, Morgan had skills that were valued in several of the nineteenth century's most prestigious professions. He had been a commander of black troops in the Civil War, a Baptist minister, a professor of theology, the principal of the New York State Normal School at Potsdam, and an officer in the National Education Association. While the connections between the battlefield, the pulpit, and the classroom may seem obscure a century later, they were clear to Morgan and his contemporaries. The new commissioner was captivated by the potential for moral uplift within the public schools and eager to focus their power on the job of "civilizing" the Indians.

Morgan's superintendent of Indian education was the Reverend Daniel Dorchester. Like his superior, Dorchester had been both a minister and an educational reformer before coming to Washington. The new team's faith in the schools was revealed in a special pamphlet issued with Morgan's first annual report: "Education is to be the medium through which the rising generation of Indians are to be brought into fraternal and harmonious relationship with their white fellow-citizens, and with them enjoy the sweets of refined homes, the delight of social intercourse, the emoluments of commerce and trade, the advantages of travel, together with the pleasures that come from literature, science and philosophy, and the solace and stimulus afforded by a true religion." The commissioner went on to describe how "the condition of this whole people [could] be radically improved in a single generation." First, every Indian community or village should have a day school for its children. These institutions would provide an "impressive object lesson" in the virtues of civilized living and serve as a center for funneling students into a second tier of facilities, the primary schools. The primary schools would provide boarding and be located at most agencies and population centers. Their mission was to lay the "foundation work of native education." For this reason, Morgan wrote, the primary schools had to take students "at as early an age as possible, before camp life [had] made an indelible stamp on them." At about age ten, students would advance to grammar schools, which would "accustom pupils to systematic habits" by making them adhere to a rigid daily schedule and begin learning a trade. Finally, at about fifteen, academically inclined Indians would enter government high schools, which, Morgan wrote, "should uplift the Indian students on to so high a plane of thought and aspiration as to render the life of the camp intolerable." He added that this fourth level of school would thus serve as "a gateway out from the desolation of the reservation into assimilation with natural life."[39]

The editors of the *Journal of Education* applauded Morgan's proposal, calling it "the key-note so long desired by all thoughtful well-wishers of the Indian."[40] Congress was not so enthusiastic, and lagging appropriations left many of the commissioner's proposals on the drawing board. Nevertheless, he and Dorchester accomplished a great deal of the "systemization" envisioned in his first report. Grades were established in all government schools and a uniform series of textbooks was adopted for each level of instruction. In 1891 all school personnel came under the provisions of the Civil Service Act, and "professional" employees began attending federally sponsored summer institutes to sharpen their skills and hear lectures by prominent educators. Finally, Congress adopted a compulsory attendance law that gave Indian agents and policemen the power to force children into Morgan's new system.

While hailed by progressive educators and most Indian reformers, Morgan's program was not universally popular among policy makers. His harshest critic was the celebrated headmaster of Carlisle. Richard Pratt argued that schools like his own, which were self-contained and far away from the Indians' traditional surroundings, were the only institutions that could "civilize" native children. "Morgan's Public School for the Indian craze," Pratt told Alice Fletcher in 1893, "is in my judgment worse than no school at all." He felt that the new civil service rules prevented him from selecting a compatible staff and that grading the government schools would reduce Carlisle itself to a trade school. The carloads of bereft children would soon be replaced by shipments of students who already had received a basic education near their homes. (A law passed in 1893 required all off-reservation students to complete three years at agency schools before going elsewhere.) "I despise the plans of my good friend Gen. Morgan more than I can tell you," Pratt wrote.[41]

But it is the symbolism of this conflict rather than its size that is significant. By the early 1890s Pratt's opinions had little influence in policy making. Commissioner Morgan's successor at the Indian Office left Daniel Dorchester in charge of the Indian schools for a full year before replacing him with a Democrat, and that man, William Hailmann, shared his predecessor's preference for a modern national school system. As Hailmann told the National Education Association in 1895, the day when "the few philanthropic men and women missionaries" guided the Indians' progress were past. In recent years, "they gradually stepped aside and the schoolmaster stepped in." In keeping with this trend, Hailmann proposed a final step in the government's program: the integration of native children into local public schools.[42]

There was of course a practical aspect to Hailmann's proposal. The Democrats continued to oppose increases in the Indian budget (cuts were made in 1894, 1895, and 1896), and the economic crisis of the 1890s made larger expenditures unthinkable. Still, the superintendent believed his plan was "in line with the enlightened policy that labor[ed] to do away with tribal life, reservations, agencies, and military posts among the Indians." A small number of Indian students had been attending public schools during Morgan's term. In 1892 the commissioner had seen "no insuperable obstacles" to expanding the practice, so when Hailmann took office in 1894 he proposed to place as many children as possible in public schools.[43]

To facilitate this process, Hailmann drew up a general contract that spelled out the responsibilities of both the Indian Office and the receiving institutions. It committed the government to pay county school boards ten dollars per quarter for each child; it required local authorities to give native students the same education they gave the children of tax-paying citizens; and it called on teachers and administrators "to protect the pupils included in this contract from ridicule, insult and other improper conduct at the hands of their fellow pupils, and to encourage them . . . to perform their duties with the same degree of interest and industry as their fellow pupils, the children of white citizens." This remarkable document made explicit what professional Indian educators in the late nineteenth century believed was the logical extension of their efforts: the complete absorption of Indian children into white society. Emulating the nation's modern common schools rather than the lonely missionary outposts of the past, policy makers envisioned a comprehensive system that would admit "savages," expose them to the nation's most powerful assimilating institution, and graduate "civilized" men and women who would be treated with respect by their white peers.[44]

In 1892 Commissioner Morgan wrote of Indian education, "I doubt if there is a question before the public in which there is more general consensus of opinion. Even the Western States and Territories, where the feeling against the Indians has been exceedingly bitter, show a surprising and most gratifying change in public sentiment." This certainly appeared to be true. The haphazard arrangments of the previous decade, based as they were on a revivalistic notion of immediate conversion to white ways, had been replaced by an impressive national system of native schools. These institutions were organized by grade level, supplied with special materials, and staffed by nonpolitical professionals. The new system appeared cheap, practical, and up-to-date. While politicians continued to differ over the extent of the commitment that should be made to Indian education, most of them endorsed the new approach and embraced its assimilationist goals. "If every Indian child could be in school for five years," the *Journal of Education* predicted in 1893, "savagery would cease and the government support of Indians would be a thing of the past."[45]

The national Indian school system was an integral part of the new assimilation campaign. It sought to extend the institutions of the majority culture so that they could surround and absorb Indian communities. It was designed explicitly to incorporate native people into the larger society and to "raise" them to a common standard of civilization. In this sense, Native American education bore a striking resemblance to the urban school reforms then underway in many parts of the United States. People like Thomas Jefferson Morgan and William Hailmann moved from public to Indian education, and the two systems shared a number of concepts and expectations.

Michael Katz has argued that in late-nineteenth-century America, urban school systems emerged that were "universal, tax-supported, free, compulsory, bureaucratic, racist and class biased." These characteristics may not have been as universal (or as self-consciously repressive) as Katz asserts, but they summarize accurately the goals (and much of the reality) of the new government schools for both Indians and whites. The comprehensive program of the Indian Office was universal. The new facilities were supported by tribal funds and congressional appropriations ("tax supported"), and were "free" to native children. Attendance was compulsory. Finally, Indian schools were "racist" and "class biased" in the sense that their explicit goal was the overthrow of traditional cultures and the imposition of "civilized" lifeways. Neither Indian nor white children were to be exposed to haphazard, personalized learning. Rather, they were to be introduced systematically to a common version of life in modern America.[46]

Many of the Indian Office's educational programs also ran parallel to those being instituted in the public schools. The trend toward a centralized nonpolitical hiring system was common to both systems, as was the popularity of summer teachers' institutes. Carlisle became famous both because of its success with Indians and because it was an example of Calvin Woodward's new theories of manual education. From his post at Washington University in St. Louis, Woodward taught that manual instruction should be the basis for all learning. He was interested not in vocational skills but in habits of work and concentration that could be transferred to academic areas. If students received the "symmetrical training" he advocated, Woodward told the National Education Associaiton, "this age of scientific progress and material wealth [would] be also an age of high intellectual and social progress." Pratt adopted these ideas and provided both industrial and academic training. Carlisle offered instruction in a number of trades and established an "outing" program that placed students on nearby farms for several months at a time.[47]

Perhaps the most telling indicators of the similarities between native education and the "modern" public schools were the many differences between the programs offered by the Indian Office and the instruction available to blacks and Asians. While southern blacks saw the promises of Reconstruction reduced to the shabby reality of inadequate segregated schools, and Asians on the Pacific Coast were either ignored or excluded by white educators, Native Americans became the favored focus of a national "civilization" program.

Throughout the late nineteenth century, reformers and humanitarians proposed the extension of a common-school education to blacks. These proposals usually relied on private philanthropy, but during the 1880s congressional Republicans, led by New Hampshire senator Henry Blair, suggested federal assistance. The Blair bill promised to aid all poor school districts, but its supporters believed blacks would be its principal beneficiaries. Congress approved geometrical increases in the annual Indian school budget during the same years that the Blair bill floundered and died. Asians met a similar fate. When anti-Chinese rioting occurred in a number of western towns, federal authorities took little or no action. Ultimately, in 1882, Congress responded to its white constituents rather than the embattled minority by passing the Chinese Exclusion Act.[48]

It would be misleading to overstate the differences between white attitudes toward Indians and other racial minorities in the late nineteenth century. Native Americans were considered less than civilized, and a number of officials expressed doubt over their ability to adapt to modern living. Nevertheless, the Indian education program constituted a unique level of federal activism on behalf of a nonwhite minority. There were several reasons for this. First, the advocates of Indian education did not arouse local opposition. Many southerners viewed the Blair bill as a federal intrusion into state politics and southern race relations. An attempt by Washington to aid Asians on the Pacific Coast would have met a similar reaction. Most Indian groups lived in areas that were still federal territories in the 1880s; interests that might have objected to the government's programs were unrepresented in Congress. And the sparsely settled West often welcomed federal spending as a prop to the region's fragile economy. Thus, men like Dawes could succeed in Indian affairs where they had failed with the Blair bill or the Chinese Exclusion Act. Indian reform allowed whites to adopt "principled positions" while taking few political risks.

But there was more at work in this area than a political calculus. Indians were a relatively small group. They numbered roughly 250,000 in 1900, compared to 4 million blacks and 100,000 Asians.

And they were scattered across several states and territories. For these reasons, and because of the special hold they had on the white imagination, politicians and educators could argue that, unlike other nonwhite peoples, Native Americans might be absorbed by the majority. Captain Pratt imagined that 40,000 young people would be educated and employed by the country's booming new industries. Secretary Teller fashioned a federal school system to accommodate them. And William Hailmann planned for their eventual incorporation into the nation's public schools.

Thomas Morgan was right: there was a "general consensus of opinion" regarding Indian education. Building on the assumption that schooling was an essential component of assimilation, policy makers worked within the political boundaries of the 1880s to erect a national program. The new institutions were patterned after common schools; they were run by professionals, opened to all, and designed to spread the values of the majority culture. They profited by the Native American's dearth of political enemies in Congress, as well as the educators' expectations that systematic instruction would produce rapid "progress." By the end of the decade this aspect of the government's assimilation policy was fixed. Policy makers now waited for the Indians to respond as the experts had predicted.

Henry Dawes's General Allotment Act was the final part of the government's new assimilation campaign. The law, which was approved in February 1887, established a pathway for the legal, economic, and social integration of Native Americans into the United States. It was the first piece of legislation intended for the general regulation of Indian affairs to be passed in half a century, and it remained the keystone of federal action until 1934, when the Indian Reorganization Act replaced it.

Because supporters of the Dawes Act hailed it as the "Indians' Magna Carta," and because it governed Indian affairs for nearly fifty years, historians have treated its passage as an event that produced drastic shifts in policy. This was not the case. Congress passed the allotment law toward the end of a decade of reform activity. Consequently its provisions embodied a number of ideas and expectations that already had gained acceptance and become a part of government action. In addition, the new severalty statute was a remarkably plastic document; it required no immediate action and gave administrators considerable discretionary power. The law set general goals and ignored many of the problems of implementation. It is properly viewed as a statement of its sponsors' common assumptions about the Indians' place in American society rather than as a technical prescription for prompt change.[49]

In January 1881, Democratic senator Richard Coke of Texas, Dawes's predecessor as chairman of the Indian Affairs Committee, introduced the first general allotment bill of the decade. Although Congress never approved Coke's proposal, the bill initiated a six-year public debate, during which three major allotment schemes were considered. By 1887 this debate produced a document that had such wide support that it passed both the House and Senate on a voice vote. In its final form, the severalty law represented the consensus view of policy makers. It set out general plans for Indian land administration, Indian education, and Indian citizenship. And in each area it proposed actions that promised to hasten native assimilation.

As we have seen, virtually all policy makers endorsed the idea of reducing the size of the reservations. Differences arose over how—and how quickly—to proceed. Prospective settlers cared little for legal niceties. As one of their leaders in congress explained, the westward movement could not be delayed. "Its march," he added, was as "irrestible as that of Sherman's to the sea." Thus, "no Indian treaties, no Interior Department regulations, no Indian Bureau contrivances [could] stop the onward flow of white emigration." A number of reformers also accepted this expansionist perspective; they believed the swift replacement of reservations with individual homesteads would end the rule of corrupt agents and hasten the civilization process. Lyman Abbott, editor of the *Christian Union* in New York, was the most outspoken of this group. The reservation system, he wrote, was "hopelessly wrong" and could not be reformed. "It can only be uprooted, root and branch and leaf, and a new system put in its place."[50]

Two dissimilar groups opposed Abbott and the expansionists. Senator Dawes and his congressional supporters argued that any plan to put Indians on individual tracts of land should be implemented gradually. In addition, he pointed out that allotment had to be accompanied by continued federal support and protection. "If we are to set an Indian up in severalty," he told his fellow senators, "we must throw some protection over him and around him and aid him for awhile in this effort; we must countenance the effort; we must hold up his hand." This gradualist position was shared by other legislators who were pessimistic about the ability of Native Americans to survive as individual farmers. John Tyler Morgan of Alabama, for example, saw forced allotment as an attempt "to substitute in place of the traditional and simple and ancient form of government obtaining among these various tribes the proud and magnificent system which has been built up to accommodate itself to the most enterprising and enlightened nation in the world." In the House, Charles Hooker of Mississippi echoed Morgan as he called for the establishment of permanent tribal homelands in the West.[51]

The original Coke bill emphasized the gradual approach to allotments. It gave each tribe the right to choose—by a two-thirds vote—between allotment and the issuance of patent that would guarantee common ownership of a specific tract of land (presumably of a size approximating 160 acres per person). Thus, no group would be allotted until they became "civilized" enough to ask for individual lands. A revised version of the Coke bill that Senators Dawes and Coke sponsored jointly in 1884 also contained this tribal consent provision. The Coke-Dawes proposal passed the Senate, but opponents prevented it from reaching the floor of the House. The resulting stalemate continued until 1886, when a third proposal eliminated the consent clause in favor of two other forms of protection. This third proposal became the Dawes Act. It stated that allotment would occur only at the president's direction—"whenever in his opinion" the Indians were ready for it. In addition, the new statute retained a provision of the earlier bills which stipulated that allotments would be "inalienable" for twenty-five years. An Indian's land would thus be exempt from taxation and ineligible for sale for a generation. Finally, the Dawes Act stated that it did not apply to the Five Civilized Tribes of Indian Territory or to the New York Indians. Thus the debate over severalty was separated from the more complicated argument over how to reduce the size of those older reservations.[52]

Western expansionists and the more aggressive reformers could now look forward to a succession of presidential proclamations initiating the allotment of attractive reservations. But those with a gradualist view could assume that most of the Indians' white neighbors were politically impotent and unlikely to influence the chief executive. Further, the inalienable title would prevent surrounding non-Indian communities from raiding the allottees' new property. Senator Dawes's law also required that any future sale of "surplus" lands (lands not needed for allotment purposes) would require the approval of the tribes. The Dawes Act contained no timetable for the dismantling of the reservations and the creation of individual Indian homesteads. The issue was neatly blurred and tossed into the hands of future presidents.

In addition to disputes over the administration of tribal lands, the Dawes Act also revealed—and compromised—disagreements over Indian citizenship. Policy makers endorsed the ultimate goal of total assimilation but differed over its timing, as they had in the case of the reservation lands. Many of the same factions were involved in the two disputes. Just as the pious Lyman Abbott and David Payne's rabid Oklahoma "boomers" agreed that reservations should be abolished immediately, so the Reverend William J. Harsha, chairman of the Omaha Citizenship Committee, found his allies among Colorado miners and Dakota sodbusters when he called for the immediate extension of the Fourteenth Amendment to Native Americans. Their opponents—southerners concerned with an invasion of state's rights and reformers uncomfortable with eliminating all federal protection for the tribes—also tended to speak out against rapid allotment. Both Florida's Senator Wilkinson Call and Secretary Carl Schurz, for example, opposed an immediate granting of the franchise.[33]

The original Coke bill proposed placing allotted Indians under state law without granting them citizenship. The bill's author defended this unique arrangement by saying that it would allow the Interior Department to continue to "aid the Indian in his attempts to become civilized." The effect of Coke's proposal was to put Indians in a position comparable to that of blacks, whose national citizenship had been voided in the years since the Civil War. That process in fact reached its logical end in the *Civil Rights* cases, decided in the midst of the debates over the severalty law. In its 1883 decision the Supreme Court had promised that national standards of citizenship would not be enforced in the South. Under the Coke bill, Indians, like southern blacks, would be unable to appeal to federal courts for protection. Not surprisingly, therefore, the measure called forth support in Congress from the New South.[54]

But southerners like Coke were not the only opponents of rapid citizenship. The Ponca controversy in 1879 indicated that there were deep divisions even among the Indians' "friends" on this issue. Carl Schurz opposed Judge Dundy's order to release Standing Bear because he believed an immediate grant of citizenship would destroy the government's ability to aid the tribes. John Wesley Powell also endorsed gradual citizenship, arguing that Indians needed "a period of probation prior to assuming the responsibilities and obtaining the privileges of citizenship." Apparently a majority of the Senate shared this view, for when a proposal to grant Indians immediate citizenship was brought up in January 1881, it was defeated by a vote of twenty-nine to twelve.[55]

Other reformers divided over the question of how rapidly to grant citizenship. The *Nation* and the *American Law Review* (defenders of Schurz in the *Standing Bear* case) continued to advocate gradualism. George F. Canfield, a Columbia University law professor, was an outspoken member of this group. He pointed out that the franchise would expose the Indians to a variety of risks. They "would be withdrawn from the power of Congress to keep them exempt from taxation, to prevent the introduction and sale of liquor among them, and, in general, to regulate and control our intercourse with them." Supporters of immediate citizenship—the Boston Indian Citizenship Committee, the Indian Rights Association, and others— thus faced "humanitarian" justifications for limiting citizenship as well as cynical ones. Schurz and his supporters asserted that the status quo should continue until the Indians themselves gave up their old ways and demonstrated individually their readiness for the franchise.[56]

The debate over citizenship changed dramatically in 1884, when the Supreme Court decided the case of *Elk* v. *Wilkins*. The case grew out of an attempt by John Elk, a "civilized Indian," to vote in Omaha, Nebraska. Local election officials argued that Elk was not a citizen and therefore was ineligible for the franchise. The Supreme Court agreed, stating that Indians were not born within the jurisdictional boundaries of the United States and that Congress had never established a naturalization process for them. The justices declared that it was up to the legislative branch to decide the issue: "The question whether any Indian tribes, or any members thereof have become so far advanced in civilization that they should be let out of the state of pupilage, and admitted to the privileges and responsibilities of citizenship, is a question to be decided by the nation whose wards they are and whose citizens they seek to become; and not by each Indian for himself."[57] Those who had supported Schurz's benign notion of gradual citizenship or Powell's concept of a "probation" period now were on the spot. They could leave the Indians without federal guarantees, as the Coke bill had proposed, or they could suggest a substitute. Without new legislation the Indians would continue under the absolute control of the Indian Office; the "tyranny of the reservation" would be absolute.

Faced with an explicit choice between leaving the Indians in limbo and providing for their legal assimilation, policy makers chose the latter. Both the Dawes-Coke bill of 1884 and the final Dawes Act declared that all allottees would be granted citizenship. There were many reasons for this. In the face of the *Elk* decision reformers who had advocated gradualism could no longer argue that individual natives would become citizens as they rose to "civilization." Again, the group's relatively small numbers and generally positive public image worked in favor of "humanitarian" treatment. And finally, the alternative of *not* granting citizenship was unacceptable. A denial of the franchise would maintain the Indians' wardship indefinitely and embarrass those who saw total assimilation as a vindication of the universality of American institutions.

Despite its commitment to citizenship, the Dawes Act continued to satisfy a wide variety of interests. Under the new law Indians would not become citizens until after they received allotments. And allotment presumably would not occur before they had demonstrated the ability to manage their own farms. As Senator Dawes explained shortly before his bill passed the upper house in 1886, the franchise was granted "in order to encourage any Indian who [had] started upon the life of a civilized man and [was] making the effort to be one of the body-politic in which he live[d], giving the encouragement that if he so maintain[ed] himself he [would] be a citizen of the United States." The extent of congressional support for this position was demonstrated soon after Dawes spoke. Samuel Bell Maxey of Texas proposed an amendment to strike the citizenship provision. He argued that there was ample precedent for barring natives from membership in the polity. "Look at your Chinamen," he cried, "are they not specifically excepted from the naturalization laws?" But Maxey's colleagues would not extend the Chinese Exclusion Act to the Indians. They rejected his proposal by a voice vote and sent the severalty bill to the House. There the section was approved without significant opposition.[58]

In a commentary on the new law published early in 1887, the Indian Rights Association observed that the Dawes Act had "thrown wide open the door to Indian citizenship. . . . The native [was] invited and even urged to enter whatever places he [might] choose to occupy as a citizen of this free Republic." The law provided a general procedure for enfranchising Indians but—as in the sections on dividing up the reservation lands—it contained no specific timetable or regulations. Instead, policy makers had seized on—and been satisfied with—a general commitment to Indian citizenship.[59]

Indian education was the final policy area affected by the new severalty law. While the Dawes Act did not refer directly to the native school system, it assumed that Indians should become citizens and that they would adopt the habits of the white majority. Allotment, the House Indian Affairs committee observed in 1885, would "be such an incentive to labor that the Indian [would] gradually but surely abandon his nomadic habits and settle down to a life of comparative industry."[60] But there was considerable disagreement over what the government should do to foster the process.

Supporters of the growing Indian school system believed that allotment would require a new level of government activity. As Alice Fletcher observed, the reservations "reduced . . . mental life to a minimum" and Indian farmers therefore would need both training and support. Otherwise, Carlisle's Captain Pratt warned, the allot-tee's land would "remain like himself, barren and waste." Simply di-viding the land among tribal members would not create "civilized" natives. Olin Welborn of Texas told his House colleagues that while allotment was the "great goal" of government action, assigning lands in severalty was "the final step, and before it [was] taken the Indians [had to] be prepared for it."[61]

But critics of the new education programs had a very different view of allotment. They welcomed the severalty law because it promised to end decades of government "coddling," and they urged the Indian Office to reach the goal of Indian self-sufficiency as rapidly as possible. Senator John Ingalls of Kansas typified this position. He endorsed the original Coke bill because it meant a reduction in the annual budget. "I am not an advocate of butchery," he explained, "I am in favor of some humane policy that shall relieve the Treasury from the annual imposition of millions of dollars to support these people in unproductive idleness, and I assented to the reporting of this bill in the hope that something might be done in that direc-tion."[62] The final Dawes bill did not specifically endorse either view of education. Nowhere was the government's future role in fostering "civilization" spelled out; everything passed by implication.

Despite the power it exerted over Indian-white relations for nearly half a century, the Dawes Act was little more than a statement of intent. It contained no timetables and few instructions as to how it would be implemented. At its core, the law was an assertion that the gap between the two races would be overcome and that Indians would be incorporated into American society. They would farm, par-ticipate in government, and adopt "higher" standards of behavior. The statute assumed that landownership, citizenship, and education would alter traditional cultures, bringing them to "civilization." What is more, the new law was made possible by the belief that In-dians did not have the "deficiencies" of other groups: they were fewer in number, the beneficiaries of a public sympathy and pity, and capable of advancement.

The passage of the General Allotment Act completed the organi-zation of the new campaign to assimilate the Indians, but its imme-diate impact was unclear. Ambiguous provisions echoed the proposals of dozens of reformers and reform groups; thus the law left a number of important issues unresolved. When would the president "direct" allotment to begin? How much power would tribes have when they "negotiated" for the sale of their surplus lands? Furthermore, who would decide which tribal lands were surplus and which were needed for future allotments? How would the Indians' citizenship rights be enforced? And how much assistance could the new allottees expect from the government schools? While answers to these questions would change dramatically during the years ahead, the first decade of the Dawes Act's existence was marked by a clear pattern: the new law was implemented slowly and in a manner consistent with the assimilationist assumptions that inspired it. Lands were opened to settlement at a relatively slow pace, native citizenship rights were generally protected, and the Indian Office continued to accept responsibility for fostering Indian "progress."

Most students of the severalty era have concluded that "the application of allotment to the reservations was above all characterized by extreme haste."[63] While in the long run this was the case, it was not true of the period immediately following the passage of the act. During those early years, most administrators and lawmakers were willing to allow allotment to proceed slowly and selectively. By 1895 only twenty-four reservations had been surveyed and allotted. Of these, fifteen required more than two hundred parcels of lands to accommodate the entire tribe, and but ten required more than three hundred. Most groups allotted in this period were quite small (allotments went to every tribal member—men, women, and children). What is more, with the exception of the Cheyenne and Arapaho reservation in Oklahoma, most of the allotted tribes were living in areas that had long since been settled by whites. Of course the Indian Office was usually acting unilaterally, but it was not proceeding precipitately.

John Atkins, the first Indian commissioner to administer the severalty law, established guidelines for allotment that appear to have been followed by both his Republican and Democratic successors for the next decade. Commenting on the new law in 1887, he wrote, "Too great haste in the matter should be avoided, and if the work proceeds less rapidly than was expected the public must not be impatient. . . . Character, habits, and antecedents cannot be changed by an enactment." To his general statement Atkins appended a list of twenty-four reservations that the president believed were "generally favorable" to allotment. Nineteen of those were allotted in the next eight years. In 1895 the original nineteen accounted for three-quarters of all allotted reservations. In other words, despite the tragedies it produced, the severalty law was not applied initially in the "feverish hurry" many historians have observed.[64]

The Indian Office followed a general plan. Commissioner Thomas Morgan, for example, reported in 1892 that, with the exception of the Sioux, "the allotment of land to all of the Indians to whom application of the severalty law would be for their interest [could] be made and completed within the next three or four years." Morgan's statement was based on a comprehensive review of the allotment process. He was aware that large areas in Utah, southern Colorado, Arizona, Montana, and Indian Territory were as yet untouched. In 1887 the Indian Rights Association suggested, "Reservations should be taken first which are ripest for the work, where the way is clear, the risks small, the complications few." During its first decade of administering the Dawes Act, the Indian Office generally took that advice.[65]

Few allotments were leased before 1895. An amendment to allow Indians to lease their individual holdings had been rejected in the Senate in 1881 and was not reintroduced. The Dawes Act therefore contained no provisions for leasing allotments. But in 1891 Congress gave those Indians who for reasons of "age or disability" could not work their land the right to rent it with the approval of their agent. Only 2 such leases were approved in 1892; 4 were granted in 1893. The following year Congress added a new, elastic category—"inability"—to the list of reasons that justified leasing. That year the number of approved rentals rose to 296, although 223 of them took place on a single reservation. The following year the secretary of the interior approved 328 leases. While this figure represented a substantial increase, it amounted to barely 2 percent of all allotments.

Leasing was not yet the great evil it was to become in the twentieth century. The Indian Office generally opposed the practice, viewing it primarily as an administrative convenience that enabled agents to maximize production on native lands. Reformers like Captain Pratt also justified it as an instrument for freeing "progressive" Indians from their farms. Such people, "who have the disposition to build themselves up out of and away from the tribal connection," he wrote Senator Dawes, "ought not to be discouraged by any governmental hindrances whatsoever."[66]

The early allotment years also were marked by a continuation of federal protection for the tribes, despite the grant of citizenship. In Nebraska, the Omaha and Winnebago agent ordered squatters and unapproved lessees who had insinuated themselves on newly allotted land to leave the reservation. When the affected people resisted and threatened violence the commissioner proceeded against them with the aid of the army and the federal courts. Reformers continued to advocate federal protection for Indians. The most vocal among them was Harvard Law School professor James Bradley Thayer, who wrote a series of articles on the subject for the *Atlantic Monthly* in 1891. Thayer's thesis was that Native Americans "need, and [would] need for a good while, the very careful and exceptional protection of the nation." While Dawes pointed out to Thayer that such protection already existed, there was little dissent from the idea that assimilation would result from the judicious application of the severalty law. This was not to be an era of termination; federal guardianship would continue until the Indians appeared ready to stand on their own.[67]

Finally, it should be noted that the period immediately following the passage of the Dawes Act saw the rapid expansion of the native school system and the first extension of civil service reform to the Indian Office. The innovations of school superintendents Oberly and Hailmann and Commissioner Morgan occurred in the context of concern over the success of allotment. "Preparation for citizenship" and "education for the future" were common themes of their administrations. Increasing emphasis was placed on the quality of federal employees. "Right intentions, experience, and sound judgment . . . on the part of the resident agent," Herbert Welsh wrote in 1892, "are most necessary to a successful operation of the severalty law." Not only would the local agents oversee the assignment of homesteads but they would also direct various "civilization" programs and mediate between tribesmen and local non-Indian settlers. While the struggle over civil service classifications continued into the twentieth century, the reformer's initial victories came in the early 1890s. President Harrison placed the Indian Service under civil service regulations in 1891. And two years later Congress empowered the Indian Office to make school superintendents the agents for their reservations. Since these people already came under the civil service laws, that step seemed to signal the eventual end of patronage appointments in the Indian Service.[68]

Both the formulation and the initial administration of the General Allotment Act reflected a broad popular interest in total Indian assimilation. The law promised to achieve goals that policy makers agreed were appropriate for Native Americans: private landownership, education, and citizenship. In this sense it embodied the attitudes of the public, interested scientists, politicians, and reformers. There would continue to be differences between those who sympathized with the Indians and those who did not, and between those who wanted a gradual process and those who were more impatient. But for the moment there was universal agreement that an assimilation campaign that was both practical and comprehensive was finally underway.

Chapter 3

The Transformation of the Indian Question

Four hundred years after Columbus set sail for the New World, the city of Chicago organized a world's fair to demonstrate the significance of his voyage. The Columbian Exposition mixed an optimistic vision of the future with a nostalgic look backward. For the civic boosters who conceived it, and the millions of tourists it attracted, the Chicago World's Fair was a celebration of the power and promise of a new America. Special trains put the fairgrounds within easy reach of most sections of the country. On the midway, visitors were surrounded by marvels: entertainers arrived from across the globe, a full-scale replica of a steel battleship stood offshore in Lake Michigan, and Alexander Graham Bell conveyed his greetings from New York over the nation's first long-distance telephone line. Humming dynamos drove arc lights that shone on an elaborate collection of fountains and sculpture, providing fairgoers with dramatic nightly "illuminations." By far the most impressive exhibit was the setting itself, a series of mammoth buildings arranged around broad lagoons.

Built in the space of a few months, their plaster facades towered over the displays and cast gleaming reflections across the water. The White City conveyed a vision of the future.

But the exposition also celebrated the past. The White City itself, a wonder of modern construction, was built to resemble a series of Greek temples, and the statues that shimmered under the electric floodlights were executed in the classical style. An evocation of the American past was found on an artificial island in the central lagoon. There the Boone and Crockett Club, an organization of hunters and conservationists led by Theodore Roosevelt and the naturalist George Bird Grinnell, presented a scene from what they called a "typical and peculiar phase of American national development . . . life on the frontier." Like keepers of a shrine, the two men supervised the construction of a display that they believed to be accurate in every detail. As they reported to their fellow members, "The club erected a long, low cabin of unhewn logs . . . of the kind in which the first hunters and frontier settlers dwelt." Inside the building there was "a rough table and settles, with bunks in one corner, and a big, open stone fireplace." To the furniture they added artifacts: "Elk and deer hides were scattered over the floor or tacked to the walls. The bleached skull and antlers of an elk were nailed over the door outside; the head of a buffalo hung from mid-partition . . . and the horns of other game, such as mountain sheep and deer, were scattered about." In front of the cabin stood a "white-capped prairie schooner."[1] Visitors to the island would also see stuffed elk and deer staring unblinkingly at them from behind hastily planted trees.

The Boone and Crockett Club display, standing literally in the shadows of the White City, suggests the extent to which Americans of the 1890s were beginning to realize that their cities, telephones, and battleships were purchased with the space and homogeneity of the past. The message of the club's exhibit resembled the one Frederick Jackson Turner brought to a meeting of historians that same summer: the frontier, the "crucible" that had formed the American character, was slipping into history. Like Turner's view of a national past, the island, with its elk hides and prairie schooner, its stone fireplace and animal skulls, was not an accurate representation of the American experience. Nevertheless it captured public attention because it conveyed an attractive, compelling image that offered an alternative to the mechanical whir and bustle of the Chicago midway.

The frontier was taking on new meaning. At the exposition it became an object men like Turner and Roosevelt could grasp as a counterpoise to the present—a model for the American character. Within this context, the public perception of the Indian was bound to undergo a subtle but significant metamorphosis. Like the prairie schooner and the roughhewn cabin, the Indian too would slip into history. The race would become more important for what it represented than for what it might become. As the frontier began to evoke nostalgia rather than dread, Native Americans would cease to be an immediate threat that required bludgeoning or "civilization." The need to eradicate native cultures faded with the memory of the frontier struggle. In the new century, Indians would be redefined as vital players in America's dramatic past. They would become a valued part of a fading, rustic landscape.

In the early twentieth century, these shifts in public image promised to have an important effect on the Indians' future. The laws and policies adopted in the 1880s had been intended to define a new, permanent relationship between Native Americans and the United States. Land, education, and citizenship awaited those who walked the "white man's road." But the reforms of that era were effective only as long as the assimilationist expectations fueling them were widely shared. If the commitment to rapid "civilization" began to fade, federal programs—like the treaties that preceded them— would become mere paper commitments to be altered, avoided, or ignored. An optimistic view of natives was crucial to the implementation of the reformer's agenda. So long as policy makers viewed Indians as people in transition—moving "upward," from one stage of culture to another—the total assimilation campaign would continue uninterrupted. If that perception shifted, the ambiguously worded laws and policies would lose their initial meaning, and the "Indian question" of the 1880s would be transformed.

While public images are as elusive as they are invisible, it is possible to trace their reflections through time. One canvas against which the image of the Indian was projected vividly at the turn of the century was the American world's fair. In the forty years following the Philadelphia Centennial in 1876, at least ten fairs were staged in the United States. The Philadelphia and Chicago events, the Louisiana Purchase Exposition in St. Louis (1904), and the Panama-Pacific International Exposition in San Francisco (1915) were truly international extravaganzas, while the shows in New Orleans (1884), Atlanta (1895), Nashville (1897), Omaha (1899), Buffalo (1901), and San Diego (1915) were smaller and more regional in focus. Nevertheless, all the fairs were founded on grand expectations. Among those was the hope that the exhibits would be (in one organizer's words) the "university of the masses."[2] An important element in this educational conception was a presentation of Indian life. Every fair devoted space to an exhibition of the Native American's place in American culture. These self-conscious displays are an excellent measure of the public's shifting perception of the Indians.

The Philadelphia exposition was held in honor of the nation's centennial. Between the opening day in March, when President Grant and the Emperor of Brazil trooped through the exhibits, and the rain-drenched closing ceremonies in November, more than 9 million people came to Fairmount Park to marvel at the United States' achievements. Most visitors went first to Machinery Hall to see the amazing new telephone and the massive Corliss steam engine. But close by—and no doubt second on many itineraries—was the barn-like Government Building with its displays organized on the theme "A Century of Progress." The building was a hit. As the *New York Times* correspondent wrote: "It will convince the world that the future of America is based upon a rock and will endure." Fully half of the Government Building was given over to a display of Indian life. Local newspapers reported that the Smithsonian Institution and other federal agencies had collected "all manner of curious things," including totem poles from the Northwest, "Esquimaux artifacts, and a series of plains warriors made from papier-mache."[3]

But the exhibit did not concentrate solely on traditional culture. In keeping with the fair's theme, a large part of the Indian area was devoted to evidence of native "progress." A number of display cases contained descriptions of missionary work, public education efforts, and government programs to encourage farming. The *Philadelphia*

Bulletin noted, "The whole [Indian exhibit] is completed by numerous photographs of Indian life . . . representing the progress made in the schools established among the tribes." The effect of this emphasis on Indian advancement was quite striking. As one of the Centennial guidebooks explained, "It is odd to see these pet enemies of the country seated calmly in front of the school-houses . . . Their educational varnish is warranted by those who are applying it to stand, and some of them look as though it might, even under the trying conditions it remains for them to encounter." Former commissioner of Indian affairs Francis A. Walker, who wrote a multivolume summary of the fair, was even more enthusiastic:

This exhibit has contributed much to a solution of the vexed question, "What shall be done with the Indians?" For if not only the Creeks, Choctaws and Cherokees can be tamed and civilized to this degree, but even the savage Modoc, and the fierce Apache, when brought together and held under the civilizing influence of civilizing agencies, have not the friends of humanity gained a powerful argument?

Another observer put it more simply: "We could not but fancy we saw a future in the pleasant and gentle faces of some young Pawnees."[4]

The optimistic tone of the exhibit indicated that its designers believed the Indians' future was a national responsibility. Apparently fairgoers agreed that Native Americans deserved both sympathy and assistance. In the summer of Custer's death at the Little Big Horn, the Indian display summarized both the hopes of the public and the expectations of policy makers. These groups imagined Native Americans were entering a period of rapid change. It seemed that a nation devoted to progress could promise nothing less.

By 1893, when the Columbian Exposition was staged in Chicago, some of the optimism in evidence in Philadelphia had begun to fade. As the Boone and Crockett Club exhibit suggested, new attitudes were reflected in the Midwest's first fair. Actually there were two Indian displays at Chicago. Frederick Putnam, director of Harvard's Peabody Museum, organized one exhibit for the exposition's anthropology department. The second was supervised and designed by Commissioner of Indian Affairs Thomas Morgan, the former preacher who had been widely praised for his reform of the Indian school system. In 1876 the scientists from the Smithsonian and the administrators at the Indian Office had worked together; their exhibits in 1893 were separate. Each group was more intent on presenting its own work than on hewing to a common theme.

According to Professor Putnam, his presentation was "the first bringing together on a grand scale of representatives of the people who were living on the continent when it was first discovered by Columbus." He added that his displays would be arranged chronologically so that "the stages of the development of man on the American continent could be spread out as an open book from which all could read." In this sense the exhibit would follow the theme presented in Philadelphia. But unlike the 1876 exposition, the Chicago showing included a feature rejected by the Centennial's apostles of progress: living natives from Indian reservations. These people included Navajos, Senecas, Kwakiutls, Penobscots, and Pueblos (the last group lived on the midway in plaster replicas of their adobe homes). Smaller groups of Sioux, Apaches, Nez Perces, and others settled along the lake front, demonstrating and selling their handicrafts. Their presence, wrote Hubert Howe Bancroft, demonstrated in "a series of object lessons the development of various phases and adjuncts of civilization."[5]

The Indians' tribal past was no longer to be presented by glass cases filled with implements and clothing. The "object lessons" of the Chicago fair were alive. They could teach something about "the development of man on the American continent" only if the public could imagine them as objects from the past—breathing substitutes for artifacts on a shelf. Peabody and his colleagues were diverting the fairgoer's attention from the future to the past and identifying their Native American contemporaries as relics and throwbacks.

The Indian Office saw the fair as an opportunity to demonstrate the promise of its new assimilation program. Its principal exhibit was a two-story frame schoolhouse. During the fair, delegations from government schools occupied the building; each group spent a few days in the model classrooms, demonstrating "civilized" skills and enduring the stares of the curious. These were considerable, for the school attracted over one hundred thousand visitors a week during the summer. Commissioner Morgan proudly announced that the display vindicated the government's efforts. "It sets forth the future of the Indian," he wrote; "it shows concretely and unmistakably his readiness and ability for the new conditions of civilized life and American citizenship upon which he is entering."[6]

Obviously, dividing the Indian exhibit between the anthropology department and the Indian Office was more than a bureaucratic convenience, for the themes of the two displays were strikingly different. One conveyed the idea that Indians were members of an exotic race with little connection to modern America. The other, by stressing education and native "progress," pointed to the possibility of Indian assimilation. What is more, there seemed to be a good deal of uncertainty—among the organizers of the fair as well as the public—over which focus was more appropriate.

Captain Richard Pratt, still headmaster at Carlisle, was outraged by Putnam's living "object lessons." He viewed them as reminders of the Indians' "barbaric" past, and feared that they would distract the public from the evidence of progress on display in the Indian schoolhouse. In fact, the old cavalryman was so incensed that he demanded a special room for Carlisle in the Liberal Arts Building. He did not want to be associated with the other exhibits. His demand was met, as was a request that Carlisle students be invited to march in the opening day parade. Pratt took that occasion to demonstrate the reality of Indian "progress." Ten platoons of students participated, each representing one of the skills taught at the school. The front row of each platoon carried the tools of a trade while those in the rear held high samples of finished products they had made.[7]

Some of the displays of traditional life produced reactions similar to Pratt's. On seeing a Kwakiutl dance performed during the first week's festivities, a *Chicago Tribune* reporter complained that "right in the midst" of an event "that marks the progress of mankind were these ceremonies of this strange and semi-barbarous race carried on." Similar protests surfaced throughout the summer. An August editorial perhaps epitomized this disapproval: "Those in authority have gone to the farthest extreme and sanctioned a so-called entertainment which may be the height of amusement among the Kwakiutl or the Dahomen cannibals, but which should have no place in the beautiful White City."[8]

The most sustained attack came from Emma Sickles, a Chicagoan who had been fired by Putnam from a position on his staff. She launched a newspaper campaign to shut down all of the "primitive" presentations. "The exhibit of Indian life now given at the fair," she wrote, "is an exhibit of savagery in its most repulsive form." While her campaign ultimately failed, her cries that the Indians should not be viewed as "helpless specimens" were heard—and printed—by newspapers in New York and Chicago.[9]

The unified picture of a people in transition presented at Philadelphia had been altered. "Backward" natives were now an important part of public displays, even though the physical presence of traditional Indians disturbed those who predicted the rapid "civilization" of the race. The government schools attracted large crowds, but so did the native villages and the anthropology building. (Buffalo Bill's Wild West Show played to enthusiastic audiences elsewhere in the city throughout the summer.) The public appeared as interested in exotic "savages" as it was in Indian "advancement."

By 1904, when the Louisiana Purchase Exposition opened in St. Louis, these divergent themes had been resolved. Interest in the Indians' "primitive" character was paramount, and—more important—both the government and the public greeted the exotic displays with enthusiasm.

St. Louis tried to imitate the successes of the White City. The city fathers promised that their displays would be larger and their buildings more elaborate than anything seen in Chicago. Old dreams of becoming the Midwest's chief metropolis revived and were nurtured. Henry Adams described the result in his autobiography:

One saw a third-rate town of half-a-million people without history, education, unity, or art, and with little capital—without even an element of natural interest except the river which it studiously ignored—but doing what London, Paris, or New York would have shrunk from attempting. This new social conglomerate with no tie but its steam-power and not much of that, threw away thirty or forty million dollars on a pageant as ephemeral as a stage flat. . . . One enjoyed it with iniquitous rapture, not because of the exhibits, but because of their want.[10]

The Indian exhibits in St. Louis were more elaborate than those in Chicago. As it was in 1893, the major display was the product of the exposition's department of anthropology. When the Smithsonian's W. J. McGee was appointed chairman of this department in 1901 he quickly set about organizing a "Congress of the Races" that he promised would be a "comprehensive exhibit of the primitive peoples of the globe." When the fair opened, Ainus from Japan, African pygmies, Patagonian natives, and several groups of Native Americans were assembled on a hillside in the center of the anthropology area. McGee wrote that he selected these people because they were "least removed from the sub-human or quadrumane form" and would therefore serve as living illustrations of human progress. "In brief," the chairman declared, "one may learn in the indoor [museum] exhibit how our prehistoric forebears lived, and then see, outside, people untouched by the march of progress still living in a similar crude manner."[11]

At the top of McGee's hillside exhibit stood a government Indian schoolhouse, like the one the Indian Office had constructed in Chicago. The scientist explained the significance of its location:

The outdoor exhibit, beginning at the foot of a sloping hill, where the bearded men and the tattooed women of the Ainu sit outside their thatchwork huts and carve bits of wood into patterns, employing their toes as well as their hands, and ending with the Government Indian school at the top of the hill, where Sioux and Arapaho and Oneida attend kindergarten and primary and grammar classes, and build things so fitted to modern needs as farm wagons—this exhibit tells two living stories. It presents the race narrative of odd peoples who mark time while the world advances, and of savages, made, by American methods, into civilized workers.

Within the school, students demonstrated their ability to cook, do laundry, and operate a printing press, as well as their skill at wagon-making, carpentry, and blacksmithing. A forty-piece Indian band gave daily concerts, and a battalion of cadets paraded every afternoon at 5:30. The aim of the exhibit, McGee noted, was to present "a practical illustration of the best way of bearing the white man's burden."[12]

The "Congress of Races" suggested how American scientists and policy makers resolved their disagreements over the proper way to present American Indians to the public. No longer portrayed as both a "people in transition" and a breed of primitive exotics, Native Americans had become members of one of the world's many "backward races." Nearly "subhuman," the Indians of 1904 needed nothing more than simple training to become "civilized workers." Like the Ainus and the pygmies, they were a different order of being, a people who could not be expected to "progress" as far as those from more "civilized" societies.

McGee's hillside exhibit attracted three million visitors; none of them appear to have protested his presentation of traditional Indian life. In fact, the St. Louis newspapers found the encampment thoroughly entertaining. Early in the summer, Joseph Pulitzer's *Post-Dispatch* ran daily photos of the Indians. These staged shots appeared under headlines such as "Real Thing in the TeePee Line" and "Patagonian Giants Start To Run When They See Philippine Midgets." Traditional natives were accepted as anthropological curios: harmless objects to be ridiculed without fear or embarrassment.[13]

Fairgoers also demonstrated their interest in "backward races" by flocking to the exhibit from the United States' new colony in the Philippines. This forty-seven-acre display was the largest at the fair. It included a plaster reproduction of the old walled city of Manila, replicas of native villages, a government school, a military garrison (complete with loyal Philippine soldiers), and eleven hundred natives in traditional dress. The similarity of this exhibit to the Indian encampment was pointed out by Secretary of War William Howard Taft, when he observed at the ribbon-cutting ceremony that the Archipelago's annexation promised Americans a reenactment of the winning of the West. According to Taft, "[America has] reached a period . . . in which we find ourselves burdened with the necessity of aiding another people to stand upon their feet and take a short cut to the freedom and civil liberty which we and our ancestors have hammered out."[14]

Superficially, the Indian exhibits changed only slightly between

1876 and 1904. All three fairs presented Native Americans as "un-civilized," and each of them assumed that members of the race could enter white society only by shedding their traditional cultures. But beyond these similarities, the presentations in Chicago and St. Louis revealed an important shift in popular perceptions. By 1904 the Indian's future—which a Philadelphia observer had seen "in the pleasant and gentle faces of some young Pawnees"—appeared limited. Native Americans now appeared handicapped by their race and limited by their "backwardness." Positioned in the center of a bizarre anthropological curio shop and described as an element of the "white man's burden," the tribesmen seemed best suited for a life of manual labor. In 1876, journalists had dwelt on the Indian's future; a visitor to the Indian exhibit in St. Louis called it "The Last Race Rally of the Indians."[15]

When the Panama-Pacific International Exposition opened in San Francisco in 1915, the metamorphosis of the Indians' public image was complete. At this final American fair before World War I, Native Americans appeared as people whose future was of only marginal concern to the white majority. There was no Indian encampment in San Francisco, nor was there an elaborate anthropological presentation. The only living Indians in evidence were some Zunis hired by the Santa Fe Railroad to grace their Grand Canyon show. The Smithsonian sponsored a modest display in the government pavilion, but it contained only a few archeological artifacts. The model villages of St. Louis and Chicago became plaster dioramas portraying scenes of traditional life under glass. And exhibitions of student work—furniture, canned fruit, needlework—replaced the Indian Office's model schoolhouse.

By far the most popular presentation of native life at the San Francisco fair was in bronze: James Earle Fraser's statue, "The End of the Trail." Fraser's work portrayed a nameless, exhausted Indian slumped in the saddle of a worn-out pony. With remarkable candor, the artist later explained the message of his work: "It was [the] idea of a weaker race being steadily pushed to the wall by a stronger that I wanted to convey."[16] To emphasize its symbolic meaning, Fraser's piece was placed beside a statue of an American frontiersman. "Pioneer" was a symbolic figure who (according to one guidebook) had a "challenge in his face," as he stared "into early morning." The guide added that the pioneer was "typical of the white man and the victorious march of civilization." The effect of this juxtaposition was not lost on fair-goers. One reviewer wrote, "So it has been with the Indian. His trail is now lost and on the edge of a continent he finds himself almost annihilated."[17]

"The End of the Trail" won a gold medal and became a major at-traction. At the close of the fair a citizen's group tried to acquire it for a park overlooking the Pacific, but their campaign was cut short by World War I. Years later, Fraser himself said that it was still his dream to find a home for the horse and rider on the California coast. "There he would stand forever," he said, "driven at last to the very edge of the continent." The public message contained in the statue was clear: the pioneer was victorious; the Indian race was on its way to extinction.[18]

The popularity of Fraser's pathetic Indian indicated that despite a generation of reform-inspired optimism, the romantic Indian of Cooper and Longfellow was coming back into vogue. In 1876, the presentation of Native American life had emphasized the changes taking place among the tribes. The public supported this optimistic view, but by the 1890s interest in Indian "progress" was coexist-ing with curiosity about the tribal past. Exhibitors in Chicago and St. Louis returned to a static, romantic view of the native life and stressed the notion that traditional culture was antithetical to modern civilization. And the "living specimens" put on display raised anew long-standing doubts about the Native American's abil-ity to survive assimilation. By 1915 the public was growing accus-tomed to viewing Indians as members of one of the world's many "backward races." "Pushed to the wall," they could look forward to little besides manual labor and extinction.

Fair exhibits are historical artifacts, mute displays that might be read differently by different observers. Other areas of the nation's popular culture provide evidence that places the expositions in a broader context. In the press, for example, despite the fact that the level of interest in Indians varied considerably between 1890 and 1920, books and articles dealing with native life appeared regularly and projected a consistent point of view. Moreover, new reform groups and clubs interested in Indian life continued to be organized. Both areas communicated an image of the Indian that was remarkably similar to the one produced by the world's fair displays.

In the 1880s, Helen Hunt Jackson and Alice Fletcher often used the new mass-circulation weeklies to advertise their cause. A generation later, the practice continued, but the reformers' optimism was replaced with darker judgments. For example, in 1907 *World To-Day*, a picture-filled monthly under the editorial control of the University of Chicago's William Rainey Harper, published an article entitled "Shaping the Future of the Red Man." After surveying conditions on the reservations, the piece concluded that the "crudeness" and "shortcomings" of the Indian were "insuperable deterrents to the success of our new policy of standing [him] upon his feet and teaching him to walk alone." This pessimistic view of the Indians' future was echoed elsewhere. The following year, *Harper's*, in an article entitled "Making Good Indians," argued the Indian was hampered by a "strong streak of childishness," while the *Atlantic Monthly*, once a platform for Senator Dawes and Professor Thayer, promised that "the epic of the American Indian has closed."[19]

Perhaps most surprising, the muckrakers—journalists sympathetic to Jackson and other reformers—shared the popular disenchantment with Indian progress. Ray Stannard Baker, whose *Following the Color Line* revealed the evils of segregation and questioned the accuracy of many Jim Crow stereotypes, exemplified the change of heart. His description of the allotment of the Fort Hall reservation in Idaho, written for *Century Magazine* in 1903, observed, "It is the fate of the Anglo-Saxon that he go forever forward without resting; he stands for civilization, improved roads and cities." As for the Indians, they were invulnerable to the government's good intentions. Following their allotment at Fort Hall, he noted that the tribesmen there went on "exactly as before, looking on imperturbably, eating, sleeping, idling, with no more thought of the future than a white man's child."[20]

Fiction writers developed a similar theme. Helen Fitzgerald Sanders, for example, a Montanan who traveled widely in the West, published "The Red Bond" in San Francisco's *Overland Monthly* in

1911. The short story described Judith, a mixed-blood woman who had attended eastern boarding schools before settling in a small town on the plains. In the hands of a Helen Hunt Jackson, Judith would have resembled Ramona, the lacemaking heroine of her 1884 reform novel. But in Sanders' story, Judith abandoned her education after witnessing the arrest of a young Indian for the drunken murder of a white man. The young woman helped the boy escape and then followed him into the hills. "The red bond of her forefathers," Sanders wrote, "held her as relentlessly as though she had never left the blanket and the teepee." The implications of this reversion were unsettling. Sanders wrote that Judith "had clung to those newer teachings of the adopted race, but at last the old, old yearnings surged up, and she forgot all but the crooning songs her mother used to sing and the spell of the wilderness." *The Virginian*, Owen Wister's immensely popular portrait of a gallant cowboy, contained similar observations, as did his short story "Little Big Horn Medicine," Elliot Flower's "Law and the Indians" (which appeared in the *Atlantic Monthly*), and Honore Willsie's novel, *Still Jim*.[21]

When they imagined the Indian's place in contemporary society, popular writers concluded that Native Americans were destined to live on the fringes of civilization. The successful Indians of the early twentieth century were not the teachers, ministers, or yeomen farmers promised by the nineteenth-century reformers. Now the highest praise was saved for hired hands and construction laborers. Such Indians, *Munsey's Magazine* reported in 1901 (in an article entitled "Making the Warrior a Worker"), were "learning the gospel of work." In her novel *Still Jim*, Honore Willsie put it more poetically. She praised the Apaches who wielded picks and shovels on modern road crews: "The last of Geronimo's race was building new trails for a new people." Just as the organizers of the St. Louis fair had found it most appropriate for Indian students to be carpenters and blacksmiths, so the popular writers of the early twentieth century matched their pessimistic view of Indian capabilities with a call for Native Americans to pursue a life of unskilled labor.[22]

Hamlin Garland made this modern view of Native Americans a central theme in *Captain of the Grey Horse Troop*, by far the most popular Indian book of the early twentieth century. Based on extensive research on the Tongue River Reservation and a great deal of genuine sympathy, the novel was serialized in the *Saturday Evening Post* before its publication by Harper and Brothers in 1902. It described that experiences of Captain George Curtis during his tenure as an Indian agent for the imaginary "Tetongs" of Montana. Garland's hero started his charges on the road to "civilization" while combatting corruption in Washington, greed in a nearby cattle town, and the indifference of the beautiful Elsie Brisbane. In the end, everyone was overwhelmed by the captain's courage and charm. While hardly great literature, the story provided Garland with a vehicle for discussing the Indians' future.

The "Tetongs," Curtis explained, were good-hearted but backward. "I like these people," the captain announced. "It touches me deeply to have them come and put their palms on me reverently—as though I were superhuman in wisdom—and say: 'Little Father, we are blind . . . Lead us and we will go.'" A scientist visiting the reservation agreed, reminding Garland's hero that "fifty thousand years of life proceeding in a certain way results in a certain arrangement of brain-cells which can't be changed in a day, even in a generation." People with such handicaps required a protector; they could not survive on their own because education had no impact on them and citizenship had no meaning. Captain Curtis, with his benevolent control over their reservation, would save them. Garland wrote that the cavalryman "felt himself in some sense their chosen friend— their Moses, to lead them out of the desolation in which they sat bewildered and despairing."[23]

Garland's vision of the solution to the tribe's plight appeared in the novel's closing scene. Having defeated his foes and won young Elsie's promise to marry, Curtis took his fiancée and his sister Jennie on a walk through a "Tetong" village. He passed among them like an antebellum overseer; the reservation had become his plantation.

Everywhere they went Curtis and his friends met with hearty greeting. "Hoh—hoh! The Little Father!" the old men cried and came to shake hands, and the women smiled, looking up from their work. The little children, though they ran away at first, came out again when they knew that it was the Captain who called. Jennie gave hints about the cooking and praised the neat teepees and the pretty dresses. . . . Here was a little kingdom over which Curtis reigned, a despotic monarch, and [Elsie] if she did her duty, would reign by his side. . . .

There were tears in Elsie's eyes as she looked up at Curtis. "They have so far to go, poor things! They can't realize how long the road to civilization is."

"I do not care whether they reach what you call civilization or not; the road to happiness and peace is not long, it is short; they are even now entering upon it. They can be happy right here."

Landownership, citizenship, and adequate schools do not complicate the tableau. Rather than a racial group "rising" to civilization and joining white society, Garland's natives defined a western version of the plantation Sambo. They were "happy right here."[24]

Garland repeated his attack on total assimilation in his short stories and an essay in the *North American Review*. There he argued that government schools separated children from their parents and that allotment destroyed tribal life and sentenced inept farmers to lonely starvation. Significantly, he pointed out that Indians—because of their backwardness—deserved the same pity and concern as blacks: "We are all answerable for them, just as we are answerable for the black man's future," he wrote. "As the dominant race we have dispossessed them, we have pushed them to the last ditch which will be their grave, unless we lay aside greed and religious prejudice and go to them as men and brothers; and help them to understand themselves and their problems; and only when we give our best to these red brethren of ours, do we justify ourselves as the dominant race of the Western continent." Garland's writings present a vivid example of the modern view of Indians. He ascribed the cultural differences that separated the Native American from the rest of society to racial backwardness, expressed sympathy for the tribesmen's poverty, and called on whites to guide their less fortunate brethren with Captain Curtis's mosaic leadership. His position mixed compassion with ethnocentrism; it suggested that Indians must understand their own shortcomings before they could rise from their poverty. And while he spoke of progress, Garland clearly rejected the evangelical optimism of Henry Dawes and Alice Fletcher.[25]

There was more to the popular view of Indians than pity. Harsh racial judgments coexisted with fascination and sympathy in literature as they had in the exhibition hall. Not suprisingly, then, in the early twentieth century tribal mythology and handicrafts gained in popularity even as the Indian was being indicted for childishness and ignorance. As the symbol of America's heroic history, Native Americans represented virtues the nation risked forgetting in the headlong pursuit of wealth and power. Safely confined in the past, Indians could be a tonic for the country's old age, a living remnant of a younger America. As one journalist wrote in 1917, "Many of us cannot help regretting the fact that we are witnessing the effacement of what we have known as the real American red man, the wild Indian."[26]

George Bird Grinnell and Charles Lummis were among the most outspoken of those who viewed the passing of the Indians' traditional lifeways with regret. The attitude of both men arose—at least in part—as a consequence of personal experience. Lummis and Grinnell were members of the last generation to have experienced life on the American frontier. Grinnell, whose New York boyhood had included a friendship with the famous Audubons, accompanied his Yale mentor, Othniel C. Marsh, on the first paleontological expedition to the Dakotas in 1870. And Lummis, a Massachusetts native, "discovered" the Southwest in 1884, when he walked from Ohio to California. Both men became journalists—Grinnell edited *Forest and Stream* and Lummis owned a California magazine called, successively, *Out West* and *Land of Sunshine*—and their early adventures remained central to their work. Grinnell was an eager advocate of forest and game preservation, while Lummis used his magazine to promote the beauties of the Southwest and to campaign for the protection of the region's historic sites. The two men were captivated by Indian culture and eager to insulate Native Americans from the press of modernity. Unlike the reformers of the previous generation, they viewed the Indian as a victim of progress, not its beneficiary. Lummis believed that "the Indian, poor devil, will presently die off." Grinnell agreed, writing that the Indian's way of life had "passed away and will not return."[27]

To Grinnell and Lummis the Indians were doomed because, like the redwoods and the buffalo, they could neither resist the white man's advances nor adapt to his civilization. Echoing Hamlin Garland's captain, the two men believed Indians to be lovable but backward; their outdated way of life was a badge of their primitive nature. Grinnell noted, for example, that the Indian had "the mind and feelings of a child with the stature of a man," while Lummis observed that one of his favorite tribes, the Hopi, "are ethnically in about the development of a ten year old." The transplanted westerner went on to suggest that whites should abandon their hopes of assimilating the Indians. He called instead for a "modest forbearance" that would "lead us to 'let nature take her course' and not kill [the Indian] before his appointed hour."[28]

In 1902 Lummis and Grinnell joined forces to found the Sequoyah League, a reform organization with chapters in New York and Los Angeles. Their effort was short-lived. The league disappeared by 1907, but their policy suggestions illustrate the implications of their sentimental point of view. Lummis wrote that the Sequoyah League sought "not to have hysterics or to meddle, but to assist the Indian department." This "assistance" usually took the form of attacks in *Out West*. Lummis's chief complaint was that agents and teachers ignored the Indian's inability to change. "Ignorant of government and history," he wrote, "the government insists that the Indian shall civilize as much in twenty years as our own Saxon or Teuton ancestors did in five hundred." Such an effort, he added, tried to "subvert the law of gravitation."[29]

The Sequoyah League focused on two areas: education and land policy. Grinnell wrote that government schools were not necessarily a blessing. "In many cases," he observed, "the attempt to educate the Indian beyond a certain point tends to injure rather than to help him." Lummis was even more direct; he added, "We should not educate [Indians] to death." An institution like Carlisle, charged by nineteenth-century reformers with the "civilization" of native children, was to them a "peon factory" doomed to failure. The Sequoyah League called instead for training in traditional handicrafts. Baskets and pottery for sale to tourists, not land and citizenship, would enable the Indians to be self-supporting. As for allotment, Lummis and Grinnell pointed out it was not a panacea. Referring to the Dawes

Act, Grinnell argued that in the administration of Indian Affairs, "no hard and fast rule of treatment [could] be established."[30]

Undoubtedly the founders of the Sequoyah League shared a genuine concern for the Native American's future. Nevertheless, it is equally true that their interest stemmed from what the Indians represented as well as from their actual condition. For Grinnell and Lummis it was important to protect the first American's picturesque way of life both because the people—being backward—could live no other way and because they represented an important element in the American past. The Indians could not be educated beyond a certain point and, indeed, they should not be; the rapid "civilization" of the Indian would call into question the racial struggle that was basic to the American experience. Lummis and Grinnell believed that conquest of the West represented the triumph of Anglo-Saxon civilization over unbending barbarism. History proved that the races could not intermingle. Thus, the best that could be hoped for in the present was the gradual "improvement" of the defeated inferior races. Lummis wrote in 1904, for example, that the reformer's enthusiasm for education was generous, but naïve. It was absurd, he argued, to "go on butting [their] heads against history and the attraction of gravitation—trying to make Chinaman, darkey and Indian into hand-me-down white men." For these men, it was both practical and altruistic to preserve racial differences.[31]

The Sequoyah League's blending of racism and nationalism surfaced often in the early years of the twentieth century. In 1906, for example, Edward S. Curtis launched his famous forty-volume study, *The North American Indian*. With the financial backing of J. P. Morgan and the technical assistance of the Bureau of American Ethnology, Curtis spent twenty-five years recording the habits and costume of dozens of tribes. The finished books were an artistic triumph, but they were also a monument to Indian extinction. From the opening photograph, labeled "The Vanishing Race," through scores of images of old warriors, young maidens, and Indian encampments, Curtis demonstrated both the beauty and the transience of the old ways. Theodore Roosevelt added the expected note of patriotism in the "foreward" he wrote for the first volume. The president told Curtis his books were a "good thing for the whole American people." He welcomed the project because the Indian's life had "been lived under conditions through which our own race passed so many years ago that not a vestige of their memory remains. It would be a calamity if a vivid and truthful record of these conditions were not kept."[32]

In the years before World War I other Americans expressed a similar interest in vivid—if not entirely accurate—records of the Indian's role in the national past by supporting a number of projects as monuments to the race. Among these was a campaign organized by the president of Stanford University and the leader of the Boy Scouts to preserve a bison herd on part of Montana's Flathead reservation. Another project was completed in 1912, when Chicago sculptor Lorado Taft unveiled a 50-foot-high cement statue of Black Hawk on the banks of the Rock River in Illinois. Monuments also appeared in Minnesota, Colorado, Oregon, and Massachusetts. But the grandest plan of all was conceived by department store executive Rodman Wanamaker. At a New York banquet honoring Buffalo Bill Cody, Wanamaker announced that he intended to erect a bronze statue of a young Indian at the entrance to the city's harbor. The figure would be 165 feet high, posed with his hand raised in a sign of peace. The monument to the "departed race" would be 15 feet taller than the Statue of Liberty and built entirely with private funds. All that was needed was land for a site. Congress obliged in 1911, setting aside a section of Fort Wadsworth on Staten Island.

That a monument to a vanishing race would be a source of national pride might seem ironic, but there was no irony intended when Wanamaker selected February 22, 1913—George Washington's birthday—for the groundbreaking ceremony. At the appointed hour thirty-two aging chiefs gathered to watch President Taft break ground for the project and to hear him say that the statue "tells the story of the march of empire and the progress of Christian civilization to the uttermost limits." That the public Indian had become a national treasure was made more explicit at the close of the morning's festivities, for the U.S. Mint had chosen the occasion to begin distributing the new Indian-head nickel. The shiny coins, with an Indian profile on the front and a buffalo on the reverse, were passed with great ceremony to Taft, Wanamaker, and the assembled Indians.[33]

James Baldwin once asked a white audience, "Why do you need a nigger?" He spoke with the anger and frustration of someone who felt that America refused to recognize his humanity and his past. Native Americans must have had similar feelings in the early twentieth century as they witnessed the emergence of a new public image of themselves. Apparently, white artists and writers needed to see the Indian as someone burdened by his race and limited by his "backwardness." And the white public needed to preserve a vestige of the vanishing race as a symbol of the nation's past victories. As one reporter wrote of the New York Indian memorial, it would be a reminder of the people "to whom we are indebted for the great, free gift of a continent." But Baldwin's question remains: Why was the new image needed? Why did the optimism of the reform era fade so quickly? What made racial explanations of Indian behavior so attractive? And why should Americans equate patriotism with a bronze memorial? To answer these questions fully, one must turn from art to politics.[34]

When told of President McKinley's assassination, so the famous story goes, Republican boss Mark Hanna exclaimed that the White House now belonged to "that damned cowboy." Whether apocryphal or not, the incident reveals that in his brief political career Theodore Roosevelt had successfully identified himself as a roughrider, a man of the West. While he had spent less than three years ranching in the Dakotas, the new president studiously cultivated his frontiersman image. Every schoolboy knew that Teddy was a big-game hunter and a cowpuncher.[35]

Roosevelt brought a westerner's perspective to the administration of Indian affairs and supported the nostalgic version of Indian life that was emerging in the public press. What is more, throughout his time in office, the young president drew on the advice of an informal "cowboy cabinet" he had gathered around him. The "cabinet" had six members: Hamlin Garland, George Bird Grinnell, Charles Lummis, Frederic Remington, Owen Wister, and Francis Leupp. With the possible exception of Garland, none of the men were native-born westerners, but like Roosevelt they had all discovered the region on trips across the plains during their youth. They shared a paternalistic concern for the Indians and believed they should protect the Native American from the naïve reformers who preached total assimilation.[36]

Like other cabinets, the president's cowboy advisers were not always crucial to policy making. In his second term, as his confidence in his own judgments increased, TR relied less on the group. But in his first years, Roosevelt called on them often. They were old friends. He had known Lummis and Wister at Harvard; Grinnell, Garland, and Remington he had met in New York in the 1880s and 1890s; and he had worked with Leupp in Washington while Roosevelt was serving on the civil service commission. They were also loyal. Soon after TR's inauguration Lummis had written, "I am glad you are in the saddle when the hard days come." All the men visited him in Washington; Grinnell, Wister, and Remington arrived within the first few weeks after he took office.[37]

Roosevelt consulted with his friends over appointments and policy decisions, but the significance of the group lay in what it reveals about the president's approach to Indian affairs. For the first time since 1880, an administration saw the assimilation effort as a regional concern rather than a national obligation. Grinnell spoke for the group when he urged the president to appoint someone familiar with the West to head the Indian Office. He argued that such a person "would do more to transform the Indians into working, earning people than anything else that could be devised." Grinnell and others also called for a reorientation of federal programs and a new, more cautious approach to Indian "uplift."[38]

Less than a year after taking office Roosevelt discussed the problem of selecting Indian agents with one of his advisers. While observing that the best agents were often men who were *not* from the areas adjoining a reservation, he pointed out that "in the long run the success of a governmental policy . . . must depend upon the active good will of those sections of people who take the greatest interest in the matter." Federal meddling in local affairs was ultimately self-defeating. "Wise eastern philanthropists can do a good deal," he added, "but many . . . are anything but wise; and these are in the aggregate very harmful." Under the Rough Rider, government actions would take into account the interests of white westerners as well as the Indians. The "active good will" of the tribe's neighbors would be more important to policy making than the dictates of eastern philanthropists.[39]

A regional approach to racial issues was characteristic of both Theodore Roosevelt and his era. The president told an audience at all-black Tuskegee Institute in Alabama, for example, "The white man who can be of most use to the colored man is that colored man's neighbor. It is the southern people themselves who must and can solve the difficulties that exist in the South." And he repeated the theme in reference to the Pacific Coast when he completed the Gentleman's Agreement with Japan in 1907 and wrote that the exclusion of Asian immigrants was "the only sure way to avoid . . . friction." With the passing of nineteenth-century reformers and their rhetoric of equality, and the rise of a politically powerful white population in the West and South, politicians like Roosevelt began arguing that accommodation to local prejudices was more realistic than federal "philanthropy."[40]

Like most westerners, the president's chief concern was the economic development of the frontier. His *Winning of the West* argued that it was the United States' destiny to "civilize" the continent, a message Roosevelt repeated in 1903, when he asserted that it had been the nation's task "to wage war against man, to wage war against nature for the possession of the vast lonely spaces of the earth which we have now made the seat of a mighty civilization." TR initiated efforts to establish a national reclamation program, develop a scientific approach to forest management, and adopt a systematic approach to mining on the public domain. The purpose of these activities, he wrote in 1907, was "to promote and foster actual settling, actual homemaking on the public lands in every possible way. Every effort of this administration [had] been bent to this end." He replaced the nineteenth-century idea that the West and the Indians would develop together with regional boosterism.[41]

But Roosevelt's approach to Indian assimilation was not simply a product of his deference to regional chauvinism. He also maintained a pessimistic view of Native American abilities, a view supported by his cowboy advisors. In 1893 the Rough Rider returned from a tour of the West with a conclusion that would be echoed in the writings of Lummis, Grinnell, and Garland: "To train the average Indian as a lawyer or a doctor is in most cases simply to spoil him." While continuing to support universal schooling, Roosevelt called on eastern reformers to lower their expectations.[42]

Roosevelt's views on Indian education were consistent with his advocacy of American imperialism and his support for racial segregation. Roosevelt was an outspoken defender of overseas expansion. He believed that the white races had a duty to raise less powerful nonwhite nations to a better standard of living. This is what Roosevelt believed Americans had set out to do in the Philippines, despite the fact that the archipelago was a military "heel of Achilles" and the Filipinos would need a "succession of Tafts [to] administer them for the next century." TR believed that participation in world trade and contact with efficient businessmen would teach natives the advantage of civilization and stimulate them to improve themselves.[43]

He also thought American blacks would benefit from an extended period of domination by whites. "Negroes," Roosevelt wrote an English friend, should only have "the largest amount of self-government which they can exercise." With this axiom in mind the president had little difficulty justifying segregation, disenfranchisement, and—a bizarre paradox—the maintenance of the color bar at the 1912 Progressive party convention. "I have the most impatient contempt," he wrote, "for the ridiculous theorists who decline to face facts and who wish to give even to the most utterly undeveloped races of mankind a degree of self-government which only the very highest races have been able to exercise."[44]

And Indians belonged to a nonwhite race. In his speeches and correspondence TR emphasized that the Indian, like his Filipino and black brothers, should learn to labor at the lower echelons of the white man's industrial society. "No race, no nationality ever really raises itself by the exhibition of genius in a few," he told a graduating class of blacks and Indians at Hampton Institute in 1906; "what counts is the character of the average man and average woman." He urged the students to develop "courage, willingness to work, [and] the desire to act decently." When presenting this message to whites, the president was more direct and less benign. Responding to a critic of his imperialistic views, Roosevelt snapped, "If we were morally bound to abandon the Philippines, we were also morally bound to abandon Arizona to the Apaches."[45]

Near the end of his life, TR wrote: "Some Indians can hardly be moved forward at all. Some can be moved both fast and far. . . . A few Indians may be able to turn themselves into ordinary citizens in a dozen years. Give to these exceptional Indians every chance; but remember that the majority must change gradually, and that it will take generations to make the change complete." This analysis reveals how profoundly Roosevelt differed from the evangelical reformers and Republican stalwarts who had fashioned the assimilation campaign of the 1880s. Viewing the Native American's future in the context of twentieth-century political realities, the former president saw no alternative to his pessimistic judgments. Popular writers applauded his "realism," and his cowboy advisers nodded their approval.[46]

The years following Roosevelt's presidency were marked by political turmoil. William Howard Taft, whipsawed between warring factions within his own party, was quickly dumped by the electorate. TR returned from his famous safari and launched the most successful third-party movement of the century. In its aftermath the Democrats placed the first southerner in the White House in over half a century despite his failure to win more than 42 percent of the popular vote in the 1912 election. And the Socialists, gaining strength at every election, hovered on the verge of respectability. Nevertheless the two men who followed Roosevelt into the White House shared his view of the Indian question. The new "realism" of the Rough Rider replaced the assimilationist consensus of the 1880s and 1890s. Backward but beautiful, the Indian stirred little controversy among the leading political warriors of the progressive era.

As TR's hand-picked successor, Taft shared many of his predecessor's attitudes and continued most of his policies. Like Roosevelt he addressed the students at Hampton, praising their instruction in "manual dexterity" and complimenting them for recognizing that "the best home for the negroes [was] on the farm." As a former governor general of the Philippines, Taft was also a firm defender of what he called the "altruistic work" being carried out in the colony. And the new president agreed that Indians, like blacks and Filipinos, should be protected by their more "civilized" countrymen. In what was probably his only appearance before an entirely Indian audience during his four years in office, the president told students at the Haskell Institute, "You are under the guardianship of the United States which is trying in every legitimate way to fit you to meet what you have to meet in future life." Taft added that Indians who received an education should be an example to their tribesmen "in industry, in loyalty to the country, in law abiding character, and in morality."[47]

When Woodrow Wilson took office it was obvious that the total assimilation of the Indians had ceased to be a public concern. Greeting a delegation from the new Society of American Indians in 1914, the president confessed, "Problems have crowded upon me so fast and thick since I became President that this is one of the problems to which I have not as yet been able to give proper study." He dismissed the group with a promise to give their concerns his "very serious consideration." Significantly, however, despite his ignorance, Wilson agreed with Roosevelt that Indian affairs were best administered by westerners. Franklin K. Lane, a San Francisco lawyer endorsed by the Los Angeles Chamber of Commerce and the Asiatic Exclusion League, served as the Democrat's secretary of the interior. Lane's first assistant secretary in charge of the Indian Office was Andrieus Jones of New Mexico, and Cato Sells, a banker and party official from Texas, became commissioner of Indian affairs. Wilson rejected the idea that the federal government had a special responsibility to oversee and encourage Indian progress. The concerns of white westerners were foremost in his administration; little would override their influence in Indian affairs.[48]

Important changes were also taking place in Congress. Once the cost-free plaything of eastern reformers, Indian legislation was becoming the special province of western politicos. The transition began in 1889, when four new states—the Dakotas, Montana, and Washington—began sending representatives to Washington. It continued through the 1890s as Utah, Wyoming, and Idaho received their statehood, and was completed when Oklahoma (1907), Arizona (1912), and New Mexico (1912)—each with a significant Indian population—entered the union. Since most of the new states were sparsely populated, their impact on the House of Representatives was slight. But in the Senate, the arrival of eighteen new senators in an arena where power was already evenly balanced altered that body's treatment of issues affecting the West.

In the first ten years of the twentieth century there was no single senator who dominated policy making in the Senate the way Henry Dawes had in the 1880s. Nevertheless, a study of the voting behavior of senators from 1900 to 1910 reveals a group of fourteen men who voted together at an average rate of more than 65 percent. Twelve of the fourteen were from states west of the Mississippi. While these senators served for varying lengths of time, they all participated in at least five of the eleven roll call votes held on questions affecting Indians during the decade. And they influenced the outcome of those votes; on nine of them a majority of the group voted with the winning side. Lists of voting blocs are inherently artificial—men who voted infrequently may have been influential, and members of the group may have believed they were acting independently—but the list in Table 2 contains most of those who guided Indian policy in the Senate during the Roosevelt era.

Voting behavior during the Wilson administration followed a similar pattern. Eleven roll call votes were held on legislation affecting Indians between 1913 and 1921. Of the fifteen senators who participated in at least five of those votes and voted identically 50 percent of the time or more, nearly half were from the West. The group listed in Table 3 also includes two men who chaired the Senate Indian Affairs Committee: insurgent Republican Moses Clapp (1907–11) of Minnesota and Arizonan Henry Ashurst (1915–19). Perhaps most significant, the Wilson years marked a sharp decline in congressional involvement in Indian affairs. An average of nearly half the Senate was absent during the eleven roll call votes held during the Democrat's two terms, and on *none* of them did more than fifty-five members of the upper house register a vote. Thus no more than twenty-eight senators were needed to carry any issue. Even a moderately cohesive group of fifteen senators could be confident of deciding the important Indian policy issues that arose.[49]

Men from beyond the Mississippi did not snatch control of Indian policy away from their eastern colleagues; it was handed to them.

Table 2. Indian Policy Makers, c. 1900–10 *

Senator	Years in Senate	Mean Agreement Score
Elmer Burkett, R–Nebr.	1905–11	77
Samuel Piles, R–Wash.	1905–11	77
Chester Long, R–Kans.	1903–9	76
Frank Flint, R–Calif.	1905–11	73
Porter J. McCumber, R–N.Dak.	1899–1920	71
George Perkins, R–Calif.	1899–1915	70
Jacob Gallinger, R–N.H.	1891–1918	64
Henry Teller, R, Silver Democrat–Colorado **	1885–1909	64
Henry Burnham, R–N.H.	1901–13	62
Alfred Kittredge, R–S.D.	1901–9	62
Fred T. Dubois, Populist–Idaho	1891–97, 1901–7	59
William Stewart, R–Nev.	1887–1905	58
Robert Gamble, R–S.Dak.	1901–13	56
Clarence Clark, R–Wyo.	1893–1917	52

* Information presented here is based primarily on votes 44–55 in Appendix 1.

** left GOP in 1896

As presidential attitudes and the high rate of abstentions on Indian-related roll call votes indicate, lawmakers increasingly were prepared to view Native Americans as the special concern of the westerner. The chairmanship of the Senate's Indian Affairs Committee also became theirs. Between 1893, when Henry Dawes retired, and 1920, nine men held that influential post. All were from states west of the Mississippi, and three were from states that had not existed before 1889. Beset by dozens of pressing issues, and faced with a group that claimed to "know" the Indian better than they, eastern legislators agreed with the New York congressman who responded to the Indian office's proposed budget for 1907 by calling on his colleagues to "approve a bill as a whole without discussion or change of

Table 3. Indian Policy Makers, c. 1913–20 *

Senator	Years in Senate	Mean Agreement Score
James Martine, D–N.J.	1911–17	75
Frank White, D–Ala.	1914–15	73
Henry Ashurst, D–Ariz.	1913–41	72
Nathan Bryan, D–Fla.	1911–17	69
Key Pittman, D–Nev.	1913–40	66
Morris Sheppard, D–Tex.	1913–41	65
William Thompson, D–Kans.	1913–19	64
Henry Hollis, D–N.H.	1913–19	64
Ollie James, D–Ky.	1913–18	58
Henry Myers, D–Mont.	1911–23	57
Joseph Ransdell, D–La.	1913–21	56
William Chilton, D–W. Va.	1911–17	55
Atlee Pomerane, D–Ohio	1911–23	55
Thomas Walsh, D–Mont.	1913–33	54
Moses Clapp, R–Minn.	1899–1917	53

* The eleven votes taken during the Wilson administration are numbers 57–67 in Appendix 1.

any character." He added that appropriations in this area were "absolutely safe in the hands of the committee."[50]

Like the popular writers who dwelt on Native American racial handicaps and the presidential advisers who called for "practicality" rather than "eastern philanthropy," the western legislators who came to dominate policy making were hostile to an elaborate campaign to achieve total assimilation. "The only element that can elevate the Indian," South Dakota's Senator Richard Pettigrew argued, "is that of showing him how to help himself. No assistance can be given him that will advance him one particle in civilization along any other lines." In the opposite wing of the capitol, Democrat John Stephens of Texas preached a similar gospel to the House of Representatives.

"We should reverse our Indian policy," he cried, "cease making these great annual appropriations; break up their tribal relations; allot their lands among them, and open up the surplus lands on their reservations for settlement." These lawmakers believed that the Indian's only hope for survival lay in becoming self-sufficient actors in the new communities now dotting the western landscape.[51]

Finally, western politicans acquired a firm control over appointments in the Indian Office. While Roosevelt put Francis Leupp in the commissioner's chair because the former reporter had traveled widely in the West, Wilson found the genuine article in Texan Cato Sells. Sells, who served from 1913 to 1921, was succeeded by Charles Burke, a South Dakota congressman who had chaired the House Indian Affairs Committee. Appointments at the lower levels of the Indian Office were almost entirely controlled by local congressman and senators. "I simply cannot get a man confirmed," Roosevelt wrote in 1903, "unless the senators from that state approve of him."[52]

In the early twentieth century, shifts in popular perceptions reshaped the public image of the Indian and his place in American society. Writers and politicians turned away from the hopeful view they had created a generation before. They began doubting the speed with which the Native American might "rise" to a civilized state and questioning whether total assimilation was desirable at all. For many, the Indians had ceased to represent a challenge to the assimilative capacities of their dynamic industrial society. Instead, the race came to symbolize the country's frontier past. In this new context, traditional lifeways were less disturbing, and the eradication of old habits ceased to be an overriding policy objective.

Sources of attitudinal change are elusive. Political and economic pressures mold—but do not determine—them. And while ideas often gain endorsement on their own merit—even when they run against the logic of events—it is equally true that people do not form perceptions in a social vacuum. Events and ideas interact with one another. In the case of the Indian in the early twentieth century, popular curiosity about native life reinforced a growing nostalgia for the lost frontier. These ideas in turn profited from the rise of westerners to political power. Although each trend produced its own image of

Native American life, they all shared and reinforced a common core of beliefs. Among these was the notion that Indians viewed the world differently from whites, that they were not likely to change, and that ambitious assimilation programs could not succeed. In retrospect, the evangelical reformers of the 1880s now seemed both naïve and out of date. The old faith that Native Americans would magically "rise" to civilization struck people like Theodore Roosevelt and Hamlin Garland as praiseworthy, but foolish. And policies based on that faith would not win side support.

White perceptions of the Indian have always been characterized by ambivalence—contempt mixed with admiration, rejection tempered by compassion—but these uncertainties should not obscure important shifts in attitude. Of course the rhetoric of assimilation and the activities of reformers continued, but in the first decade of the twentieth century the balance of opinion appeared to waver and move. Optimism and a desire for rapid incorporation were pushed aside by racism, nostalgia, and disinterest. Total assimilation was no longer the central concern of policy makers and the public. The Indian question had been transformed.

Chapter 4

Frozen in Time and Space

Undergirding the policy reforms of the late nineteenth century was a faith in the immediacy of Indian progress. Policy makers believed that the path from "savagery" to civilization was difficult to traverse, but they set out to mark it and to guide the Indians along its upward track. Shifts in public attitudes were not likely to destroy the faith of America's leaders, for their belief was rooted in science as well as popular intuition. Nevertheless, as the generation of John Wesley Powell and Henry Dawes left the scene, confidence in the Indians' future receded with them. New scientists appeared. They wrestled with new problems and reached new judgments about human history. In the twentieth century, these scholars shattered the old evolutionary orthodoxy and cast aside the view that progress was a natural human condition. Inevitably, this change of heart undermined support for total Native American assimilation. In the 1880s, the Indians had been viewed as a people moving from a lower to a higher stage of development. By 1920 they were frozen in time and space.

Two broad areas of historical change established the context for changes in the scientific perception of Indians. First, during the early twentieth century racial and ethnic differences attracted the attention of a growing number of scholars. Their interest reflected a rising public concern. In the nation's cities, immigrants continued to arrive at unprecedented rates, creating social enclaves that seemed unconnected to the rest of society or to the American past. At the same time southerners were furiously throwing up legal levees to control a flood of social crises that threatened to sweep away a social order founded on white supremacy. They fashioned a universe of segregation statutes to separate the races and buttressed these with demagoguery and violence. Finally, in the West successive rounds of anti-Asian hysteria produced a similar pattern of fear and exclusion. Just as their counterparts in the late nineteenth century were preoccupied with progress—its causes, its virtues, and its future—so the anthropologists and sociologists of the succeeding generation could not escape an obsession with diversity: were the races equal? Should they mix? Could several cultural groups share the same political system?[1]

Within the academic world a second sequence of events was taking place: the social sciences were passing out of the hands of self-taught amateurs. In the twentieth century, university professors would dominate scholarly inquiry. Their rise to dominance brought with it national associations, new academic journals, and the modern graduate school. These institutions in turn fostered and sustained a cadre of intellectuals who valued rigorous inquiry, shunned abstract speculation, and were loyal to their profession rather than to religious or political ideologies. Among modern scientists there was a new emphasis on scientific inquiry and standardized training and a general disenchantment with a priori schemes and assertions.

Rising racial tensions and the professionalism of the social sciences produced disenchantment with social evolutionary thinking. While usually confining nonwhite people to the lower stages of development, evolutionists like Lewis Henry Morgan had explicitly rejected racial classifications; they argued instead that progress was inevitable and that human development followed a single pattern. Modern scientists concerned themselves with the physical differences between groups and criticized their predecessors for minimizing the importance of race. Others argued that too little was known about individual societies to support Morgan's grand theory of human development. They called for detailed investigations and were willing to postpone attempts at synthesis.

Under these pressures the old social evolutionist orthodoxy broke apart and four competing schools of thought took its place. First, a group of anthropologists associated with the Bureau of American Ethnology began to modify evolutionary theory in order to take into account new research and the supposed importance of racial differences. A second party of social scientists concluded that racial differences alone determined social behavior. They believed that non-white peoples had little chance of joining a "civilized" society led by their racial superiors. Third, scholars in the emerging field of sociology looked to the physical and social environments to explain human differences. And finally, in the first two decades of the new century a number of young anthropologists trained by Franz Boas proposed a new concept—culture—to explain the existence of different racial and ethnic traditions. Rather than producing a single new orthodoxy, modern social scientists produced several.

Where politicians concerned with Indian policy had once found unanimity, they now found confusion and disagreement. In the 1880s, the anthropologists' faith in progress had been reflected in a wide array of federal programs; inevitably, the erosion of that faith called the programs into question. Doubts about the wisdom of total assimilation gained scientific support, and, when called upon, scientists gave negative advice. The ambitious assimilation campaign was a mistake and should be restrained—of that they were sure. They were less certain about what should take its place.

In the early twentieth century, social evolution continued to be the credo of the Bureau of American Ethnology. The scientists who worked there labored to incorporate new data from field research sites and new attitudes toward racial differences into the evolutionary framework that was the legacy of John Wesley Powell. While their modifications of Powell's teachings allowed them to continue to view themselves as his heirs, their efforts produced a significant shift in the office's attitude toward total assimilation.

Political pressure and advancing age forced John Wesley Powell from the U.S. Geological Survey in 1893. He remained chief of the Bureau of American Ethnology until his death in 1902, but he had very little day-to-day contact with it. The administration of the office fell to "Ethnologist in Charge" W. J. McGee (1853–1912), a self-educated geologist with eccentricities to match those of his mentor. Like the major, McGee grew up on the Middle Border and began his scientific career as an energetic collector of "specimens." His Iowa home was filled with cases containing rocks, insects, stuffed animals, and Indian artifacts. McGee also shared Powell's belief in the need for a partnership between science and government. At the age of twenty-four the young amateur organized a geological survey of his home state. He completed the project in four years, in the process winning the attention of the U.S. Census Bureau (for whom he next worked). In 1883 McGee became Powell's assistant at the geological survey; work with the Bureau of Ethnology followed.

It was McGee who took the lead in reconciling Powell's dynamic view of social evolution with the changes taking place in the social sciences. The major's protégé recognized that human progress was not as evident at the turn of the century as it had been when Powell had organized the Bureau of Ethnology twenty years before. McGee explained this predicament in the presidential address he delivered at the founding meeting of the American Anthropological Association. "The Trend of Human Progress" began with the recollection of an incident from his Iowa boyhood. One summer day McGee had walked to the bluffs overlooking the Mississippi and "for the first time looked down upon the broad Father of the Waters." He remembered, "I already knew from the books and the talks of my elders that it was a river." He continued to the water's edge and there came upon a group of boys, lounging on a pile of lumber. "I inquired of these long-time residents on the river bank which way the river ran. The voluble lad with feet nervously dangling from the edge of the lumber-pile answered promptly, 'Huh! it don't run nowhere; it stays right here.' . . . the lesson was not lost; I had learned how hard it is to find which way the current runs." Like the boys in the parable, McGee pointed out that observers with "conviction transcending experience" often misperceived the course of human history. He saw himself and his fellow anthropologists as people who would take seriously the data being gathered by scientists and reject blind allegiance to a theoretical school. "The direction of flow of the Mississippi might have been learned from a practical boatman," he noted, "and it is meet to inquire whether the trend of human progress may not be gained from actual workers in man's experience of Man."[2]

McGee did not reject the evolutionist's faith in ongoing progress. He told the American Association for the Advancement of Science in 1897 that the evolutionary framework tended "to bring order out of that vast chaos of action and thought which [had] so long resisted analysis and synthesis." And his presidential address contained the assertion that "it should be self-evident that motion involves progression." McGee went on to describe that forward movement in the fields of anthropology (or "somatology": McGee also shared Powell's love of new scientific terms), psychology, ethnology ("demonomy"), philology, and the history of ideas ("sophiology"). But as his image of the muddy Mississippi suggested, McGee was also aware that the evolutionist could ignore contradictory evidence and overstate the speed of progress.[3]

McGee suggested that scholars appreciate the distance between stages of culture. Different rates of progress, he noted, produced the "difference in modes of thinking [that] form of the strongest bar against the union of tribes and nations." The anthropologist quickly added that such differences were "the expression of brain rather than blood," but his observation would hardly be encouraging to a government schoolteacher or a defender of land allotment. Even though McGee promised that "thought [was] extending from man to man . . . toward a higher plane than any yet attained," his emphasis on the gaps that separated "tribes and nations" pushed the unification of human society—something Powell had predicted—far into the future.[4]

According to McGee, the existence of racial differences raised additional barriers between stages of culture. He asserted that each of the major races had evolved independently. Polygenesis, with its suggestion that different races constituted different orders of beings, undermined the prospects for rapid progress. "The progenitors of the white man," he observed, "must have been well past the critical point before the progenitors of the red and the black arose from the plane of beastiality to that of humanity." Progress might be "self-evident," but it was neither uniform—whites evolved before blacks—nor steady. The races of the world might be blending into a single entity, he noted, but this was occurring "through the more rapid extinction of lower races" as well as through intermarriage.[5]

Indeed, progress might not come to everyone. McGee defended American imperialism in the early twentieth century—pointing out that the "lamp of civilization" was shining on the "dark-skinned peoples"—but he did not believe all "barbarians" could be saved. As the civilized nations rose in efficiency and size, their rate of advancement quickened; progress was "decidedly slower among civilization's subjects." Although there was a great deal in "The Trend of Human Progress" that echoed Powell and Lewis Henry Morgan, its emphasis on racial and cultural differences offered a variant on the social evolutionist theme that might be exploited in the increasingly tense atmosphere of the early twentieth century.[6]

After 1899, McGee's pessimism deepened. His theoretical writings often returned to the gulf between culture groups and the importance of race as an indicator of civilization. In 1901, for example, his presidential address to the Anthropological Society of Washington noted, "The savage stands strikingly close to sub-human species in every aspect of mentality. . . . The range from the instinct and budding reason of higher animals to the thinking of lowest man seems far less than that separating the zoomimic [animal-like] savage from the engine using inventor." The distance separating civilization from the world of the "zoomimic savage" seemed to be getting greater. Three years later, he was referring to "aliens" of "foreign or ill-starred birth and defective culture" as the "mental and moral beggars of the community." Such people, he added, "may not be trusted on horseback but only in the rear of the wagon."[7]

Powell died in the fall of 1902, and McGee awaited his appointment as chief of the Bureau of Ethnology. When he was passed over in favor of William Henry Holmes, a curator at the Smithsonian's National Museum, the major's protégé appealed to the Institution's board of trustees. Franz Boas was one of his most outspoken defenders. In a series of letters to the Columbia University anthropologist, McGee spelled out how he intended to organize the bureau's programs should his appeal be successful. His chief interest was to apply scientific methods to problems confronting American society. He suggested developing a "practical branch" to study the different races living within the United States. Examining the physical and psychological make-up of these groups, he argued, would allow the bureau to "discuss race problems on a scientific rather than a sentimental basis." He wished to extend the bureau's research to "mulattoes as well as to Chinese, Japanese, and other peoples," and to take on such specific tasks as "determining the citizenship value of both pure and mixed Indians."[8]

The changing racial composition of the United States suggested to McGee that the simple line of progress laid out by Morgan and Powell was in need of further examination. One could neither expect assimilation to operate automatically nor confidently predict the outcome of the process. "This country has become a melting pot of humanity," McGee wrote his German-Jewish immigrant colleague. "Without definite foresight on anybody's part, we are working out the greatest experiment in all the world's history in the blending of types of both blood and culture; thereby we are introducing half unwittingly, vital alloys whose properties no one can predict with confidence." He hoped that scientists like himself would be able to guide American statesmen, but his appeal was fruitless (the trustees of the Smithsonian wanted to steer clear of political controversy) and he left the bureau in 1903 to direct the "Congress of Races" at the Louisiana Purchase Exposition in St. Louis.[9]

McGee never produced a comprehensive restatement of social evolutionist theory. His dispute with the Smithsonian's board of trustees cut him off from future work with the Institution, and his lack of professional credentials made securing an academic position unlikely. Theodore Roosevelt appointed him vice-chairman of the Inland Waterways Commission in 1907, and he held that office until his premature death in 1913. But the self-taught Iowan was not the

only scientist concerned with the effects of racial differences on social progress. William Henry Holmes (1846–1933) continued his
predecessor's questioning when he took control of the Bureau of
Ethnology.

With a background as a museum curator, Holmes focused most of
his attention on the proper form and organization of displays. He advocated arranging exhibits according to an evolutionary plan. "By
this method of presentation," he told one gathering of anthropologists, "we teach . . . the succession of peoples and culture and convey a general notion of mutations of fortune and the slow process
from lower to higher phases of existence." His comments on the
"process" by which American Indians were moving from lower to
higher "phases of existence" were most fully developed in an essay
published in the *American Anthropologist* in 1910.[10]

Holmes agreed with McGee that each race had evolved separately
and the most "primitive" peoples had separated earliest from a central line of development. He speculated that "the African and Asiatic
may be the result of the first branching, taking permanent form
in well-separated environments, the Caucasian and especially the
American developing later." But Holmes moved beyond McGee in
his estimation of what polygenesis implied for the future of the individual races.[11]

McGee had acknowledged that some nonwhite races could learn
from the "lamp of civilization," but aside from his desire to keep
such people in the "back of the wagon," and his observations regarding racial intermarriage, he had made no predictions regarding their
assimilation into "civilized" society; Holmes did. "Our people have
been witnesses of a hundred years of vain struggle ending with the
pathetic present," the government's chief ethnologist wrote. He believed the bureau's researches enabled him to predict the Indian's future: "We are now able to foretell the fading out to total oblivion in
the very near future. All that will remain to the world of the fated
race will be a few decaying monuments, the minor relics preserved
in museums, and something of what has been written." Holmes allowed that some "peaceful amalgamation" might take place, but for
the majority "extinction of the weaker by less gentle means will do
the work." Like McGee, Holmes believed racial differences raised

the barriers between stages of culture. He carried that belief to its logical conclusions. "The final battle of the races for the possession of the world," Holmes warned, "is already on."[12]

Holmes made the issue plain. The only way to accept evolutionist doctrine while at the same time accepting deep differences between the races was to predict the "fading out to total oblivion" of backward peoples like the Indians. The issue of race had always been an ambiguous element in the writings of American evolutionists, but earlier scientists like Morgan and Powell had suggested that the conflict between "civilized" whites and uncivilized nonwhites could mean advancement for the "inferior" races. Holmes, faced with the "pathetic present" and a century of failed government programs, preferred to exclude the Indians from his blueprint for social progress.

On the few occasions when they turned from scientific speculation to contemporary policy, the twentieth-century evolutionists repeated their warnings. In a letter to Carlisle's Captain Pratt, McGee defended himself against charges that he opposed Indian education. The scientist explained that he simply had lower expectations. "By reason of the intimate acquaintance with the Indian mind," he observed, "I may differ from some Indian educators as to the rate at which the old should be put off and the new taken on." Other scholars were more pessimistic. An article appearing in the *American Anthropologist* in 1919, for example, stated that "primitive peoples [could not] stand an enforced civilization." The author contended, "No better example of this can be cited than that of the American Indians, who even on their own soil have resisted civil conditions unto death." A generation earlier, Major Powell had called for a partnership between science and the Indian Office. In 1919, evolutionists had only bad news: "Many proud tribes have perished, one after another, before the march of civilization, and the remainder at times seem surely destined to ultimate extinction." Believers in total assimilation and ambitious federal programs would have to look elsewhere for support.[13]

While McGee and Holmes attempted to reconcile a dynamic view of social evolution with their estimate of the great distances separating racial and cultural groups, other social scientists looked to race as the ultimate source of human diversity. These racial formalists were a varied lot. They ranged from Daniel Garrison Brinton, who never abandoned his faith in social progress, to Madison Grant, whose narrow racism predicted unending conflict among the races. All of them classified American Indians as a single race with specific inherited characteristics. All inveighed against "race mixing" and predicted the imminent extinction of the Indian.

Brinton (1837–99), who in 1886 became the first professor of anthropology in the United States, was one of the nineteenth century's last great amateur scholars. He shared a number of traits with his contemporary, Lewis Henry Morgan. Like Morgan, he put aside a boyhood interest in Indians when he embarked on a professional career. Morgan became a lawyer; Brinton practiced medicine. Both men also retired from those careers at a relatively early age so that they could devote all of their time to anthropological study. Although Brinton held a chair in anthropology at the University of Pennsylvania, he did no teaching. He devoted the last decade of his life to research and writing.

Daniel Garrison Brinton does not fit neatly into the racial formalist category. He considered himself an evolutionist, his principal interest was linguistics, and he devoted relatively little time to theoretical speculation. It would be wrong to group Brinton with the eugenicists of the early twentieth century or to forget that there were a number of other aspects to his career. Nevertheless, his point of view—particularly as expressed in his published lectures—prefigured the more explicitly racial approaches to Indian life that appeared after 1900.[14]

During the 1890s, three themes appeared in Brinton's work and formed the basis for the racial formalists' perspective. He argued first that one's capacity for progress was determined by race. This capacity was inheritable and changed so slowly that it was a virtually permanent characteristic of each racial group. Second, Brinton predicted that the Indians' racial inferiority would bring about their extinction. And finally, he warned against intermarriage. He argued that unions of Indians and Europeans would damage the "white race."

Although he accepted the fact that all humanity was "of one blood by the judgment of a higher court than anatomy can furnish," Brinton believed that environment and the "differentiation of the species man" had produced wide differences within the world's population. "Certain mental traits and faculties are broadly correlated to . . . physical features," he wrote in 1898, "and no amount of sentimentality about the equality of all men can do away with this undeniable truth." According to this view, "ethnic characteristics" were established early in the evolution of the species and were "hence impressed indelibly on its members."[15] Race preceded culture. As a consequence, the "indelible" qualities of a group limited its progress. Naturally, Brinton viewed all Indian tribes as one, regardless of their social complexity or the sophistication of their technology. The Indian race had some strengths: it was not as dark as the African race, and the "average cubical capacity" of their skulls lay about midway between that of whites and blacks. But there were also weaknesses. Most significant was their inability to create complex social organizations. Aztec and Maya civilization, the good doctor wrote, were simply large versions of "the simple and insufficient models of the cruder hunting tribes of the plains."[16]

In isolation, the Native Americans would survive; their limitations would not impair the race's ability to feed and clothe itself. In the presence of civilized folk, however, the "pathological condition" of the Indians' "ethnic mind" doomed the group to extinction. Most destructive, Brinton argued, was the Native American's "ineradicable restlessness." Indians were easily excited. This trait led to "scenes of the wildest riot," as well as to nervous disorders and alcoholism. The physician's ingenious diagnosis turned the cries of reformers like Helen Hunt Jackson on their head. The dishonor was not the white man's—*he* was not the one with the "nervous disorders" that provoked frontier violence, and *he* was not excitable. White men had different "indelible" characteristics.

Finally, the lesson Brinton drew from the past was antithetical to the guilt-ridden sermonizing of Dawes and Fletcher. Native Americans were locked in a downward trajectory that could not be altered. "If he retains his habits he will be exterminated," Brinton wrote; "if he aims to preserve an unmixed descent, he will be crushed out by disease and competition." Of course intermarriage with those from more progressive races might change this fate, but Brinton quickly sealed that exit. He believed that neither pity, sympathy, nor love should divert whites from marrying their own kind: "That philanthropy is false, that religion is rotten which would sanction a white woman enduring the embrace of a colored man."[17]

In the years following Brinton's death in 1899, the use of racial characteristics to explain social and cultural differences became widespread. Most of the writing in this area, however, focused on European ethnic groups and American blacks because of their greater numbers and political significance. William Z. Ripley's *Races of Europe* (1899) and Madison Grant's *The Passing of the Great Race* (1916) were the most popular of these books that called for the preservation of northern European culture in the United States in the face of mounting numbers of newcomers from Italy, Greece, and the Balkans. Ripley and Grant insisted that southern Europeans belonged to inferior races that should be barred from entry into the New World by restrictive immigration laws. Other social scientists carried the theme to the American South, asserting that the inherent inferiority of blacks precluded their participation in the country's political or social institutions. Although Indians, because of their smaller numbers and relative political unimportance, did not attract wide attention, racial formalists like Ripley and Grant referred to Native Americans and repeated Brinton's three themes. These scholars described a world of racial castes in which Indians were fixed in a subordinate position.[18]

Belief in the inheritance of acquired characteristics was fundamental to the racial formalists' position. "Civilized" races had an inborn respect for law, while "savage" peoples naturally passed their "backward" habits on to their children. Versions of this view ran from Madison Grant's belief that race lay at the base of all social phenomena to Franklin Giddings's more moderate conception that racial characteristics were the product of environmental pressure. Nevertheless all formalists agreed that a racial hierarchy existed and would continue unchanged into the future. Grant favored northern

Europeans on purely racial grounds. Giddings and others believed climate and social traditions shaped racial characteristics, but they reached similar conclusions. According to Giddings, the "Scotch" were the most "critical intellectual" race while "Negroes and other colored peoples" were largely "instinctive," "imitative," and "emotional."[19]

When scholars like Grant and Giddings turned to contemporary Indian life they continued to wear their formalist blinders. Like Brinton, most of the racial theorists of the early twentieth century were quick to point out that Native Americans were superior to blacks. Some writers, such as Lindley Keasbey of the University of Texas, based their judgment on color. "Arranged in an ascending series," he noted in 1907, "we rank the Negro or Black race lowest; next the American, or Red race; then the Mongolic [sic], or Yellow race, and finally the caucasic [sic] or White race." Others, like Madison Grant, refined the scale by grouping Indians with Mongoloids. This was a step up from the bottom, for "the Mongol is not inferior to the Nordic in intelligence, as is the Negro." The third means of differentiating Indians from blacks was to refer to the achievement of native civilizations. Lothrop Stoddard of the American Museum of Natural History in New York was an advocate of this last view. In *The Rising Tide of Color*, a defense of Anglo-Saxon supremacy published in the aftermath of World War I, the scientist wrote, "There can be no doubt that the Indian is superior to the Negro. The Negro, even when quickened by foreign influences, never built up anything approaching a real civilization; whereas the Indian . . . evolved genuine polities and cultures." Regardless of their base, however, these comparisons between the inherent character of blacks and Native Americans served only to emphasize the supposed permanence of their nature. Scientists like Grant and Stoddard might view the Native Americans more sympathetically than they did blacks, but Indians too were prisoners of their race.[20]

Specifically, racial formalists found America's natives unable to reason in the abstract, lacking in creativity, and less adventuresome than the European "empire builders." These deficiencies produced what Lothrop Stoddard called the Indians' great conservatism. "The

Indian possesses notable stability and poise," the scientist wrote, "but the very intensity of these qualities fetters his progress and renders questionable his ability to rise to the modern plane." As a result, the Indian "exhibits dull indifference to alien innovation." More benign than the lurid accounts of black Americans that titillated the white public at the same time, these descriptions of the Indian personality still relegated natives to an inferior station and sanctioned permanent segregation. In their popular textbook, *Applied Eugenics*, Professors Paul Popenoe and Roswell Johnson stated the lesson clearly for all who cared to study it: "We do not mean, of course, to suggest that all natives who have died in the New World since the landing of Columbus have died because the evolution of their race had not proceeded so far in certain directions as that of their conquerors. But the proportion of them who were eliminated for that reason is certainly very large."[21]

Although they opposed all intermarriage (Grant argued that such union produced "a race reverting to the more ancient, generalized and lower type"), formalists were far more concerned about southern European immigrants and American blacks than they were about Indians. Since Native Americans were bound for extinction, they posed no threat. Their passing, noted one theorist, would spare the country "at least one source of racial impoverishment." In the interim, the Indian Office would be wise to tailor its programs to the race's particular characteristics. In the field of education, for example, racial formalists pointed out that "too much must not be expected of one generation." In an essay entitled "On the Education of the Backward Races," Ernest Coffin pointed out that lowered expectations were the key to a successful school program. Educators should teach only what Indians were capable of learning. "Thus will the indigenous capacities be shaped," he concluded, "not in a mold of our fashioning, but in one of indigenous material, purified and enlarged by the touch of the genius of a higher culture." Stripped of its racism, a proposal of this kind might be interpreted as a call for what educators now call bicultural education. But in the early years of the century, Coffin's ideas were intended as a correction to the belief that Indians could be taught the same subjects as whites. Consideration of what one author called the "ethnic factors in education" would help the Indian Office improve "a race that is in its childhood."[22]

Racial formalists seized on the physical differences between native and white Americans to explain their social differences. Race alone, these scholars argued, explained the Indians' slow progress and justified their "speedy extinction." Natives were destined to remain behind and below the white man during whatever time the race remained on earth. Consequently, government policies based on the assumption that all people might reach a common plane had no scientific basis. There were no evolutionary promises of assimilation from the racial formalists, only imprisonment in an "ineradicable" past.[23]

During the early twentieth century, America's growing cadre of professional social scientists produced a large body of reliable data about human societies. The new evidence often raised questions about the accuracy of social theories. For example, people who were "savages" but who lived on opposite sides of the globe were found to have relatively little in common. At the same time other groups on different cultural levels turned out to share a number of values and practices. The races of the earth, supposedly distinct and bound by their "ineradicable" past, often possessed strikingly similar characteristics. The new science of anthropometry proved that head sizes and brain weights varied hardly at all from race to race. Analysts were beginning to conceive of races as complexes of constantly shifting subgroups rather than fixed populations. Such discoveries raised doubts in many minds about the accuracy of social evolutionary theory as well as the reliability of simple racial formalism. In this atmosphere of doubt, a new line of research—one that concentrated on the role of the environment in determining behavior—began to attract wider attention.[24]

The early social evolutionists of course had been mindful of environmental influences. Both Morgan and Powell had described the contrasts between the Old World and the new, pointing out, among other things, that the absence of large domesticated animals had nudged the Americans away from large permanent settlements and intensive agriculture. Naturally, then, Otis T. Mason (1838–1908), the first of the country's anthropologists to discuss the primacy of the environment, did not set out to destroy evolutionism. In fact Mason was part of the Washington establishment's stable of self-made scholars. Originally a high-school teacher, Mason began working in the ethnology department of the National Museum in 1872. He became curator of ethnology twelve years later and served as head anthropological curator from 1902 to 1908. Mason also contributed to the publications of the Bureau of American Ethnology and was active in the Anthropological Society of Washington. Like Daniel Garrison Brinton, Mason was essentially an evolutionist, but—also like Brinton—he was curious about the importance of factors other than a group's social organization. Brinton became preoccupied with race; Mason turned to the environment.

Curatorial work formed the basis for Mason's ideas about cultural development and the environment. He believed material objects—tools, cookware, and weapons—should form the basis for the organization of exhibits. And Mason carried his thinking a step further; it occurred to him that the "artificialities of human life" also determined a group's social structure. For this reason, he argued in 1908, cultural development should be measured by a people's technical skill. Technological progress required "an appropriation of all the material of which the earth is composed and the domination of the forces of nature for the help of man." The elaborate technology of western societies revealed their high level of cultural development. The crude tools of "backward" societies were a measure of their barbarism. Mason agreed with other evolutionists that culture was singular—there was one standard of progress—but he suggested a new way of gauging a group's achievements.[25]

Mason thus translated social evolutionism into material terms: material culture could be used to determine where a society fit on the scale of human development. Furthermore, to the extent that the products of a society were a function of its physical environment—climate and resources—Mason asserted that a people's surroundings determined their cultural development. "Culture," he concluded, "has had to do from first to last with the physical universe for its resources, environment, and forces, chiefly in the earth, the waters and the air." He recognized that human ingenuity was vital to cultural development (nature is "a servant not a master"), but he continued to recognize the centrality of environmental influences.[26]

When the Bureau of Ethnology prepared its monumental *Handbook of American Indians* in the first decade of the new century, Mason was the obvious choice to prepare an entry on environment. The assignment provided an opportunity to apply his theoretical speculations to North America. Mason wrote that the "natural phenomena" of the continent surrounded the aborigines, "stimulating and conditioning their life and activities." The arrangement of the stars and planets was significant ("since lore and mythology were based on them"), but the most important factors were physical geography, climate, and the dominant plants and animals. He concluded that these factors "determine cultural development." Using this approach, Mason delineated twelve "ethnic environments" and asserted that "in each area there is an ensemble of qualities that impressed themselves on their inhabitants and differentiated them." While he did not throw over the study of social arrangements or reject the significance of racial differences, Mason delineated a position different from that of his colleagues at the bureau. He provided a broad definition of the environment, and suggested that the diversity of Indian cultures could be explained by the diversity of the American landscape itself. These ideas promised an alternative to the rigid orthodoxies of McGee and Madison Grant.[27]

When he turned to contemporary Indian affairs, Mason extended his environmental argument, recommending that the Indian's surroundings be arranged in such a way as to encourage "civilized" habits. An understanding of anthropology, he told the American Association for the Advancement of Science, would "be of practical value in devising methods for the management and evolution of the Indians, Negroes and Chinese within [the United States'] borders." Schools would benefit most from his advice, for scientists like himself could serve as consultants "pointing out the elements of civilization and the order of their normal evolution." Although Mason cautioned that the "middle steps" of development could not be ignored—native schooling must cover each rung in the ladder of progress—he maintained that Indian education could raise Native Americans to civilization.[28]

Like Brinton, Mason developed his ideas in the 1880s and 1890s. His essay presented variants on the dominant evolutionism of his day. Nevertheless, the curator's environmentalism soon attracted scholars who questioned the old orthodox view. The idea that culture is rooted in the physical universe suggested to them a new basis for the study of human history.

Opponents of southern and eastern European immigration often argued that people from these economically less developed areas were unfit for life in the United States. Scholars who supported this position—Franklin Giddings, John Commons, Richmond Mayo-Smith, Sarah Simons, and others—argued that the so-called new immigrants had been molded by different forces than those acting on the peoples of England, Germany, and Scandinavia. Mayo-Smith, for example, a leader among immigration restrictionists, believed that America's educational, political, and legal systems formed a "super-organic environment" that arrivals from feudal and peasant societies would have difficulty understanding. Like Mason, Mayo-Smith and his colleagues held that one's surroundings shaped mental attitudes as well as technological innovations. They agreed with W. I. Thomas, who wrote in the *American Journal of Sociology*, "When society does not furnish the stimulation, or when it has preconceptions which tend to inhibit . . . attention in given lines, then the individual shows no intelligence in these lines."[29]

When it came to modern Indians, scholars like Mayo-Smith had a ready explanation for the tribes' resistance to the assimilation campaign. The Native American was "not like the white man of any class or condition," George Bird Grinnell wrote. The source of the "difference of mind" between the races lay beyond social organization or genetics. The gap between the races indicated that "the Indian, like every other human being, receive[d] his knowledge and his mental training from his surroundings." Grinnell had little contact with academic sociology, but his view of Indian life attracted Fayette McKenzie, a former reservation schoolteacher who in 1906 earned a Ph.D. in sociology at the University of Pennsylvania with a dissertation on Indian assimilation. McKenzie was the only sociologist of his generation to devote most of his attention to Native Americans. His thesis praised Grinnell for properly defining the distance between whites and Indians as "not a fundamental difference in mental constitution, but a difference in tradition—a difference in the social mind."[30]

McKenzie's assertion that the environment shaped a "social mind" that in turn influenced an entire society led him to a relatively optimistic view of Indian assimilation. The young sociologist helped organize the Society of American Indians and worked with educated Native Americans to promote allotment, education, and the enforcement of native citizenship. New conditions, he believed, would surely stimulate a new Indian civilization. McKenzie attacked scholars who were skeptical of federal intervention. "Is culture a product of biology and blood or one of psychology and tradition?" he asked in 1912. "The pessimist and the indifferentist work from the former premise, the optimist from the latter. . . . We have only to effect a considerable change in circumstances (material and psychic) to bring about a corresponding change in ideas and culture." By granting the environment a central role, McKenzie could imagine that "changes in circumstance" would induce social programs. A colleague writing in the *American Journal of Sociology* put it more succinctly. Because of new conditions "the character of the Indian himself [was] undergoing a change."[31]

McKenzie continued to act on his "optimistic" assumptions throughout his career. He was active in the public recreation and settlement house movements while on the faculty at Ohio State; in 1915 he became president of Fiske University. Following his retirement from Fiske, the sociologist returned to Indian affairs, serving as a member of Lewis Meriam's survey staff that investigated reservation life and government policies in the mid-1920s.

But in the years before World War I few environmentalists were optimists. Grinnell believed the gap between Indians and whites was so great that "the attempt to educate the Indian beyond a certain point tended to injure rather than to help him." Like John Commons and the opponents of immigration, Grinnell believed that social habits, once formed, could not simply be erased by plunging someone into new surroundings. And he was supported in this position by sociologist Frank W. Blackmar, who argued in the *American Journal of Sociology* that "social and tribal conditions" as well as "biological heredity" produced distinctive "traits and temperaments" in Native Americans. Environmentalism apparently could cut two ways: methodologically it might avoid the rigidities of earlier theories, but it could be used to defend absolute cultural and racial hierarchies.[32]

The great achievement of the environmentalists was their insight that a wide range of external factors could produce traditions that would hold a people's loyalty for generations. These social scientists rejected the one-dimensionality of social evolution and the constraints of racial formalism. Soon other scholars were studying the environmentalists' innovations and trying to devise new ways to express their insights. The culture concept that emerged in the years before World War I was the product of these deliberations. And its rising influence marked the victory of a conceptual framework that could explain the diversity of North American Indian society while remaining free of the preconceptions of social evolution and racial formalism.

The development of the modern concept of culture was intimately linked to the career of Franz Boas (1858–1942). Boas, a German physicist who earned his Ph.D. at the University of Kiel in 1882, was driven from Europe by antisemitism and limited professional opportunities. He first came to America in 1886 to carry out field studies among the Indians of Vancouver Island for the British Association for the Advancement of Science. Between 1886 and 1896 he continued this project; he also worked on the staff of *Science* magazine and taught briefly at G. Stanley Hall's new Clark University. Boas became a professor of anthropology at Columbia University in 1896, a position he held until his death. At Columbia, Boas organized the first comprehensive graduate program in anthropology in the United States. He also published influential studies in the areas of ethnology, linguistics, anthropometry, and folklore. Both his scholarly output and the fact that he trained more anthropologists than any of his contemporaries made him a central figure in the discipline. It was Boas who first suggested that culture alone—not race, evolutionary development, or physical surroundings—shaped the lives of Native Americans. In the years before 1920 he did not explicitly reject the superiority of western culture or repudiate racial inequality, but his fresh approach to anthropological inquiry eventually accomplished both tasks.

Boas brought a physicist's precision to his field. He recognized from the outset that the data rapidly accumulating in museums and libraries disproved widely held racial and evolutionary theories. In response to those theories he suggested the adoption of a more scientific method. "Anthropology has reached the point of development where the careful investigation of facts shakes our firm belief in the far-reaching theories that have been built up," he wrote in 1898. "Before we seek what is common to all culture," he warned, "we must analyze each culture by careful and exact methods." He repeated this position often, telling a correspondent in 1907, for example, that he was "not very much given to speculations relating to things that cannot be investigated, but rather to work backward from the known to the unknown." Thus, while his work in the years before World War I laid the groundwork for ambitious theories, his preoccupation with the specific meant that he would have little immediate impact on public debate or government policy making.[33]

Boas's major statements on race and culture appeared in *The Mind of Primitive Man*, a collection of essays published in 1911. The book approached racial differences statistically. Carefully reviewing the evidence of brain weights and head size that the racial formalists had amassed to defend their hierarchies, Boas demonstrated that most of their conclusions were based on averages derived from widely varying samples. Consequently there was a great deal of overlap between groups and "the differences between different types of men were, on the whole, small as compared to the range of variation in each type."[34]

Boas conceded that it was "probable" that a difference in brain weight "causes increased faculty," but he could find no conclusive evidence that differences in intelligence coincided with racial categories. Referring to the world's population, he argued that "their faculties may be unequally developed but the differences are not sufficient to justify us to ascribe materially lower stages to some peoples, and higher stages to others." Like the environmentalists, Boas would not accept rigid boundaries between groups or place limits on a race's ability to change or progress.[35]

If racial and cultural categories had no precise meaning, how then to account for the staggering diversity of human society? Boas trod lightly here. "It may . . . be," he wrote, "that the organization of the mind is practically identical among all races of men; that mental activity follows the same laws everywhere, but that its manifestations depend upon the character of individual experience." He avoided the word *environment*, for he intended to avoid simple determinism. "Individual experiences" could be shaped by many forces; their common element was their impact on the human mind.

The bulk of the experience of man is gained from oft-repeated impressions. It is one of the fundamental laws of psychology that the repetition of mental processes increases the facility with which these processes are performed, and decreases the degree of consciousness that accompanies them. This law expresses the well-known phenomenon of habit. . . . When a certain stimulus frequently results in a certain action, it will tend to call forth habitually the same action. If a stimulus has often produced a certain emotion, it will tend to reproduce it every time.

Boas stepped beyond environmentalism by suggesting that "oft-repeated impressions" could derive from religion and mythology as well as physical surroundings or social relationships. He asserted that the totality of individual forces acted on individual people and formed their distinctive approach to life. That totality Boas called culture. Moreover, because the world contained many groups, each experiencing a different collection of "impressions," there were many cultures. The evolutionists' faith in a uniform path of cultural development had no foundation.[36]

At this early stage of his career Boas did not explicitly reject the idea that physical differences might influence the achievements of racial groups, but he argued forcefully that culture explained most of the variety evident in the data before him. "The differences between civilized man and primitive man are more apparent than real," he concluded. "Social conditions, on account of their peculiar characteristics, easily convey the impression that the mind of primitive man acts in a way quite different from ours, while in reality the fundamental traits of the mind are the same." Such a view implied that each set of "social conditions"—each culture—was internally consistent and rational. "To the mind of primitive man," Boas wrote in 1904, "only his own associations can be rational. Ours must appear to him just as heterogeneous as his to us." While not saying that all cultures were equally worthy of admiration or protection, Boas recognized, and eloquently defended, their common humanity.[37]

As George Stocking has amply demonstrated, "Boas began his career with a notion of culture that was still within the framework of traditional humanist and contemporary evolutionist usage." Trained at a modern German university and eager to apply scientific methods to the study of man, the young anthropologist could hardly be expected to reject his own definition of civilization. That he stripped away so many preconceptions from the discipline was remarkable; that he continued to speak of "primitive" and "civilized" man was not. Thus, while *The Mind of Primitive Man* rejected a hierarchy of race or physical environment, it continued to view non-Western peoples as lacking the sophistication of those who lived in the industrial world. "There is an undoubted tendency in the advance of civilization," Boas wrote, "to eliminate traditional elements and to gain a clearer and clearer insight into the hypothetical basis of our reasoning. It is therefore not surprising that, with the advance of civilization, reasoning becomes more and more logical." Thus primitive people like the American Indians would have to become more "logical"—more Occidental—in order to become more "civilized." Boas believed the study of anthropology would teach a "higher tolerance" toward other ways of life. He did not assert that it would teach greater respect.[38]

The culture concept gave social scientists a new tool with which to explore tribal societies. It opposed racial formalism and called for an expansion of the environmentalists' framework to include everything that might condition an individual mind. As Boas presented it in 1911, culture served the same function in all societies. Most significant, the concept—together with the scientific approach that produced it—opened countless paths of inquiry for the scholars beginning to emerge from Columbia's graduate school. Three of the scholars, Clark Wissler, Alfred L. Kroeber, and Robert H. Lowie, were particularly interested in how the culture concept might affect the public perception of Indians and other non-western people.

Clark Wissler (1870–1947), the oldest of the three, became Boas's student at Columbia in 1896. Although Wissler never earned a doctoral degree, he lectured at Columbia and assisted his mentor in curatorial work at the American Museum of Natural History. In 1906 Boas decided he could no longer tolerate the museum's indifference to his research proposals, and he resigned; Wissler succeeded him as curator of anthropology. The incident occurred early in both men's careers and it strained relations between them for many years. Nevertheless Wissler had absorbed his professor's devotion to the scientific method and was eager to join in the search for an alternative to the dominant social theories of his day.

The young curator's chief ambition in the period before 1920 was to use Boas's outlook to compile a general classification of American tribes. This was needed, he believed, because of the confusion wrought by the "speculation" of the amateur anthropologists who had preceded him. Wissler argued that the evolutionists' search for a single organizing theme was futile: "The number of social groups in the New World is so large, that no one can hope to hold in mind more than a small portion of them." He also rejected the environmentalists because their preoccupation with physical surroundings was too mechanistic. "The solution of the environment problem," he wrote in 1912, "depends upon our conception of culture. . . . it is difficult to see how the mere external world could be an important factor in determining cultures." Like Boas, Wissler suggested beginning with the experiences that shape individual persons in a community. "The chief explanation of this phenomenon," he wrote in reference to the origins of culture, "lies in man himself. A group of people having once worked out processes like the use of acorns, maize, manioc, etc., establish social habits that resist change. Then the successful adjustment of one tribe to a given locality will be utilized by neighbors." The landscape tended to set boundaries beyond which certain lifeways could not pass, but it did not determine how people would organize their lives.[39]

Wissler presented his cultural approach to Native American life in *The American Indian*, which appeared in 1917. He divided the hemisphere into culture areas—regions where tribes maintained similar institutions and beliefs. Each culture area had a center, where scholars could observe its characteristic traits more clearly. Moving away from that center, tribes exhibited fewer and fewer of those traits, eventually blending into the neighboring culture areas. Using this framework, and taking "all traits into simultaneous consideration," Wissler delineated fifteen culture areas in North and South America.[40]

Scholars have disputed Wissler's culture areas ever since. Boas himself apparently thought they were too narrowly conceived, and several of his students tried to revise or replace them. Despite its alleged faults, however, Wissler's scheme enabled anthropologists to use the culture concept in a comprehensive description of native societies. He thus fixed in his colleagues' minds a picture of the Americas that was sufficiently complex to incorporate the racial, linguistic, environmental, and societal data that had destroyed earlier theories.

In 1901 Columbia University awarded its first doctoral degree in anthropology to Alfred L. Kroeber (1876–1960). The founding chairman of the anthropology department at the University of California, Berkeley, and president of both the American Folklore Society (1906) and the American Anthropological Association (1917, 1918), Kroeber was the most prominent Boas protégé of the period. His long career produced important achievements in several areas, but the chief contribution of his early years was an elaboration of his teacher's attacks on racial formalism and social evolution. In a series of bold essays that appeared between 1915 and 1917, Kroeber defended racial equality and asserted the primary importance of cultural traditions.

Boas had attacked scientific racism with numbers; Kroeber was more direct. He argued that the study of human society was essentially the study of cultures; race was irrelevant to the enterprise. This assertion was one of a list of professional principles—"Eighteen Professions"—he published in the *American Anthropologist* in 1915: "*The absolute equality and identity of all human races and strains as carriers of civilization must be assumed by the Historian.* The identity [of all races] has not been proved nor has it been disproved. . . . All opinions on this point are only convictions falsely justified by subjectively interpreted evidence." To ascribe a people's culture to their race, he wrote a year later, was "untenable except on the preconception that social forces as such do not exist and that social phenomena are all ultimately . . . resolvable into organic factors." Kroeber acknowledged many differences between "primitive" and modern peoples, but he viewed those differences as a function of culture, not race.[41]

Kroeber's insistence on cultural explanations of behavior was the central theme of "The Morals of Uncivilized People," another essay published before World War I. There he asserted that all societies share a common set of "instinctive" moral ideas: condemnation of incest and murder, care for elders, and community self-protection. He asked, Why are so many different standards of conduct built on this common core of beliefs? The answer, he noted, was that each culture encourages and prohibits specific acts on the basis of its own needs and dangers. "There is every reason to believe," Kroeber concluded, "that uncivilized and civilized men practice what they respectively regard as virtue to the same degree." Cultures were not uniform; they existed everywhere.[42]

The centrality of culture as an explanatory tool was repeated and emphasized a few years later by another Columbia scientist. In *Culture and Ethnology* Robert H. Lowie (1883–1957) wrote that pyschology, race, and geography were all "inadequate for the interpretation of cultural phenomena." The inference is "obvious," he told his fellow scientists: "Culture is a thing *sui generis* which can be explained only in terms of itself. . . . the ethnologist would do well to postulate the principle, *Omnis cultura ex cultura*." With the boldness that is the special possession of young Ph.D.s Lowie added that believers in social evolution were clinging to a "pseudo-scientific dogmatism."[43]

Boas and his growing band of students brought both rigor and creativity to anthropological inquiry. Although they often disagreed among themselves, they shared an enthusiasm for professionalism (standardized training, scientific research methods, a common code of conduct) and a disenchantment with abstract speculation. Their energy and productivity propelled them to positions of leadership in the discipline. But the supporters of the culture concept were a relatively small group. The Bureau of American Ethnology had a near monopoly on research funds and its leadership was hostile to Boas after he publicly criticized William Henry Holmes's appointment as Powell's successor in 1902. Moreover, during World War I, scientists from the Bureau even led a move to oust the immigrant professor from the American Anthropological Association for making "disloyal statements." This hostility, together with the resentment of colleagues from competing universities, prevented the "scientific students of culture" from attaining a position of dominance until well after the war. Before 1920 the "Boas faction" operated in an arena controlled by others. They operated in the same intellectual milieu as the evolutionists, the racial formalists, and the environmentalists. Like the others, they were concerned primarily with explaining the differences between "primitive" and "civilized" peoples. And when they discussed the government's campaign to assimilate the American Indians, they had similar complaints.[44]

The discovery of Ishi in 1911 provides a vivid example of the cultural anthropologists' attitude toward contemporary issues. Ishi was a California Indian who had lived his entire life in the wild. His appearance in the corral of a slaughterhouse in the foothills of the Sierra Nevada was his entrance into "civilization." A generation before, Alice Fletcher had taken one of her Omaha informants home to Washington. Francis LaFlesche became her adopted son and the coauthor of a number of her books. In 1911 Alfred Kroeber took Ishi to the University Museum in San Francisco. The museum became his new home. Kroeber's affection for his Indian friend was no less than Alice Fletcher's for LaFlesche, but his sense of what was "best" for the man who came under his care was remarkably different. Kroeber believed that Ishi was the physcial and intellectual equal of any man, but he also held that there were differences between the "primitive" and "civilized" worlds that could not be overcome quickly. Describing his new friend for a popular magazine, Kroeber asserted, "Ishi has as good a head as the average American; but he is unspeakably ignorant. . . . He has lived in the stone age, as has so often been said." The anthropologist went on to explain that the Indian's ignorance involved "an almost inconceivable difference in education, in opportunity, in a past of many centuries of achievement on which the present can build. Ishi himself is no nearer the 'missing link' or any other antecedent form of human life than we are; but in what his environment, his associates, and his puny native civilization have made him he represents a stage through which our ancestors passed thousands of years ago." Kroeber agreed with those who saw a deep chasm separating natives and whites even as he cautioned that the differences between the two groups were not permanent.[45]

Like Kroeber, most supporters of the culture concept concentrated their energies on refuting racial and evolutionary speculation. They denied the Indians' inferiority by stressing their "primitiveness." In *The Mind of Primitive Man*, for example, Franz Boas insisted that it was European civilization—not the white man—that had conquered the globe. "Several races," he noted, developed lifeways similar to those of Europe. Europeans were successful primarily because conditions on the continent facilitated the spread of innovations. Of these conditions, "common physical appearance, contiguity of habitat, and moderate difference in modes of manufacture were the most potent." He added that as Western culture spread, it destroyed the "promising beginnings" of development in other areas. "In short," Boas concluded, "historical events appear to have been much more potent in leading races to civilization than their faculty." An advanced culture had overwhelmed the peoples of North America. Their fate was not a function of physical weakness or a hostile environment; they were primitives only in relationship to the expanding power of "civilization."[46]

Although Native Americans might have been pleased to learn that modern anthropologists had rejected the idea of a racial hierarchy, they would not have been heartened by the scientists' predictions for their future. Boas believed that the Indian population was so "insignificant" that it would soon disappear through intermarriage. And Livingston Farrand, a colleague in the Columbia University anthropology department, wrote in his textbook on the history of Native Americans, ~"Gradual absorption by the surrounding whites seems to be the Indian's most probable fate."[47]

In the short term, students of culture urged the government to demonstrate its sensitivity to primitive people by toning down its assimilation program. Farrand, for example, pointed out, "The failure to understand and appreciate the workings of the Indian mind and the nature of many of his customs, . . . has often produced serious disturbance, unrest and revolt." The wisdom of improving the Indian's "mind," or "civilizing" his "customs" was no longer self evident. John Swanton, a Harvard-trained anthropologist who also studied under Boas, agreed. He cautioned that the work of "the historian of human culture—the anthropologist in the broad sense—is . . . an important element in determining future action, lack of which may result in unproductive and ill-considered change." These scholars did not question the ultimate objective of assimilation; they called instead for restraint and patience. Alfred Kroeber typified this ambiguous position when, in 1908, he introduced an old Mojave man to a meeting of Indian reformers and Bureau of Indian Affairs officials. "He is a man I am proud to call my friend," the anthropologist exclaimed, "not only because he is the only person who wears long hair, but also because he is a Christian and a good American." Kroeber was pleased that the man retained a part of his traditional costume *and* that he was adapting to the presence of the majority culture. If the officials would be patient with people like Kroeber's friend, it seemed, they could look forward to a time when all Indians were "Christians and good Americans."[48]

During the 1880s, anthropologists played a vital role in the conception of the assimilation campaign. Government scientists created an atmosphere of support for the reduction of tribal landholdings, the erection of a national Indian school system, and the extension of citizenship. A generation later, their endorsement of a single set of policy goals had vanished. Social scientists no longer spoke with one voice when discussing the future of Native Americans in the United States.

Scientific opinion was divided over the significance of the Indians' race. While formalists viewed racial characteristics as decisive, environmentalists were undecided. Some, like Fayette McKenzie, wanted to discount race entirely. Others, like John Commons, believed both race and physical surroundings shaped character. The evolutionists were also of two minds: they hewed to the doctrine of universal progress while consistently placing nonwhites in the lowest categories of development. Amid this indecision students of culture rejected the influence of race altogether.

Scholars were also unsure of the Indian's future. In the 1880s faith in evolutionary development led to predictions of the imminent "civilization" of the tribes. By the early 1900s that faith contained an element of doubt. Racial formalists joined with evolutionists like William Henry Holmes to predict the disappearance of the Indian race. Boas expected intermarriage to wipe out the natives' separate existence. Fayette McKenzie, the optimistic sociologist, was the only scholar to maintain a buoyant attitude; he called for the transformation of tribal life through the manipulation of the Indians' social environment.

The disarray among American intellectuals dealt a silent blow to the assimilation campaign. Disagreement and doubt replaced certainty and support. Scholars who confidently moved between science and policy making had been succeeded by professional academics, cautious in their prescriptions and skeptical of "ill-considered" federal intervention. If there was any agreement among modern social scientists or any advice they could give, it was reflected in their warnings. The differences between Indians and whites were great. Native societies were not "in transition" to civilization, they were adapting slowly—if at all—to the forces of modernity. Primitive man would cling to his old ways for as long as he could. The lesson of these insights was clear: the assimilation process was an exceedingly problematic enterprise.

While the existence of competing points of view prevented social scientists from advocating specific new legislation, their collective disenchantment encouraged government officials to revise their expectations for the future. The total assimilation envisioned in the late nineteenth century might be desirable, but it would not occur rapidly or automatically. Anthropologists and sociologists agreed that Western European culture represented an improvement over primitive lifeways, and they favored Indian progress towards that standard. But they did not believe that policy reforms—allotment, education, or citizenship—would transform the race. Instead they suggested extending the timetable for Indian advancement and re-defining the assimilationist's expectations.

By 1920 it was clear that social scientists had switched sides. No longer cheering the advancement of a people in transition, they now reminded the public that Indians belonged to primitive, static cultures that would require years of instruction and training before they could join a complex industrial society. Modern academic opinion suggested that total assimilation was an unrealistic goal; perhaps partial accommodation to "civilized" standards was all that policy makers should hope for.

Chapter 5

The Emergence of a Colonial Land Policy

On the day after Christmas 1854, Governor Isaac Stevens of Washington Territory and sixty-two headmen representing the Nisqually, Puyallup, and other Puget Sound tribes signed a treaty of friendship and mutual aid. In this agreement, as in dozens of others negotiated in the heady aftermath of the nation's push to the Pacific, the United States committed itself to the maintenance of a reservation. Qui-ee-metl and his fellow tribesmen promised to relinquish all claims to land outside the new preserve, to "exclude from their reservations the use of ardent spirits," to stop trading with the British at Vancouver Island, and "to be friendly" to the Americans. Stevens's promises were few, but among the most important was his assurance that the tribe's new home would be protected by his government for the Indians' "exclusive use." No white man would live among them without their permission.[1]

None of those who gathered that day at Medicine Creek (or three months later in Washington, D.C., when the treaty was ratified) foresaw the changes that were to overtake Qui-ee-metl and his people during the next half-century. No one discussed the government's obligations in the event of a 200-percent population increase in Washington Territory or the arrival of a transcontinental railroad. Nevertheless the Indian Office seemed ready to live up to its commitments. Reservation boundaries were maintained until 1886, when the booming city of Tacoma grew to the edge of Puyallup lands and those Indians were allotted under a provision of the original agreement. Like the people who received their lands under the Dawes Act, the Puyallups acquired trust patents that protected their homesteads and declared that they were now citizens of the United States. The government began providing for the tribe's "civilization" while continuing to preserve an area for is "exclusive use."

Unfortunately for the Puyallups, the Pacific Northwest continued to experience dramatic economic growth. The Northern Pacific Railroad carried crops and raw material to Tacoma from farms and mines a thousand miles inland, and the Pacific steamer trade made the city a global crossroads. Soon after the allotment of the tribe was completed, demands for Indian lands began afresh. This time the Indian's neighbors would not be satisfied with a simple reduction of the tribal domain—they began to argue that the treaty of Medicine Creek had run its course and should be abandoned.

In the early twentieth century, Tacoma's challenge to the Puyallups was repeated in communities across the West. The region was booming. The states beyond the Mississippi, containing 70 percent of all Indians, led the nation in population growth. Between 1890 and 1920 the number of people living in California doubled. During the same time in Arizona the increase was 300 percent, in Washington, 400 percent. Economic expansion accompanied these demographic changes. Single-crop farming, made possible by railroad transportation and the rise of urban markets, stimulated the cultivation of land previously considered marginal or unproductive. As a result, more area came under the plow in the half-century following the Civil War than had been broken in all of the years since the landing at Jamestown. Only rarely did tribal allotment and its accompanying land sales stem the demand for land. "Surplus" areas made available by the Dawes Act served primarily as reminders that with the closing of the frontier, the last untapped source of land in the West would be the areas previously held by Indians.

Responding to their constituents, Washington's state congressional delegation introduced legislation to terminate the trust titles by which the Puyallups held their land and to end the relationship established at Medicine Creek. Their bill came before Congress in 1892, but debate on the measure continued off and on for six years. Although it had little significance beyond Puget Sound, the Puyallup bill focused the lawmakers' attention on the rising demands that the government alter its policy toward the Indian lands.

Now—unlike 1854—the future was clear. Population growth, railroad construction, and urbanization were sure to continue. There would be no more large tracts of free land over which to scatter new settlers. How long, legislators asked, would the Indian Office stand between native landowners and enterprising farmers eager to buy their property? How could the government reconcile its grant of citizenship with its maintenance of federal protection? Were Indian lands private or public; was the Indian a citizen or not?

During the Puyallup debates the bill's sponsors increasingly defined the issue of Indian lands as a regional one. Seattle's congressman, John L. Wilson, charged that federal protection of the Puget Sound tribe was hampering the westward movement. Referring to the residents of Tacoma, he cried, "Here are 40,000 Anglo-Saxons, flesh of your flesh and bone of your bone, your kin and kindred who are seeking to . . . develop their interests and increase their commerce upon the public highways." John B. Allen, the state's senior senator, described the trust patents as a "policy of paternalism" that had been "interposed" between two groups of citizens. In his view that paternalism was both illogical and unfair. "They are regarded as qualified to vote for President," Allen said of the Indians, "but not competent to manage their personal affairs."[2]

Western politicians responded to this appeal. "There is no greater friend of the Indian," Charles Manderson of Nebraska assured his Senate colleagues, "no man who desires his advancement more than the white man who lives by his side." Manderson (who was born in Philadelphia) argued that people like himself had seen the Indians and knew them "for what they [were] worth." And he resented the

Indian Office when it ignored white men while aiding their Indian neighbors. "The contrast . . . between the Indian . . . pampered and . . . sustained," he noted, "and the white man who on the very next farm struggles for life is most marked and most significant, and we of the West are growing most tired of it."[3]

Volatile political issues ran just beneath the surface of Manderson's argument. In his speech supporting the Puyallup bill, Nebraska's senator was reminding his colleagues that the Indian Office was tampering with relations between white men and their nonwhite neighbors. Congress had only recently exorcised the spirit of reconstruction, and there was little interest among lawmakers in reviving what they believed were the demons of that era. Republican proposals to aid southern schools and supervise the conduct of federal elections had gone down to defeat and the GOP was now eager to cut its losses. If the South knew the Negro best, westerners argued, was it not appropriate that they be granted a similar free hand with the Indians?

Westerners also appropriated the language of assimilation for use in their cause. The Indian Office was breaking up reservations, extending the protection of citizenship, and crowing over the success of its education programs. If Native Americans were truly ready for civilization, why hold their land under federal supervision? If some assimilation was good, was not more better? Oregon's Joseph Dolph pointed out to the Senate that the trust patent could not continue indefinitely. "The sooner the Indians are absorbed in the body politic the better," he exclaimed; "we shall never be able to solve the Indian problem until that is done." Under these attacks the burden of proof began to shift from the opponents to the defenders of federal supervision. Increasingly, advocates of federal protection would be required to defend themselves before a skeptical public.[4]

Congressmen who opposed opening the Puyallup lands insisted that canceling trust patents would produce a riot of speculation and fraud. "Not only would it result in [the Indians'] financial ruin," wrote Indian Commissioner Browning, but it would "tend to their moral destruction." Unfortunately, however, the commissioner's predictions (which turned out to be accurate) had broad—and disturbing—implications. The tribe's "financial ruin" would occur either because the businessmen of Tacoma were grafters and cheats, or because the native landowners were incapable of handling their own affairs. The first explanation insulted the integrity of the Washington delegation and—by extension—the honor of the seven western states that had joined in the fight. To make such an argument was politically disastrous. The alternative challenged the assumptions on which all Indian assimilation programs were based. To adopt it would be self-defeating. Thus the defenders of federal protection over Indian lands found themselves in a box of their own making. Once they supported allotment and assimilation, they could not step in to protect the tribe without provoking cries of federal "tyranny," a slogan the reformers themselves had used when working to overthrow the reservation system a generation earlier.[5]

The Puyallups' defenders were largely holdovers from the reform era of the 1880s. Older senators like John M. Palmer, the Illinois "gold bug," and Arkansas' James K. Jones insisted that the government should honor its obligations to the tribe. They were joined by Henry Dawes (who retired from the Senate in 1893) and Herbert Welsh, the tireless founder of the Indian Rights Association, who told the association that the government should reject "any sudden or arbitrary act" that would upset the "gradual operation" of the allotment law. Together these men were able to hold off the westerners for a time. The Puyallups did not begin to lose their allotments until the late 1890s; attacks on other tribes would come later.[6]

The Puyallup case prefigured the debates over Indian land that were to occur during the next two decades. Western politicians, increasingly restive over federal restrictions on the taxation and sale of allotments, would call for the termination of the Indian Office's protective role and the abolition of old treaties. Defenders of government protection would find it difficult to answer the assertion that they were "coddling" the tribes and blocking the region's economic growth. In the end, officials charged with implementing assimilation programs would find themselves on the defensive, confronted with a growing demand that they limit their activities.

The land policy that emerged from both the Puyallup debate and the dozens of controversies that followed was never summarized in a single statement or law, but its shape could be discerned in administrative decisions and programs for the development and administration of tribal lands. The policy's central theme was consistent and unmistakable: federal authorities no longer had an obligation to encourage Indians to control their property. Surrounded by prosperous white neighbors and hampered by their backwardness, Native Americans would be better off taking economic directions from others. The consequence of this shift in policy was a gradual redefinition of the broader goals of the Indian Office. Total assimilation—the incorporation of independent Indian landowners into American society on an equal footing with their fellow citizens—appeared to be an illusory objective. Instead, partial assimilation—bringing Native Americans into limited contact with the majority society while dropping the goal of equality—seemed a more reasonable alternative. As pressure on tribal holdings mounted and the political costs of continuing the old campaign became more evident, political leaders fashioned a new policy toward Indian lands and launched a new phase in the assimilation effort.

William Jones, who became commissioner of Indian affairs in 1897, was hardly one to make dramatic departures in policy. A willing, round-shouldered cog in William McKinley's political machine, Jones had no qualifications for the office other than his loyalty to the GOP. During his eight years in Washington, the former mayor of Mineral Point, Wisconsin, tried to remain a man without enemies. He was equally cordial to western politicians, eastern reformers, powerful railroad executives, and eager white farmers. He had little contact with the Indians, but that was to be expected, for Jones believed his principal duty was to manage the political forces acting on him and to implement the policies he inherited from his predecessors.

There is no better measure of Commissioner Jones's passivity than his approach to the Indian lands. Between 1897 and 1905 he responded to the growing demand for white access to native property by supporting an acceleration in the pace of allotment and working to open the tribal domain through land cessions and changes in Indian Office procedures. By the end of his tenure, hundreds of thousands of acres had passed out of native control. And, perhaps more important, the commissioner's amiable attitude had inspired a new approach to the allotment process. Policy makers no longer talked of a gradual implementation of the severalty law or the civilizing influence of individual landownership. Government assistance and sympathy passed from Native Americans to the white men who "knew them best."

Although poorly administered and ultimately disastrous, the first division of land in severalty at locations such as the Omaha and Winnebago agency in Nebraska and reservations in Wisconsin and Minnesota were at least defensible in terms of allotment's goals. They involved relatively small agricultural areas and affected tribes with long histories of interaction with whites. During the 1890s, however, larger, more isolated preserves became the focus of attention, and westerners began to press the Indian Office to speed up the rate at which these areas were surveyed and divided. The first important departure from the cautious approach to allotment came in Indian Territory. There thousands of settlers gathered on the unassigned lands of Oklahoma—the western portion of the territory—while equally large groups of squatters camped out on unused portions of the area inhabited by the Five Civilized Tribes. Together these "boomers," and the businessmen who supported them, demanded that Washington open the land to white settlement. Although land cessions involving the unoccupied tracts were approved in 1889, 1890, and 1891, it was not until 1891 that the government used the Dawes Act to dispossess a tribe in the territory. For two years, five special agents moved methodically down the roll of the 3,294 people at the Cheyenne and Arapaho agency, assigning each of them a piece of western Oklahoma. At noon on April 19, 1892, the signal was given and more than twenty-five thousand new "neighbors" stampeded onto the surplus lands of the old preserve.

When it occurred, the Cheyenne and Arapaho allotment was an anomaly. It involved more than twice as many Indians as had been assigned homesteads at any other agency, and it was the first application of the law to a major plains tribe. It also prompted criticism from people who normally supported Henry Dawes's law. General Hugh Scott, the reform-minded commander of Fort Sill, held that the tribe was "degraded" by its contact with the greedy whites who kept arriving from the East. And Dawes himself told a meeting at Lake Mohonk in 1895 that the government was abandoning its responsibilities at the Cheyenne and Arapaho agency. Allotment, he warned, had "fallen among thieves."[7]

Commissioner Jones shared none of these anxieties. His first year in office coincided with the final push to dissolve the tribal governments in Indian Territory. Congress approved the Curtis Act in June 1898. This new law established a timetable for the eventual allotment of all the Indians in what later became Oklahoma. Many of those who supported the measure worried about its impact, but Jones was not one to equivocate under such circumstances. He welcomed the new law, calling it "the most important piece of legislation . . . that [had] been passed by Congress relative to Indian affairs since the passage of the [Dawes] Act."[8]

The commissioner also demonstrated his indifference to an acceleration of the allotment process during the controversy over the Kiowa and Comanche reservation. That dispute began with the Jerome Agreement, a fraudulent land cession rejected by the Indians in 1892 but approved by Congress in 1900. Samuel Brosius, the Indian Rights Association's Washington lobbyist, described the pact as a "monstrous measure," a "steal and great wrong to the Kiowas." But the Interior Department—acting on the instructions of Congress— began to prepare for the opening of the reservation.[9] Unable to persuade the government to reconsider, the Kiowa's principal chief brought suit in federal court. Lone Wolf asked for an injunction to halt the implementation of the Jerome Agreement. The case moved quickly to the Supreme Court for a decision.

The issue in *Lone Wolf* v. *Hitchcock* was plain: could Congress ignore the provisions of the Treaty of Medicine Lodge Creek (ratified in 1868), which stipulated that all land cessions must be approved by the tribe? George Kennan, a muckraking critic of the Indian Office, warned that a decision in favor of the government would "mark the beginning of a new departure in [U.S.] Indian policy. There [would] be no legal bar to the removal of all the American Indians from their reservations and the banishment of every man, woman and child of them to Alaska or Porto Rico." A defeat for the Kiowas would strike at one of the fundamental assumptions underlying the Dawes Act—that tribal land was the Indian's private property.[10]

The court's unanimous opinion left little doubt as to the extent of Congress' legal prerogatives. "Plenary authority over the tribal relations of the Indians has been exercised by Congress from the beginning," the justices explained, "and the power has always been deemed a political one, not subject to be controlled by the judicial department of the government." After stating the issue in these terms, the Court moved quickly to a decision: "The power exists to abrogate the provisions of an Indian treaty." The outcome should not have been a surprise; after all, the Cherokee removal crisis in the 1830s had established the supremacy of the U.S. government. But the Supreme Court in *Lone Wolf* went much farther than had John Marshall in its defense of congressional power. The modern view of Indian-white relations stressed the legislature's "plenary" power rather than its responsibilities as a guardian or trustee. The safeguards Henry Dawes had inserted into his law—presidential descretion over initiating allotment and the requirement that tribes consent to the sale of their surplus lands—could now be ignored. "The Supreme Court has virtually given Congress full power to take Indian lands without the Indians' consent," George Kennan explained. And he predicted, "Attempts will undoubtedly be made in all parts of the West to get possession of desirable Indian reservations."[11]

William Jones knew better than to buck the tide. "The decision in the *Lone Wolf* case," he told the House Indian Affairs Committee, "will enable you to dispose of [Indian] land without the consent of the Indians. If you wait for their consent in these matters, it will be fifty years before you can do away with the reservations." Henceforth the Indian Office would offer little support for a gradualist interpretation of allotment. To make his position plain, the commissioner employed a revealing analogy: "Supposing you were the guardian or ward of a child 8 or 10 years of age, would you ask the consent of a child as to the investment of its funds? No; you would not." If Indians were children, then there was no need to use caution in the implementation of the Dawes Act or to expect rapid progress among the tribes. There was no reason to put off the task of dividing the reservations into homesteads and opening the "surplus" to white settlement.[12]

In the years ahead, pressure from western politicians, the dissolution of Indian Territory, and the devastating consequences of the *Lone Wolf* decision altered the context in which allotment occurred. Land cessions and severalty programs were no longer based on the assumption of native ownership or the goal of quick and total assimilation. Since Congress could now initiate the breakup of a reservation, Washington decision makers would no longer be insulated in their responsibilities as guardians by layers of bureaucracy. The Indians' neighbors would be heard clearly, and federal authorities would be unable to ignore their call.

Congress was ready to exercise its new power. As early as 1896 the legislature had expressed its impatience with the Indian Office by adopting a resolution directing a commission to negotiate land cessions with the Crow, Flathead, Northern Cheyenne, Fort Hall, Uintah, and Yakima Indians. But these early efforts were largely stymied by the intransigence of the tribes. The Crow Indians, for example, agreed to sell 1.5 million acres of surplus land, but demanded one dollar per acre in payment. Previous treaties required the tribe's consent in order for the land transfer to be valid. The high fee and the natives' unanimous resistance infuriated the lawmakers. "How," sputtered one apoplectic Congressman, "can [the Indian] have more than a possession of title simply by making moccasin tracks over it with his bow and arrow?" The Crows refused to budge, and the agreement lay unratified until after the Supreme Court's decision.[13]

The first victims of *Lone Wolf* were the Rosebud Sioux, who, like the Crow, had insisted on a fair market price for their land. The tribe signed an agreement to sell four hundred thousand acres for $2.50 an acre in 1901, but Congress balked at their demands. The changing times were typified by Connecticut's aging Senator Orville Platt, who now took the floor to attack the practices he and Henry Dawes had defended twenty years earlier. Like distorted echoes, his old arguments floated into the twentieth century in an inverted form. "I think that when we make an Indian tribe rich," Platt exclaimed, "we delay its civilization." He argued that "the easiest Indians in the country to civilize" were those who had "no money, no funds, no land, no annuities." The seventy-five-year-old lawmaker went on to suggest that Congress should "improve" the Rosebud bill by simply opening the four hundred thousand acres to white settlers and passing their land payments on to the Indians. The Great White Father would become a real estate agent, acting as the tribe's bursar rather than its benefactor. Platt's amendment violated the original agreement, but it was not forgotten, and in February 1904—after the Supreme Court had affirmed the legislature's "plenary power"—his proposal was dusted off and enacted into law.[14]

The 1904 Rosebud Act's proclamation that "the United States shall in no manner be bound to purchase any portion of the land" won the support of Commissioner Jones, despite opposition from the Indians and Herbert Welsh's charge that the law was "the first attempt under the Lone Wolf decision to steal Indian lands." The logjam was now shattered. Within weeks the stalled Crow agreement came to the floor of the House shorn of its purchase provisions and containing new language lifted directly from the Rosebud bill. Again, William Jones blessed the scheme. "It will be noted, he wrote, "that the bill makes no provision for the consent of the Indians." The omission, he added, should not worry the Crow people: "Believing that the bill . . . will fully safeguard and protect the interests of the Indians, it is not believed that such consent will be necessary or need be obtained." A few days after the Crow bill won approval, a similar measure affecting the Devil's Lake Reservation passed the House without debate. In April, Congress opened the Flathead reservation, and in the following session two other land measures were approved.[15]

In the fall of 1905 four large reservations—Uintah, Crow, Flathead and Wind River—were opened to white settlement. Just as Henry Dawes had envisioned, lands were allotted to their Indian occupants while surplus tracts were made available to outsiders. But the methods used to effect these openings revealed that the process at work was not the senator's original scheme. The Rosebud bill had established a new pattern for allotment and staked out a new approach to Indian land policy. The initiative for dividing each reservation into homesteads had come from Congress and had not been delayed by negotiations. The Indian Office did not purchase the unallotted land; it invited whites to come in and promised to pass their payments on to the tribes. Lawmakers now were concerned principally with western development. Typically, Wyoming's congressman, Frank Mondell, told the House that the opening of Wind River was vital to his state's economic future. Passage of the bill, he testified, meant "the development of [his] State . . . its defeat means that a large portion of [the] state [would] for years remain undeveloped."[16]

Commissioner Jones obligingly swung into line: "The pressure for land must diminish the reservations to areas within which [the Indian] can utilize the acres allotted to him, so that the balance may become homes for white farmers who require them." There was no longer the annoying insistence that the government prepare the tribes for landownership. Officials still spoke of assimilation, but the shifts in policy suggested that the term was taking on new meaning.[17]

The Indian Office also adapted to the rising influence of western politicians by adopting new rules for leasing and selling native-owned property. Leasing had begun early in the nineteenth century. Tribes granted rights of way to travelers and railroads and rented pastures to cattlemen and sheepherders. But the early twentieth century brought new customers to the Indians: farmers eager to cultivate and "improve" the land.

The original Dawes Act prohibited the leasing of allotments, and despite a later modification of this restriction few homesteads were rented before 1895. But by the end of the decade the demand for farms—and the willingness of many Indians—began to overcome government resistance. Agents encouraged this process, pointing out that rentals provided their charges with capital for equipment and seed and suggesting that industrious neighbors stimulated Indian advancement. The superintendent of the Sac and Fox agency spoke for a number of his colleagues when he wrote, "Direct contact between these lessees and the Indians will, I am confident, cause the latter to become more industrious and economical, as well as to elevate their moral and social status."[18]

But leasing subverted the original purpose of allotment. Native American landlords had no reason to farm or become self-sufficient. They remained aloof from the non-Indian communities that sprung up around them, and they had few reasons to change their traditional lifeways. "Not one acre of allotted agricultural land should be leased," wrote one agent in 1898. He added that "it would be far better to burn the grass on the allotted lands than to lease them for pastures to the white man." The Indian Rights Association agreed, pointing out that rental agreements often encouraged bribery and corruption.[19]

The ever cooperative commissioner Jones resolved these conflicting points of view by establishing a new procedure that, typically, bowed in both directions at once. In July 1900, he announced that all future leases running for more than a year had to involve payment in the form of permanent improvements to the property. Two years later he added a provision that able-bodied Indians be required to retain forty acres of their allotment for family gardens. In practice, these new regulations facilitated a dramatic increase in the number of allotments that were worked by whites. A succession of renewable one-year leases made it possible for farmers to avoid the first rule, while the second freed unwilling Indians from the necessity of cultivating their land. All they were required to do was keep forty acres for themselves. And the Indian Office's easygoing enforcement of these procedures made it clear that while the form of the original allotment scheme might be retained, its content was changing. "The results," the Indian Rights Association announced, "are disastrous."[20]

The sale of Indian allotments also grew more frequent during the Jones era as both Congress and the commissioner wrote new rules concerning the disposition of property assigned to deceased allottees. Previously, if the fee patent had been issued, the land was automatically disposed of through a will or probate proceeding. But most allottees still held their lands in trust; their wills had no legal force, and according to the Dawes Act the Indian Office had the task of distributing their holdings among the heirs. The result was a massive backlog of intricate heirship cases and subsequent division of land into tiny, uneconomical units. With the commissioner's support, Congress attempted to simplify the process in 1902 by allowing inherited lands to be sold. Jones assured the public that "every practicable safeguard" had been included in the new law, but, as had happened in other areas of land administration, he was swept away by the forces of progress. Ownership of these holdings swiftly passed to non-Indians because allottees were still prohibited from including trust lands in their wills and the Indian Office required that all lands be sold for cash at public auction. No assistance was offered to family members wishing to buy a relative's farm. In effect, an allottee's heirs could do anything with their inherited property as long as they sold it—for cash. A letter from Jones's successor to President Roosevelt makes the impact of these new regulations clear. "Under the present system," Francis Leupp reported, "every Indian's land comes into the market at his death, so that it will be but a few years at most before all the Indians' land will have passed into the possession of the settlers."[21]

The 775,000 acres of inherited land sold between 1902 and 1910 represent only a fraction of the total territory lost during those years. But the figure is significant, both because it represents the loss of land specifically allocated to individual Indians and because it reflects the Indian Office's shifting attitude toward allotment and assimilation. Policymakers no longer considered the Indian homestead a vital element in Native American advancement.

A generation earlier, politicians had agreed that assimilation was a natural process. For example, reformers like Henry Dawes fought bitterly with Alabama's Senator John Tyler Morgan over civil rights and the tariff, but Dawes agreed with the white-maned southerner that the government should "draw [the Indians] through their affections, their instincts, and their tastes up to our civilization, and get them to dissolve their relations with the tribe." From this perspective, there was ample time for the tribes to find their way to civilization. Even William Holman, a Democratic congressman from Indiana who was a regular and fierce opponent of the Indian Office's ever mounting budget, called for a "liberal policy" of patience and federal support. "For myself," he wrote in 1894, "I am not anxious for the present that these Indian lands shall be opened to white settlement. I am not willing that the interests of the Indians shall be impaired by the efforts of the white men to get their lands."[22]

While he never repudiated the reformers who preceded him, William Jones clearly followed other voices and responded to different interests. In addition to western politicians, there were impatient young easterners like Henry Cabot Lodge, who wanted to "get away from this business of reservations," and advocates of American imperialism, who rejected the idea of rapid assimilation. These critics called for a more authoritarian approach to Indian uplift. "Freedom and liberty in every land and in every age has been established and maintained by spear, sword and bayonet," Congressman Joseph Sibley asserted during one debate on Indian policy; there was little reason to delay allotment or to complicate the government's efforts by consulting the Indians. "We go forth with the plowshare and the pruning hook; with the Bible and the spelling book," the Pennsylvania Republican continued, "not to stifle liberty but to give nobler ideas of liberty; not to forge fetters, but to break them."[23]

Jones's willingness to reduce the government's protective role reflected a more pessimistic view of Indian abilities. He wrote in 1903 that Native Americans had two choices. Either they could remain a "study for the ethnologist, a toy for the tourist, a vagrant at the mercy of the State and a continual pensioner upon the bounty of the people," or they could place themselves under the control of the Indian Office and be "educated to work, live and act as reputable, moral citizens." The commissioner did not believe that progress was inevitable or that it came from gentle prodding or the passage of time. Force and necessity would cause Native Americans to change their ways; federal largesse would not.[24]

When William Jones left office in 1905 it appeared on the surface that he had carried out the land policies established in the 1880s. Allotment continued, and officials repeated their support for assimilation. But the Indian Office had initiated new approaches to both severalty and assimilation. Congress now played a major role in the decision to allot reservations and open them to white settlement. Indians lost control over tribal lands as well as individual allotments. And policymakers increasingly viewed Native Americans as people whose progress did not require federal protection. The official view of native property was passing from the idea that it was a birthright to the notion that it represented a part of the public domain. As such, Indian lands should foster regional economic growth rather than serve the narrow needs of their "backward" inhabitants.

In many respects Francis Leupp was an unusual candidate for the office of Indian commissioner. He had no experience in government or national politics and was a model of progressive rectitude. The product of an old New York family, schooled in public piety by Mark Hopkins at Williams College, Leupp had devoted most of his life to gentlemanly reform. He was a journalist by profession, trained as an editorial assistant by William Cullen Bryant on the *New York Evening Post* and seasoned as the publisher of his own newspaper in Syracuse. Leupp soon tired of management, however, and drifted to Washington, where in 1889 he became the *Post's* bureau chief. The stately pace of government in the nineteenth century left the future Indian commissioner ample time to pursue other interests. He joined the National Civil Service Reform League and before long became editor of the group's newsletter. Friendship with the organization's chief political backer—Theodore Roosevelt—quickly ensued.

Roosevelt and Leupp shared a number of interests besides civil service reform. They came from similar backgrounds, had traveled extensively in the West, and were careful observers of the Indian policy debates that were going on around them. The two men endorsed the government's new assimilation campaign and supported Herbert Welsh's Indian Rights Association. In 1895, when Welsh (who was also active in the Civil Service Reform League) was looking for a new Washington lobbyist for his association, Roosevelt recommended Leupp as the "very man for the job." Alice Fletcher also endorsed the hiring of Leupp.[25]

Leupp proved an enthusiastic employee. Believing that "the Indian question seems to be the most important with which the government is faced from a humanitarian point of view," he spent his three-year term hounding administrators who ignored the civil service rules, appearing at hearings on appropriations, and investigating charges of corruption and mismanagement. In the process Leupp became an expert, called on to carry out special missions for the Indian Office, and in 1896 he was appointed by President Grover Cleveland to the Board of Indian Commissioners. When, a few weeks after the

1904 election, Roosevelt appointed his fellow New Yorker to suc-ceed William Jones, it seemed that the government was about to re-place an aging hack with a modern, disinterested administrator. As one reform journal put it, "Mr. Leupp is the first Commissioner of Indian affairs, we believe, since Grant made his first appointment, who was chosen because he was an expert on the subject."[26]

Jones had been a cipher, buffeted by economic and political pres-sure groups. Leupp anticipated those groups by downplaying the old assimilation agenda and endorsing bold new government policies. Under Jones the Indian Office had been reactive, responding to the demands of western settlers and businessmen. Under Leupp the gov-ernment became more aggressive. "The commonest mistake made . . . in dealing with the Indian" he wrote in his first *Annual Report*, "is the assumption that he is simply a white man with a red skin." The commissioner went on to argue that it was foolish to expect too much of Native Americans; landownership and citizenship would not produce equality and racial integration. The assimilation pro-gram should be less ambitious; it should have "improvement, not transformation" as its goal. According to Leupp, the Indian was a burden the government should bear gracefully; there were no easy solutions to the problem of native backwardness and there should be no expectation of rapid native progress. "The duty of our civiliza-tion," he believed, "is not forcibly to uproot his strong traits as an Indian, but to induce him to modify them."[27]

In the 1880s, the Indians' alleged handicaps were used to defend the reservation system. Carl Schurz had argued that Standing Bear and others like him should remain under federal protection because they could not survive on their own. Leupp held a similar view of the Native Americans' capacity for "civilization," but he argued that there was no alternative to severing the government's ties to the In-dians. "The question whether to begin setting the Indian free is no longer before us," he wrote in 1899; "that process is now under way." The commissioner added that rapid allotment might even prove a positive benefit. "When the last acre and last dollar are gone," he wrote, "the Indians will be where the Negro freedmen started thirty-five years ago." Unable to progress with government protection, the Indians would be better off on their own.[28]

Leupp's "expert" administration produced land policies to match his "realistic" assessment of the Indians' future. He applauded Congress' growing power over allotment and land openings. Political pressure to dissolve reservations meant farmers were eager to live among the Indians. And, as he wrote about the opening of the Rosebud Reservation, white neighbors were an important source of native progress. They were, he told the Indian Rights Association, "of vastly more real value to the Sioux in their present stage of development than would be all the wealth of the Orient poured into the tribal treasury." To promote the interaction of settlers and allottees, Leupp also called for a reduction of federal protection for Indian homesteads. For those lands that were not allotted or that belonged to people who could not develop them, Leupp proposed an active program of federal management to improve their productivity and tie them more closely to the American economy.[29]

Like his predecessor, Leupp advocated transferring control of native lands from Indians to whites. But unlike William Jones, Leupp articulated a policy that reconciled the goal of assimilation with the Native Americans' dwindling power over their own resources. For him the key to this reconciliation lay in the Indians' backwardness. Since he believed the Indians' racial traits could not be overcome, he proposed that natives accept the control of outsiders in the name of progress. For some that control would come from the local whites who purchased their allotments and directed the local economy. For others it would appear through federal management of their lands. In any event, non-Indians would provide both long-term guidance and a model to emulate. Leupp recast the meaning of assimilation to allow for the expansion of white control over Indian resources. "I have kept steadily in view," the commissioner wrote on leaving office in 1909, "the necessity for turning the Indian into a citizen . . . realizing the importance of his conforming in his own mode of life generally with the mode of life of his fellow countrymen of other races, but never forcing him into such conformity in advance of his natural movement in that direction."[30]

The pace of allotment, which had accelerated after the *Lone Wolf* decision, continued at a rapid rate under Leupp. Major land cessions, such as the May 1908 opening of 2.9 million acres of the Standing

Rock and Cheyenne River reservations, now followed a routine. They were proposed by western politicians, approved by a voice vote in Congress, and greeted with cheers from local settlers and businessmen. "The best that friends of the Indian often hope to secure," an Indian Rights Association official wrote in 1907, "is an adequate price for the lands to be sold." Old hopes of gradual allotment were overwhelmed by new political alignments and the increasingly popular notion that Indians would be better off if made to fend for themselves.[31]

Nevertheless, debate over allotment had not ended. In fact during the Roosevelt administration policy makers continued to argue over federal protection. But the focus of their attention was now allotments rather than reservations. How long, they asked, should the government continue as the guardian of individual landholdings? The Indian Rights Association declared in 1905 that the "Indian homestead . . . [was] the one asset that should be most scrupulously guarded," but this position had a familiar weakness. If the Indian was to be assimilated, why should he be coddled and protected on his homestead? And if it was good that Native Americans were on their own, why limit their freedom by guarding their land? Fayette McKenzie, the young sociologist who helped organize the Society of American Indians, put the argument simply. "The Indian who can speak English and who has been educated by the government should be free to sell his lands and to sink to the bottom."[32]

Leupp agreed with McKenzie's opinion. Insulating the Indians from their white neighbors would only retard the economic development of the West and deprive Native Americans of the opportunity to rub shoulders with a superior race. "Whatever upbuilds the country in which the Indian lives," Leupp asserted, "upbuilds the Indian with the rest." With these ideas in mind, the commissioner set out to eliminate the twenty-five-year trust period stipulated by the Dawes Act. He succeeded in May 1906, when Congress approved the Burke Act, which amended the allotment law by giving the secretary of the interior the power to issue fee-simple titles to any allottee "competent and capable of managing his or her affairs." A fee-simple title meant that "all restrictions as to sale, incumbrance, or taxation of said land [would] be removed."[33]

In a letter of protest against the new measure the Indian Rights Association's Washington lobbyist charged that it was unconstitutional because it changed an agreement "without the consent of both parties to the contract." The protest had no effect. The *Lone Wolf* decision recognized the legislature's plenary power over native lands, and the lawmakers themselves, of course, welcomed the statute. The Senate committee reporting the bill noted that ending the trust period by executive order would place control over allotments in the hands of "the Secretary of the Interior and the Indian Department who [knew] best when an Indian [had] reached such a stage of civilization as to be able and capable of managing his own affairs." The commissioner agreed. "Through such measures," he wrote, "the grand total of the nation's wards will be diminished and at a growing ratio."[34]

During the remainder of his term, Leupp devoted considerable energy to extending the principles of the Burke Act. The law exempted allotments in Indian Territory from its provisions, but the commissioner insisted that restrictions be lifted there as well. Referring to the territory's Indians, he wrote, "Not until the surplus spaces in their country are settled by a thrifty, energetic, law respecting white population, can the red possessors of the soil hope to make any genuine advancement."[35]

In 1907 Congress gave Leupp the power to sell allotments belonging to "noncompetents." Although the language of the new statute implied that it would affect only those with specific disabilities, the commissioner urged that it be interpreted liberally. In a circular sent to all agents, he wrote that it should apply to "special cases where it [was] shown that Indians [were] unable to properly develop their allotments." Such cases would include those who, "through their own mental incompetency and ignorance," chose poor homesteads and were therefore rendered "noncompetent." Such sophistry had a single purpose: the rapid sale of as many homesteads as possible.[36]

Although Leupp's campaign to eliminate trust patents was generally successful, the depth of his commitment to ending federal guardianship was most evident in a proposal that failed to win congressional approval. In 1908 he and Secretary of the Interior James Garfield suggested that fee-simple titles be issued to any Indian "who, after [a] warning in writing by the Commissioner of Indian Affairs . . . persist[ed] in disobedience to the laws of the State in which he reside[d] or of the United States." Landownership, once the goal of the assimilation program, was now to be a punishment. Clearly, Leupp had little expectation that Indian landowners would be the equal of their white neighbors. Their property was no longer a mark of their progress—the endpoint of the civilization program—it had become the ante in an economic contest Native Americans were sure to lose. The Indian Rights Association declared that Leupp's proposal would "reverse the humane policy of a quarter of a century of protecting the allottee in his weakness," but the commissioner was unmoved. He insisted that the efforts of his administration were "directed toward the emancipation of the red man from the shackles fastened upon him by the artificial and misdirected paternalism of our Government." The cries that Tacoma's greedy representatives once had raised against the Puyallups now were being mouthed by the commissioner of Indian affairs.[37]

The proposal to punish disobedient allottees with fee patents died in committee. Leupp's arguments were so crude that the tragic impact of his proposals could not be ignored. Nevertheless, his suggestion was a mark of how far the Indian Office had come from Commissioner John Atkins's statement that "too great haste" in the administration of the Dawes Act "should be avoided." Leupp viewed gradualism and the protection of native control over their own lands as "misdirected paternalism" that would undermine economic growth and hamper Indian "improvement." He not only supported the shift in control over Indian resources that had begun under William Jones, he trumpeted the departure as an innovative contribution to the assimilation campaign.

The philosophy behind Leupp's attacks on the trust patent also was evident in his administration of the tribal lands that remained under federal control. The commissioner facilitated the leasing of these holdings to non-Indian farmers and developed reservations by including them in federal conservation and irrigation projects. His efforts lowered the barriers surrounding Indian property and encouraged the Native American's metamorphosis from rising citizen to dependent subject.

Leupp believed that "all primitive peoples [were], from [the United States'] economic point of view, grossly wasteful of their natural resources." Leasing would provide a remedy for this malady by turning the Indians' lands over to efficient white businessmen. The lessees would use native lands wisely and provide the Indian landlords with an object lesson in civilized behavior. There was no limit to the commissioner's vision. He supported a mineral leasing bill that would allow prospecting on previously closed tribal lands, agreeing with the secretary of the interior that "lands lying dormant" should be opened "on such terms as [would] promote their development." He suggested that the Choctaws develop their large coal holdings by forming a mining corporation. The tribal stockholders could hire white experts to operate the mines and eventually—when their trust protections were lifted—they could sell their shares in the company to non-Indian investors. And Leupp encouraged white businessmen to contract for the "harvesting" of tribal timber.[38]

The commissioner's most successful scheme involved American sugar-beet companies who received long-term leases to tribal lands in exchange for a pledge to employ Indian laborers. Leupp was convinced that field work was the best thing for the Native American. "Our first duty to the Indian is to teach him to work," he wrote in 1906. "In this process the sensible course is to tempt him to the pursuit of a gainful occupation by choosing for him at the outset the sort of work which he finds pleasantest; and the Indian takes to beet farming as naturally as the Italian takes to art or the German to science. . . . Even the little papoose can be taught to weed the rows just as the pickaninny in the South can be used as a cotton picker." Thinning and weeding sugar beets would do more for the nation's wards, he concluded, than "all the governmental supervision and all the schools, and all the philanthropic activities set afoot in his behalf by benevolent whites, if rolled into one and continued for a century." A leasing project was desirable, therefore, because it demanded simple tasks and placed the Indians under the supervision of their white neighbors. By laboring in the fields, Indians would contribute to the economic development of the West while acquiring the habit of working.[39]

In 1908 Congress authorized Leupp to negotiate long-term leases for the Fort Belknap, Uintah, and Wind River reservations. These agreements were to run for up to twenty years and, it was hoped, would provide the incentive for large companies to enter the sugar-beet business. Although these early leases were successful, they did not attract sufficient corporate interest to launch a widespread movement. His proposals for bringing the gospel of conservation to the reservation had a more lasting effect.[40]

Conservationists in the progressive era were as concerned with the efficient use of the wilderness as they were with its preservation. Irrigating arid western lands thus appealed both to reformers and to advocates of regional development. In the nineteenth century, irrigation had been pursued on an ad hoc basis, usually to carry out a pledge made in a treaty. Appropriations for irrigation did not become a regular part of the Indian Office budget until 1894, and did not exceed one hundred thousand dollars until 1901, when the Indian Office hired its first engineer. As the size of the government's programs grew, however, their focus shifted from agricultural reservations to areas that previously had been nonproductive. Water and careful planning, experts like Leupp believed, could spread prosperity into areas that had been beyond the reach of the United States' burgeoning industrial economy.

The Shoshone and Arapaho Indians at Wind River, Wyoming, were the first to experience this new, ambitious version of irrigation-based development. In March 1905, Congress approved the use of money derived from the sale of surplus lands for a system of ditches and canals that would irrigate forty-five thousand acres of the reservation. The lawmakers also stipulated that reservation residents should receive first priority in hiring for the construction crews. The tribe's agent declared the outlook for his charges was "brighter than at any time in their history," and promised that they would soon be able "without much trouble, to raise large crops of grain and hay and vegetables." The popular press looked forward to tangible results. *Outlook* magazine, often a critic of the Indian Office, was certain that the Wind River project would make the Indians "self-helpful and one of the world's workers." Disenchanted by airy promises of equality, policy makers seemed pleased with the practical notion of turning a bleak Wyoming reservation into productive farms.[41]

Apparent success at Wind River led Leupp to repeat the formula elsewhere. In June 1906, the newly opened Uintah reservation in eastern Utah became the site for a two-hundred-thousand-acre irrigation project. Leupp asked that Congress appropriate five hundred thousand dollars of the tribe's money for the project, arguing, "The future of these Indians depends upon a successful irrigation scheme, for without water their lands are valueless, and starvation or extermination will be their fate." Always generous with tribal funds, the lawmakers allocated six hundred thousand dollars. During the same session Congress authorized the Reclamation Service to include the Yakima agency in a large system being built on the Yakima River, and the following year three hundred thousand dollars from the Blackfoot treasury was earmarked for that tribe's reservation water system. In 1908 a similar project was launched for the Flatheads.[42]

Non-Indian enthusiasm for these new irrigation systems overrode all opposition. When the residents of Wind River protested the appropriation of their tribal funds without their consent the chairman of the House Indian Affairs Committee replied, "Under the *Lone Wolf* decision we have ample authority . . . to provide that this money expended for the Indians shall be reimbursed to the treasury." But the rationale for "reimbursing" the government for expenditures made on behalf of the tribe was more than legal. The chairman added, "[The government will] place the Indians in possession of lands now substantially worthless, but which will be worth a million and a quarter dollars." The desert would bloom, and who was to say that this achievement was less important than obedience to old treaties or adhering to the protests of a few "wasteful" Indians? The tribe was to be saved along with its arid homeland. That non-Indian farmers would also benefit was a welcome dividend.[43]

The irrigation projects subsidized the development of new agricultural land, but they also led directly to the leasing and sale of native property. Rather than make the tribes "self-helpful," these ambitious schemes led to greater outside control of Indian resources. The leading cause of Indian land loss in connection with irrigation was the legal doctrine of beneficial use. Early in the history of the West, state governments responded to the frequent inadequacy of the local water supply by dividing the resource among its citizens.

Individual persons acquired rights to specific amounts of water, thus assuring themselves of a constant supply for their needs. States usually used the concepts of prior claim and beneficial use as the basis for making their awards. Early applicants took precedence over later ones, and landowners receiving a water right agreed to use the water—make beneficial use of it—within a specific time limit. Settlers could claim water for their homesteads, but they could be certain of maintaining that water only if they actually used it.

Every law providing for the irrigation of reservation lands stipulated that local regulations would govern the Indians' access to water. Beneficial use was sure to control water assignments on the new projects. Thus, reluctant allottees or those unable to farm could lose their water to their "energetic" white neighbors who would begin farming later than the Indians, but who would stand ready to make beneficial use of their water. In addition, all of the projects were constructed with appropriations from tribal accounts. When a group's treasury was inadequate, the Indian Office would advance the money in anticipation of a reimbursement. To ensure the repayment, it was essential that the surplus lands within them—the lands not assigned to allottees—be sold. When water rights were in danger, the value of those surplus lands was nil.

Local water laws forced the Indian Office to develop newly irrigated reservations as quickly as possible. But how was this to be done? The superintendent of the Uintah agency provided an answer in his annual report for 1906. "It will be necessary," he warned, "to make the most persistent efforts in causing all land to be cultivated." Where the Indians themselves would not farm, there was "but one course open, and that [was] to lease all surplus lands at a very reasonable figure." Leupp agreed, and ordered the agent "to make every possible effort to lease all allotted land which could be irrigated, whenever the allottees were making no use of it." He supplemented this order with a request to Congress that the Indian Office be empowered to grant long-term leases at both Wind River and Uintah. The lawmakers responded promptly: ten-year rentals were negotiated at Uintah, and twenty-year agreements were made at Wind River. Similar solutions to the water-rights issue were implemented at Yakima, Flathead, and Blackfoot agencies.[44]

In the years after Leupp left office, disputes over water rights continued to bedevil the irrigation effort. In 1908 the Supreme Court recognized the Indians' prior claim to water in its resolution of a dispute between the Indians at Fort Belknap and their white neighbors on the Milk River. *Winters* v. *U.S.* based its finding that reservations had inherent water rights on the supposition that Congress intended the Indians to farm their lands. "It would be extreme to believe," the justices wrote, "that within a year Congress destroyed the reservation and took from the Indians the consideration of their grant, leaving them a barren waste, took from them the means of continuing their old habits, yet did not leave them the power to change to new ones." Nevertheless, the decision spoke only of water necessary to "change old habits," and said nothing about allottees who refused or were unable to farm. The Court did not recognize a specific tribal share of the river. It also did not clarify the federal government's power over water on the opened portions of the reservations—the portions where sales to non-Indians presumably would subsidize the Indians' dams and ditches. Despite the Indians' victory in *Winters*, their claims to water for future needs and the value of their surplus lands remained in doubt. The Indian Office continued to lease irrigable land on the assumption that the tribes had to prove beneficial use quickly, just as white settlers did. This assumption—which a federal court upheld in 1916—was the tool that undermined native control of the newly irrigated lands.[45]

Throughout the irrigation effort the Indian Office blurred the distinction between tribal land and the public domain. Both tribal and federal lands were opened to private development and managed for maximum return; in both, federal experts guided policy. The Roosevelt administration also demonstrated that it perceived the two areas as one when it turned the administration of forest lands on Indian reservations over to the Forest Service in January 1908. Secretary of the Interior James R. Garfield intended the transfer "to improve the forest and yield the full market value of timber cut" as well as to protect the resource for future development. This arrangement foreshadowed the termination movement of the 1950s, as experts in coordinate branches of the federal system were asked to combine Indian affairs with their other responsibilities. Such cooperation,

Commissioner Leupp reported, prevented "much duplication of work" and hastened "the day . . . when the [Indian] Office [might] be abolished as an anomaly which there [was] no longer any excuse for maintaining." The forestry plan succumbed to departmental rivalry after eighteen months, but its demise did not darken the popularity of bureaucratic cooperation. Secretary of the Interior Walter Fisher wrote Leupp's successor that he wanted "to simplify and strengthen in every way practicable the cooperative relations between various bureaus of the department, and also those with the bureaus of other departments doing closely allied work." Sentiments such as these marked a retreat from the old assumption that trust lands were protected vehicles for the Indians' "civilization." Instead, government officials were now suggesting that national goals—efficiency and economic development—should override the specific work of the Indian Office. Accelerated land sales, sophisticated forestry programs, and grand irrigation projects might benefit the Indians, but they also served a larger goal: the rapid development of the western states. In this context, Native Americans were no longer specially protected landowners who gave up part of their property in exchange for equal admission to the "white man's road." They were evolving into a dependent group that lived under the control of their powerful governors.[46]

In a number of areas, then, Leupp articulated the subtle shifts that had been taking place in Indian land policy during the previous decade. The commissioner welcomed reforms that reduced the Indians' role in decision making. Moreover, he advocated the efficient development of tribal lands, either by federal managers or the Indians' white neighbors. Certainly the goal of assimilation—that is, greater contact between the races—remained, but its content continued to change. The new land policies assumed that Indians were peripheral: they would be tolerated if they survived, but they would not be protected as private landowners. It was no longer expected that natives would rise quickly to the level of the white man or that they would be incorporated totally into the majority culture. Leupp imagined that Indians would be only partially assimilated and that they would remain on the fringes of American society—behind and below their enterprising new neighbors:

When only the Indians who are fit to farm and want to farm are farming, when the multitude who take naturally to the mechanic arts are launched in trades, when those whom nature has not bent in any particular direction have entered upon the first stage of normal human development as hewers of wood and drawers of water, and those who are too old or too weak to work are frankly fed, clothed, and sheltered at the public expense, we may look for a more rapid upward movement by the race as a whole than it has ever yet made.[47]

The reformers who gathered at Lake Mohonk in the fall of 1910 had been meeting annually for nearly thirty years. Activists from Henry Dawes to Alice Fletcher had used these occasions to fire their audiences and excoriate the foes of assimilation. But at the end of the first decade of the twentieth century Matthew Sniffen of the Indian Rights Association had a new message for the faithful: "The Indian problem has resolved itself into one of administration." Careful management had become the key to native progress. The years following Leupp's resignation from the commissionership in June 1909 demonstrated the broad appeal of Sniffen's assessment. Policy makers routinely rejected tribal protests when allotting new reservations or opening surplus lands to homesteading. Officials removed trust restrictions on Indian homesteads at a record rate and expanded the leasing program to include mineral rights, timber, and pastureland. Administrators now held Native American resources firmly in their grasp and acted in the interests of efficiency and regional progress. By 1920 this approach had completed the process by which the Indians' lands had devolved from protected property to areas resembling the Unites States' overseas colonies.[48]

Robert Valentine, Leupp's successor, whose officious punctilio ideally suited the executive style of the Taft regime, contributed substantially to the change in the status of Indian lands. He had little training in Indian affairs, but his Harvard education prepared him for public life, and his brief experience as a settlement worker in Greenwich Village convinced him that the Indian Office should be engaged in a "non-political work of social service." He came to the capital from his settlement work to serve as Leupp's personal secretary. In 1908, after three years at that post, he became assistant commissioner. He rose to the commissioner's job with Leupp's blessing soon after Taft's inauguration.

Valentine was a man of order. During his first year in office he reorganized his staff and created a "Methods Division" which was "charged with the betterment of all methods and organization of the Indian Service." The chief concern of this office was how to administer thousands of allotments and millions of acres of tribal land. The new commissioner agreed with Leupp's objectives—maximum use of native property, efficiency, and a minimum of Indian interference—but he wanted the government to adopt regular procedures and cut overhead costs. These efforts consolidated Leupp's many initiatives and fixed his attitudes in policy.

Despite the passage of the Burke Act in 1906, Valentine believed that too many Indians were hiding behind their trust patents. He argued that tribesmen often remained under federal protection so that they could avoid taxes and rent their lands to white farmers. To combat this tendency, he recommended new, more aggressive policies designed "to place each Indian upon a piece of land of his own where he [could] by his own efforts support himself and his family or to give him an equivalent opportunity in industry or trade, to lead him to conserve and utilize his property . . . rather than to have it as an unappreciated heritage."[49] James McLaughlin was an enthusiastic backer of Valentine's ideas. The agent who supervised the arrest of Sitting Bull (an event that set off a tragic chain reaction leading to the Wounded Knee massacre), McLaughlin was the Indian Office's most experienced field officer. Under Jones, Leupp, and Valentine he served as the government spokesman in major land cession negotiations and an inspector of reservations. In a memoir entitled *My Friend the Indian*, published during the second year of Valentine's term, McLaughlin wrote that the government could do the greatest amount of good by "giving to the Indian his portion and turning him adrift to work out his own salvation." In Congress, McLaughlin's position was endorsed by westerners like South Dakota's Charles Burke, who told his colleagues in the House that the Indian could not hope to progress "if the Government for all time keeps its hand on him and assures him that no matter what happens he will be taken care of." Like Senator Platt, who argued that wealth would delay the Indians' civilization, these men urged Valentine to go ahead with his plans to "set the red man free."[50]

Within his first year in office, Valentine proposed legislation to systematize the issuance of fee patents. "The Indian problems must ultimately be solved by the Indians themselves and the white communities in which they live," the commissioner argued. Valentine's proposal provided for competency commissions to tour the agencies and issue fee patents to qualified allottees. Rather than wait for natives to apply for titles, the government would issue them on its own. The commissioner believed that tribesmen should sell all land they did not cultivate and receive their individual shares of the tribal treasury. His ideas were incorporated into the Omnibus Act, which was passed on the last day of the session, in June 1910.[51]

Beginning in the summer of 1910, competency commissions began making the rounds of the reservations. Many Indians were uncooperative, but the next two years brought over two hundred thousand acres of trust land onto local tax rolls. The commissioner reported that only 30 percent of those who received clear title to their allotments "failed to make good." But conflicts between Native Americans and their white neighbors persisted, and Indian land loss continued. In a letter to the secretary of the interior the superintendent of the Uintah agency explained why this was so: "Full satisfaction to the local people cannot be encompassed, and at the same time protect the interests of the Indians . . . the conflict with settlers [is] almost continuous, due to settlers endeavoring to obtain all sorts of rights over possessions of the Indians."[52]

The Omnibus Act also allowed for the "segregation" of tribal funds: "competent" Indians could receive their portion of the tribal treasury just as they received full title to their land. Like rapid fee patenting, the distribution of tribal funds had wide support among western politicians and bureaucrats like James McLaughlin. McLaughlin wrote that closing out the tribe's accounts would "relieve the government of the care of these funds and build up manhood and individual self-reliance, which [could] never be realized under the present doling out process." Even the reformer-sociologist Fayette

McKenzie supported the idea, as did the Indian Rights Association, which announced in 1907 that tribal treasuries delayed the "proper development of the Indian character." The Indian Office was cautious, noting that the distribution of funds often led to "orgies of drink and disease", but it remained confident that dividing the Indians' money would "speed up their competency."[53]

Valentine's systematic approach created two categories of Indians—the competent and the incompetent. "Competent" Indians had received some education or had some experience with whites and therefore could be expected to survive on their own. It was not necessary for a competent Indian to be the equal of his white neighbor, but only to be "healthy" and a "good laborer or other workman." The incompetent were a "mere waste element," requiring constant supervision and support. Protection for the incompetent was justified by their backwardness. In the debate over the status of allotments in the new state of Oklahoma, for example, Senator Porter McCumber argued for a continuation of trust patents to protect individual landholdings. "Our error," he declared, "has been attempting to do something that was impossible in all our history, and that is to make a white man out of an Indian; to so educate him . . . that he could compete in the business or professional enterprises of the world with the white civilization." Because the Indians were not "progressive," he believed they required continued federal supervision. Pessimism and pity were now the principal rationales for federal protection.[54]

Guardianship was no longer intended for those "rising" to the level of the white man; it would be reserved for individual Indians incapable of progress. What had been a trend in the government's land policies was now a central concern. Federal trust protections would be extended to the worst cases; anyone demonstrating the ability to survive would be judged competent and set "free." Nineteenth-century reformers had viewed every Indian as potentially competent. Consequently, protection had been extended to the entire group and was to be withdrawn gradually as the group progressed. Now protection was reserved for the incompetent; the rest could survive on their own. "It may be that we are keeping the Indian in a fool's paradise," one reform journal explained, "as long as we treat him entirely differently from the way we treat any ignorant foreigner who comes to our shores."[55]

Valentine left office to stump for the Bull Moose cause in September 1912, leaving his organizational plans only partially fulfilled. It fell to his successor to define precisely the difference between competent and incompetent Indians. Woodrow Wilson's choice for the job, a Texas banker named Cato Sells, had little knowledge of the field, but he soon heard from those who were eager to instruct him. Sells joined an administration that had minimal interest in racial equality. Constrained by the powerful southern wing of his party and led by a president who traded deference to party bosses for legislative success, the new Democratic commissioner saw no reason to paddle against the political current. In the aftermath of Valentine's reforms, the direction of that current was clear: the new commissioner would be expected to speed up the competency hearings and reduce the level of federal protection over Indian lands.

At the outset of the Wilson administration, a number of lawmakers were calling for the abolition of the Indian Office. A bill introduced in 1912 by Oklahoma's Robert Owen directed the Interior Department to complete the allotment process and end all federal guardianship in ten years. Montana's Henry L. Meyers was typical of those who supported this sort of direct action. "The solution of the Indian problem," he once declared, "lies in throwing Indian reservations open to allotment and settlement." Uninterested even in the "incompetents," he called on the government to encourage white farmers to "mingle with the Indians and show them by example how to farm and conduct their affairs." Owen's bill failed, for his ideas constituted too radical a break with the past and were opposed by the Indian Office, but he succeeded the following year in gaining congressional approval for the Joint Commission to Investigate Indian Affairs. The commission received full subpoena power and a two-year budget of fifty thousand dollars. Senator Joe Robinson of Arkansas became the group's chairman. He was joined by fellow Democrat Harry Lane from Oregon and Michigan's Republican senator, Charles Townsend. The House also named two Democrats, John Stephens of Texas and Charles Carter of Oklahoma, and a Republican, South Dakota's Charles Burke, to serve on the committee.[56]

Franklin K. Lane, the California civic reformer whom Wilson had appointed secretary of the interior, welcomed the creation of the Joint Commission. In a letter to one of the western congressmen who had advocated it, Lane even suggested that the Indian Office could be dispensed with entirely. "The Indian Bureau should be a vanishing Bureau," he wrote, adding, "Tens of thousands of so-called Indians . . . are as competent to attend to their affairs as any man or woman of the white race," and thousands more "should be given their property and allowed to shift for themselves." Federal guardianship should be reserved only for the "mature full-blood Indian." The secretary accepted the idea that competence, not equality, should be the goal of the government's efforts. "The Indian," Lane wrote in 1915, "is no more entitled to idle land than a white man."[57]

The Joint Commission called for a "material reorganization" of the Indian Office, but its recommendations did little to dampen the termination sentiment in Congress. Harry Lane and others continued to file their bills and to argue that if the Indians were "given their freedom . . . and then they frittered it away and came to poverty, it might be said that they had had a fair chance, and it was up to them." None of Lane's proposals were passed, but they were received with increasing sympathy. "I am not prepared to . . . go at one step to the length which the Senator from Oregon proposes," one western lawmaker warned, "but I do concur . . . that there is a vast amount of needless and worse than needless expenditure of money in the administration of Indian Affairs."[58]

Attacks on the Indian Office did not come from Congress alone. The Indian Rights Association complained that the government was dragging its feet in the distribution of the fee patents. The organization's annual report for 1913 criticized the persistence of wardship on several reservations and called for the distribution of all "communal property" at a fixed time. Two years later, the group was more insistent. "The time has come," the association declared, "for a change." Other reformers such as Warren K. Moorehead, a self-trained anthropologist who served on the association's Board of Directors, and Frederick Abbott of the Board of Indian Commissioners suggested placing Indian affairs in the hands of an expert commission. "Competent men who understand Indians," Moorehead wrote, would be the best ones to create the "broad highway upon which the Red Man [might] safely travel to his ultimate destination—the civilized community." These critics opposed extreme proposals for the termination of all federal assistance because they continued to believe that the government had a special obligation to the tribes, but they agreed that the time had come for "a reformation in our system of Indian administration."[59]

Commissioner Sells responded to his critics with an energetic and highly visible program of liberalized fee patenting. A new competency commission crisscrossed the West, and the Interior Department promised to put more men in the field as soon as Congress appropriated money to support them. By the end of 1916 Sells was predicting that if the current rate of granting fee-simple titles continued, the Indians would be "practically self-supporting" in ten years.[60]

To publicize its efforts, the Indian Office also began the practice of distributing fee-simple titles to allottees at elaborate pageants called last-arrow ceremonies. These proceedings always began with an order to the entire reservation to assemble before a large ceremonial tipi near the agency headquarters. The crowd would look on while their "competent" brethren were summoned individually from inside the lodge. The candidates for land titles were dressed in traditional costume and armed with a bow and arrow. After ordering a candidate to shoot his arrow into the distance, the presiding officer, usually the agent, would announce, "You have shot your last arrow." The arrowless archer would then return to the tipi and reemerge a few minutes later in "civilized" dress. He would be placed before a plow. "Take the handle of this plow," the government's man would say, "this act means that you have chosen to live the life of the white man—and the white man lives by work." The ceremony would close with the new landowner receiving a purse (at which point the presiding officer would announce "This purse will always say to you that the money you gain from your labor must be wisely kept") and an American flag. Secretary Lane presided at the first of these rituals at the Yankton Sioux reservation in the spring of 1916. Through the following summer the press covered similar proceedings at the Crow, Shoshone, Coeur d'Alene, Fort Hall, Sisseton, Fort Berthold, and Devil's Lake agencies.[61]

But Sells's upbeat projections and last-arrow ceremonies did not end congressional impatience. Charges of excessive protection and inefficiency persisted and by early 1917 threatened to bring the government's programs to a halt. In January three western senators—Henry Ashurst of Arizona, Key Pittman of Nevada, and Thomas Walsh of Montana—blocked the passage of the annual appropriations bill, relenting only after their colleagues agreed to appoint a new joint commission. Two months later the Indian Rights Association indicated that it was willing to join the recalcitrant westerners. In a letter to the commissioner, Herbert Welsh observed that there was "formidable opposition to the present policy and management of the Indians," much of which came from "persons with ulterior motives." But the old reformer added, "There are points of weakness in our Indian administration. . . . These disturbing conditions should be closely studied in order that [their] causes may be determined." Throughout this effort, he concluded, one object should remain above the "detail of routine work"; that was a "complete severance of government control of Indians." Welsh added that despite the growing pressure in Congress there was still time to act: "While there is increased agitation of the need of liberating the Indians from Government wardship, we feel that if your Bureau would favor legislation embodying these principles sufficient influence may be brought to bear upon Congress to secure favorable consideration."[62]

Three weeks later, Sells acted. On April 17, 1917, he issued his "Declaration of Policy," which set out the criteria for issuing fee-simple titles in the future. "Broadly speaking," the commissioner announced, "a policy of greater liberalism will henceforth prevail in Indian administration to the end that every Indian, as soon as he has been determined to be as competent to transact his own business as the average white man, shall be given full control of his property." Competence would now be measured by race and years of schooling. Persons who were less than one-half Indian or who had graduated from a government school would receive fee patents immediately. Incompetent Indians (the uneducated and those whose ancestry was more than 50 percent Indian) would continue to hold their property in trust, but they would be "urged to sell that portion of their land which [was] not available for their own uses." Sells promised that his new policy was the "dawn of the new era in Indian administration" and the "beginning of the end of the Indian problem." An Indian Office circular accompanying his memo ordered all agency superintendents to submit a list of candidates for fee patents "at the earliest practicable date."[63]

With his "Declaration," Sells captured the initiative from his critics. The Indian Rights Association's Washington agent admired the tactic. "I guess," he wrote a colleague, "[Sells] has seen the handwriting on the wall." The press was less cynical. *Outlook* magazine, which sported Theodore Roosevelt on its masthead and took pride in a long involvement with Indian reform, quickly endorsed the measure and editorialized, "There is no hope for the Indians as a race if they are forever kept in tutelage as wards of the Nation . . . it is better that some Indians should be lost as the result of a courageous policy than that the whole Indian race should be denied . . . freedom." These sentiments were echoed in Congress and the Indian Office bureaucracy. The termination movement subsided, and agents in the field applauded. "As soon as the nation rids itself of dependents," one superintendent wrote, "the more virile it can become."[64]

In the ensuing months, as the rest of the nation busied itself with the European war, Sells made good on his promise. By the spring of 1918 he revealed that nearly 1 million acres had been patented and "thousands of Indians [had] been given their freedom." In 1919 he declared that more fee-simple patents (10,956) were issued in the previous three years than had been granted during the previous decade. Competent Indians also received title to a share of their tribe's treasury. Under powers granted by Congress in 1918 and 1919 the Indian Office began dividing tribal funds into individual accounts and placing them in local banks. Patented Indians had free access to these accounts, but those owning trust lands made withdrawals only with the permission of the agent. Finally, the commissioner carried out his promise to "urge" noncompetents to sell their unused lands. In the first four years of his administration, more than 155,000 acres of trust lands had been sold; during the second four years (1917–20) that figure more than doubled. The same increase occurred in sales of inherited allotments. By the time he left office, Sells had presided over the sale of more than 1 million acres of trust land.[65]

Although Sells often declared that there "would be no wisdom" in terminating all federal ties with the Indians, his administration of native lands hastened the end of many forms of governmental protection. Congressional critics attacked his "Declaration" by saying "Nothing more will come of this than has come from the promises heretofore made." But the commissioner parried every thrust with new assertions that he was ending his office's guardianship function. His approach mollified western settlers eager to purchase Indian lands, comforted Welsh and those who attacked bureaucratic inefficiency, and promised to fulfill the administration's prediction that it was beginning the "end of the Indian problem."[66]

In the 1890s, during the debates over the Puyallups, western congressmen had asked how the government could maintain its paternal protection over the Indians while sustaining the economic development of their region. The Sells administration provided a conclusive answer. Assimilation would be redefined as the process of setting Native Americans "free" to seek their own destiny in an expanding society. Policy makers now believed that landownership and economic independence were less important to native advancement than daily interaction with white settlers amid a growing economy. Federal protection would be reserved only for those judged unable to function in that setting.

Both groups—the competent who received titles to their lands and the incompetent who remained under federal supervision—lost control of their resources. While specific figures are not available, reports from the agencies indicated that once the last arrow had been fired, tax collectors, auto dealers, and equipment salesmen descended on the newly patented Indians. Pressures of this kind combined with the Indian Office's support for the "law of necessity" to produce a rapid decline in native landownership. Officials witnessed the impoverishment of allottees with sympathy buttressed by the belief that patented Indians had to survive on their own. They agreed with Theodore Roosevelt, who wrote that the suffering of Indian farmers was "their own fault and not that of whites." He added, "Let them suffer the hardships which their own fault brings."[67]

Indians living on trust land faced a similar loss of control over their resources. Cato Sells expanded the Indian Office's leasing program and extended the list of resources available for exploitation by outsiders. Commissioner Valentine extended the limit of agricultural leases to five years and encouraged rental by white farmers, but it was the prosperity associated with World War I that invigorated the program. The war in Europe caused a dramatic rise in commodity prices and made many Indian lands economically attractive. Once the United States entered the war, Sells launched a patriotic campaign to increase the production of all trust lands. By the end of 1917 he announced that his "aggressive steps" had produced a two-hundred-thousand-acre increase in the amount of land under lease. The Indian Office also repeated Leupp's argument that leasing would surround the tribes with energetic white neighbors. The superintendent of the Crow reserve, for example, reported in December 1917, "The introduction of white owners and white lessees with attractive leases will tend to improve the roads, scatter public schools throughout the Reservation and in every way improve the industrial condition of the Reservation." By 1920, 4.5 million acres of trust land were under lease.[68]

The continuing precariousness of the government's irrigation campaign on the reservations also contributed to the growth of agricultural leasing. Enthusiasm for the program continued—one popular magazine called it "Rescuing a People by An Irrigation Ditch"—but it continued to suffer from legal and financial complications. Uncertainty surrounded the Indians' water rights, for westerners refused to recognize that Indians had first call on the water whether or not they had made "beneficial use" of it. The region's lawmakers insisted that individual states retained complete authority over water, and Congress would not overrule them. Idaho's William E. Borah told his colleagues in the Senate, "The Government of the United States has no control over the water rights of the state of Idaho." As for the *Winters* decision, in which the Supreme Court upheld the tribes' first claim to water, Utah's Senator George Sutherland spoke for many others when he dismissed it as "one of those unfortunate statements that sometimes courts, and the highest court, lapse into."[69]

Completion and maintenance of the water projects also required a steady supply of funds. When land sales failed to produce adequate revenues, Congress refused to make up the difference. The Indian Office believed that both problems could be solved by opening newly irrigated Indian lands to outsiders, as the superintendent at the Fort Hall agency explained: "We will have to resort to quicker means of developing land than is possible through the encouragement of Indian allottees themselves." The result was a change in the law, allowing rentals of irrigated land to run for ten years instead of five, and a new drive to lease as many irrigated tracts as possible was begun. By 1920, nearly 50 percent more land on Indian irrigation projects was cultivated by whites than by natives.[70]

Commissioner Sells also presided over an unprecedented increase in timber leasing. Robert Valentine began the process in 1910, when he succeeded in inserting a section on timber leasing into the Omnibus Act. The law gave the Indian Office full authority to dispose of mature trees on trust lands and stipulated that Indians should receive the proceeds of all timber sales once deductions for maintenance and fire fighting had been made. These rules governed the disposition of the Indians' timber for the remainder of the decade. When a proposal was made in 1914 to give individual tribal councils authority to approve the sale of their own resources, Sells offered what had become a standard response: "I am confident that a successful administration of Indian affairs is dependent upon a maintenance of the principle that the United States has juridiction over tribal property."[71]

The administration maintained a similar attitude toward mineral leasing. Interest in prospecting for minerals was greatest among the congressmen from Arizona and New Mexico, because the large reservations in their states had been created by executive orders and therefore could not be "opened" without federal action. In 1915, Arizona's Henry Ashurst, the new chairman of the Senate Indian Affairs Committee, proposed allowing the secretary of the interior to grant mineral leases on all reservations on the same terms as on public lands. Ashurst's bill died in committee, but the following year his colleague in the House, Carl Hayden, attempted to attach a similar measure to the annual appropriations bill. This second effort failed as well, but the westerners regrouped, and in June 1918 Ashurst introduced a new bill. He defended it as a war measure (he promised that it would increase the government's output of manganese), and it passed the Senate after three days of debate. The House did not act on the measure, but Hayden succeeded in attaching it to an appropriations bill, which carried it into the statute books in 1919.[72]

The new rules allowed twenty-year mineral leases on Indian lands in every state except Utah and Colorado and stipulated that miners pay royalties of at least 5 percent on their net proceeds. Within four months of its passage, the mineral-leasing bill had opened twenty-four reservations—including the vast Navajo and Apache territories—to prospecting. Proposals soon appeared to expand the law to cover oil and gas exploration, but these additions did not come until later in the 1920s.

Despite its greater size, the leasing program under Sells only extended the practices of Leupp and Valentine. Indian Office administrators intended to develop the Indians' trust lands without the direct involvement of their proprietors and with minimal financial return to the tribes. Government officials justified their efforts by pointing out that they were "improving" the Indians' holdings and providing the nation's wards with an income they otherwise might not have. Carl Hayden, the young congressman from Arizona, welcomed this position, for he believed that encouraging the rental of native lands was the government's duty: "To do otherwise is to deny that there shall be advancement by either the red man or the white man in the West."[73]

By 1920 the Indian Office was implementing a land policy that bore only a superficial resemblance to the program spelled out by the Dawes Act a generation earlier. The idea that Native Americans would control their lands and rise to "civilization" with the aid of the federal government now was rejected. Economic and political pressures, together with changes in white perceptions of who the Indians were and what they could accomplish, had produced a new approach to Native American resources. Like an imperial power, the American government would "develop" native property by opening it to white farmers and businessmen, "freeing" the Indians to participate in the process as they could. Natives who adapted quickly might survive under the new regime; those who failed deserved their fate. People who remained under federal wardship would also be managed by others: white leaseholders would develop the Indians' property and instruct them by example while government officials looked after the "incompetent" tribesmen's basic needs.

A campaign for equality and total assimilation had become a campaign to integrate native resources into the American economy. Assimilation was no longer an optimistic enterprise born of idealism or faith in universal human progress; the term now referred to the process by which "primitive" people were brought into regular contact with an "advanced" society. When this process produced exploitation and suffering, it seemed logical to believe that it was teaching Native Americans the virtues of self-reliance and the evils of backwardness. The land policies of Jones, Leupp, Valentine, and Sells thus placed the Indians on the outskirts of American life and promised them a limited future as junior partners in the national enterprise. The race's relationship to the majority culture was to be far more tenuous than what Helen Hunt Jackson, Henry Dawes, and Alice Fletcher had imagined, for in the twentieth century there was to be a new category of Americans—those who did not share in the dominant culture, but who served it and were expected to benefit from their peripheral attachment to "civilization."[74]

Chapter 6

Schools for a Dependent People

Indian education remained a vital part of the government's assimilation campaign during the early twentieth century. Public officials continued to believe that organized instructon would smooth the Indians' entrance into American society even as they abandoned their predecessors' optimism and designed lessons more appropriate to a "backward" race. Professional educators, journalists, and politicians shared the old reformers' faith in the power of federal activism, but they attacked and changed the school system Richard Pratt and Thomas Morgan had created. In the modern view, Indians were incapable of rising to the level of their civilized countrymen. The Indian Office therefore should abandon its hopes of bringing the common school to the reservations; realism demanded a more modest approach.

By 1895 the reform drive of the previous decade had produced an impressive educational program. The national government was spending over $2 million annually to support two hundred institutions. Day schools, agency boarding schools, and large nonreservation establishments like Richard Pratt's showplace in Pennsylvania served more than eighteen thousand students. In the words of the superintendent of Indian schools, each of these institutions shared a "common concern" for Indian education and all "had an equally important share" in the enterprise. The scale of the government's program was matched by its idealism. The men and women who designed and supervised the system believed they had found a method of molding people anew. "Education has become a great potency in our hands," the U.S. commissioner of education told the reformers at Lake Mohonk in 1895. "Give us your children," he asked the Indian parents; "we will give them letters and make them acquainted with the printed page . . . With these comes the great emancipation, and the school shall give you that."[1]

Two decades after the founding of Carlisle, the Indian Office's commitment to a national school system appeared intact. In 1894 William Hailmann, a professional educator known nationally for his advocacy of public kindergartens, took command of the Indian school system and pledged to continue the work of his evangelical predecessors, Thomas Morgan and Daniel Dorchester. Hailmann promised to upgrade the curriculum (replacing "schoolroom pedantry" with "really vital work") and to place native children in white public schools "within a comparatively short time." His goal was civilization, his emphasis was uplift, and his predictions were upbeat.[2]

But as the turn of the century approached, doubters appeared. The first critics were those expected to welcome native children into their previously all-white classrooms. Commissioner Morgan had launched his integration scheme in 1891 with the assertion that there were "no insuperable obstacles in the way of blending Indian children with white children."[3] He was wrong. In 1895 forty-five school districts were participating in the program; five years later that number had declined by more than half. Eight years after that only four districts in the entire country were contracting with the government to instruct Indian children who lived among them.

The failure of Morgan's program deflated government optimism. Policy makers and educators could no longer point to integrated classrooms as representative of their goal: preparing children to live in a socially integrated society. The assertion that Indian education might raise Native Americans to equality was proven false by whites who wanted to keep the races apart. "It is clearly apparent," William Jones observed in 1899, "that the groundwork at least of Indian education must be laid under government auspices and control."[4] In the future native schools would continue to be self-contained systems that admitted Indian children to segregated classrooms and returned them to segregated lives.

Disillusionment with the grand designs of the nineteenth century soon spread to Congress. When Henry Dawes chaired the Senate Indian Affairs Committee, he knew his proposals to expand the government's educational programs would win widespread support. Disputes might occur over the rate of expansion, but relatively few policy makers questioned the Native American's ability to learn or to "rise to civilization." A generation later the atmosphere was different. Educators, journalists, and even reformers now doubted the appropriateness of common-school training for Indian children. And lawmakers frightened by the ballooning cost of the nineteenth-century programs began to argue that more modest expectations would require a smaller budget. Westerners—particularly Democrats who had been denied the patronage jobs that were the dividends of a growing Indian Office—often led this group, complaining that "civilized" instruction was wasted on "crude minded Indian youth." Arizona's delegate to Congress, for example, charged that the Interior Department was "frittering away . . . money in a humane chase after a dream."[5] But even those who disagreed with this view and supported the government's programs wondered aloud how long the Indians would require federal support.

Congressional critics of Indian education often were aided by interests otherwise not directly involved in the issue. Advocates of the new Jim Crow legislation in the South, for example, saw no reason for federal authorities to be involved in what they viewed as a local problem of race relations. John Stephens, who chaired the House Indian Affairs Committee, pointed out that western states were in the same position as the members of the old confederacy at the close of the Civil War. He noted that in the South "4,000,000 Negroes (who were as much wards of the Government as the Indians are now)" were "turned loose . . . without one cent ever being appropriated by Congress . . . Likewise why should not the red man be cared for in the States where they live?" Permanent, segregated, inferior schools in the Indians' own communitites would be more fitting than a continuation of the evangelical policies of the 1880s.[6]

Imperialists in Congress also questioned the wisdom of native schools. They reasoned that Indians should learn the art of survival in the same way as the Puerto Ricans and Filipinos, who had recently become U.S. subjects. If elaborate civilization programs were impractical in the colonies, did they make any more sense on federally administered reservations? The joining of imperialism with criticism of the government's educational program often occurred in the abstract, but in 1903 the link between the two issues was made explicit when the House defeated an administration proposal to bring Puerto Rican and Filipino students to Carlisle. Joe Cannon, the autocratic chairman of the appropriations committee, told his colleagues, "The taking of children and at public expense educating them above the sentiment of the people from whom they sprang and with whom they must live is demoralizing and pauperizing . . . This whole experiment with the Indian children has worked disastrously, and I do not want to inflict an outrage upon the Porto Ricans."[7] In the minds of the majority that supported him, Cannon was right in pointing out that the "sentiment" of both the Indians and the Puerto Ricans made them unfit for Captain Pratt's model boarding school.

Critics of Indian education were not always negative. They shared a common faith in self-reliance, arguing that federal beneficence insulated Indian children from white society and failed to teach them independence. "The American boy," Congressman Theodore Burton exulted, "loves to spend his time in the clear sunlight and is not penned up within the walls of a boarding school. He does not take his bath in a government bathtub; he goes to the running brook and plunges in." The lesson of this image was clear: "If we do our duty to the Indian we will give him something of the selfsame reliance." Critics like Burton were skeptical of the power of institutions to remake a person. "Paternalism," wrote Lyman Abbott, "assumes that civilization can be taught by a primer . . . this is not true." Like the critics of the trust patent, men such as Abbott and

Congressman Burton believed experience—even work at a menial job—was superior to federal assistance. In their eyes the intervention of the Indian Office inevitably led to stagnation.[8]

Pessimism in Congress was matched by a growing feeling among educational experts that Indians and whites were separated by barriers far greater than literacy or dress. The journal of the American Academy of Social and Political Sciences pointed out, "There is a wide gulf between the civilization of the Indian and that of the white race . . . he who attempts to solve the problem of Indian education . . . must recognize that the circumstances surrounding the Indians are so different from those surrounding our own race that the two races may not be placed in the same category." In the first decade of the twentieth century arguments of this kind became common, even among those who earlier had endorsed the government's program. Herbert Welsh, an early supporter of Hampton and Carlisle, wrote in 1902 that the Native American race was "distinctly feebler, more juvenile than ours." Hollis Frissell, the principal of Hampton Institute, told an audience of educators in 1900 that "Indians [were] people of the child races," adding, "In looking forward to their future I believe we should teach them to labor in order that they may be brought to manhood." And the Board of Indian Commissioners, a group established to give the evangelical reformers of the nineteenth century a voice in policy making, announced in 1898 that while a few Native Americans "might push their way into professional life, . . . the great majority must win their living by manual labor."[9]

What could be done? Educators insisted the solution was vocational training. Learning manual skills would help Indian children overcome their racial handicaps. Frissell told the National Education Association, "those of us who have to do with the education and civilization of Indians can learn many things from the dealings of our southern friends with the plantation negro." The plantation system was a "much more successful school for the training of a barbarous race than [was] the reservation." The Hampton educator believed that while "the Indian [could] never be an Anglo-Saxon," he would benefit from a term of labor under strict supervision.[10]

Other experts stressed job-related skills. In 1901 Calvin Woodward, one of the original advocates of manual training, gave a major address at the annual National Education Association convention. He told the gathering that educating Indians in literature or the arts would "sow seeds on stony ground." Woodward also observed that the vocational programs used in eastern cities were entirely inappropriate for native children. "Their very high merit for our use," he explained, "unfits them for the Indian home." He therefore recommended that the Indian Office simplify its vocational lessons. Two years later Hamlin Garland addressed the same association and repeated Woodward's advice: "Our red brethren . . . cannot be transmuted into something other than they are by any fervor or religious experience, or by any attempts to acquire a higher education. They must grow into something different by pressure of their changed conditions."[11]

Beyond the precincts of Congress and the professional societies there appeared to be considerable support for a more modest approach to Indian education. In the West, Charles Lummis, the Ohioan who published his "magazine of the West" in Los Angeles, asserted that the government's schools were run by "easterners who do not understand the frontier." He condemned Carlisle as a "machine for making machines." San Francisco's *Overland Monthly* expressed its disenchantment with federal programs by recommending that Indians and blacks be mustered into the armed forces and shipped overseas. "The military offers the best employment we can give the Indian," a 1901 article argued. Significantly, these suggestions were often echoed by easterners. *Outlook* chastised the Indian Office for offering native children "the same sort of book education . . . as [was] set before white children," and *Harper's* warned that anyone trying to "hurry up" the Indian's transition to civilization surely would "botch the job." A 1902 article entitled "How to Educate the Indians" probably summarized the popular view when it noted, "Occupations congenial to the white man can never be successfully undertaken by the savage." Manual training would enable tribesmen to take menial jobs while "the white men at the present engaged in these occupations could turn their attention to more intellectual employments."[12]

Bureaucrats, especially those committed to an established program, often are slow to respond to shifts in public attitudes. The leaders of the Indian school system were no exception. Nevertheless, during the first few years of the twentieth century, while their efforts were being denounced as extravagant, inefficient, and even futile, the government's schoolmen (and women) began to alter their course. The process began in 1898, when Estelle Reel replaced William Hailmann as superintendent of Indian education. In contrast to her predecessor—the Swiss-trained apostle of kindergarten reform—Reel came to Washington from Wyoming, and brought with her a practical rather than theoretical approach to schooling. "The theory of cramming the Indian child with mere book knowledge has been and for generations will be a failure," she wrote, "and that fact is being brought home every day to the workers in the cause of Indian regeneration." She accepted the system she inherited from Hailmann, but during her tenure in office Reel worked to reconcile the government's programs with her estimate of native abilities.[13]

The new school superintendent's chief conviction was that native children were different from white children. "The Indian teacher," she explained, "must deal with the conditions similar to those that confront the teacher of the blind or the deaf. She must exercise infinite patience." Reel agreed with those who used the race's alleged backwardness to justify an emphasis on manual training. In an office circular issued in 1900, she reminded her field personnel that half of each school day should be devoted to work and half to classroom learning. She left little doubt which of these areas should receive the most attention. Children should receive a "thorough groundwork in the English branches," the superintendent noted, warning that any further literary training had to be "by special authority of this Office." She emphasized her disapproval of violations of this order a few years later, when she reported to the commissioner that several girls at the Chemawa, Oregon, boarding school were being excused from their chores to practice the piano. "I sincerely hope that the Office will require the superintendents of all Indian schools to see that their large Indian girls become proficient in cooking, sewing and laundry work," she wrote, "before allowing them to spend hours in useless practice upon an expensive instrument which in all probability they will never own."[14]

Under Reel the Indian school system continued to expand, but its curriculum and objectives changed. Although the number of students attending nonreservation boarding schools grew by more than one-third, admission was limited to graduates of other schools. Carlisle would no longer work to transform the children who arrived there; its mission became specialized training in a few manual trades. Teachers were urged to dismiss students who remained in government schools for six or seven years. Such a child, Commissioner Jones wrote in 1901, "had fair opportunity to develop his or her characteristics," and should not be retained any longer.[15]

Most significantly, Superintendent Reel announced a new course of study in 1901 that the commissioner was confident would "bring the Indian into homogeneous relations with the American people." The Indian Office's new curriculum covered twenty-eight subjects. In each area, the superintendent's orders were the same: teach only those subjects that apply directly to the students' experience; focus all learning on skills that will promote self-sufficiency. Under agriculture, for example, she ordered, "Do not attempt anything but what can be successfully raised in the locality." Reel's five-year program of farming instruction began with "light chores"; progressed through learning to "fix broken tools" by the third year; and culminated, in the fifth year, when students learned to plow. "Upon this work more than any other," the superintendent said of the plowing lessons, "depends the advancement of the condition of the Indian." Her program covered additional fields such as baking (every girl should learn to bake bread and "must be taught how to cut bread into dainty, thin slices and place [them] on plates in a neat, attractive manner"), blacksmithing, canning, history ("they should know enough about it to be good, patriotic citizens"), hygiene, reading, and upholstering.[16] Hers was a curriculum of low expectations and practical lessons.

George Bird Grinnell, the Indian expert who joined Charles Lummis and Theodore Roosevelt in criticizing earlier evangelical programs, praised the new blueprint. "The average American citizen and legislator is so thoughtless and so little familiar with the operation of natural laws," Grinnell wrote Superintendent Reel, "that he believes it possible to transform the stone age man to the twentieth century man by act of Congress." The cofounder of the Boone and

Crockett Club went on to assure the superintendent that her program would surely be appreciated "by those who [were] best acquainted with the Indian and his needs."[17]

Reel's curriculum had one vocal critic. Former commissioner Thomas Jefferson Morgan attacked the plan as an attempt to "discredit the whole Indian school system and to call for its abandonment." The old reformer made his charges at the 1902 meeting of the American Social Science Association. He told his audience of academics that limiting Indian children to a rudimentary education would condemn them to a permanent inequality. "Why should the national government offer to its wards so much less in the way of schooling than is offered by the states to the pupils of the public schools?" Morgan asked. "The Indian child has a right that he shall not be hopelessly handicapped by such an inferior training as from the very beginning dooms him to failure in the struggle for existence." Morgan's outrage revealed the distance between the assimilationist zeal of his administration and the "realism" of Estelle Reel. A five-year course ending with plowing lessons? Baking instruction devoted to "dainty slicing"? Morgan approved of manual training, but he had never conceived of it as a central objective. Like other nineteenth-century reformers, he believed industrial training should teach the "habits" of civilization—punctuality, persistence, and attention to detail; in short, industry. Reel's curriculum seemed to do nothing but prepare students for jobs. To accept her course of study was, in Morgan's eyes, to give up the assimilation effort and to sentence native children to life on the fringes of American society.[18]

Morgan delivered his assault a few weeks before his death. The old reformer's complaints were an echo from an earlier generation; the experts of the new century approved the superintendent's plan. Soon the Indian Office was reporting that every federal school had adopted the new course of study. The curriculum, officials declared, was leading to "increasing progress." The Indian Rights Association, in the person of its Washington lobbyist Samuel Brosius, argued that since manual trades were the "only avenues open," Indians "should be encouraged to take up these in earnest." But the most convincing endorsement came in 1904, when Reel summoned teachers and administrators from government schools across the country to the

Louisiana Purchase Exposition for the "Congress of Indian Education." The delegates were uniform in their praise of her new emphasis on manual training. One educator expressed the sense of the gathering when he urged his colleagues to "make [the Indian] understand that there is dignity in toil and the best thing he [could] do [was] labor in the field." Another speaker pronounced a familiar benediction. The superintendent of the Chilocco, Oklahoma, school was confident that the government's new commitment to practical vocational training "solved the Indian problem."[19]

Despite their conviction that Indian education had improved dramatically in the early twentieth century, the delegates at St. Louis could point to few concrete changes in their school system. The curriculum now emphasized manual training, but the structure created a generation before remained intact. Students still traveled to distant boarding schools, and their teachers still stressed the goal of "civilization." Estelle Reel was an energetic advocate of "practical" skills, but her superiors, while sympathetic, did not give school reform a very high priority. It was not until Francis Leupp became commissioner in 1905 that the Indian Office embarked on a comprehensive reorganization of its educational programs. During Leupp's administration, complaints about the naiveté of nineteenth-century schoolmen became the basis for policy.

Roosevelt appointed Leupp commissioner because he believed that the journalist was his kind of expert. If the president had any doubts on this score, they were swiftly allayed by his appointee's first annual report. It called for lowered expectations and attacked those who believed in racial equality. In the area of education, Leupp wrote, "The foundation of everything must be the development of character. Learning is a secondary consideration." Although he allowed that Native Americans should not be "classed indiscriminately with other non-Caucasians, like the negro," he insisted that they occupied a station inferior to that of white Americans. "The Indian is an adult child," he told the National Education Association. "He has the physical attributes of the adult with the mentality of about our fourteen-year old boy."[20]

Like Reel, Leupp held that teaching Indians was a specialized call-

ing. Instructors in Native American schools were to receive specialized training and realize that the Indian "[would] always remain an
Indian." As a result the government schools "should not push him
too rapidly into a new social order and a new method of doing
things." He noted in his first report, "Nothing is gained by trying to
undo nature's work and do it over."[21]

As Leupp took office, respect for "nature's work" was becoming a
popular theme among educators and social scientists. The United
States' new colonies provided a vast testing ground for the education
of "backward races," and the lessons educators were learning overseas seemed to support the commissioner's insights. Charles B.
Dyke, for example, taught at Hampton Institute before going to Ha-
waii to administer Kamehameha, an industrial training school for island natives. In 1909 he reported on his experiences to the National
Education Association and offered some general guidelines for educating nonwhites. A "knowledge of the race characteristics" of one's
students was fundamental, he explained, and low expectations were
essential: "It is absurd to theorize about the propriety of a college
education for the mass of negroes, or Indians, or Filipinos or Hawai-
ians. They lack the intellect to acquire it . . . The races of men feel,
think, and act differently not only because of environment, but
also because of hereditary impulses. . . . Education does not eliminate these differences." Dyke and the new commissioner looked at
Hampton's most famous graduate for confirmation of their views.
Booker T. Washington, Leupp wrote in 1902, was successful because
"the black man [was] to him a black man, and not merely a white
man colored black."[22]

Psychologist G. Stanley Hall translated Leupp's views into scientific terms. Hall argued that the development of races was similar to
the development of individual persons; some groups had advanced
to "adulthood" while others were less "mature." "It is just as essential," he told a gathering of Indian educators, "that [the Indians]
should evolve along the lines of their own heredity and traditions as
it is for us to do so." In a paper entitled "On the Education of Backward Races," one of Hall's students extended the argument by pointing out, "If there is a need that the teacher know something of the
contents of children's minds on entering school in our cities and

towns of the East, there is much greater need that the teacher of the barbarian spend long months in long and intensive study of the aboriginal child-mind." With lessons properly tailored to their limited capacities, Native Americans could reach their appropriate level of development and find their places on the margins of American society.[23]

Unlike Estelle Reel's early efforts to temper the older evangelical approach to Indian education with "practical" concerns, Leupp and his colleagues attempted a thoroughgoing reconstruction of the government's program, based on a belief in Indian backwardness. Some of the new commissioner's proposals were not implemented. For example, his suggestion that wood-frame schoolhouses be replaced by open pavilions because "Indians are little wild creatures accustomed to live in the open air" found few takers. Other innovations were cosmetic. He announced in 1907 that teachers should be tolerant of tribal traditions—"I do not consider that their singing little songs in their native tongue does anybody any harm," he wrote. But the most important of Leupp's reforms occurred in three areas: vocational education, job placement, and a reduction in the number of government schools.[24]

Leupp observed that "most natives [would] try to draw a living out of the soil." Those that did not would "enter the general labor market as lumbermen, ditchers, miners, railroad hands or what not." These observations governed Indian Office planning. Immediately after his appointment, Leupp dispatched Superintendent Reel on an extensive survey of government installations. Throughout her travels Reel made a special effort to—in her words—"eliminate from the curriculum everything of an unpractical nature." She recommended building a model housekeeping cottage at Haskell and instituting a cooking department at Carlisle. And for all the schools she recommended a graduation ceremony patterned after the one at Tuskeegee, where students rejected speeches and songs in favor of rough clothes and demonstrations of their manual skills.[25]

By 1908 vocational instruction had become the central purpose of Indian school curricula and commencement speeches such as "What I Will Do With My Allotment" were commonplace. Like their counterparts in the nation's burgeoning cities, government educators now preached the gospel of practical instruction. Vocational training programs, guidance officers, and testing programs placed students in "appropriate" areas of study and pointed them to a place in the nation's work force. As Marvin Lazerson has pointed out, educators at this time were eager to "integrate the schools into the industrial society." Thus the *Journal of Education* editorialized in 1909, "To give the Indian of today culture without industry is only another way of meting out agency rations and blankets as a premium upon idleness . . . When the red man becomes skilled at bench, lathe, or anvil he is not anchored to a life of toil but he is ballasted for a successful voyage on civilization's sea." In the years ahead, the "ballast" of manual skills would be the white man's gift to his "backward" compatriots.[26]

To complement the government's work in vocational training, Leupp established an Indian employment bureau early in his term. He placed Charles Dagenett, a thirty-three-year-old Carlisle graduate, in charge of the program, instructing him, "Gather up all the able-bodied Indians who . . . have been moved to think that they would like to earn some money, and plant them on ranches, on railroads, in mines—wherever in the outer world, in short, there is an opening for a dollar to be gotten for a day's work." In its first year (1905–6) Leupp asserted that the employment office was the area where he had placed "greatest stress," and he pointed with pride to the five thousand tribesmen who had recently found work in Colorado sugar-beet fields, on southwestern sheep ranches, and on government building projects.[27]

The employment bureau specialized in migrant labor. Employers contracted for a specific task or time period and agreed to provide transportation and a place to camp. Wage rates varied, but they generally fell below the pay scale for whites doing similar work. One gang spent six weeks in a Colorado sugar-beet field in 1906 and returned home with an average of eighty-nine cents a day to show for their toil. "Indians are employed," the superintendent of the Pima school reported in 1908, "because they are cheaper than the same grade of white help."[28]

The success of the employment bureau confirmed Leupp's estimate: "[The Indian] does not know anything and will not attempt anything but to do as he is shown." Unskilled labor taught Native Americans to follow a daily routine and to survive in a cash economy. These rudimentary lessons, the commissioner noted, would make the race a "very valuable industrial factor in our frontier economy." Leupp was confident that the sight of Indians working patiently on their farms and ranches would convince whites that the tribesmen could be used "for the upbuilding of the country" and should not be dismissed "as nuisances."[29]

According to Leupp, manual labor promised to be a popular way to bring Indians into American society. The employment bureau would reduce the need for federal handouts and foster learning outside the "artificial" environment of the boarding and training schools. Naturally the program won wide support in Congress and among western employers. It spread to the northern plains in 1907 and the following year the board of trade in California's rich Imperial Valley requested crews to harvest cantaloupes and other fruit. By 1909 the employment bureau was operating in Wisconsin as well. "The experiment has proved a marked success," Leupp reported, "because it recognized certain racial traits of the Indian, such as his lack of initiative, his hereditary lack of competition, etc., and wooed him into the labor mart."[30]

The third phase of Leupp's effort to restructure Indian education was his campaign to replace all boarding schools with day schools. The commissioner believed that the local school was the logical place to teach the government's wards the habits necessary for self-sufficiency. Training that was more elaborate, or that drew children away from the realities they would encounter after graduation, created unhealthy distinctions between tribesmen and their white neighbors and alienated Indian children from their homes. The boarding schools, in short, taught "false, undemocratic, and demoralizing ideas."[31]

Leupp of course realized that he could not close all boarding schools immediately. But he began to undermine their position by ordering his agents to stop sending day school graduates on for further schooling. "Day schools are to be maintained," he wrote, "without any reference to their effect on the boarding school attendance." In 1908 he took another step by prohibiting all nonreservation schools from recruiting students at the agencies. "When parents or guardians wish to give their children the advantages of a term of training in a nonreservation school," he told the agency employees, "they will make their wishes known to you." Later that year in a magazine article, the commissioner reported that he was "getting rid of the boarding schools as fast as practicable." He made good on the pledge by eliminating four of the off-reservation installations from his 1909 budget request. "The abandonment of these four schools," he told Congress, "is preliminary to a gradual obliteration of an expensive system which has outgrown its usefulness."[32]

Congressional reaction to Leupp's requests reflected broad sympathy for his point of view. Westerners opposed boarding schools, both because they were "extravagant" and because they diverted federal dollars to eastern communities. Arizona's territorial delegate, for example, placed a rider on the 1908 Indian appropriations bill that would have prohibited the transportation of students more than one hundred miles from their homes to attend school. The amendment was defeated, but it won considerable support. William Hepburn, the progressive Republican who chaired the House Interstate Commerce Committee, spoke for men on both sides of the aisle when he charged that boarding schools served "no purpose in lifting up the great mass of Indians." Another colleague suggested that a better alternative would be "to give all the Indians a proper education instead of giving to a few a pampered education." Fueled by these sentiments, boarding-school attendance declined between 1905 and 1910 by over 10 percent while day school attendance rose by more than 47 percent.[33]

Attacks on the boarding institutions also breathed new life into Thomas Morgan's long forgotten scheme of placing Indian students in public schools. Morgan had commended native children to the public schools in the name of social integration; Leupp was far more practical. His nineteenth-century predecessor insisted on guarantees of equal treatment and complete mixing of the races; Leupp did not. "The enforcement of such stipulations," he noted in 1906, "caused the school authorities to give up their contracts." In the twentieth century no stipulations were required. Moreover, recent innovations in public education such as the introduction of vocational and commercial training made it possible to segregate students by ability and interest. In the 1890s, bringing Native Americans into common schools meant introducing them to a single curriculum. A decade later Indian children could be insulated in the lower branches of a compartmentalized program. Modern schools reserved a special place for the unskilled, unlettered Native American.[34]

Francis Leupp left office in 1909. But in the decade that followed his successors pursued his vision of practical education. Vocational training continued to attract government schoolmen. When Robert Valentine succeeded Leupp, he observed in his first annual report, "The Indian Service is primarily educational. It is a great indoor-outdoor school with the emphasis on the outdoors." Cato Sells was equally forthright. He called for a "happy correlation" between the lessons learned in native schools and the Indian's daily environment. "Our aim at our schools," Sells wrote, "is not the perfect farmer or the perfect housewife, but the development of character and industrial efficiency." Both men agreed that the reforms of the nineteenth century had been well-meaning but naïve, and that "improvement," not transformation, should be the government's goal.[35]

Largely because he had served as Leupp's private secretary, Valentine was devoted to his predecessor's reforms. In 1910—his first full year in office—Valentine divided the school department into six districts and assigned a superintendent to each. The superintendents were to consult with local educators, facilitate curricular reforms, and upgrade their professional staffs. The former settlement-house worker also directed his teachers to devise new courses of study that would reduce the differences between Indian schools and local public institutions as well as to continue work in industrial training.[36]

Cato Sells expanded on these developments by ordering that non-reservation schools become specialized institutions offering training in specific trades (Carlisle was to prepare students for the mechanical trades and apprentice them to Ford Motor Company) and overseeing the development of still another course of study. Unveiled in 1916, his model curriculum promised to respond to a "vital deficiency" in the government's program. "There has been a chasm," Sells wrote, "between the completion of a course in school and the selection of a vocation in life." The new program would "provide a safe and substantial passage from school life to success in real life."[37]

The 1916 course of study went beyond the description of new courses. It divided Indian schools into three categories: primary, prevocational, and vocational. During their first three years the students' time would be divided between rudimentary English and arithmetic and "industrial work." A second three-year period would include more specific lessons (such as geography and hygiene) and an introduction to a trade. The final stage, consisting of four years, would be devoted chiefly to "industrial training," with one hour per day spent in "military and gymnastic drills," and occasional periods devoted to "vocational arithmetic," "industrial geography," and "farm and household physics." Sells observed: "The course has been planned with the vocational aim very clearly and positively dominant, with especial emphasis on agriculture and home making. The character and amount of academic work has been determined by its relative value and importance as a means of solution of the problem of the farmer, mechanic, and housewife." He assumed that the Indians' future had sharp limits and that the government should work to "improve" its wards by "training Indian boys and girls for efficient and useful lives under the conditions which they must meet after leaving school."[38]

But the new curriculum signified more than a victory for vocational training. It also marked an important shift in the management and direction of the government's schools. Throughout the nineteenth century, missionaries and politicians had approached the Indian Service with proposals to "save" Native Americans from barbarism and "raise" them to "civilization." Congress responded. By the end of the nineteenth century the reformers and their allies had laid the foundations of a federal educational bureaucracy. By 1916 that bureaucracy had acquired a life of its own. Experts in Indian education defined the goals of the system and generated reforms themselves. In contrast to Thomas Morgan's grand design—in large part a projection of ideas about public education onto the Indians—modern reforms like the 1916 course of study were internal documents. The architects of the new program were employees of the Indian Office who believed that great "gaps" separated the races and gradual "improvement" was the only practical mission for the Indian schools. The bureaucratization of the Indian schools was also reflected in the backgrounds of the people who became superintendents of the system. When Estelle Reel retired in 1910 she was replaced by Harvey Peairs, a veteran teacher and administrator from the Chilocco Training School in Oklahoma. Peairs left in 1917. His successor was Oscar Lipps, who had served as one of Peairs's assistants. The government's schools generated their own leaders as well as their own reforms.

In the second decade of the twentieth century Leupp's employment bureau became a fixture in the Indian Office. Commissioner Valentine believed that the bureau could assist in the "bridging over of that critical period in a boy's life when he leaves school and starts to work," and that its success would mean the "economic and moral salvation of many boys and young men." Sells agreed. During their administrations the two men worked to expand the number of jobs available through Charles Dagenett's office. Most of the program's clients continued to be offered work as low-paid migrant laborers (the exception to this pattern was the scheme to place Carlisle graduates in automobile plants during World War I). Valentine reminded a dissatisfied Colorado beet farmer in 1909, "If you were hiring white labor to do this work, in all probability you would have to pay them more wages than you do the Indians." The "happy correlation" between the Native Americans' schools and the "lives they must lead" was being achieved.[39]

Robert Valentine and Cato Sells also continued to direct attention away from boarding schools and toward day schools. They shared their predecessor's disenchantment with off-reservation institutions and were encouraged in their beliefs by congressional budget cutters. Texan John Stephens, who chaired the House Indian Affairs Committee, was particularly vocal on this issue. He observed in 1910 that federal funds "would be better spent in industrial and day schools, teaching the children . . . how to make a living by farming and stock raising than in any other way." Stephens fought to end the practice of sending native children to Virginia's Hampton Institute. Carlisle also was a target for congressional attacks. The school's alumni and the eastern reformers who had long supported it rallied to the institution's defense, but in 1918, when the army repossessed the Carlisle plant for use as a hospital, there was little interest in saving it. Cato Sells did not believe the matter was worth discussing. "The educational system of the Indian Department will not suffer because of the abolishment of the Carlisle School," he wrote.[40]

Finally, Robert Valentine and Cato Sells implemented Leupp's suggestion that native children attend public schools without the bothersome "stipulations" Thomas Morgan had insisted on in the 1890s. In his first annual report, Valentine issued an open invitation to local educators to apply for subsidies for Indian students. "Whenever application [was] made for government aid," he promised, the Indian Office would "enter into a contract for the Indian pupils at the same rate per capita as that allowed by the State or county for white children." The agreement with the government was to be strictly a business proposition. On reservations such as Walker River, Nevada, where (according to the local agent) whites were "almost entirely lacking in sympathy for the Indian," the Indian Office made no effort to alter local prejudices by insisting that Native American students attend public schools. And where placements did occur, such as at the Cheyenne and Arapaho agency in Oklahoma, officials made sure that students did not arouse white protests. Children "against whom complaint was made" were returned immediately to agency schools. An incident in Montana illustrated the pervasiveness of this pattern.[41]

Early in 1911 the agent for the newly allotted Crow tribe learned that white communities near the reservation were organizing public schools. He requested permission for Indian children (dependents of people who were now citizens) to attend. When the attorney general of Montana refused, asserting that the Indians were neither citizens nor taxpayers, the agent appealed to Washington. Robert Valentine responded in August with an extensive review of the tribe's legal status, but no support for the agent. The commissioner conceded that Crow children had the right to attend local schools, but he observed, "It is not the intention or desire of this Office to force the attendance of children of Indians in the public schools . . . in direct opposition to the manifest wishes of the people." Valentine urged the agent to plead again with state authorities, but without federal action little could be expected. Montana's segregationist policies continued. In 1913 the Crows' agent reported, "There is practically no intercourse between the public and the Indian schools."[42]

The principal reason local authorities accepted Native American children in their schools was financial. At Fort Lapwai, Idaho, for example, a growing community of white landowners and lessees living on the old Nez Perce reservation took advantage of federal support by converting the agency boarding school to a community high school. To make the conversion feasible, two government teachers were retained, their salaries paid by the Indian Office. Indians were eligible to attend the new high school, but were barred from the local grammar schools. Consequently the number of Nez Perce students in the upper grades soon declined. The federally funded teachers spent most of their time instructing the children of local whites. A similar situation developed at Washington's Yakima agency, where the local agent reported in 1913, "It is only by having the revenue derived from the enrollment of Indian children that the county has been able, especially throughout the reservation, to increase the standard of the county school system." And from California came the report that "where the local white people [did] not have enough children of their own to maintain a school they usually let in enough Indian children to make up the required number."[43]

When the children of citizen Indians did attend local schools, little was done to ensure that they received adequate instruction. Commissioner Sells praised public schools as the "trysting place in the winning of the race," but felt no obligation to monitor attendance figures or inspect the facilities provided. Once responsibility for educating native children passed to state and local officials, the commissioner saw no reason to look back. An exchange of correspondence between Sells and one Carl Price was typical. Price, a white man, wrote to Washington in 1916 to complain that his mixed-blood children had been denied admission to the local South Dakota schools. He asserted that he paid taxes and that his children were even enumerated in the school census. Sells's response, conveyed through his assistant, was direct: "This is a matter that depends upon the South Dakota state law."[44]

The Indian Office had no more interest in noncitizens who were admitted to public institutions. Substandard conditions and local prejudices were beyond the concern of an administration eager to set the tribes "free" from federal protection. At the Uintah and Ouray reservation, the superintendent reported in 1915 that only 50 percent of school-age children were attending classes. The agency school was dilapidated and attendance at public institutions was "negligible." He also noted that the Utah compulsory attendance law was "inoperative" for native children and there was "no tie existing between the two school systems." Sells refused the Uintah superintendent's call for help.[45]

Sells and his colleagues equated success with reductions in enrollments at federal schools. The nature of the interaction between Indians and their white neighbors did not interest them. Complaints from the Crow agency that "very few full-blood Indian children [were] enrolled" in public schools and that "prejudice against such enrollment" existed went unanswered. And persistent evidence that state attendance and truancy laws were unenforced throughout the West failed to arouse official interest. If the two groups did not use the opportunity to bring about the kind of total assimilation envisioned by nineteenth-century reformers, federal intervention would not alter the outcome.[46]

By the second decade of the twentieth century, policy makers no longer viewed Indian education as a great lever to raise Native American children to positions of equality in American society. Cato Sells believed that the nation's schools would be "a nursery of one American speech and of the simpler but fundamental lessons of civic virtue, social purity and moral integrity." These institutions would do nothing to alter the Indians' marginal economic existence or to equip tribesmen with skills that might enable them to challenge the political power of their non-Indian neighbors. To modern educators, the Indians were radically handicapped, surrounded by powerful interests, and badly served by the naïve romantics of the nineteenth century. There was a government responsibility to educate native children, but no obligation to hasten their integration into the dominant culture.[47]

Commissioner Sells wrote in 1920 that educational policy makers had "no other choice than to regard the Indian as a fixed component of the white man's civilization." His statement carried a message for both races. He was telling Native Americans that they could look forward to continued domination by the majority culture; they would have a "fixed" role in the "white man's" society. And the former banker was reassuring his non-Indian constituents that they would continue to be on top. For Sells, assimilation did not imply wide-ranging social change; it was simply a label for the process by which aliens fit themselves into their proper places in the "white man's" United States. As they found their slots, Indians would not alter existing social relations or overturn accepted notions of Anglo-Saxon superiority. Instead they would be taught to follow the direction of their "civilized" neighbors and labor patiently on the fringes of "civilization." In the twentieth century, schools would not transform the tribesmen; they would train them to live on the periphery of American society.[48]

Chapter 7

Redefining Indian Citizenship

Extending citizenship to Indians was perhaps the first feature of the assimilation campaign to win wide support. The men and women who gathered in Boston and New York to hear Standing Bear tell of his plight believed the law would protect Native Americans far better than agents or missionaries. Westerners agreed, for an expansion of the natives' rights promised to reduce federal interference in their local affairs. Thus there were few objections when the Dawes Act proposed that each allottee should receive all the legal rights and privileges of United States citizens.

But the same environment that altered land and education reforms undermined the appeal of Indian citizenship. In the twentieth century, politicians and judges began to argue that "backward" races were not fit for citizenship: they would either abuse their new freedoms or be victimized by the unscrupulous. Just as the government lowered its expectations in the areas of economic development and education, so did it retreat from the idea that Native Americans could exercise their legal rights effectively. Gradually, Indians saw many of those rights slip back into the hands of federal administrators. By 1920, Indian citizenship had been redefined. The law, like the schools and the economic system, now promised the race a peripheral role in American life.

Soon after the general allotment act took effect, Indian Office administrators began to point out that tribesmen owning valuable property required legal protection. It seemed naïve to expect Indian allottees to defend their property interests without assistance. At the Cheyenne and Arapaho agency in Oklahoma, for example, individual Native Americans acquiring plots of land were quickly surrounded by aggressive settlers who scorned the Indians' property rights and refused to recognize the new allottees as fellow citizens. "It is impractical," the agency superintendent wrote two years after the reservation had been allotted, "nay, more, I respectfully submit that it is impossible to make good citizens of reservation Indians . . . by the simple act of allotting them in severalty." If this agency proved representative, the severalty law guaranteed a future of white encroachments and Indian suffering.[1]

As critics of citizenship grew more outspoken, it became clear that a return to tribal guardianship was impossible. Westerners would resent any reimposition of federal authority in their growing states, and the reformers who had lobbied for assimilation would surely oppose a return to the "anomaly" of separate Indian nations. Convinced that the problems such as those in Oklahoma were temporary and that most injustices could be overcome by legal means, reform groups continued to advocate universal citizenship. The report of the American Bar Association for 1891 contained a typical statement of this optimistic point of view. Demanding that all Indians immediately become subject to the laws of the states and territories they inhabited, it concluded: "Let the fiction be abolished. Let us enact laws suitable for the present situation, and place the legal status of the Indian upon a rational and practical basis." In a similar vein, the Board of Indian Commissioners noted, "We have entire faith that before very many years shall have passed the Indians of the United States will be better off under the general laws of our States and Territories and by incorporation with the great body of our American citizens, than they can possibly be under any system of 'paternal' government and peculiar and separate administration which could be devised." From this perspective there was no alternative to the individual protections guaranteed each person by the law.[2]

The problem, then, for people like the agent at the Cheyenne and Arapaho agency was to devise a means of providing greater federal protection without appearing to retreat from the government's commitment to Indian citizenship. The predicament was a new version of the question that had confronted policy makers involved with the management of Indian lands and the administration of native schools: how to modify early expectations about the ease and speed of Indian "progress" without returning to the federally enforced separatism of the reservation era. Supporters of the Dawes Act wanted to dismantle the reservations while continuing to supervise the management of individual allotments. Their solution had been the trust patent, which continued federal control but confined it to small areas. Similarly, educators argued for universal schooling, but suggested new kinds of training that stressed practical skills and vocational objectives. In short, in the early twentieth century the promise of Indian assimilation had been modified to allow for what were believed to be the Native Americans' "special" characteristics. Homesteads might be owned by Indians, but would be managed by whites; and the school system could expand, even as it narrowed its goals and objectives.

Indian citizenship followed a similar evolutionary path. Abandoning the goal of full equality (articulated in the 1880s as an echo of the abolitionist crusade) federal bureaucrats, lawyers, and judges gradually developed the idea that the government had an obligation to supervise and protect native citizens. The basis for their claim was the doctrine of guardianship. Guardianship provided a justification for federal intervention that did not compromise Indian citizenship. Nevertheless, in the legal arena—as in other areas of policy where federal action was based on a reaffirmation of Native American "backwardness"—the guardianship concept would have distinctly negative consequences. It would justify undermining the civil rights of individual Indians and excuse a wide range of state statutes that limited their legal prerogatives. In the early twentieth century, the guardianship doctrine was the basis for a redefinition of Indian citizenship.

Of course, the application of the law of guardianship to Indians was not new. The Supreme Court first recognized it in 1831 in *Cherokee Nation* v. *Georgia*, when it declared that a tribe was ineligible to sue a state government because Indians did not constitute a "foreign state." Instead, Chief Justice John Marshall wrote, they were a people "in a state of pupilage; their relation to the United States resemble[d] that of a ward to his guardian." For the remainder of the nineteenth century, Marshall's words were used to justify federal control of the tribes and to defend actions that overrode treaty guarantees. His meaning was less clear, however, after the allotment law made individual Indians landowners and U.S. citizens. Was it legal for federal authorities to hold individual Americans in such a unique trust relationship? Could Indians be both political equals and federal wards?[3]

The first answer to these questions came in response to a challenge to the trust patents by which allottees held their land. *U.S.* v. *Mullin* (1895) arose when a white farmer refused to recognize the Indian Office's right to remove him from land he had leased from an allotted member of the Omaha tribe. Mullin's lease was negotiated without the approval of the tribe's agent, who subsequently ordered the enterprising Nebraskan off the allotment. Mullin's lawyer argued that the Indian landlord who made the unauthorized lease was a citizen with complete freedom to handle his property as he chose. The district court denied this claim and held that the trust title was simply an extension of the treaty relationship between the Omahas and the United States. "It has never been held," Judge George Shiras wrote, "that the acquisition of the status of citizenship deprives the individual of his right to insist that the treaty obligations . . . should be observed and fulfilled." His decision also contained an apparent warning to other potential challengers of the trust title: "The United States . . . is yet bound by its treaty stipulation, to protect the Indians, whether citizens or wards of the nation, in the use and occupancy of the reservation lands which have never yet been opened to occupancy by the whites." Regardless of the grant of citizenship, then, federal authorities reserved the right to determine how Indian allotments would be used. At least in the area of land titles, Native American citizens would continue in an "anomalous"—and protected—position.[4]

In the decade after *Mullin* the courts further clarified the Indian Office's power as the sole trustee of native-owned land. Although they defended the Indians' inalienable title to the allotments themselves, judges ruled that federal supervision extended to timber on individual homesteads, proceeds from the sales of that timber, and even to the cattle provided by the government to hasten the tribesmen's "civilization." As this doctrine developed, however, a significant change occurred in the legal reasoning behind it. Judges gradually shifted their justification for guardianship from treaty guarantees to racial backwardness. In 1904, for example, a federal appeals court dismissed a suit by Big Boy, an Ojibwa allottee who sued Secretary of the Interior E. A. Hitchcock in an effort to gain control over the proceeds from the sale of timber on his allotment. Although the lower court had accepted Big Boy's claim that his citizenship entitled him to the cash, the District of Columbia Appeals Court ruled against him. Granting that the plaintiff "might well be a citizen, with all the rights and privileges of citizens," the court asserted that government regulations were "analogous to ordinary trusts wherein it [was] sought, by restricting the right of disposition, to guard the beneficiaries against the results of their own improvidence." Justice Marshall's language of guardianship was applied to an individual person; and the Indian Office was placed in the role of trustee with complete authority to act on behalf of their "improvident" wards. "The matter of citizenship is an entirely extraneous thing," the court concluded in *Hitchcock* v. *Big Boy*, "and has had nothing to do with the case."[5]

Basing federal guardianship on Indian backwardness rather than treaty obligations seemed logical in the first decade of the new century. It was a view consistent with the Burke Act's extension of the trust period and delay of citizenship and with the growing pessimism regarding the Indians' intellectual abilities. Not surprisingly, the courts spoke repeatedly of the nation's obligation to its wards and widened steadily the authority of federal officials to act on the natives' behalf. Rather than refer to treaty obligations, the courts stressed the government's duty to educate and protect its charges.

The leading example of the expansion of federal guardianship in property cases involved Marchie Tiger, a citizen Creek who had inherited an allotment in 1903, which he sold four years later to an Oklahoma real estate company. Aided and encouraged by M. L. Mott, the tribe's attorney, Tiger decided in 1908 that he had been swindled; he sued for return of his property. The Oklahoma Supreme Court denied Tiger's claim, citing a 1901 law that placed a six-year limit on all trust patents in the territory. Tiger appealed to the U.S. Supreme Court, pointing out that Congress had passed a second law in 1906 restricting land sales by full-bloods such as himself. In their May 1911 decision, the justices reversed the Oklahoma court and buttressed their findings with an extended discussion of the power of federal authorities and weakness of citizen Indians. "It may be taken as a settled doctrine of this Court," Justice William R. Day wrote for the majority, "that Congress . . . has the right to determine for itself when the guardianship which has been maintained over the Indians shall cease." Congress had every right to pass a second law removing the earlier promise of fee-simple ownership. Echoing *Hitchcock*, the Court insisted that guardianship was not altered by a grant of citizenship: "Incompetent persons, though citizens, may not have the full right to control their persons and properties. . . . [T]here is nothing in citizenship incompatible with this guardianship over the Indians' lands."[6]

The *Tiger* decision quickly became the governing authority in disputes over federal supervisory power. A year after it was announced, a federal appeals court in Utah ordered a white man to return the wool he had purchased from a Ute man without agency approval. "The United States has the power," the judges declared, "to protect the Indians and their property from the force, fraud, cunning and rapacity of the members of the superior race." This guardianship power derived from the trust patent as well as from the government's desire to "teach [Indians] to abandon nomadic habits and become farmers, laborers, clerks and businessmen." The U.S. Supreme Court repeated that theme the same year in yet another Oklahoma land case. Writing for the majority, Justice Charles Evans Hughes declared that federal guardianship "traces its source to the plenary control of Congress in legislating for the protection of the Indians under its care, and *it recognizes no limitations that are inconsistent with the discharge of the national duty.*"[7]

Throughout these legal disputes, a broad definition of the government's "duty" to supervise the property of Indians won general endorsement from reformers and policy makers. Lyman Abbott, an early and active supporter of rapid allotment, noted in 1901 that the law of guardianship provided a humane way of protecting the new citizen. "He should be treated as a ward of the courts," Abbott wrote in *Outlook*. "He is not to be condemned to barbarism because he is not equal to the competitions involved in civilization." With encouragement from Abbott and the Indian Rights Association, government officials were quite willing to act. Every commissioner of Indian affairs between 1900 and 1920 worked for greater federal control of trust lands.[8]

Once the courts had freed the doctrine of guardianship from the idea of treaty obligations and had redefined it as an instrument for defending Indians from members of the "superior race," it could be applied to a wide range of situations. Early in the allotment era, for example, the county governments organized by the Indians' settler neighbors attempted to overturn the tax-exempt status of native-owned property. No one disputed that trust land was tax-exempt, but several of these new western communities taxed the personal holdings of citizen allottees. In its efforts to resist these levies, the Indian Office relied on a broad interpretation of its obligation to protect its wards.

The first defense of Indian tax exemptions came in *U.S.* v. *Rickert* (1903). The Justice Department brought suit against James A. Rickert, the county treasurer of Roberts County, South Dakota, to enjoin him from selling property belonging to allottees on the Sisseton reservation for nonpayment of taxes. Roberts County—which encompassed the Sisseton allotments—had adopted a levy on all farm improvements in 1900 and its lawyers argued that since the tax was not on land, all citizens—Indian as well as white—were obligated to pay up. In rejecting this position, the Supreme Court noted that allotments were the "instrumentality employed by the United States for the benefit and control of this dependent race." Farm improvements, the justices reasoned, were simply an extension of that instrumentality and therefore should also be tax-exempt. "It is evident," Justice John Harlan wrote for the majority, "that Congress expected that the lands . . . allotted would be improved and cultivated by the allottee. . . . that object would be defeated if the improvements could be assessed and sold for taxes." As for the county's claim that all citizens were obligated to support their government through taxes, Harlan responded, "It is for the legislative branch of the Government to say when these Indians shall cease to be dependent and assume the responsibilities attaching to citizenship."[9]

The *Rickert* decision settled disputes over the direct taxation of allottees, but the issue continued to plague the Indian Office because county governments—often strapped for funds—tried to enforce indirect levies. Thurston County, Nebraska, which included the old Omaha and Winnebago reservations, taxed the bank accounts of Indians who had recently inherited land from deceased relatives. While the district court approved the practice, a federal appeals court rejected it in 1906. Even though individual Indians might have funds on deposit in local banks, the court declared, "They are still members of their tribes and of an inferior and dependent race." The government's efforts to protect the tribesmen "from want and despair" meant that they were "not subject to taxation by any state or county."[10]

In the years that followed, the courts declared that property protected by federal authorities, purchased with federal funds, or acquired through federal assistance was tax-exempt. Exemptions extended to the landholdings of citizen Indians in Oklahoma, profits white lessees derived from the oil and gas extracted from native allotments, and supplies delivered annually by government extension agents to Native American farmers. In 1919 the Supreme Court even upheld the right of the Interior Department to set aside property taxes on fee-simple land occupied by citizen Indians if those taxes appeared "arbitrary, grossly excessive, discriminatory, and unfair." A guardian must protect his wards from "spoliation," the justices held, and this duty necessarily included "the right to prevent their being illegally deprived of property rights."[11]

But what of the Indian's personal rights? Federal intervention to protect his property was justified by appeals to native backwardness, federal sovereignty, and the plenary power of Congress. Courts could argue that the guardianship relation simply carried forward from the reservation era, when it had provided protection for tribal lands, to the period of allotment, when it helped individual Indians retain control of their property. In effect the courts had said that allotments were miniature reservations. None of this reasoning was directly applicable to the personal liberties of citizen Indians. The Dawes Act was intended to assimilate Native Americans, to set them free from the control of the Indian Office. In the nineteenth century it had been thought that, like their black contemporaries in the South, tribesmen who took land in severalty would rely on state courts for justice. Thus when the subject changed from property to personal freedoms, it appeared that the Indians were on their own.

The Supreme Court affirmed the rights of the nation's new citizens in 1905, when it overturned the conviction of Albert Heff, a white man accused of selling liquor to a group of allottees in Kansas. The prosecution had argued that Heff's customers were "not citizens of full competence, just as . . . citizens under personal or legal disabilities are not *sui juris* in other respects." But the justices were unmoved. Congress had made the allottees citizens, they noted, and the government was "under no constitutional obligation to perpetually continue the relationship of guardian and ward." To decide otherwise, to consider all natives only partial citizens, as Heff's accusers had suggested, would be to sentence all Indians to a condition of permanent wardship. "Can it be," Justice Brewer wrote, "that because one has Indian, and only Indian blood in his veins, he is to be forever one of a special class over whom the General Government may . . . assume the rights of guardianship . . . whether the State or the individual himself consents?" A decade would pass before the Court answered yes.[12]

The Court's declaration in *Heff* that allotment brought Native Americans to full legal equality alarmed Washington's policy makers. The Indian Office feared it would soon be completely incapable of enforcing its prohibition orders or carrying out other actions that might protect allottees from the evils of modern life. And congressmen predicted that the decision would slow the recently accelerating pace of allotment. Undoubtedly administrators would be reluctant to divide reservation lands if they knew they were thereby ending all forms of federal guardianship. To answer these concerns Charles Burke, the South Dakota Republican who chaired the House Indian Affairs Committee, proposed two amendments to the original severalty act. The first would replace the twenty-five-year trust period with a statement that the secretary of the interior might issue a fee-simple title whenever he saw fit. Burke also suggested that Indians not become citizens until they had received their fee-simple titles to their homesteads. The new regulations, he told his colleagues, would reverse the "demoralization" that had followed the *Heff* ruling and restore the practice of treating allottees as if "they were still wards of the nation and subject to the jurisdiction only of the United States." The congressman wanted to make the prosecution's argument in the *Heff* case the law of the land.[13]

Burke's proposal was immediately endorsed by Commissioner Francis Leupp. Leupp wrote, "Citizenship has been a disadvantage to many Indians. They are not fitted for its duties or able to take advantage of its benefits." Because of their infirmities, the commissioner urged that tribesmen continue as wards of the Indian Office until they were "fitted" for political equality. In his view, the Burke Act removed the legal barriers to federal supervision and allowed the allotment process to continue. Such was the expectation when the Burke Act became law in May 1906.[14]

But the "solution" provided by the new statute soon proved unsatisfactory. Political enemies of the Indian Office and westerners who supported the rapid leasing or sale of Indian lands were suspicious of the law's open-ended promise of federal supervision. Senator Henry Teller, long a critic of government "paternalism" and one of the West's oldest apostles of expansion, opposed the measure because it created the anomaly of a specially protected racial group. "When you depart from the principle that every citizen is the equal of every other citizen under the law," he warned, "there is an end to free government." As they had in the debates over the pace of patenting and allotment, western men like the Colorado senator urged an end to the "distinctions" between the protected Indians and their white neighbors.[15]

Equally outspoken were the eastern reform groups who had long viewed citizenship as the key to Indian progress. In their *Annual Report* for 1906 the Board of Indian Commissioners expressed their "regret" over the passage of the new law. "We think that this prolonged period of exclusion from the duties and rights of citizenship is too heavy a price for the Indians to pay for protection by the Indian Bureau." The Indian Rights Association repeated this criticism, calling the statute "detrimental" to the Indians. In the years after 1906 the association's opposition to the Burke Act underlay its campaign to speed up the patenting process and reduce the size of the Indian Office.[16]

Opposition from westerners and reformers, together with the ongoing pressure to issue fee-simple patents at a rapid rate, doomed whatever long-term protection the Burke Act might have provided the Indians. Delays in granting citizenship could only be a temporary solution; the Indian Office needed a new definition of federal guardianship that would extend the controls already available.

The most pressing need was a way to suppress the liquor traffic. The *Heff* decision left the Indian Office with no way to keep liquor dealers away from citizen Indians. After *Heff*, federal restrictions on Native Americans' behavior were unenforceable among allottees. Prosecution was left to state authorities, who, as one agent put it, took "little interest in the suppression of the liquor traffic among the Indians, and [would] only prosecute when a case [was] presented in such form that the defendant [had] no alternative but to plead guilty." Faced with these handicaps, the Indian Office turned to the courts. In a series of cases decided between 1908 and 1916, the government succeeded in expanding the doctrine of guardianship so that federal officials could restrict liquor sales to both citizen and noncitizen Indians. At the end of this effort, the *Heff* verdict was overturned.[17]

The Supreme Court first modified *Heff* in 1908, when it approved the conviction of George Dick, a Nez Perce Indian, for liquor dealing even though both the defendant and his customers were citizens. *Dick* v. *U.S.* pointed out that the severalty law's promise that allottees would "be subject to the laws . . . of the State or Territory in which they may reside" was superseded by a separate agreement the tribe had negotiated with the Indian Office in 1893. That document stated that after the severalty process was complete, all "surplus" lands within the boundaries of the old reservation would be sold, but that they would continue under federal prohibitions against liquor dealing for twenty-five years. Justice John Harlan, writing for the Court, insisted that the conviction of Dick did not undermine the Indians' constitutional rights. Instead, he noted, it was "demanded by the highest considerations of public policy." The following year the Court further amended *Heff* by deciding (in *U.S.* v. *Celestine* and *U.S.* v. *Sutton*) that every allotment would be considered "Indian country" until a fee-simple title was issued for it. Federal officials could forbid the introduction of liquor into those areas and prosecute Native Americans who committed crimes within their boundaries.[18]

The question of limiting liquor consumption by citizen Indians was next addressed in 1911, when the high court reviewed the conviction of Simeon Hallowell, an Omaha allottee. Hallowell had been arrested for bringing whiskey to his farm. The defendant argued that Indian Office personnel had no authority to regulate his behavior since he was a citizen subject to state law. The court disagreed, and the justices reminded Hallowell that the grant of citizenship did "not necessarily end the right or duty of the United States to pass laws in their interest as a dependent people." Hallowell's farm stood on trust land that, while granted to him, remained under federal control. The court ruled that "within its own territory" the national government had the right to "pass laws protecting . . . Indians from the evil results of intoxicating liquors." The trust patent, then, would provide the courts with the necessary means for supervising allottees without appearing to interfere with their rights as citizens. But there was still no clear authority for federal intervention in cases involving citizen Indians on their fee-simple lands.[19]

The high court laid the groundwork for a decision giving the government power to supervise Indian behavior wherever it occurred in

Mosier v. *U.S.* (1912). A federal appeals court in Oklahoma upheld the conviction of Eugene Mosier for selling liquor to Hazel Grey, an enfranchised Osage woman. Referring to Grey, the court noted that a grant of citizenship "would not sever the relationship of guardian and ward existing between her and the government" and that Congress "could not delegate the power granted by the Constitution of the United States to exercise guardianship towards her to the state of Oklahoma." While the facts in the case loosely paralleled those in *Hallowell*, the court chose to take its stand on the grounds of guardianship; it avoided any discussion of the trust title.[20]

A year later the Supreme Court followed the same course in a case involving the Santa Clara Pueblo in New Mexico. The Santa Clarans held their land in fee simple under a Spanish grant that preceded the U.S. conquest of the Southwest. They had become citizens under the Treaty of Guadalupe Hidalgo in 1848. In 1913 no other tribe could claim to be freer of federal control. *U.S.* v. *Sandoval* addressed the legality of a federal prohibition statute on Pueblo land. Lawyers for Felipe Sandoval pointed out that the tribe had never been a ward of the U.S. government and had no formal ties to Washington. Unable to tie their case to trust lands, the attorneys for the Indian Office turned to the argument presented in *Mosier*: the nation's duty to act in the best interest of a "backward people." Without dissent, the Court accepted this plea. "The people of the pueblos," Justice Willis Van Devanter wrote, "although sedentary rather than nomadic . . . and disposed to peace and industry, are nevertheless Indians in race, customs and domestic government. . . . they are essentially a simple, uninformed, inferior people." Once the people of Santa Clara were portrayed in these terms, the decision could follow in rapid order, despite the precedent of *Heff*: "Not only does the Constitution expressly authorize Congress to regulate commerce with the Indian tribes, but long continued legislative and executive usage and an unbroken current of judicial decisions have attributed to the United States as a superior and civilized nation the power and the duty of exercising a fostering care and protection over all dependent Indian communities within its borders." The *Sandoval* decision did not specifically endorse *Mosier*, but it made clear that in the future officials would not have to show that the government retained a trust title to the Indians' lands in order to prosecute liquor dealers. As long as the individual Indians involved were shown to be "simple, uninformed and inferior people," federal authorities could take whatever steps they deemed appropriate to exercise their control.[21]

But despite the government's victories in *Hallowell* and *Sandoval*, the *Heff* decision stood. It applied to the actions of those who had become citizens under the Dawes Act; the later rulings were based on agreements affecting single tribes. Thus they were all considered exceptions to the *Heff* ruling. A categorical reversal of *Heff* did not come until 1916, in *U.S.* v. *Nice*, a case involving the sale of liquor to a group of allottees on the Rosebud Sioux reservation. Citing a number of recent precedents, including *Dick* v. *U.S.*, *Tiger* v. *Western Investment Co.*, *Hallowell*, and *Sandoval*, the Court held that since guardianship and citizenship were compatible, the government's general responsibility to protect Indians continued after the granting of the franchise. According to Justice Van Devanter, it was "obvious" that the Dawes Act's provisions placing Indian allottees under the control of state laws "were to be taken with some implied limitations, and not literally." The severalty law was hereafter to be interpreted in this light. "The Constitution invested Congress with the power to regulate traffic in intoxicating liquors with the Indian tribes *meaning the individuals composing them*," the Court declared. It went on to warn that the government "could not divest itself" of this responsibility.[22]

However benevolent in intent, the effort to prohibit liquor sales among Indians limited their rights as citizens. The Supreme Court's announcement that guardianship over "backward" Native Americans could not be limited or terminated helped stem the destructive flow of alcohol into Indian communities, but it raised the specter of federal control over other aspects of life. If individual liberties could be circumscribed in an area in which the Indian Office felt Native Americans did not measure up to their fellow citizens, they could surely be limited in others. In the first two decades of the twentieth century federal involvement in criminal cases affecting citizen Indians followed the pattern established in disputes over liquor sales. Here too, the guardians' role expanded, and the rights of their newly enfranchised wards contracted.

The Major Crimes Act of 1885 had established the federal courts' exclusive jurisdiction over serious crimes committed by Indians on reservations. In the late nineteenth century, allotment altered this absolute control. The Dawes Act provided that "upon the completion of . . . allotment and the patenting of the lands to said allottees," Indians would "have the benefit of and be subject to the laws, both civil and criminal of the State or Territory" in which they resided. Under this statute most early criminal cases involving allotted Indians were taken directly to state courts. Attempts to continue treating allottees like their kinsmen on unallotted reservations were rebuffed, as was the argument that state jurisdiction should begin only after fee-simple titles had been granted.[23]

At first judges and lawyers welcomed this new trend. The supreme court of Kansas observed that whites who settled on newly opened reservations should be protected against Indian lawbreakers by state laws. "We are not to presume," the justices declared, "that Congress would encourage the white man to go with his family among . . . the Indian . . . and not protect him, his family, and his property against the depredations and lawlessness of the Indian." The American Bar Association's Committee on Indian Legislation agreed. In the first years of allotment the association—largely at the urging of Harvard's James Bradley Thayer—had advocated continued federal jurisdiction, but by 1903 attitudes had changed and the association called for an expansion of state power. The Indian, the committee's report noted, was an "object of pity," and their belief was that "he would meet with justice, and often with favor and indulgence, before the juries of the neighborhood." As in the area of liquor sales, the prevailing belief was that, for better or worse, citizen allottees must be free from federal control.[24]

But despite this optimism, there continued to be a significant undercurrent of doubt over the wisdom of transferring Native Americans to the "juries of the neighborhood." Reports of police apathy and discrimination were unsettling. Typically, once allotment had taken place, a tribe's own law enforcement apparatus was disbanded and the group forced to rely on the county sheriff. In this situation Indians frequently suffered the fate of other politically powerless racial minorities. In 1898, for example, two Oklahoma Seminoles suspected of murder were burned at the stake by a white mob. The case was investigated by U.S. marshals and the tribe paid an indemnity, but territorial officials took no action against the murderers.[25]

The tribesmen's new neighbors often exhibited less "favor and indulgence" than the bar association had predicted. The agent for the newly allotted Kiowas reported a typical sequence of events that might occur when a white man filed a suit against an allottee for nonpayment of a debt. "A warrant is served," the agent noted, "and [the defendant], not having understood a word read to him, fails to appear and the case goes against him, by default. His property is ordered sold to cover costs and the amount of the debt claimed."[26] As reports of this kind multiplied, the Indian Office began to question the wisdom of abandoning its jurisdiction over citizen Indians. Despite enfranchisement, it appeared that many tribesmen would continue to require the protection of their former guardian.

The 1906 Burke Act reversed the trend toward rapid citizenship for allottees. Although the new law did not address the issue of criminal jurisdiction directly, it promised to extend federal guardianship beyond the point when Indians received their homesteads. It was this pledge that the Indian Office intended to honor. But there were those who criticized the new statute. The Indian Rights Association believed Burke's law would undermine the civilization effort, declaring in its *Annual Report* for 1906 that the new act was "detrimental" to the nation's wards. The association's opposition soon became quite strident, however, for Leupp began acting in a way that confirmed the reformers' long-standing fear that an increase in the commissioner's power would encourage authoritarianism and produce a repetition of the tragedies of 1879.[27]

In late 1906, Leupp severely punished a group of Hopi parents who refused to send their children to the government's schools. The following year he publicly defended an agent at the Crow reservation who was being accused of corruption by the Indian Rights Association and defended by the leaders of the Montana GOP. In 1908, relations between the commissioner and his old comrades reached the breaking point.

Leupp had ordered a group of recalcitrant Navajos, led by one Bai-a-lil-le, to be jailed for repeatedly refusing orders to disband and return to their homes. The Indian Rights Association leadership, already angry at the commissioner for his handling of the Hopi and Crow cases, criticized Leupp for holding the Indians without formal charges. Secretary of the Interior James Garfield responded in April by asking General Hugh Scott, an old cavalryman respected by both reformers and Indians, to investigate the Navajo affair. Scott's report, which exonerated Leupp, only added to the association's suspicions. Its officers continued to protest.

The association believed that the Bai-a-lil-le case would be a good vehicle for expressing its opposition to the renewed popularity of federal guardianship. "If the Indians can be stilled by such injustice," Samuel Brosius wrote about Bai-a-lil-le's warrantless arrest, "there is no hope for bringing them out of their slavery . . . The Navajo case is the golden opportunity to teach the Indian Commissioner a lesson." The association's Washington agent set out on his own tour of the Southwest and in the fall of 1908 began preparations for a habeas corpus proceeding in the Arizona courts. Leupp remained unmoved, though certainly he was exasperated. "If you understood fully the situation," he wrote an old friend in the association, "you could appreciate the difficulties encountered in dealing with these uncivilized Indians."[28]

Bai-a-lil-le's arrest brought sharply into focus the issue of criminal jurisdiction over Indians. Leupp, insisting that federal control should remain absolute, refused the Indian Rights Association's demand for a formal hearing of the charges against the renegade Navajos. He argued that the reformers were "painfully uninformed concerning the Indian and his traits." To the association's leadership, Bai-a-lil-le was a modern Standing Bear, and they intended to revive the case they had ridden to glory thirty years before. Significantly, the dispute brought the Boston Indian Citizenship Committee—founded during the Ponca crisis and long since moribund—briefly back to life. With aging figures such as John Davis Long presiding, the Bostonians met and published a circular asserting that the Navajos were "entitled to a fair hearing."[29]

The Boston Committee's reappearance brought a quick response from Theodore Roosevelt. In a letter to the group's leaders, the president repeated his commissioner's assertion that Indians could not be governed like white men. "Devoutly as all of us may look forward to the day when the most backward Indian shall have been brought to the point where he can be governed just as the ignorant white man is governed in one of our civilized communities," the Rough Rider observed, "that day has not yet arrived." TR and Leupp rejected the assumption of the 1880s—the Indians would become a part of white society as soon as they gained their legal rights—and replaced it with a more pessimistic view. Like the modern scientists who taught that racial and ethnic minorities possessed limited abilities, these policy makers argued that "wild" Indians would inevitably occupy an inferior place in the social order. Presumably the group's station might improve as society advanced, but its members would continue to be imprisoned by their racial heritage. To believe anything else was naïve. In this sense, the Navajo's "uncivilized behavior" justified new criminal procedures no less than the *Heff* case had demanded new liquor regulations. In 1880, *Standing Bear* had demonstrated the need for bringing Indians into the white legal system. The *Heff* decision and the Bai-a-lil-le episode proved (at least to Leupp and Roosevelt) the need to exclude them from it.[30]

Although the Indian Rights Association won its legal argument (Bai-a-lil-le was freed in March 1909), it failed to reverse the trend toward greater federal control. Even the judge who released the Navajo leader agreed that increased supervision might be justified on practical—if not legal—grounds. "However salutary in its results and desirable such a method of dealing with recalcitrant Indians may be," he wrote of the commissioner's action, "it cannot be sanctioned." In the years after 1909, the notion that wider guardianship in criminal matters would be "salutary" and "desirable" helped expand the power of federal guardians. The authority for this expansion came not from Congress, but from two important decisions of the Supreme Court.[31]

U.S. v. *Celestine*, decided in the same year that Bai-a-lil-le was set free, was a review of the conviction of a citizen Indian who had committed a murder on the allotted Tulalip reservation in Washington. Bob Celestine's lawyers argued that since the *Heff* decision had removed federal jurisdiction over citizen Indians who violated federal statutes, their client should be set free from federal jurisdiction and retried in a state court. The justices disagreed, noting that the Major Crimes Act gave the national government exclusive jurisdiction over Indians on reservations. "Notwithstanding the gift of citizenship," they wrote, "both the defendant and the murdered woman remain Indians by race, and the crime was committed . . . within the limits of the reservation. . . . It cannot be said to be clear that congress intended by the mere grant of citizenship to renounce entirely its jurisdiction over the individual members of this dependent race."[32]

The second decision, U.S. v. Pelican (1913), broadened the application of Celestine. In the wake of the Sandoval decision—which held that federal liquor prohibitions were enforceable on fee-simple Pueblo lands—the Court was asked to review the convictions of two citizen-Indian murderers. The crimes had been committed on allotted land, and the defendants cited the Dawes Act's provision that allottees were subject to the laws of the state in their attempt to have federal charges dropped. Citing the growing body of decisions supporting liquor prohibitions on trust lands, and apparently reversing several lower-court rulings, the justices declared that all allotments held in trust remained under federal jurisdiction. The old reformers' argument—that allotment would set Native Americans free from federal control and incorporate them into the larger society—was now explicitly rejected. Allotments, the Court announced, "remained Indian lands set apart for Indians under governmental care; and [the Court was] unable to find ground for the conclusion that they became other than Indian country through their distribution into separate holdings." Justice Hughes declared, "The fundamental consideration is the protection of a dependent people."[33]

By the second decade of the twentieth century it was clear that federal guardianship would not be terminated. While native landowners were receiving their fee patents and being "set free" to compete with their non-Indian neighbors, the authorities in Washington were completing their redefinition of Indian citizenship. The popularity of this new—if contradictory—policy was revealed in a study of Indian life commissioned during Robert Valentine's term. The commissioner asked Arthur Luddington, a Columbia University political scientist, to investigate conditions at each of the nation's 105 Indian agencies. Luddington designed a detailed questionnaire, which he sent to every superintendent. One question referred to the enforcement of liquor laws. Only 11 agencies reported that state authorities enforced the prohibition statutes adequately. "There is little, if any sentiment in favor of enforcing such laws," the agent at Fond du Lac, Wisconsin, reported. In response to another item, 42 superintendents conceded that state courts protected the interests of allotted Indians in some areas, but indicated that the quality of this protection was often uncertain. The superintendent at Neah Bay, Washington, noted, "There is prejudice, and always will be, against individual Indians . . . and it is right that this prejudice should continue, as it makes for the improvement of the Indian."[34]

Not surprisingly, when asked if it would be "wise to grant citizenship during the trust period to the allotted noncitizen Indians," only 21 of the 105 superintendents answered in the affirmative. Citing the need for federal supervision of the liquor traffic, as well as the laxity of state courts, the majority of the respondents urged the Indian Office to delay the grant of citizenship. Their position became a central element in Luddington's final report. Noting that recent court decisions allowed the "Federal Government to limit citizenship in almost any way which [could] be shown to be important for the welfare of the Indians," the government's expert analyst concluded: "As a general principle, the Federal Government should retain the legal right to exercise certain kinds of control or obtain for the Indians certain kinds of exceptions to existing laws."[35]

The Indian Office no longer based its obligations on treaty commitments or the need to protect new landowners. The Indians' "unfitness" for modern life—their susceptibility to alcoholism and their ignorance—made them "dependent" people whose personal freedoms might legitimately be curbed by their guardians. These limitations redefined Indian citizenship, replacing the nineteenth-century notion of full equality with the idea that political liberties were contingent on one's "civilization." Skepticism concerning the Indians' ability to adapt to American society had produced a new category of partial citizenship.

The redefinition of Indian citizenship proceeded on more than the federal level. State and local authorities shared the pessimism of the Supreme Court and the Indian Office, and they joined those institutions in fashioning an appropriate legal status for what they believed were backward, dependent people. And local lawmakers had an additional incentive: to maintain their control over a minority whose freedom might disrupt the racial status quo within their communities. State officials were most active in the areas of voting rights, laws affecting school attendance, and regulation of interracial marriage.

Indian voting received little attention in the early twentieth century. The Indian Office never made voting a part of its "civilization" campaign, and Native Americans did not vote in large numbers. In 1919 it was estimated that only 25,000 of the nation's 336,000 Indians cast ballots. Even the most fervent reformers argued that suffrage was a privilege the Indian might forego. Fayette McKenzie, an energetic founder of the Society of American Indians, assured those who might feel threatened by the extension of citizenship to Native Americans by noting, "If there be any considerable danger in giving the franchise to the illiterate Indian, every state is still free to exercise its duty to enact an educational qualification for the franchise." The sociologist and his allies appeared to agree with the supreme court of Oklahoma when it defended that state's famous grandfather clause by asserting that "suffrage [was] purely a political right granted by the sovereign power to those worthy and competent to participate in governmental affairs."[36]

The universal belief that individual states could set discriminatory eligibility requirements of course lay behind much of the disinterest in Indian voting. The Supreme Court had demonstrated in the *Civil Rights* cases and *Plessy* v. *Ferguson* that federal police powers could not affect local social arrangements, and the successful disfranchisement movement in the South during the 1890s confirmed the power of state authorities to control access to the voting booth. If individual states were as eager to bar Indians from the polls as they were to exclude blacks, they were legally capable of accomplishing their objective.[37]

Every state with a significant Indian population had voting regula-

tions that limited Native American participation in elections. These
limitations fell into four categories. Colorado, Montana, Nebraska,
Oregon, South Dakota, and Wyoming had the sole restriction that
electors be citizens of the United States. Tribes such as the Oregon
Umatillas and the Omahas of Nebraska, who had been admitted to
citizenship en masse when their reservations were allotted, thus had
access to the polls. In an 1893 decision that seemed to settle the
issue for a number of these states, the Nebraska Supreme Court declared citizen allottees eligible to vote. But in Wyoming, South Dakota, Colorado, and Montana, where most Indians remained on un-
divided reservations or were allotted after the Burke Act had delayed
the granting of citizenship, the impact of the requirement was probably different. In Corson County, South Dakota, for example (which
covered a substantial part of the Standing Rock Sioux reservation)
the 1910 census revealed there were 503 Indian and 591 white males
of voting age. In that fall's election, 545 ballots were cast. With voter
turnout customarily high in the early twentieth century, it is likely
that almost all of those 545 voters were non-Indians.[38]

A decision in the California Supreme Court issued in 1917 endorsed the practice of barring noncitizens from the polls and gave
voice to the argument—which had not been heard since *Elk* v.
Wilkins in 1884—that Indians could not participate in politics until
they were naturalized "Ordinarily," the California justices wrote in
Anderson v. *Matthews*, "every person residing in the United States
. . . if born here is, by that fact a citizen. The only exceptions to this
rule are persons . . . who . . . are subject to the jurisdiction of some
other country or political community." Echoing the leaders whom
the reformers of 1879 had villified, the state tribunal concluded that
Indians could be prevented from voting because they were "under
the control and protection of the United States." The court noted,
however, that because the plaintiff in *Anderson* v. *Matthews* belonged to a group of "wild and uncivilized Indians" and had never
been a part of a recognized tribal group, he had no apparent ties to
the United States and should be allowed to vote in California. Nevertheless, it is significant that in 1917 few people refuted the court's
assertion that tribesmen could be barred from the polls. In 1884,
when the *Elk* decision was announced, the reformers in Congress

had responded quickly with the grant of citizenship contained in the Dawes Act. Thirty-three years later, policy makers were moving in the opposite direction, expanding the government's guardianship role and delaying the extension of full citizenship to allottees.[39]

In another method of limiting Indian participation in elections, Minnesota, North Dakota, California, Oklahoma, and Wisconsin declared that all voters must be "civilized." Oklahoma and California required electors to be both "civilized" and citizens; the others allowed one's "civilization" to substitute for citizenship. In California literacy was the test of a person's "civilization," but in Minnesota, North Dakota, and Wisconsin, voters were expected to have "adopted the language, customs and habits of civilization." In Oklahoma Indians came under the state's infamous grandfather clause. Descendants of the Five Civilized Tribes were eligible to vote, but all others—whose ancestors were viewed as "blanket" Indians— were restricted.[40]

The stipulation that voters be "civilized" gave states the power to qualify native citizenship. Just as southern states could set their own definitions of what constituted literacy, so westerners could say—as one agent reported—that Indians had "not adopted to a sufficient degree the pursuits and habiliments of civilization." The Minnesota Supreme Court outlined how the rule would be used in a decision handed down in 1917. "Tribal Indians," the court announced, "have not adopted the customs and habits of civilization . . . until they have adopted that custom and habit which all other inhabitants must needs adopt when they come into the state . . . This the Indian may do by taking up his abode outside the reservation and there pursuing the customs and habits of civilization." Residency in an Indian community—even on an allotted reservation—created the presumption that a person was not civilized and therefore could not vote.[41]

A third means of keeping Native Americans from the polls was the provision in the constitutions of three states—Idaho, New Mexico, and Washington—that Indians "not taxed" were excluded from suffrage. Because Indians did not contribute to the support of the government, these states reasoned, they did not belong to the polity. The taxation test also was incorporated into the regulations of the most restrictive states—Arizona, Nevada, and Utah. This final group required all voters to be taxpayers, residents of the state (not reservations), and citizens. The effect of these restrictions can be seen in Apache County, Arizona, where the 1910 census reported a potential electorate of 2,075, roughly half of whom were Indians. Only 253 ballots were cast in the 1912 elections. If Apache County, with the largest concentration of Indians in the state, is any indication, Indian participation in the political life of the more restrictive states was probably nil.[42]

Arizona defended its policies on Indian voting by arguing that Native Americans were people "under guardianship" and therefore like prison inmates or patients in an asylum. The state's supreme court declared in 1928, "So long as the federal government insists that . . . [the Indians] may be regulated . . . in any manner different from that which may be used in the regulation of white citizens, they are within the meaning of our constitutional provision 'persons under guardianship,' and not entitled to vote." The doctrine of guardianship was being used here as it had been when it was applied to criminal law and liquor regulation: to delay rather than to hasten the day when Indians might enjoy full membership in American society.[43]

States with significant Indian populations maintained an ambiguous policy toward native children in their public schools. Decisions by courts in Oregon, California, and North Carolina indicated that local officials would use perceived racial handicaps to segregate Native American children from the rest of the population. The California Supreme Court relied on this type of reasoning in 1924, when it declared, "It is not in violation of the organic law of the state or nation . . . to require Indian children or others in whom racial differences exist, to attend separate schools, provided such schools are equal in every substantial respect with those furnished for children of the white race." And the U.S. Congress agreed, setting up segregated schools in Alaska in 1905. On the other hand, most states were willing to tolerate a limited amount of integrated schooling. Federal subsidies made accepting those students possible, and there was usually the option of returning undesirable children to Bureau of Indian Affairs institutions. Once again federal guardianship was turned against the Indian population; it provided a rationale for state limitations on their personal freedom.[44]

Miscegenation, like public school attendance, produced mixed reactions in states with large Indian populations. Only four states—Arizona, Nevada, North Carolina, and Oregon—had statutes forbidding sexual relations between Indians and whites. But, as in the case of education, there was general agreement that the states could limit Indian freedom if they wished. The Arizona and Oregon laws were tested and upheld in their state supreme courts; three of the states continued their restrictions until well after 1920.[45]

By 1920, the redefinition of Indian citizenship was complete. A version of federal guardianship had been applied to Native Americans that protected them from exploitation by limiting their freedom. Guardianship allowed federal controls on land to continue after allotment, perpetuated the regulation of the Indians' personal life, and allowed states to discriminate against their native populations.

In the nineteenth century, the United States had considered itself the guardian of tribes. In the *Crow Dog* decision, the Supreme Court decreed that the murder of one Indian by another was beyond the reach of federal authorities; the tribes were separate entities whose internal affairs were their own concern. In the twentieth century, as the government worked to destroy tribal life, the meaning of guardianship changed. Rather than being a device to protect the interests of a group, guardianship was now applied to individual Indians. In its modern form, guardianship enabled the government to oversee the behavior of members of a "backward" race.

Shifting the impact of guardianship from tribes to individual Indians won the support of those who called for universal allotment and the abolition of the Indian Office. Nineteenth-century reformers had expected federal officials to supervise native progress and to intervene on the Indians' behalf when they were victimized. But in the twentieth century—after Indian citizenship was redefined—there was less call for interference from Washington. The Indian Office might still administer the remaining trust lands and regulate the liquor traffic, but most property would be "set free" from control and the Indians urged to adapt to local conditions. Questions concerning legal rights would be settled in the courts. Ironically, as individual persons under guardianship Indians required less supervision than they would have if the ambitious campaign of the 1880s had continued uninterrupted. As wards, Indians were a static group. They posed no threat to their non-Indian neighbors. Their peripheral role in American society was clear, and potential disputes with local officials over voting rights, liquor laws, criminal jurisdiction, and school admissions were defused. The modern definition of guardianship fit neatly into the process of peripheralization that was occurring in all areas of federal Indian policy. As the natives' power over their own lands was reduced and their "place" in white society defined, their political rights were altered and the list of their freedoms was shortened. Their legal status, like their economic and social position, became fixed on the fringes of American society.

A final measure of the impact of the new meaning of guardianship on the Native American's "place" in twentieth-century society was the response of legal commentators to Congress' decision in 1924 to grant citizenship to all Indians. Scholars have traditionally considered that action the instrument by which white America finally admitted Native Americans to political equality, but two essays written in the late 1920s suggest that this view falls short of the truth. The authors of these commentaries did not focus on the rights of the newly enfranchised natives. Instead, they reminded the public of what by then was settled legal doctrine: that the extension of citizenship to Indians did not alter their status as legal wards of the government. And the existence of the guardianship relation could limit their rights as citizens.

Chauncey Shafter Goodrich, a San Francisco lawyer, explained the legal status of California Indians in the 1926 *California Law Review*. "It was assumed in the past," he wrote, "that the grant of citizenship to an Indian would make him, politically speaking, as other men." But this was no longer true: "The court gradually came to take the definite position that the guardianship continued in force, regardless of citizenship, until expressly surrendered by Congress." Goodrich observed that "this curious combination of citizenship and tutelage . . . naturally called forth criticism," but he pointed out that "each new case presented to the Supreme Court . . . resulted in a stronger statement of the doctrine." As for the 1924 citizenship act, the lawyer argued that it "[did] not seriously affect the status of the Indians concerned, save, perhaps, further to confuse confusion." Goodrich saw no necessary conflict between native citizenship and a continuation of the limitations imposed on individual Indians by guardianship.[46]

Guardianship was the focus of a second *California Law Review* essay that appeared in 1930. Citing the recent Arizona case of *Porter v. Hall*, in which disfranchisement of the state's Indians was upheld on the grounds that natives were federal wards, Professor N. D. Houghton of the University of Arizona noted, "There appears to be ample ground for similar discrimination by the state government whenever it may be deemed to be necessary or desirable." Houghton agreed with Goodrich's interpretation of the 1924 law. The political scientist asserted that "unless specific provision were made for termination of the conditions of 'guardianship,' that condition, in all its vigor, would attach to the newly made citizen Indians." Both men held that guardianship was the key to the Native American's legal identity and would remain so until Congress specifically repealed all of the laws and treaties that had created their status in the first place.[47]

In the early twentieth century, federal officials became the guardians of individual Indians. The original grant of citizenship in the 1880s had proved inadequate; it had not brought Native Americans to political equality, nor had it removed the necessity of federal intervention to protect them from exploitation. Unwilling to guarantee Indians the rights promised under the Dawes Act, federal policy makers chose a different tack: the extension of guardianship to individual members of a "backward" race.

With the new century came a rise in racial tension in the South and Far West, ethnic pressures in dozens of urban centers, and demands for the creation of a new American empire. The nation altered its view of itself. Policy makers and reformers no longer spoke of incorporating disparate groups into American society by exposing them to the schoolroom and the ballot box and trusting progress. Faced with the job of managing overseas possessions, deluged by a seemingly endless stream of exotic immigrants, they devised a new solution. American society seemed incapable of assimilating its alien populations or of overcoming class divisions. Conditions made a mockery of the confident expectations that had been the gospel a generation before. In this anxious environment, lawyers and politicians began to describe their society hierarchically. They reasoned that each racial and ethnic group had specific strengths and weaknesses. Consequently assimilation became equated with locating each group in a discrete place within the social structure. Each should have a role in the life of the whole nation, yet each had a natural limit as to what it could achieve and contribute. Guardianship would define the proper "place" for Indians. It would hold them in a spot appropriate to their racial characteristics, at once protecting them from exploitation and limiting their progress. Policy makers could now declare that the campaign for assimilation was complete.

Chapter 8

The Irony of Assimilation

In June 1920, Walter M. Camp, a railroad engineer and self-taught authority on the Indian wars of the late nineteenth century, submitted a brief report to the U.S. Board of Indian Commissioners. Entitled "The Condition of Reservation Indians," Camp's statement was based both on information gathered during seventeen years in the West and data supplied by "hundreds of intelligent and honorable people."[1] The contents of this document serve as a fitting coda to the Indian assimilation campaign.

While Camp admitted that his evidence came primarily from Montana and the Dakotas, he argued that his conclusions were applicable to Native Americans throughout the country. He concluded that the Indians' fundamental problem was their inability to become self-sufficient. Native Americans were notoriously poor farmers, stockraisers, and businessmen. They lacked the drive and talent necessary for moneymaking. The source of these shortcomings, Camp wrote, was not the economic, social, or legal arrangements that had been forged in the previous half-century. Instead, the natives' failures could be traced to their personal weaknesses:

Right here I am minded to express, as pertinent to my subject, my own conclusion as to the fundamental difference between the so-called 'civilized' man and the so-called 'savage,' for the latter of whom 'primitive man' is, I think, a better designation. The savage is concerned only with the immediate necessities of life, while the civilized man looks not only to the future, but beyond mere subsistence. In other words, the Indian is not a capitalist. It matters not which way this fact is stated. One might say that he is lacking in industry, and that the dearth of capital is an effect and not the cause of his poverty. Whichever way one puts it, the fact remains that it has not been in the nature of the Indian to accumulate either property or stores of goods as a reserve against adverse conditions. It has not been the way of the Indian to fortify himself against temporary failure of effort, as is the habit of the more sagacious element of civilized peoples. We thus see a difference of mental attitude as between the two races that, fundamentally, accounts for all of the industrial differences.[2]

Like the anthropologists and popular writers of the early twentieth century who became obsessed with the wide "gap" between Indian and white societies, Camp explained contemporary social conditions by referring to the Indians' racial "traits." It was the Indians' characteristic "mental attitude" and not the government's policies or their own cultural traditions that kept them in poverty.

Because he believed that the Indians' failures were the "natural" result of their "primitive" mind, Camp cautioned the members of the board to lower their expectations for native "progress." To expect "very considerable industrial advance in the short space of one generation," he wrote, would be a mistake. Indians suffered from "communistic ideas" that led them to share their resources unwisely. And their habit of traveling and visiting revealed an "excess of hospitality." These habits, Camp noted, created great "obstacles to progress" that could only be overcome by years of effort. Federal guidance was also required if natives were to "grow out of" their present habits. Echoing contemporary policy makers who defended leasing, vocational education, and qualified citizenship, Camp asserted that most Indians were incapable of speedy adaptation to western habits. In his view it would not be harmful—indeed, it would be beneficial—if Native Americans served extended terms as menial laborers in a society dominated by whites.[3]

Walter Camp was confident that the future would bring gradual progress. After all, he wrote, "the effect of school education, association with white people, living with white neighbors and of much intermarriage of the races [was] beginning to tell in the social and economic status of these people." These influences would slowly raise the level of "civilization" among Indians. On this point, Camp agreed with the progressive politicians and bureaucrats who believed that native "advancement" could only be secured if the Indians remained under the guidance of whites. Even though the "mental attitudes" of the subject group were "primitive," a persistent policy of education and increased "white association" was bound to show results. Camp concluded, "We should do all that is within our power to elevate him!"[4]

"The Condition of Reservation Indians" illustrates the extent to which Indians had come to be perceived as peripheral members of the nation. The optimistic expectations of the 1880s by now were long forgotten. Assimilation no longer meant full citizenship and equality. Instead, the term now implied that Indians would remain on the periphery of American society, ruled by outsiders who promised to guide them toward "civilization." "Primitive" customs would be tolerated while Indian lands were leased or sold, Indian children were taught manual skills, and limitations were placed on Indian citizenship. The United States' natives were being assimilated, but the modern redefinition of that term meant that they were not expected to participate in American life as the equals of their conquerors.

The redefinition of Indian assimilation in the early twentieth century reflects a fundamental shift in American social values. In the two decades before World War I, politicians and intellectuals rejected the notion that national institutions would dissolve cultural differences and foster equality and cohesion. The optimism and confidence of the Gilded Age faded to doubt and defensiveness. In place of the old ideals appeared a new hierarchical view of society that emphasized the coexistence and interaction of diverse groups. Confronted with growing ethnic diversity, badgered by malcontents protesting economic inequality, and chastened by the apparent failure of their programs, policy makers rejected the old goal of complete homogeneity and equality. They came to believe instead that each racial and ethnic group—and each class—possessed specific skills and characteristics; a group's "nature" could not be erased by exhortation or government action.

In the twentieth century American leaders argued that each group should play its proper role and work with others to preserve the social order. Blacks should take on manual tasks and keep to themselves in the rural South. Eastern Europeans should be small merchants and tradesmen. Native-born whites should be professionals and political leaders. Each group should contribute to the maintenance of the whole. The key to assimilation was no longer the act of becoming part of an undifferentiated, "civilized" society; instead, assimilation had come to mean knowing one's place and fulfilling one's role. In this sense, the Indian assimilation campaign had succeeded by 1920, for the Native Americans' place in the United States had been fixed and policies devised for holding the race to its duties.

The extent of the human suffering that was the chief feature of tribal life in the early twentieth century became known in stark detail when the Institute for Government Reseach published *The Problem of Indian Administration* in 1928. Commonly known as the Meriam Report, this document described an infant mortality rate double that of the general population, a death rate from tuberculosis seven times the national average, and an illiteracy rate that ran as high as 67 percent in one state. Finally, the institute's field workers estimated that two-thirds of all Indians earned less than one hundred dollars per year. Here was the reality that awaited a people "set free" from government "paternalism."[5]

One feels uncomfortable dwelling on the ironies of the assimilation campaign, for what is ironic to a well-fed historian was disastrous for the Indian people subjected to the government's policies. To shift attention from their plight seems both insensitive and sophistic. Nevertheless, the ironies are significant—both of them. First, the "assimilation" that whites advocated in 1920 was an inversion of what the policy makers of the 1880s had intended. Cynics might assert that the inversion was intentional (Dawes and Fletcher were not serious, they would say), but the early reformers were not so far-sighted or so clever. They organized a campaign to incorporate Indians into American life, and their goal—total assimilation—was a mirror of what they believed was possible. By 1920 their campaign was over. Like generals who claim victory while retreating, men like Walter Camp accepted the marginal place that scientists, educators, and politicians had assigned to native people and announced themselves satisfied. Assimilation had come to mean its opposite.

The second irony is more interesting. The assimilation effort, a campaign to draw Native Americans into a homogeneous society, helped create its antithesis—a plural society. Despite Walter Camp's smug assurance that education and association with civilized citizens was "beginning to tell," the decades following his report were marked by the persistence, rather than the disappearance, of tribal cultures. First in the buoyant days of the Indian New Deal and again in the activism of the 1960s and 1970s, a renewed tribal spirit moved to the center of Indian life. In the process, those native traditions that endured taught the non-Indian world that humanity is not divided into "civilized" and "primitive" camps.

Although the history of the tribal revivals is complex and largely unwritten, its basic outlines are clear. Missionaries and school-teachers failed to stamp out tribal languages and ceremonies. Those features of Indian culture continued to serve tribal members and provide invisible storehouses for values and traditions. Economic and political pressure produced new generations of native leaders who defended the interests of the group. Family ties continued to insulate individual Indians from alien cultures and provide a source of history and identity. And the land—assaulted, stolen, leased, bulldozed, and flooded—continued as a source of group cohesion and an inspiration for continued activism. Each of these aspects of cultural reorganization was encouraged by the government's decision in the early twentieth century to "lower" its expectations and relegate the Indians to a peripheral role in American life.[6]

Because they believed that Native Americans would take generations to "appreciate" modern ways, politicians and policy makers grew more tolerant of traditional practices. And as long as tribal traditions survived, they could encourage the retention of tribal values, make possible the rise of a new generation of Indian leaders, and provide the cultural space necessary for individual Native Americans to chart their course through the twentieth century. The transformation of the assimilation campaign thus contributed to the survival of native communities and the emergence of modern incarnations of traditional cultures.

Other groups traveled this path to cultural survival. Blacks experienced a new form of rejection in the "nadir" of the early twentieth century, but reemerged as a cultural force in the vibrancy and genius of the Harlem renaissance. Jews reinvented their traditions in the urban ghetto, and Catholics forged a potent political interest group amid the nativist hysteria of the 1920s. Rejection and exclusion—confinement in their "proper station" in the social hierarchy—bred self-consciousness, resourcefulness, and aggressive pride.

The campaign to assimilate the Indians reveals both the burden and the promise of the Native American experience in our own time. Walter Camp's summary demonstrates how satisfied white Americans could be as they relegated Native Americans to the outer ring of Society. But his report also suggests how Indian people survived the suffering and exploitation that has characterized so much of their recent history. Defined as marginal Americans, tribal members could take advantage of their peripheral status, replenish their supplies of belief and value, and carry on their war with homogeneity. We should be thankful that this is a conflict the Indians are winning.

Appendixes

Appendix 1

Senate Roll Call Votes Affecting Indians, 1880–1920

The following list is a compendium of all roll call votes taken in the U.S. Senate between 1880 and 1920 that pertained to Indian affairs. The list includes a statement of the subject of each vote, followed by an indication of the congress and session during which the vote was held, the page of the *Congressional Record* on which the vote was recorded, the date of the vote, and the outcome of the vote.

In the notation of the outcome of each vote, "Y" represents yea votes; "N," nay votes; and "A," abstentions. For example, vote number one occurred during the 46th Congress, Second Session, and was recorded on page 2199 of the *Congressional Record* of that session. The vote was taken on April 7, 1880, and the measure was passed, 35 to 11. There were thirty abstentions.

1. To add to the Ute Treaty that it will not take effect until "the President shall be satisfied that the guilty parties are no longer living

or have fled beyond the limits of the U.S." Amendment to S.1509. 46–2, 2199; April 7, 1880; Y35, N11, A30.

2. An amendment to S.1509 to establish a boarding school for Ute Indians. 46–2, 2258; April 9, 1880; Y44, N8, A24.

3. An amendment to S.1509 that would eliminate tax exemptions for Indian lands guaranteed by treaty. 46–2, 2309–10; April 12, 1880; Y5, N40, A31.

4. An amendment to S.1509 calling for the removal of all Indians from Colorado. 46–2, 2312; April 12, 1880; Y9, N41, A26.

5. An amendment to S.1509 reducing treaty guaranteed annuities to Utes in order to pay damages to white settlers in Colorado. 46–2, 2312; April 12, 1880; Y15, N33, A28.

6. An amendment to S.1509 proposing to limit annuity payments to Indians to five years so as "not to confirm them in their idleness." 46–2, 2316; April 12, 1880; Y15, N33, A28.

7. Final vote on Ute Bill—S.1509—which altered the government's role in the tribe's affairs. Indians were allotted, given special inalienable titles, and exempted from taxation. 46–2, 2320; April 12, 1880; Y37, N16, A23.

8. An amendment to H.R. 4212 calling for the retention of the Board of Indian Commissioners. 46–2, 2829; April 28, 1880; Y37, N21, A18.

9. An amendment to H.R. 6730 appropriating $1,000 annually as supplemental pay for Captain Pratt of the Carlisle Indian school. 46–3, 821; January 21, 1881; Y27, N29, A35.

10. An amendment to S.1773 granting citizenship to all Indians who took land in severalty. 46–3, 939; January 26, 1881; Y12, N29, A35.

11. An amendment to S.1773 to eliminate the requirement that tribal consent be obtained before allotment took place. 46–3, 1064; January 31, 1881, Y10, N40, A26.

12. An amendment to H.R. 4185 to appropriate $250,000 for Indian education. 47–1, 2463–64; March 31, 1882; Y29, N18, A29.

13. Final vote on S.60, a right-of-way permit allowing the St. Louis and San Francisco Railroad to build across Indian Territory. 47–1, 2856; April 13, 1882, Y31, N13, A32.

14. An amendment to H.R. 6092 to eliminate the appropriation

for Indian education in Alaska. 48–1, 4105; May 13, 1884; Y10, N30, A36.

15. An amendment to H.R. 3961 that would require the Gulf, Colorado and Santa Fe Railroad to take the "most direct practicable route" through Indian Territory. 28–1, 5445; June 21, 1884; Y16, N25, A35.

16. A motion to take H.R. 4680, a bill granting the Southern Kansas Railroad a right of way through Indian Territory without Indian consent, from the table. 48–1, 5471; June 23, 1884; Y16, N14, A23.

17. An amendment to H.R. 7970 striking out the clause empowering the president to open negotiations for the opening of Indian Territory to white settlement. The first of three votes on this issue. 48–2, 1748; February 16, 1885; Y35, N20, A21.

18. Amendment to appropriations act—H.R. 7970—to authorize the president to negotiate with Creeks, Seminoles, and Cherokees "for the purpose of opening to settlement . . . the unassigned lands in Indian Territory." 48–2, 2395; March 2, 1885; Y18, N24, A34.

19. Same as above. 48–2, 2368; March 2, 1885; Y33, N27, A16.

20. A motion to bring to the floor S.91, a bill extending the time period allowed the St. Louis and San Francisco Railroad for the construction of a line through various reservations in Indian Territory. 49–1, 1593; February 18, 1886; Y31, N13, A32.

21. Final vote on S.1484, a bill granting the Kansas and Arkansas Valley Railroad a right of way through Indian Territory without prior consent of the Indians affected. 49–1, 3250; April 8, 1886; Y36, N8, A31.

22. Vote to refer H.R. 10614, the Oklahoma bill, to the Committee on Territories rather than the Committee on Indian Affairs. 50–2, 1507; February 5, 1889; Y39, N12, A25.

23. To strike out the provision of H.R. 12578 that appropriated $1.9 million for the purchase of 2.1 million acres of Seminole land without the consent of the tribe. 50–2, 2609; March 2, 1889; Y27, N13, A36.

24. To amend S.895 to expand Oklahoma Territory to include "No Man's Land," in violation of the treaty of 1832. 51–1, 1274; February 13, 1890; Y27, N16, A39.

25. To amend S.895 to grant Oklahoma Territory legal jurisdic-

tion over all cases in "No Man's Land" except those cases involving Indians. All such cases would be tried in tribal courts. 51–1, 3721; April 23, 1890; Y50, N5, A29.

26. To amend H.R. 10726 to strike out appropriations for two Catholic boarding schools. 51–1, 7668; July 24, 1890; Y19, N27, A38.

27. To amend S.8150 by striking out "no claim shall be allowed which is based upon the unsupported testimony of an Indian." 51–1, 2909; February 19, 1891; Y37, N14, A37.

28. To amend H.R. 13388 to appropriate $2.9 million to purchase, without the tribe's consent, the Chickasaw and Choctaw title to lands at that time leased from them. 51–2, 3540; February 28, 1891; Y38, N23, A28.

29. To amend H.R. 5974 to strike out "the President shall detail officers of the United States Army to act as Indian agents at all agencies . . . where vacancies may hereafter occur." 52–1, 2758; March 31, 1893; Y29, N34, A25.

30. Another attempt to strike out provision for army officers as Indian agents. 52–1, 2998; April 6, 1892; Y25, N28, A35.

31. Motion to table Senator Squire's proposal to allow Puyallups to dispose of their land to Tacoma, Washington, residents in advance of the twenty-five-year inalienability limit. 53–2, 7678; July 19, 1894; Y26, N19, A40.

32. Amendment to H.R. 6792 guaranteeing an allotment to all Utes who did not decline one. 53–3, 1454; January 28, 1895; Y12, N32, A41.

33. Amendment to H.R. 6792 which would add, "This act shall take effect only upon the acceptance thereof and consent thereto by a majority of all adult male Indians." 53–3, 1455; January 28, 1895; Y13, N31, A41.

34. Final vote on H.R. 6792, which, without the tribe's consent, reduced the size of the Southern Ute reservation and allotted homesteads to those Indians who might ask for them. 53–3, 1456; January 28, 1895; Y36, N12, A37.

35. Amendment to H.R. 8479 to end appropriations for education contracts with Lincoln and Hampton institutes. 53–3, 2506; February 21, 1895; Y21, N32, A34.

36. Amendment to H.R. 8479 to reduce appropriations for con-

tract schools 20 percent each year for five years. Further to add that "at the end of five years all contracts for such education shall cease." 53–3, 2544; February 22, 1895; Y31, N23, A34.

37. Amendment to H.R. 6249 to add, "And it is hereby declared the settled policy of the government to make no appropriations whatever for the education of Indian children in any sectarian school." 54–1, 4259; April 22, 1896; Y38, N24, A27.

38. Final vote on H.R. 6249 to accept a conference committee report empowering the Dawes Commission to enroll and grant citizenship to Indians in Indian Territory, thereby bypassing the tribal governments and the treaty process. 54–1, 6085; June 4, 1896; Y27, N20, A42.

39. Vote on the conference report on H.R. 6249, which stated, "The Senate will recede from its statement requiring the government to sever connections with contract schools by July 1, 1898." 54–1, 6086; June 4, 1896; Y17, N31, A41.

40. To amend H.R. 10002 by inserting, "All of the Uncompahgre Indian reservation except 10,000 acres of bottom land . . . is hereby opened to public entry." 54–2, 2140; February 23, 1897; Y48, N17, A25.

41. An amendment to H.R. 10002 to extend the jurisdiction of federal courts to all inhabitants of Indian Territory, in violation of treaty agreements. Roll call over whether such an amendment would be in order. 54–2, 2340; February 26, 1897; Y36, N24, A30.

42. To strike from a proviso of H.R. 10002 extending the jurisdiction of U.S. courts to Indian Territory the words *full and exclusive* before the word *jurisdiction. Full and exclusive* would mean that federal judges would have jurisdiction over citizens of the Five Civilized Tribes. Such wording would violate treaty agreements. 54–2, 2345; February 26, 1897; Y8, N40, A42.

43. Amendment to H.R. 15 to open all of the Uncompahgre Indian reservation to settlement, excepting only those tracts that had already been allotted. As of the date of passage of this bill, no allotments had been made on this preserve. 55–1, 725; April 15, 1897; Y33, N13, A41.

44. Amendment to H.R. 7433 to continue appropriations for con-

tract schools in areas where no government schools were available. 56–1, 3919; April 9, 1900; Y16, N30, A41.

45. Amendment to S.2992, the Rosebud Agreement, to guarantee a price of $2.50 per acre for all Indian land sold to settlers. 57–1, 4971; May 2, 1902; Y19, N38, A31.

46. Vote to recommit (in effect, to kill) the Rosebud Agreement. 57–1, 5024; May 5, 1902; Y12, N35, A41.

47. Amendment to H.R. 12684 to pay J. Hale Sypher $25,000 in fees for representing the Choctaw Indians. Charges of corruption surrounded vote. Claim was first made in 1891. 58–2, 3561; March 23, 1904; Y23, N25, A42.

48. Amendment to H.R. 11128, the Devil's Lake Agreement, to allow white settlers to acquire Indian lands for free after five years of settlement. This vote was not binding because the absence of a quorum was later suggested. The amendment was finally rejected on April 18. 58–2, 4925; April 16, 1904; Y5, N31, A54.

49. Amendment to appropriations bill, H.R. 17474, to allow Indians to send children to sectarian schools with their portion of annual annuities. 58–3, 3622; February 28, 1905; Y31, N26, A33.

50. Vote on the chair's decision that a provision in the appropriations bill, H.R. 17474, giving natives who applied for enrollment in the Five Tribes the right to appeal in U.S. courts, was in order. 58–3, 3639; February 28, 1905; Y26, N20, A44.

51. Amendment to H.R. 5676, the Five Tribes bill, to prevent sale of mining rights alone. The proposal required landowners to be responsible for the entire allotment. 59–1, 3208; March 1, 1906; Y8, N38, A43.

52. To lay on the table the section of H.R. 5676 (see vote 51, above) dealing with leasing mineral lands. Mineral lands would thus be reserved under previous arrangements until a study of the area could be made. Previous arrangements required federally supervised leases. 59–1, 3272; March 2, 1906; Y38, N7, A44.

53. Final vote on H.R. 5976, a bill that continued restrictions on the taxation and sale of land by "full-blooded" members of the Five Tribes. Existing leases arrangements also continued. 59–1, 5122; April 12, 1906; Y41, N11, A37.

54. Final vote on H.R. 15331, the annual appropriations bill. Chief

objections referred to restrictions on the sale of allotted lands in Oklahoma, payments to residents of the Colville reservation, and payments to tribal lawyers. 59–1, 8264; June 11, 1906; Y30, N16, A42.

55. Amendment to H.R. 22580, the annual appropriations bill, to remove all restrictions on the sale and taxation of Indian lands in Indian Territory. Vote on whether this motion was in order. 59–2, 2414; February 7, 1907; Y22, N31, A36.

56. Final vote on S.109, a bill to allow the government to sell "surplus" lands on the Standing Rock Reservation. Objections were based on the bill's provision directing 25 percent of the revenue from the land sales to be used to build schools in settlements organized by new white homesteaders as well as the absence of a minimum sale price for the Indian land. 62–2, 1483; January 29, 1912; Y17, N30, A44.

57. Vote on a point of order made on an amendment to H.R. 1915, the annual appropriations bill, which directed the allotment of all tribal funds to members of the Choctaw, Chickasaw, and Cherokee tribes. 63–1, 2088; June 18, 1913; Y36, N15, A45.

58. An amendment to H.R. 12579, the annual appropriations bill, appropriating $100 per capita to Choctaw and $15 per capita to Cherokees from their tribal funds. 63–2, 10673; June 18, 1914; Y40, N15, A41.

59. An amendment to an appropriation for irrigation on reservations which read: "Provided, that no part of this appropriation shall be expended unless the Attorney General of the United States shall, after submission to him by the Secretary of the Interior's request for an opinion, hold affirmatively that in his opinion the Indians under existing law, are protected and confirmed in their water rights." 63–2, 11036; June 24, 1914; Y29, N20, A47.

60. Final vote on conference report on H.R. 12579, the annual appropriations bill. The report eliminated the amendment approved on June 24, (see vote 59, above). 63–2, 12610; July 24, 1914; Y27, N26, A43.

61. Amendment to H.R. 20150, an appropriations bill, striking out per capita payments to Choctaw and Chickasaw Indians. 63–3, 5156; March 2, 1915; Y15, N33, A48.

62. Amendment to H.R. 20150, an appropriations bill, allowing

appeals of enrollment applications to the Five Tribes only for those whose cases were pending on March 4, 1907. 63–3, 5162; March 2, 1915; Y33, N13, A50.

63. Amendment to H.R. 18453, an appropriations bill, to allow the purchase of automobiles for the Flathead agency. 64–2, 2117; January 27, 1917; Y33, N19, A44.

64. Amendment to H.R. 18453, an appropriations bill, to provide for relief of Seminoles. 64–2, 2123; January 27, 1917; Y14, N26, A56.

65. Amendment to H.R. 18453, an appropriations bill, to reduce the amount appropriated for the relief of the Seminoles. 64–2, 2167; January 29, 1917; Y23, N26, A47.

66. Final vote on H.R. 18453, an appropriations bill, for fiscal year 1918. 64–2, 4321; February 26, 1917; Y33, N22, A41.

67, Amendment to H.R. 8696, an appropriations bill, to provide for an irrigation project for the Flathead reservation. 65–2, 4075; March 26, 1918; Y16, N25, A54.

Appendix 2

Congressional Appropriations for Indian Schools, 1877–1920

Year	Amount (in dollars)	Percent Change	Total Average Attendance in Government Schools	Indian Schoolage Population
1877	20,000		3,598	
1878	30,000	+50	4,142	
1879	60,000	+100	4,448	
1880	75,000	+25	4,651	34,541[1]
1881	75,000	0	4,976	
1882	135,000	+80	4,714	
1883	487,000	+260	5,686	
1884	657,000	+38	6,960	
1885	992,800	+47	8,143	37,123[1]
1886	1,100,000	+10	9,630	
1887	1,211,415	+10	10,520	
1888	1,179,916	−2.6	11,420	
1889	1,348,015	+14	11,552	
1890	1,364,568	+1	12,232	40–50,000[2]
1891	1,842,770	+35	13,588	
1892	2,291,650	+24	15,167	
1893	2,317,612	+1	16,303	
1894	2,243,497	−3.5	17,220	
1895	2,060,695	−8.9	18,188	37,300[3]
1896	2,056,515	−2	19,262	
1897	2,517,265	+22	18,876	
1898	2,631,771	+4.5	19,648	
1899	2,638,390	+0.25	20,522	
1900	2,936,080	+11	21,568	37–40,000[2]
1901	3,080,368	+4.9	23,077	

Congressional Appropriations *continued*

Year	Amount (in dollars)	Percent Change	Total Average Attendance in Government Schools	Indian Schoolage Population
1902	3,244,250	+5.3	24,120	
1903	3,531,250	+8.8	24,382	
1904	3,522,950	−1.2	25,104	
1905	3,880,740	+10	25,455	42,600[3]
1906	3,777,100	−2.7	25,492	
1907	3,925,830	+3.9	25,802	
1908	4,105,715	+4.6	25,964	
1909	4,008,825	−2.4	25,568	
1910	3,757,909	−6.3	24,945	45,700[3]
1911	3,685,290	−1.9	23,647	
1912	3,757,495	+2	26,281	
1913	4,015,720	+6.9	25,830	
1914	4,403,355	+9.6	26,127	
1915	4,678,628	+6.25	26,128	49,500[3]
1916	4,391,155	−6.1	25,303	
1917	4,701,903	+7.1	25,297	
1918	5,185,290	+10.3	23,822	
1919	4,837,300	−6.75	20,492	
1920	4,992,325	+1.2	23,248	50,500[3]

[1] Government figure in *Annual Report of the U.S. Commissioner of Indian Affairs*.

[2] Government estimate in *Annual Report of the U.S. Commissioner of Indian Affairs*.

[3] Author's estimate, 15 percent of total Indian population.

SOURCE: *Annual Report of the U.S. Commissioner of Indian Affairs* (1913, 1920).

Appendix 3

The Status of the Indians' Personal Rights and Liberties

Questions and responses from Office of Indian Affairs Circular No. 612, dated March 14, 1912, sent by Arthur C. Luddington. Figures represent number of responses in each category.

How effectively are state liquor laws enforced?

not at all	46
occasionally	24
usually	19
strictly	11
no answer	3

Are the rights of the noncitizen Indians under your charge effectively protected by the federal courts?

yes	74
no	4
unclear answer	16
no answer	24

Has the grant of citizenship to Indians proved in any way a failure?

yes	29
"somewhat"	18
no	28
no answer	30

Would it be wise to grant citizenship during the trust period to the allotted noncitizen Indians under your charge?

yes	22
no	44
no answer	39

Has the introduction of white settlers among Indian allottees been on the whole a benefit or a detriment to the Indians?

benefit	62
detriment	11
unclear answer	9
no answer	23

Abbreviations in Notes

AA	*American Anthropologist*	*N.W.*	*Northwest Reporter*
AJS	*American Journal of Sociology*	*P.*	*Pacific Reporter*
ANR	Superintendents' Annual Narrative and Statistical Report, Entry 960, Records Group 75, National Archives	*Proc. AAAS*	*Proceedings of the American Association for the Advancement of Science*
ARCIA	Annual Report of the U.S. Commissioner of Indian Affairs	*Proc. NEA*	*Proceedings of the National Education Association*
		RG 75, NA	Records Group 75, National Archives
CR,–,.	*Congressional Record*, Congress–Session, page.	RG 48, NA	Records Group 48, National Archives
		S.E.	*Southeast Reporter*
F.	*Federal Reporter*	S.R.	Senate Resolution
H.R.	House Resolution	*S.W.*	*Southwest Reporter*
IRA	Indian Rights Association	*U.S.*	*United States Reports*
IRA AR	Indian Rights Association Annual Report	*U.S. Statutes*	*United States Statutes at Large*

Notes

Chapter 1

1. *Boston Post*, January 15, 1897, p. 1; *St. Louis Post-Dispatch*, January 13, 1879, p. 1.

2. *Atlanta Constitution*, January 16, 1879, p. 2. For a detailed description of the Fort Robinson incident, see Ramon Powers, "Why the Northern Cheyenne Left Indian Territory in 1878: A Cultural Analysis," pp. 72–81.

3. For descriptions of the religious disputes that undermined the administration of the Peace Policy, see Peter A. Rahill, *The Catholic Indian Missions and Grant's Peace Policy, 1870–1884*, passim. See also Robert H. Keller, "The Protestant Churches and Grant's Peace Policy: A Study in Church State Relations," chaps. 7 and 12; and R. Pierce Beaver, *Church, State and the American Indians*. For the Interior-War Department controversy, see Henry G. Waltmann, "The Interior Department, War Department and Indian Policy, 1865–1887"; and Loring Benson Priest, *Uncle Sam's*

Stepchildren, pp. 15–28. Special congressional allocations for Indian education did not begin until 1880, when $75,000 was appropriated.

4. George Crook, "The Apache Problem," p. 269.

5. Quoted in *U.S. ex rel. Standing Bear* v. *Crook*, in Henry L. Dawes Papers. For descriptions of the Ponca incident, see J. Stanley Clark, "Ponca Publicity," pp. 495–516; Thomas H. Tibbles, *The Ponca Chiefs*; and Helen Marie Bannon, "Reformers and the Indian Problem, 1878–1887 and 1922–1934," pp. 11–27. According to Tibbles, oral argument began on April 30. Local newspapers reported that the proceedings began on May 1. See Thomas Henry Tibbles, *The Ponca Chiefs: An Account of the Trial of Standing Bear*, ed. Kay Graber (Lincoln: University of Nebraska Press, 1972), p. 140.

6. *Alta California*, May 14, 1879, p. 2; *Chicago Tribune*, May 19, 1879, p. 4. For Dundy's decision, see *U.S. ex rel. Standing Bear* v. *Crook*, 25 *Federal Cases* 695–701.

7. For a popular account of the Ute War, see Marshall Sprague, *Massacre*.

8. *Chicago Tribune*, October 2, 1879, p. 1.

9. *Chicago Tribune*, October 4, 1879, p. 4; *Virginia City* (Nev.) *Territorial Enterprise*, October 30, 1879, p. 2; *Alta California*, October 3, 1879, p. 2; *Alta California*, Oct. 4, 1879, p. 2. Given the violence of the Ute incident, it is somewhat surprising to see such benign responses in the white press. Colorado and western Kansas papers were strongly anti-Indian, but elsewhere condemnations of the tribe were mixed with attacks on government policy. For a discussion of press reactions to Indian fighting, see Roger L. Nichols, "Printer's Ink and Red Skins: Western Newspapers and the Indians," pp. 82–88. Nichols shows that papers in secure areas had a more sympathetic view of Indian-white relations than those on the frontier. Robert G. Athearn, *William Tecumseh Sherman and the Settlement of the West*, pp. 345–46, also discusses this phenomenon. Another study of newspaper reactions to the Ute fighting is found in Omer C. Stewart, *Ethnohistorical Bibliography of the Ute Indians of Colorado*, app. B. Stewart lists negative responses in Colorado, Wyoming, and western Kansas, and more positive editorials in Knoxville, Tennessee; Hartford, Connecticut; and Philadelphia. For a more general discussion of the Indians' "image" at this time, see Robert Winston Mardock, "Irresolvable Enigma?" *Montana*, January, 1957, pp. 36–47; and Robert F. Berkhofer, Jr., *The White Man's Indian*, pt. 4.

10. The basic source for Thomas H. Tibbles's life is his autobiography, *Buckskin and Blanket Days.*

11. Tibbles, *Buckskin and Blanket Days*, p. 218; Clark, "Ponca Publicity," pp. 504, 505; *Chicago Tribune*, October 21, 1879, p. 4.

12. Tibbles, *Buckskin and Blanket Days*, p. 234; ibid., p. 199; and *Boston Daily Advertiser*, Nov. 26, 1879, p. 4.

13. Helen Hunt Jackson to Thomas Wentworth Higginson, quoted in Thomas W. Higginson, *Contemporaries*, p. 155.

14. See, for example, accounts of January meetings in New York in the *New York Times*, December 13, 1879, p. 2, and January 17, 1880, p. 5.

15. Carl Schurz to Helen Hunt Jackson, January 17, 1880, *Speeches, Correspondence and Political Papers of Carl Schurz*, 3:499; *New York Tribune*, February 13, 1880, p. 4. The Jackson-Schurz Affair is described fully in Robert W. Mardock, *The Reformers and the American Indian*, and its relationship to the entire reform movement is discussed in Francis Paul Prucha, *American Indian Policy in Crisis*, pp. 116–17. An extended statement by Helen Hunt Jackson not discussed in these works is a letter from her to Henry Wadsworth Longfellow, dated March 2, 1881, Manuscript 1340, 2 (2971), Houghton Library, Harvard University. For the Hayt Affair, see Roy W. Meyer, "Ezra A. Hayt," in Robert M. Kvasnicka and Herman J. Viola, eds., *The Commissioners of Indian Affairs*, pp. 161–62.

16. *Virginia City* (Nev.) *Territorial Enterprise*, February 8, 1880, p. 2; *Chicago Tribune*, January 31, 1880, p. 4.

17. See Prucha, *American Indian Policy in Crisis*, pp. 36, 132–68. The *Boston Daily Advertiser* covered the formation of the committee in its November 26, 1879, issue (see p. 4).

18. See Mary E. Dewey, *Historical Sketch of the Formation and Achievements of the Women's National Indian Association in the United States*, pp. 5–12; Mardock, *Reformers and the American Indian*, pp. 199–200; and Amelia S. Quinton to Henry L. Dawes, Janaury 23, 1885, Dawes Papers.

19. Herbert Welsh, "The Indian Problem and What We Must Do to Solve It," pp. 8–9.

20. *New Orleans Times-Picayune*, December 10, 1879, p. 4; *New York Tribune*, March 8, 1880, p. 4.

21. *Virginia City* (Nev.) *Territorial Enterprise*, Janaury 26, 1879, p. 2; ibid., February 9, 1879, p. 2; *New York Tribune*, October 4, 1879, p. 4;

Boston Daily Advertiser, November 8, 1879, p. 2; *St. Louis Post-Dispatch*, December 1879 and January 1880, passim.

22. *Alta California*, February 26, 1880, p. 2; *Atlanta Constitution*, January 14, 1879, pp. 1, 2; and *Boston Daily Advertiser*, November 8, 1879, p. 2.

23. *New York Tribune*, February 13, 1880, p. 4. For a fuller discussion of the reformers' ideas, see Bannon, "Reformers and the Indian Problem," especially chap. 5.

24. 20 *U.S. Statutes* 297 (1879).

25. See Regna Darnell, "The Development of American Anthropology, 1879–1920"; and "The Professionalization of American Anthropology," pp. 83–103. The anthropologist's decision to study Indians is discussed from the perspective of a modern black scholar in William S. Willis, Jr., "Anthropology and Negroes on the Southern Colonial Frontier," in James C. Curtis and Lewis L. Gould, eds., *The Black Experience in America*, pp. 33–50. Curtis M. Hinsley, Jr., discusses earlier studies of Indian communities in *Savages and Scientists*, pp. 34–63.

26. Henry Adams to Lewis Henry Morgan, July 14, 1877, Morgan Papers; John Wesley Powell to Lewis Henry Morgan, May 23, 1877, Morgan Papers. Hinsley notes that many researchers questioned Morgan's scheme, but agrees that social evolutionism was "formally adopted" at the BAE. See Hinsley, *Savages and Scientists*, p. 139.

27. For the role of evolutionary theory in the nineteenth century, see J. W. Burrow, *Evolution and Society*; Robert E. Bieder, "The American Indian and the Development of Anthropological Thought in America, 1780–1851," chap. 5; and the refinements of George Stocking, "Some Problems in the Understanding of Nineteenth-Century Cultural Evolutionism," in Regna Darnell, ed., *Readings in the History of Anthropology*, pp. 407–25. For the place of evolutionary thinking in the United States, see Roy Harvey Pearce, *Savagism and Civilization*; Reginald Horsman, "Scientific Racism and the American Indian in the Mid-Nineteenth Century," pp. 152–68; and Berkhofer, *The White Man's Indian*, pp. 49–55.

28. Lewis Henry Morgan, *Ancient Society*, pp. 5, 7.

29. Morgan, *Ancient Society*, pp. 39, 427–28, emphasis in original.

30. Morgan, *Ancient Society*, p. 426. Despite his success in real estate, Morgan was uncomfortable with the excesses of private wealth he saw around him. Moreover, he did not advocate the rapid, forced allotment of

individual homesteads to Indians. Nevertheless, he always viewed individual landownership as a final step in human progress, and he approved of a gradual, voluntary allotment program. See his "Factory System for Indian Reservations," pp. 58–59.

31. Leslie A. White, ed. *Pioneers in American Anthropology: The Bandelier Morgan Letters*, 2 vols. (Albuquerque: University of New Mexico Press, 1940), 2:249.

32. John Wesley Powell, "Mythologic Philosophy," *Proc. AAAS* (1879): 2788. The major biographies of Powell are William Culp Darrah, *Powell of the Colorado*; and Wallace Stegner, *Beyond the Hundredth Meridian*. For a more cautious assessment of Powell's role in policy making, see Curtis M. Hinsley, Jr., "Anthropology as Science and Politics: The Dilemmas of the Bureau of American Ethnology, 1879–1904," in Walter Goldschmidt, ed., *The Uses of Anthropology*, pp. 15–32.

33. Powell, "From Barbarism to Civilization," p. 97; idem, "From Savagery to Barbarism," p. 195; and for Powell's optimistic predictions, see idem, "Sketch of Lewis Henry Morgan," pp. 114–21; idem, "Introduction," *17th Annual Report of the Bureau of American Ethnology* (Washington: Government Printing Office, 1899), pp. xvii–xviii; idem, "On the Evolution of Language," *1st Annual Report of the Bureau of Ethnology* (Washington: Government Printing Office, 1881), p. 16; idem, "The Use of Some Anthropological Data," ibid., pp. 80–81.

34. "Statement of Major J. W. Powell, made before the House Committee on Indian Affairs as to the condition of the Indian Tribes west of the Rocky Mountains," January 13, 1874, *House Miscellaneous Document*, no. 86, 43d Cong., 1st sess., ser. 1618, pp. 7–8.

35. Powell, "Introduction," *1st Annual Report of the Bureau of Ethnology*, p. xxxii; Powell to Spencer F. Baird, April 2, 1880, National Anthropological Archives #4677. It is important to note that while Powell was convinced that the savage would disappear, he did not assume that individual natives would die off. His was one of the scientific voices raised against the idea of Indian extinction. He expressed this position most clearly in "The North American Indians," an article in Nathaniel S. Shaler, ed., *The United States of America*, 2 vols. (New York: Appleton, 1894), 1:190–272.

36. See Cyrus Thomas, "Report on the Mound Explorations of the Bureau of Ethnology," *12th Annual Report of the Bureau of American Ethnology*

(Washington: Government Printing Office, 1894), p. xlvi; Powell, "Introduction," *16th Annual Report of the Bureau of American Ethnology*, lxxxvii; idem, "Introduction," *14th Annual Report of the Bureau of American Ethnology* (Washington: Government Printing Office, 1896), p. lx.

37. Powell, "Introduction," *1st Annual Report of the Bureau of Ethnology*, p. xxix. For an example of Powell's caution, one might note his reaction to Frank Cushing's exposure of a land swindle at Zuni. When the affair showed signs of embarrassing Illinois Senator John Logan, Powell immediately recalled the young bureau researcher. See Joan Mark, "Frank Hamilton Cushing and an American Science of Anthropology," *Perspectives in American History* 10 (1976): 461. Powell's contacts with policy makers were especially strong between 1885 and 1888, when John Atkins, who as a congressman had been one of the original sponsors of the Bureau of Ethnology, served as commissioner of Indian affairs.

38. Powell to Henry Teller, March 23, 1880, Manuscript #3751, National Anthropological Archives. It is difficult to assess the impact of Powell's letter to Teller. Even though the Colorado Republican did not become a supporter of individual allotments until after 1885, he did endorse severalty plans based on tribal consent. In addition, he was a leading advocate of Indian education, overseeing an unprecedented expansion of the Indian schools during his tenure as secretary of the interior (1882–85).

39. Powell, "The Non-Irrigable Lands of the Arid Region," p. 922.

40. Alice Fletcher to Frederick W. Putnam, March 6, 1890, Putnam Papers. See Nancy Oestreich Lurie, "Women in Early American Anthropology," in June Helm, ed., *Pioneers in American Anthropology*, pp. 29–81; Lurie, "The Lady from Boston and the Omaha Indians," pp. 31–33, 80–85; Walter Hough, "Alice Cunningham Fletcher," pp. 254–58; and Joan Mark, *Four Anthropologists*, chap. 2, for descriptions of Fletcher's career. It is important to note that although Alice Fletcher was the most active, she was not the only bureau employee to speak out on policy. Frank Cushing, for example, complained of reservation corruption and hoped for peaceful assimilation. See Frank Cushing to Spencer F. Baird, December 4, 1881, National Anthropological Archives. Triloki Nath Pandey's "Anthropologists at Zuni," pp. 321–28, indicates that while Cushing was a critic of federal officials, he often supported the government's position before the tribe. Another prominent anthropologist who spoke out in the public debate was Morgan's pro-

tégé Adolph Bandelier, whose novel, *The Delightmakers*, popularized the social-evolutionist analysis of Indian life and whose speeches supported assimilation efforts.

41. Alice Fletcher to Thomas J. Morgan, May 26, 1890, Alice Fletcher Papers, box 3; "Education and Civilization," *Senate Executive Document* no. 95, 48th Cong. 2d sess., p. 173.

42. Tibbles, *Buckskin and Blanket Days*, p. 237; Alice Fletcher to Henry L. Dawes, February 4, 1882, Dawes Papers. See also Alice Fletcher to Henry Dawes, February 8, 1882, and Alice Fletcher to Secretary of the Interior James Kirkwood, same date, Alice Fletcher Papers.

43. *CR*, 47–1, 3027.

44. Alice Fletcher to William J. Harsha of the Omaha Citizenship Committee, April 3, 1883, Fletcher Papers.

45. Letters Received (Entry 79), Alice Fletcher to Hiram Price, December 13, 1883, RG 75, NA; *Red Man*, February 1887; Alice Fletcher to John E. Rhoads, April 7, 1887, Fletcher Papers, Box 1.

46. Alice Fletcher to Isabel Chapin Barrows, Nov. 11, 1894, Barrows Family Papers, Houghton Library, bMS AM1807.1 (175).

47. Alice Fletcher to Isabel Chapin Barrows, Feb. 1, 1888, Barrows Family Papers, Houghton Library, bMS AM1807.1 (175).

48. "Speech to the Massachusetts Republican Convention," 1882, Dawes Papers.

49. Henry L. Dawes to Electa S. Dawes, December 12, 1880, Dawes Papers.

50. See Chester M. Dawes to Henry L. Dawes, January 18, 1881, Dawes Papers.

51. The term *Anglo-Conformity* is taken from Milton Gordon, *Assimilation in American Life* (New York: Oxford U. Press, 1964), chap. 4.

52. Henry L. Dawes, "The Indian Problem in 1895," manuscript, in Dawes Papers.

53. *CR*, 48–1, 2565.

54. Ibid. For a more detailed discussion of Senate alignments on this issue, see Frederick Hoxie, "The End of the Savage: Indian Policy in the U.S. Senate," *Chronicles of Oklahoma* 55 (Summer 1977): 157–80.

55. John Higham, *Strangers in the Land*, chap. 2.

Chapter 2

1. *CR*, 46–2, 2128; Henry Dawes, "The Indian Problem in 1895," typescript in Dawes Papers.

2. For a description of the land cessions of these years, see Imre Sutton, *Indian Land Tenure*, pp. 115–25.

3. *Proceedings of the Convention to Consider the Opening of Indian Territory, Held at Kansas City, Mo. Feb. 8, 1888* (Kansas City, Mo., 1888), pp. 59–60. The most recent discussion of the Indian Territory opening is H. Craig Miner, *The Corporation and the Indian*. A great deal of Professor Miner's book involves what he sees as the surprising amount of Indian participation in the opening of their homeland to white settlement. My analysis differs from the one presented in *The Corporation and the Indian* and has two major themes. First, the destruction of Indian Territory was undertaken by non-Indians to serve non-Indian interests. And second, natives who participated in this destruction in the 1880s by lobbying for coal leases, building railroads, or fencing land were serving two masters—themselves and their white colleagues. Miner discusses Payne on pp. 97–100. For more on Payne and the Oklahoma "boomers," see Carl Coke Rister, *Land Hunger*; pp. 50, 71–75, and passim. For a thorough analysis of the railroads in Indian Territory, see Ira G. Clark, "The Railroads and the Tribal Lands," especially chap. 9.

4. *Railroad Gazette*, July 22, 1881, p. 402.

5. *Railroad Gazette*, ibid., September 24, 1886, p. 657; March 20, 1885, p. 184.

6. Hill's official biographer described the Great Northern's invasion of the Blackfoot and other preserves with great pride. See Joseph Gilpin Pyle, *The Life of James J. Hill*, 1:377–87.

7. *House Report* no. 1035, 52d Cong., 1st sess., p. 4. The Colville and other Washington Territory land acquisitions are discussed in greater detail in Herman J. Deutsch, "Indian and White in the Inland Empire," p. 44.

8. The Northern Pacific was the victim of the "extortion" process in 1888, when it leased the Washington and Idaho's roadbed across the Coeur d'Alene reservation, and in 1889 at Crow, where it bought the Rocky Fork and Cook City. See *Railroad Gazette*, March 30, 1888; May 18, 1888 (for the Washington and Idaho); and January 4, 1889; Feb. 15, 1889; and March 14, 1890 (for the Rocky Fork and Cook City).

9. *CR*, 47–1, 2852.

10. See *CR*, 47–1, 2856.

11. *CR*, 47–1, 6587; *CR*, 49–1, 3248. Joseph Brown (D-Ga.) was commenting on a proposal to grant the Kansas and Arkansas Valley Railroad an east-west right of way through Indian Territory that promised to link Denver and New Orleans; see *Senate Report* no. 107, 49th Cong. 1st sess.

12. See Paul W. Gates, "The Homestead Law in an Incongruous Land System," *American Historical Review*, pp. 652–81; and Roy M. Robbins, *Our Landed Heritage*, pt. 3, for a description of the abuses of the Homestead Act and the rising sentiment for reform in the 1880s.

13. *CR*, 49–1, 2317; *CR*, 52–1, 2690.

14. Henry Dawes to Henry M. Teller, September 19, 1882, Dawes Papers.

15. 25 *U.S. Statutes* 113; 25 *U.S. Statutes* 888, sec. 17; and 25 *U.S. Statutes* 642, sec. 4.

16. *House Report* no. 1035, 52d Cong., 1st sess.; *CR*, 49–1, 812, 1763.

17. The Ute agreement followed this pattern except that the tribe's original home was completely opened up and the Utes moved to the Uintah reservation in Utah. What is more, Indian Territory was also opened to whites in this way. First Oklahoma and the Cherokee Strip were acquired by the federal government, then the Nations themselves were allotted. The fact that whites wanted signed agreements from the tribes, even when the cession was a foregone conclusion, indicates something of their concern for "reforming" the Indians. Whites believed that by agreeing to a land cession, Native Americans were taking the first steps towards individual landowner-ship and "civilization."

18. *CR*, 49–1, 969. Because this study focuses on white behavior, I have not discussed the impact of Indian negotiators on the land cession agreements of the 1880s. Nevertheless, the skill and tenacity of these people deserve mention. Anyone reading the proceedings of the various negotiating sessions between the white and Sioux leaders that led up to the 1886 agreement will bury forever the notion that the tribes were passive victims of the white onslaught. The band leaders had only a few cards left in their deck, but they played each one well, refusing to concede anything without a struggle. Though less dramatic and of shorter duration, the other negotiating sessions often followed a similar course. Whites were usually insistent and impatient, and the Indians, using this impatience and the sympathies of the eastern press to their advantage, usually drove the best bargain possible.

19. For an overview of Indian education, see Martha E. Layman, "A History of Indian Education in the U.S." (Ph.D. diss., University of Minnesota, 1942). One of the few published case studies of Indian education in the nineteenth century—which emphasizes the reforming zeal of the 1880s and 1890s—is Bruce Rubenstein, "To Destroy a Culture," pp. 137–60. The promise of new schoolhouses was attached to treaties made with the Sioux, Navajo, Ute, Kiowa, Commanche, Cheyenne, Arapaho, Crow, Shoshone, and Pawnee. See *ARCIA* (1881): 30 for a description of these agreements.

20. Educational appropriations came from three sources after 1880: general educational appropriations, treaty commitments, and appropriations for contract schools. After 1883, the treaty commitments accounted for a very small part of the total. Contract funds increased at roughly the same rate as general appropriations, but did not directly affect the federal school program. The rise in general appropriations is therefore the best indicator of congressional interest in government schools for Indians. Incidentally, one should not forget that, throughout this period, the Five Civilized Tribes supported and maintained their own school system in Indian Territory.

21. Henry Whipple to Richard H. Pratt, March 24, 1876, Pratt Papers.

22. Draft of a speech, "On Indian Civilization," in Pratt Papers. Delivered c. 1878.

23. Samuel C. Armstrong to Pratt, August 26, 1878, Pratt Papers. Armstrong's request was repeated the next day. Apparently Booker T. Washington served as a dormitory counselor for the new arrivals. See Bannon, "Reformers and the Indian Problem," p. 326.

24. Pratt to Dr. Cornelius Agnew, July 19, 1881, Pratt Papers. The founding of Carlisle was summarized by Commissioner of Indian Affairs Ezra Hayt in a note to Pratt. Hayt wrote: "You are entitled to the credit of establishing the School. You found the empty barracks, you got the consent of the Secretary of War to use them, you fussed around the Interior Department until you got up sufficient steam to propel the enterprise. You got the children together, in fact did everything but get the money." Ezra Hayt to Pratt, July 5, 1880, Pratt Papers.

25. *CR*, 47–1, 6154.

26. Pratt to Henry L. Dawes, April 4, 1881, Pratt Papers.

27. *CR*, 47–1, 2456.

28. Alfred L. Riggs to Pratt, April 14, 1882, Pratt Papers; Henry M. Teller

to Alice Fletcher, August 3, 1882, Fletcher Papers. By 1890, eight additional nonreservation schools opened their doors.

29. *House Executive Document* no. 1, pt. 5, 47th Cong., 2d sess., p. xvii.

30. See votes 9 and 12, Appendix 1.

31. *ARCIA* (1884): 1.

32. *CR*, 48–1, 2565.

33. *CR*, 50–1, 2503; *CR*, 53–2, 6300. For a compilation of statistics regarding appropriations for the Indian schools, see Appendix 2.

34. *ARCIA* (1886): 99; *CR*, 50–1, 4802; *CR*, 48–1, 4074. For a fuller explication of the western position, see Senator James H. Kyle, "How Shall the Indians Be Educated?" pp. 434–47.

35. Alfred L. Riggs, "Where Shall Our Indian Brothers Go to School?" p. 200.

36. The school superintendents were J. M. Haworth (1882–85), John Oberly (1885–86), John B. Riley (1886–87), S. H. Albro (1888–89), Daniel Dorchester (1889–94), and William N. Hailmann (1894–98). It is interesting that after 1889, as civil service regulations removed the power to dispense patronage and a professional consensus on policy decreased criticism, the terms of the superintendents began to overlap presidential administrations. The statement by William Hailmann is in a letter to Herbert Welsh, January 27, 1894, IRA Papers. In 1898 Hailmann enlisted the support of Theodore Roosevelt in an attempt to retain his position under William McKinley. See Theodore Roosevelt to F. E. Leupp, January 29, 1898, Series 2, Theodore Roosevelt Papers.

37. "An Outrage," *Journal of Education* 25 (June 2, 1887): 349. The "institutionalization" of educational reform within the Indian Office is a central theme of Paul Stuart, *The Indian Office*, especially chap. 9.

38. *ARCIA* (1885): 113.

39. *ARCIA* (1889): 94, 103–4, 100, 98. For an excellent biographical sketch of Morgan, see Prucha, "Thomas Jefferson Morgan," in Kvasnicka and Viola, *Commissioners of Indian Affairs*, pp. 193–204.

40. "General Morgan's First Report," *Journal of Education* 30 (December 12, 1889): 376.

41. Pratt to Alice Fletcher, July 30, 1893, Pratt Papers; R. H. Pratt to Alice Fletcher, August 7, 1891, Fletcher Papers, Box 1.

42. *Proc. NEA* (1895): 81.

43. *ARCIA* (1894): 341, *ARCIA* (1892): 55.

44. *ARCIA* (1894): 15.

45. *ARCIA* (1892): 46–47; "Indian Education," *Journal of Education* 37 (February 16, 1893): 104.

46. Michael B. Katz, *Class, Bureaucracy, and the Schools*, p. xx. The emphasis on the total transformation of Indian children through education is also discussed in Jacqueline Fear, "English versus the Vernacular," pp. 13–24.

47. Calvin M. Woodward, "The Function of the Public School," pp. 222, 224. The curriculum at Carlisle never progressed beyond the high-school level, but the captain maintained that his students should not limit their goals. See R. H. Pratt to Alice Fletcher, August 7, 1891, Fletcher Papers.

48. For a discussion of the Blair Bill, see C. Vann Woodward, *The Origins of the New South* (Baton Rouge: Louisiana State University Press, 1951), pp. 63–64. For a description of the passage of the Chinese Exclusion Act, see Alexander Saxton, *The Indispensable Enemy* (Berkeley: University of California Press, 1971), p. 177.

49. For descriptions of the passage of the Dawes Act, see Prucha, *American Indian Policy in Crisis*, chap. 8; Henry Fritz, "The Board of Indian Commissioners and Ethnocentric Reform," in Jane Smith and Robert Kvasnicka, eds., *Indian-White Relations*, pp. 62–71; D. S. Otis, *The Dawes Act and the Allotment of Indian Lands*; and Priest, *Uncle Sam's Stepchildren*. Also helpful are Henry Eugene Fritz, *The Movement for Indian Assimilation*; and Mardock, *The Reformers and the American Indian*. For a description of the law's broad support, see William T. Hagan, "Private Property, the Indian's Door to Civilization," pp. 126–37. Of course, the idea of allotting individual tracts of land to Indians was not new. Prucha (*American Indian Policy in Crisis*, pp. 227–34) and Priest (*Uncle Sam's Stepchildren*, pp. 177–82) summarize the history of the earlier schemes. The significance of the Coke bill was the intention that it would apply generally.

50. William M. Springer (D.-Ill.), *CR*, 46–2, 178; proceedings of the Lake Mohonk Conference printed in *House Executive Document* no. 109, 49th Cong., 1st sess., pp. 95–96. Lyman Abbott's ideas were echoed by William Graham Sumner, "The Indians in 1887," p. 254. The broad consensus behind the allotment "solution" is also described in Berkhofer, *The White Man's Indian*, pp. 170–75.

51. *CR*, 47–1, 3028; *CR*, 46–3, 784; *CR*, 46–2, 499.

52. Dawes discussed his reasons for compromising with his opponents at

the 1886 Lake Mohonk Conference. See *ARCIA* (1886): 992. The "President's discretion" phrase was first adopted in 1881, during debate over the Coke severalty bill. See *CR*, 46–3, 1064–67.

53. See William Justin Harsha, "Law for the Indians," p. 272. Harsha also put his plea in the form of a novel, *A Timid Brave*. For Call's view, see *CR*, 46–3, 908; Schurz's position is described in chap. 1.

54. *CR*, 46–3, 877.

55. Powell quoted in *CR*, 46–3, 911. The vote is number 10, Appendix 1.

56. George F. Canfield, "Carl Schurz on the Indian Problem," p. 457.

57. 112 *U.S.* 648 (1885).

58. *CR*, 49–1, 1632; ibid., 1634.

59. Charles C. Painter, *The Dawes Land in Severalty Bill and Indian Emancipation*, p. 1. The ambiguous quality of citizenship provisions in the Dawes Act was very perceptively analyzed by Harvard Law School professor James Bradley Thayer in "The Dawes Bill and the Indians," pp. 315–22.

60. *House Report* no. 2247, 48th Cong., 2d sess., p. 1.

61. Alice Fletcher to Thomas J. Morgan, May 26, 1890, Fletcher Papers; *Red Man*, December 1886; *CR*, 49–1, 2470.

62. *CR*, 56–3, 1032.

63. See Otis, *The Dawes Act and the Allotment of Indian Land*, p. 82.

64. *ARCIA* (1887): 4; Otis, *The Dawes Act and the Allotment of Indian Land*, pp. 82, 83. Atkins's restraint in administering the Dawes Act is a prominent theme in Gregory C. Thompson, "John D. C. Atkins," in Kvasnicka and Viola, *Commissioners of Indian Affairs*. See pp. 182–83.

65. *ARCIA* (1892): 69–70; Painter, *The Dawes Land in Severalty Bill*, p. 5

66. See *ARCIA* (1893): 476 and *ARCIA* (1894): 421; Richard Pratt to Henry Dawes, January 22, 1892, Pratt Papers.

67. See *Beck v. Flournoy Live-Stock and Real Estate Co.*, 65 F. 30 (1894); Thayer, "A People Without Law," p. 683.

68. Herbert Welsh, *How to Bring the Indian to Citizenship*, pp. 8–9. See Laurence F. Schmeckebier, *The Office of Indian Affairs*, p. 284. In 1892 Congress also gave the president the authority to name army officers to vacant agencies. This was widely regarded as a blow to patronage. See Prucha, *American Indian Policy in Crisis*, pp. 353–72; and Stuart, *The Indian Office*, pp. 145–49.

Chapter 3

1. George Bird Grinnell and Theodore Roosevelt, "The Exhibit at the World's Fair," in *American Big Game Hunting*. The only full-length history of the Boone and Crockett Club is an uncritical house history: James B. Trefethen, *Crusade for Wildlife*. An excellent pictorial presentation of the fair is Halsey C. Ives, *The Dream City* (St. Louis: N. D. Thompson, 1893).

2. W. J. McGee, quoted in David R. Francis, *The Universal Exposition of 1904*, p. 523. All the fairs stressed the educational benefits of their displays. While much of this was hucksterism, the expositions did provide large numbers of Americans with their first look at the products of an expanding technology, samples of European art (Marcel Duchamps's *Nude Descending a Staircase* was a main attraction at San Francisco), and representatives of foreign cultures.

3. *New York Times*, March 29, 1876; *Philadelphia Bulletin*, May 23, 1876.

4. *Philadelphia Bulletin*, May 23, 1876; Edward C. Bruce, *The Century*, pp. 224–25; Francis A. Walker, ed., *International Exhibition, 1876*, 8:97; Bruce, *The Century*, p. 225.

5. Frederick W. Putnam quoted in Ralph W. Dexter, "Putnam's Problems in Popularizing Anthropology," p. 316; Hubert Howe Bancroft, *The Book of the Fair*, p. 631.

6. *ARCIA* (1893): 21.

7. *ARCIA* (1893): 22.

8. *Chicago Tribune*, May 7, 1893; ibid., August 20, 1893. See also *New York Times*, August 19, 1893.

9. *New York Times*, October 8, 1893. See also Dexter, "Putnam's Problems in Popularizing Anthropology," pp. 327–28.

10. Henry Adams, *The Education of Henry Adams* (Boston: Houghton Mifflin, 1969), pp. 466, 468.

11. W. J. McGee to F. W. Lehman, August 8, 1901, W. J. McGee Papers; W. J. McGee quoted in Francis, *The Universal Exposition of 1904*, p. 524; McGee, "Strange Races of Men," p. 5186.

12. McGee, "Strange Races of Men," pp. 5184, 5188.

13. For typical stories and photos, see *St. Louis Post-Dispatch*, May 1, 2, 4, 5, 16, 22, June 26, and August 13, 1904.

14. For a description of the exhibit, see Alfred C. Newell, "The Philippine Peoples," p. 5129; *St. Louis Post-Dispatch*, May 1, 1904.

15. Charles M. Harvey, "The Last Race Rally of the Indians," p. 4803. For more on the St. Louis fair, see Richard Drinnon, *Facing West*, pp. 333–46.

16. James Fraser quoted in J. Walter McSpadden, *Famous Sculptors of America*, p. 281.

17. Eugen Neuhaus, *The Art of the Exposition*, p. 32; Juliet James, *Sculpture of the Exposition Palaces and Courts*, p. 34.

18. McSpadden, *Famous Sculptors of America*, p. 282.

19. C. H. Forbes-Lindsay, "Shaping the Future of the Indian," p. 292; idem, "Making Good Indians," p. 13; Harvey, "The Red Man's Last Roll Call," p. 330.

20. Ray Stannard Baker, "The Day of the Run," pp. 643–55.

21. Helen Fitzgerald Sanders, "The Red Bond," p. 163. For Sanders's view of native life, see also *The White Quiver*, a romantic novel about the Piegans before the coming of the European. See Owen Wister, *The Virginian*, p. 197; idem, "Little Big Horn Medicine," in *Red Men and White*, p. 5; Elliott Flower, "Law and the Indian," p. 488; Honore Willsie, *Still Jim*. For yet another example of this theme of the "indelible" quality of one's ancestry, see Frederic Remington's *John Ermine of the Yellowstone*.

22. A. Decker, "Making the Warrior a Worker," p. 95; Willsie, *Still Jim*, 168.

23. Hamlin Garland, *Captain of the Grey Horse Troop*, pp. 56, 113, 121.

24. Ibid., 406–7, 414–15.

25. Garland, "The Red Man's Present Needs," p. 488. See also the following short stories on contemporary events: "Wahiah—A Spartan Mother" (on agency schools, 1905); "The Story of Howling Wolf" (on westeners' hatred of Indians, 1903); "Drifting Crane," (on the inevitability of white progress, 1890). All these stories were reprinted in Garland, *The Book of the American Indian*. See also "The Red Plowman," pp. 181–82. For a thorough and sympathetic account of Garland's Indian writings, see Lonnie E. Underhill and Daniel F. Littlefield's introduction to *Hamlin Garland's Observations on the American Indian*.

26. Carl Moon, "In Search of the Wild Indian," p. 545. For a discussion of this new twentieth-century attitude toward the West, see G. Edward White, *The Eastern Establishment and the Western Experience*, especially pp. 184–203.

27. Charles F. Lummis, "My Brother's Keeper," pp. 139, 264; George Bird Grinnell, *When Buffalo Ran*, p. 10.

28. Grinnell, *Blackfoot Lodge Tales*, xii; Lummis, "The Sequoyah League," *Out West*, 1903, p. 301; idem, "My Brother's Keeper," p. 264.

29. Lummis to Theodore Roosevelt, May 19, 1904, Series 1, Roosevelt Papers; Lummis, "My Brother's Keeper," p. 145. It should not be surprising that Lummis considered *Captain of the Grey Horse Troop* a "very accurate" book and recommended it to his readers. See his "Reading List on Indians," *Land of Sunshine*, March 1903, p. 360.

30. Grinnell, *The Indians of Today*, pp. 155, 156; Lummis, "My Brother's Keeper," p. 226; idem, "Sequoyah League," *Out West* 20 (April 1904): 382, 384; Grinnell, *The Indians of Today*, pp. 169, 170.

31. Lummis, "Sequoyah League," *Out West* 20 (April 1904), 384.

32. Roosevelt to Curtis, November 21, 1911, Series 3A, Roosevelt Papers; Roosevelt, Foreword in Edward S. Curtis, *The North American Indian*, 1 : xi.

33. The groundbreaking ceremony and Taft's speech were described in the *New York Times* on February 23, 1913. Wanamaker's statue was never completed. Work was postponed by the world war—apparently because of a shortage of bronze—and later abandoned for lack of interest. Wanamaker also sponsored three western expeditions. The first was devoted to the filming of a dramatization of "Hiawatha" on the Blackfoot reservation. The second was for a "last council of the chiefs," a gathering of old warriors that was also filmed. The final trip was a visit to 169 Indian communities by a special railroad car that carried recorded greetings and patriotic messages from President Woodrow Wilson and Secretary of the Interior Franklin K. Lane. The last two of these projects are described in Joseph K. Dixon, *The Vanishing Race*. See also Louis L. Pfaller, *James McLaughlin*, chap. 15.

34. Beverly Buchanan, "A Tribute to the First American," p. 30. See also Rodman Wanamaker to W. H. Taft, July 10, 1909, Case 4006, Taft Papers. The phrase "departed race" was used by General Nelson A. Miles in a letter of support to Wanamaker (dated Janaury 9, 1909) that the businessman enclosed in his July appeal to the president.

35. I agree with William T. Hagan that Roosevelt "deserves better than the occasional references to him as one of the more articulate racists of the late nineteenth century." Nevertheless, unlike Hagan, I am looking beyond TR's career as civil service commissioner and his fragile friendship with Her-

bert Welsh to his presidency. Consequently my view is somewhat harsher. See Hagan, "Civil Service Commissioner Theodore Roosevelt and the Indian Rights Association," pp. 187–201. For a general study of Roosevelt's racial attitudes that outlines his view of the Indians, see Thomas G. Dyer, *Theodore Roosevelt and the Idea of Race*, pp. 69–88.

36. On Garland and TR, see Hamlin Garland to Theodore Roosevelt, March 17, 1902, Series 1, Roosevelt Papers, and Jean Halloway, *Hamlin Garland*, pp. 130–31. On Grinnell and TR, see George Bird Grinnell to Theodore Roosevelt, September 14, 1903, Series 1, Roosevelt Papers. On Lummis and TR, see Charles F. Lummis to Roosevelt, October 8, 1901, Series 1, Roosevelt Papers. On Remington and TR, see White, *The Eastern Establishment*, passim; and Remington to Roosevelt, September, 1899, Series 1, Roosevelt Papers. On Wister and TR, see Wister, *Roosevelt*, passim. On Leupp and Roosevelt, see discussions of his special missions for the president in Leupp to Roosevelt, June 24, and September 3, 1903, Series 1, Roosevelt Papers; and June 14, 1904, Series 2, Roosevelt Papers.

37. Charles F. Lummis to Roosevelt, October 8, 1901, Series 1; Roosevelt Papers. See Roosevelt to Grinnell, September 27, 1901, Series 2, Roosevelt to Wister, June 7, 1902, Series 2; and Roosevelt to Remington, November 14, 1901, Series 2, all in Roosevelt Papers.

38. George Bird Grinnell to Theodore Roosevelt, September 14, 1903, Series 1, Roosevelt Papers.

39. Roosevelt to Grinnell, June 13, 1902, Series 2, Roosevelt Papers.

40. "Address at Tuskeegee Institute, Tuskeegee, Alabama, October 24, 1905," in Theodore Roosevelt, *Address and Papers*, p. 265; Roosevelt to King Edward VII, February 12, 1908, *Letters of Theodore Roosevelt*, ed. Elting E. Morison, 6:940. For Roosevelt's reasoning on the Japanese exclusion question, see Roosevelt to Frederic Remington, February 7, 1909, Series 2, Roosevelt Papers; and Roosevelt to Theodore Roosevelt, Jr., February 13, 1909, *Letters of Theodore Roosevelt*, 6:1520–21.

41. "Speech in San Francisco to Native Sons and Daughters of the Golden West," May 13, 1903, Series 5B, Roosevelt Papers; Roosevelt to James Wilson, secretary of agriculture, June 7, 1907, *Letters of Theodore Roosevelt*, 5:682. See also, Roosevelt to Elihu Root, ibid., 4:812.

42. Roosevelt, *Report of Hon. Theodore Roosevelt Made to the U.S. Civil Service Commission, upon a Visit to Certain Indian Reservations and Indian Schools in South Dakota, Nebraska and Kansas*, p. 12. For the progres-

sives' view of minority education in general, see Harvey Wish, "Negro Education and the Progressive Movement," pp. 184–201.

43. Roosevelt to Silas McBee, August 27, 1907, *Letters of Theodore Roosevelt*, 5:775–6. A great deal has been written about Roosevelt's racism. Howard Kennedy Beale, in *Theodore Roosevelt and the Rise of America to World Power*, and Rubin Weston, in *Racism in U.S. Imperialism*, argue for the importance of the president's racial attitudes in determining his foreign policy perspective. William Harbaugh, in *Power and Responsibility*, plays down this factor. The truth probably lies somewhere closer to Seth Schiener's statement: "It is not clear if he made his [racial] distinction for sociological or physiological reasons. In his writings, Roosevelt did not distinguish between the two; in fact, both environmental and physical explanations overlap." Seth Schiener, "President Theodore Roosevelt and the Negro, 1901–8," p. 170.

44. Roosevelt to Sir Harry Hamilton Johnson, July 11, 1908, *Letters of Theodore Roosevelt*, 6:1126. For a further discussion of Roosevelt's progressivism and imperialism, see Dewey Grantham, "The Progressive Movement and the Negro," in Charles E. Wynes, ed., *The Negro in the South Since 1865*, pp. 77–78.

45. "Speech at Hampton Institute," May 30, 1906, Series 5A, Roosevelt Papers. The comment about the Apaches is contained in Roosevelt to Charles Bonaparte, March 20, 1901, *Letters of Theodore Roosevelt*, 3:36–37. Roosevelt also defended the United States' suppression of the Philippine insurrection with the statement, "The reasoning which justifies our having made war against Sitting Bull also justifies our having checked the outbreak of Aguinaldo and his followers." Quoted in Weston, *Racism in U.S. Imperialism*, p. 557. For an extended discussion of the links between imperialism and the Indian question, see Walter L. Williams, "United States Indian Policy and the Debate over Philippine Annexation," 810–31.

46. Roosevelt, *A Book Lover's Holidays in the Open*, pp. 51, 74.

47. William Howard Taft, "Southern Democracy and Republican Principles," in *Present Day Problems*, p. 233; "Speech at Hampton Institute," November 20, 1909, Series 9A, Taft Papers; "Address of President Taft at the Indian School, Haskell Institute, Kansas," September 24, 1911, Series 9A, Taft Papers.

48. "Speech to the Society of American Indians at the White House," De-

cember 10, 1914, Series 7F, Woodrow Wilson Papers; see Arthur S. Link, *Wilson*, pp. 17–18; and A. E. Yoell to Woodrow Wilson, March 23, 1913, Series 4, Wilson Papers; Franklin K. Lane to Woodrow Wilson, May 22, 1913, Series 4, Wilson Papers; and Cato Sells to Albert S. Burleson, March 17, 1913, Series 2, Wilson Papers.

49. For a list of the votes used in the tabulation of these figures, see Appendix 1. For discussions of regional prerogatives in congressional discussions of reform legislation during this period, see Howard W. Allen, Aage R. Clausen, and Jerome M. Clubb, "Political Reform and Negro Rights in the Senate, 1909–15," pp. 191–212; and James Holt, *Congressional Insurgents and the Party System, 1909–1916*, especially chaps. 6 and 8.

50. *CR*, 59–2, 471. The chairmen of the Senate Indian Affairs Committee were James K. Jones (D-Ark.), 1893–95; Richard Pettigrew (R-S.Dak.), 1895–99; John Thurston (R-Nebr.), 1899–1901; William Stewart (R-Nev.), 1901–7; Moses Clapp (R-Minn.), 1907–11; Robert Gamble (R.-S.Dak.), 1911–13; William J. Stone (D-Mo.), 1913–15; Henry Ashurst (D-Ariz.), 1915–19; and Charles Curtis (R-Kans.), 1919–21.

51. Richard Pettigrew to E. Whittlesey, secretary of the Board of Indian Commissioners, January 25, 1897, RG 75, NA; *CR*, 57–1, 1944.

52. Roosevelt to Lyman Abbott, September 5, 1903, *Letters of Theodore Roosevelt*, 3:590. See also William A. Jones to Theodore Roosevelt, March 20, 1901, Series 1, Roosevelt Papers.

Chapter 4

1. The racial tensions of these years and their effect on social scientists are described in Barbara Miller Solomon, *Ancestors and Immigrants*; Mark Haller, *Eugenics: Hereditarian Attitudes in American Thought* (New Brunswick, N.J.: Rutgers University Press, 1963); I. A. Newby, *Jim Crow's Defense*; George M. Frederickson, *The Black Image in the White Mind*; John S. Haller, *Outcasts from Evolution*; and George W. Stocking, Jr., "American Social Scientists and Race Theory, 1890–1915." A good description of the growing interest in race in a particular area of the social sciences is Ethel Shanas, "The American Journal of Sociology through Fifty Years," pp. 522–33. The article describes a content analysis of the *Journal*; results for 1895–

1919 are on page 524. The role of scientific racism in Indian-white relations during these years is also discussed briefly in Berkhofer, *White Man's Indians*, pp. 59–61.

2. McGee, "The Trend of Human Progress," pp. 401–2, 403.

3. McGee, "The Science of Humanity," p. 323; idem, "The Trend of Human Progress," pp. 409, 424, 436, 442, 444.

4. McGee, "The Trend of Human Progress," pp. 429, 435.

5. Ibid., p. 446.

6. Ibid., pp. 446–47. For McGee's association with imperialism and scientific racism, see Edward A. Atkinson to McGee, June 10, 1899, and Hinton Rowan Helper to McGee, August 28, 1899, both in McGee Papers.

7. McGee, "Man's Place in Nature," 12, 13; idem, "Anthropology and Its Larger Problems," in Howard J. Rogers, ed., *Congress of Arts and Sciences*, pp. 461–62.

8. W. J. McGee to Franz Boas, September 18, 1903, Boas Papers.

9. W. J. McGee to Franz Boas, April 2, 1910, Boas Papers. For a description of Powell's and McGee's last years at the BAE, see Franz Boas to Carl Schurz, August 12, 1903, Boas Papers, and Hinsley, *Savages and Scientists*, chap. 8.

10. William Henry Holmes, "Museum Presentation of Anthropology," *Proc. AAAS* (1898): 487. The bureau's contacts with the Indian Office were few once Powell passed from the scene. In an exchange of correspondence with the Board of Indian Commissioners in 1911, Frederick W. Hodge, who succeeded Holmes as chief, noted that there had been only one minor incidence of cooperation in recent years. Hodge pointed out that the bureau had to be careful of its funding, and that it "hesitated to offer its services unless it could be sure they were desired." Nevertheless, he added, "the bureau is anxious to render to the Government any service, economic or otherwise, that may lie in its power, and is willing to make any reasonable sacrifice to promote the proper administration of our Indian affairs." See Frederick Hodge to Merrill Gates, January 28, 1911, and "Memorandum of a Call on F. W. Hodge, . . . May 3, 1912," both in the Board of Indian Commissioners General Correspondence, Entry 1386, RG 75, NA. Hinsley describes Holmes's tenure in *Savages and Scientists*, chap. 9.

11. Holmes, "Some Problems of the American Race," p. 166.

12. Ibid., p. 161.

13. W. J. McGee to Richard H. Pratt, August 25, 1902, Pratt Papers; George S. Painter, "The Future of the American Negro," pp. 410, 411.

Painter, who had taught at Tufts and Clark universities, was, at the time this article was published, a professor of philosophy at New York State Teacher's College. For another example of this point of view, see "What Indian Children Are Taught," *Scientific American Supplement*, April 13, 1907, p. 315.

14. The only modern study of Brinton is Regna Darnell, "Daniel Garrison Brinton." In her essay, Darnell emphasizes Brinton's evolutionism and his belief in psychic unity as an important unifying theme in his career. While I agree with her conclusions, within the context of the 1890s, Brinton's judgments of Indian culture were among the most racially oriented in the academic community. Berkhofer, in his *White Man's Indian*, shares this view; see p. 60. For an example of Brinton's evolutionism and optimism, see Daniel Garrison Brinton, *Races and Peoples*, especially p. 300.

15. Brinton, *The Basis of Social Relations*, p. 20; Brinton, "The Factors of Heredity and Environment in Man," *AA* 11 (September 1898): 273, 275.

16. Brinton, *The American Race*, p. 39; idem, *The Basis of Social Relations*, pp. 70–71.

17. Brinton, *Races and Peoples*, pp. 294–95, 287.

18. William Z. Ripley, *The Races of Europe*; Madison Grant, *The Passing of the Great Race*; Frederick L. Hoffman, "Race Traits and Tendencies of the American Negro," pp. 1–329.

19. Stocking, *Race, Culture and Evolution*, chap. 10; idem, "Social Scientists and Race Theory," chaps. 3 and 7 and app. B; Franklin H. Giddings, "A Provisional Distribution of the Population of the U.S. into Psychological Classes," *Psychology Review* 8 (July 1901): 337–49.

20. Lindley M. Keasbey, "Civology—A Suggestion," *Popular Science Monthly*, April 1907, p. 368; Madison Grant, *The Conquest of a Continent*, p. 24; and Theodore Lothrop Stoddard, *The Rising Tide of Color against White World Supremacy*, pp. 125–26.

21. Stoddard, *Rising Tide of Color*, p. 126; Popenoe and Johnson, *Applied Eugenics*, p. 132.

22. Grant, *Passing of the Great Race*, 15–16; Seth K. Humphrey, *The Racial Prospect*, p. 176; Ernest W. Coffin, "On the Education of Backward Races," p. 56; Edgar L. Hewitt, "Ethnic Factors in Education," p. 10.

23. See Henry F. Suksdorf, *Our Race Problems*, p. 51.

24. For an early attack on social-evolutionist theories in light of new research, see Talcott Williams, "Was Primitive Man a Modern Savage?"

p. 548. For the same type of attack on racial formalism, see Albion Small, "The Scope of Sociology," *AJS* 5 (1899–1900): 22–52. The general direction of these critiques is discussed in Stocking, "Social Scientists and Race Theory," pp. 295–319; and his *Race, Culture and Evolution*, pp. 163–69. Also helpful is Frederick W. Preston, "Red, White, Black and Blue," pp. 27–36; and James R. Hayes, "Sociology and Racism," pp. 330–41.

25. Otis T. Mason, "Mind and Matter in Culture," p. 187.

26. Ibid., p. 190.

27. Frederick Webb Hodge, ed., *The Handbook of American Indians North of Mexico*, 1:427.

28. Mason, "The Uncivilized Mind in the Presence of Higher Phases of Civilization," pp. 347, 355, 361.

29. Richmond Mayo-Smith, "Assimilation of Nationalities in the United States," p. 649; William Isaac Thomas, "The Mind of Woman and the Lower Races," p. 452.

30. Grinnell, *The Indians of Today*, p. 7; Fayette A. McKenzie, *The Indian in Relation to the White Population of the United States*, p. 42.

31. McKenzie, "The American Indian of Today and Tomorrow," p. 140; Sarah E. Simons, "Social Assimilation," p. 550. For an account of the Society of American Indians, see Hazel Hertzberg, *The Search for an American Indian Identity*; for a sketch of McKenzie's career, see the Brookings Institution, Institute for Government Research, *The Problem of Indian Administration*, p. 83.

32. Grinnell, *The American Indian Today*, p. 156; Frank W. Blackmar, "The Socialization of the American Indian," p. 661.

33. "The Jesup North Pacific Expedition," in George W. Stocking, ed., *The Shaping of American Anthropology*, p. 108. Franz Boas to Warren K. Moorehead, October 7, 1907, Boas Papers.

34. Franz Boas, *The Mind of Primitive Man*, p. 94.

35. Ibid., pp. 28, 122–23.

36. Ibid., pp. 102, 104.

37. Ibid., pp. 114–15; Boas, "Some Traits of Primitive Culture," *Journal of American Folklore* 17 (October–December 1904): 253.

38. Stocking, *Race, Culture and Evolution*, p. 203; Boas, *Mind of Primitive Man*, pp. 203, 206; Ibid., p. 209.

39. Clark Wissler, *The American Indian*, p. 206; idem, "The Psychologi-

cal Aspects of the Culture-Environment Relation," 224–25; idem, *The American Indian*, pp. 338–39.

40. Wissler, *The American Indian*, p. 208.

41. Alfred L. Kroeber, "Eighteen Professions," p. 285 (emphasis in original); idem, "Inheritance by Magic," p. 37.

42. Kroeber, "The Morals of an Uncivilized People," p. 446.

43. Robert H. Lowie, *Culture and Ethnology*, p. 66; idem, *Primitive Society*, p. 6.

44. See Stocking, "The Scientific Reaction against Cultural Anthropology," in *Race, Culture, and Evolution*, pp. 270–307, as well as his "Anthropology as Kulturkampf: Science and Politics in the Career of Franz Boas," in Goldschmidt, *The Uses of Anthropology*, pp. 33–50. See also Regna Darnell, "The Development of American Anthropology," pt. 4.

45. Kroeber, "Ishi, the Last Aborigine," p. 308.

46. Boas, *Mind of Primitive Man*, pp. 16–17.

47. Ibid., p. 253; Livingston Farrand, *Basis of American History*, p. 271.

48. Ibid., p. 267; John R. Swanton, pp. 469–70; Alfred Kroeber quoted in "The Spectator," *Outlook*, May 16, 1908, p. 106.

Chapter 5

1. Charles J. Kappler, ed., *U.S. Laws and Statutes; Indian Affairs: Laws and Treaties* (Washington, D.C.: Government Printing Office, 1904), 2:661–63.

2. *CR*, 53–2, 6251; *CR*, 52–1, 2951.

3. *CR*, 53–2, 7685.

4. *CR*, 53–2, 7672–3.

5. Quoted in *CR*, 54–2, 1260.

6. Welsh to members of the Indian Rights Association, January 27, 1894, IRA Papers.

7. Hugh L. Scott to "Major Davis," August 17, 1896, Hugh L. Scott Papers (Scott was the army commander at Fort Sill when he wrote these words); *ARCIA* (1895): 1023. See also the exchange between Dawes and the Cheyenne and Arapaho agent, Major A. E. Woodson, at the 1897 Lake Mohonk Conference. Major Woodson gave the assembled reformers a glowing ac-

count of the progress of his charges, while Dawes repeatedly asked skeptical questions from the floor. *ARCIA* (1897): 979–83. For a detailed description of the pace of allotment, which confirms that allotment activity was heaviest after 1899, see Leonard A. Carlson, *Indians, Bureaucrats and Land*, pp. 73–75.

8. *ARCIA* (1898): 75. For the Indian Rights Association's support for the Curtis Act, see Francis Leupp to Herbert Welsh, March 11, 1898, IRA Papers.

9. Samuel Brosius to Herbert Welsh, February 12, 1899, IRA Papers.

10. George Kennan, "Have Reservation Indians Any Vested Rights?" p. 765.

11. 187 *U.S.*, 565–6 (1903); George Kennan, "Indian Lands and Fair Play," p. 501.

12. Quoted in *House Report* no. 443, 58th Cong., 2d sess., pp. 4–5.

13. *CR*, 56–1, 1913.

14. *CR*, 57–1, 4803.

15. Herbert Welsh to Matthew K. Sniffen, February 18, 1904, IRA Papers; *House Report* no. 890, 58th Cong., 2d sess., p. 5; 33 *U.S. Statutes* 321 (Devil's Lake); 33 *U.S. Statutes* 303 (Flathead); 33 *U.S. Statutes* 1069–70 (Uintah); and 33 *U.S. Statutes* 1016 (Wind River).

16. *CR*, 58–2, 1945.

17. *ARCIA* (1903): 3.

18. *ARCIA* (1895): 34; *ARCIA* (1896): 272. For an overview of the government's leasing policies, see Sutton, *Indian Land Tenure*, pp. 125–35.

19. *ARCIA* (1898): 1113.

20. *IRA AR* (1900): 59.

21 *ARCIA* (1902): 66; Francis Leupp to Theodore Roosevelt, June 23, 1905, Series 1, Roosevelt Papers. For a discussion of land sales under the Dawes Act, see David M. Holford, "The Subversion of the Indian Land Allotment System, 1887–1934," pp. 12–21.

22. *CR*, 52–1, 2404; William S. Holman to Herbert Welsh, March 9, 1894, IRA Papers.

23. Henry Cabot Lodge to Herbert Welsh, March 15, 1894, IRA Papers; *CR*, 56–1, 1407, 1408.

24. *ARCIA* (1903): 2.

25. Theodore Roosevelt to Herbert Welsh, January 23, 1895, and Alice Fletcher to Herbert Welsh, February 12, 1895, IRA Papers.

26. Francis Leupp to Herbert Welsh, February 6, 1895, IRA Papers; "Dealing with the Indians Individually," *Independent*, December 14, 1905, p. 1419.

27. *ARCIA* (1905): 1, 8, 9, 7. Leupp's views bear a surface similarity to those of John Collier. Nevertheless, Leupp's assumption that Native Americans belonged to a "backward" race and his commitment to rapid assimilation make the connections between him and FDR's Indian commissioner more complex than most historians have imagined. For an example of the Leupp-to-Collier argument, see Donald L. Parman, "Francis Ellington Leupp," in Kvasnicka and Viola, *Commissioners of Indian Affairs*, pp. 224, 231.

28. Francis Leupp, "A Fresh Phase of the Indian Problem," pp. 367, 368.

29. Francis Leupp to Samuel Bosius, March 2, 1907, IRA Papers.

30. Francis Leupp to James R. Garfield, February 20, 1909, Garfield Papers.

31. Samuel Brosius to Ezra Thayer, June 10, 1907, IRA Papers.

32. *IRA AR* (1905): 72; McKenzie, *The Indian in Relation to the White*, p. 45.

33. Francis Leupp to James R. Garfield, February 20, 1909, Garfield Papers; 34 *U.S. Statutes* 183.

34. Samuel Brosius to Francis Leupp, March 26, 1906, IRA Papers; *Senate Report* no. 198, 59th Cong., 1st sess., p. 2; *ARCIA* (1906): 30.

35. Francis Leupp to Theodore Roosevelt, January 23, 1906, Series 1, Roosevelt Papers.

36. The law covering "noncompetent land sales" is 34 *U.S. Statutes* 1018.

37. The proposal and the Indian Rights Association's reaction are contained in Samuel Brosius to Members of Congress, March 21, 1908, IRA Papers. Leupp's defense of fee patenting is in his article, "A Review of President Roosevelt's Administration," p. 304.

38. Leupp, *The Indian and His Problem*, p. 93; James R. Garfield to the Speaker of the House of Representatives, Feb. 6, 1908, Entry 121, General Service file #013, RG 75, NA; ARCIA (1906): 27. See also Leupp, "The Red Man, Incorporated," p. 20; and idem, "The Indian Land Troubles and How to Solve Them," pp. 468–72.

39. *ARCIA* (1906): 4.

40. See 34 *U.S. Statutes* 1015–34 and 35 *U.S. Statutes* 70 for the congressional authorizations to grant long-term leases. Leupp defended his plan in his valedictory letter to James R. Garfield (February 9, 1909, p. 20, Gar-

field Papers) and in an article written after his retirement, "The Red Man's Burden," p. 750.

41. 33 U.S. Statutes 1016; *ARCIA* (1905): 382; Rev. James B. Funsten, "The Indian as a Worker," p. 878.

42. *ARCIA* (1905): 147; 34 *U.S. Statutes* 375; for Yakima, see *House Report* no. 1477, 59th Cong., 1st sess.; the Blackfoot agreement was passed on March 1, 1907, as part of the annual appropriations bill—see 34 *U.S. Statutes* 1035; for the Flathead opening, see 35 *U.S. Statutes* 448–49.

43. *CR*, 60–1, 1909.

44. *ARCIA* (1906): 369; *ARCIA* (1907): 54; 34 *U.S. Statutes*, 53–54 (Yakima); ibid., 1035 (Blackfoot); 35 *U.S. Statutes*, 449 (Flathead).

45. *Winters* v. *U.S.*, 28 *Supreme Court Reporter* 212; *U.S.* v. *Wightman* 230 F 277 (1916). See also *Sowards et al.* v. *Meagher et al.* 108 P 1112 (1910) and *Skeem* v. *U.S. et al.* 273 F 93 (1921).

46. "Plan for Cooperation Between the Indian Office and the Forest Service," enclosed in James R. Garfield to Secretary of Agriculture, January 22, 1908, Central Classified File 5–25, "Cooperation—Forest Service," pt. 1, RG 48, NA; F. E. Leupp to James R. Garfield, February 20, 1909, Container 143, James R. Garfield Papers; Walter L. Fisher to Commissioner of Indian Affairs, April 10, 1911, Central Classified File 5–25, "Cooperation—General," pt. 1, RG 48, NA. For an account of the Forest Service's handling of its responsibilities, see Gifford Pinchot to Secretary of Agriculture, July 23, 1909, Central Classified File 5–25, "Cooperation—Forest Service," pt. 1, RG 48, NA.

47. F. E. Leupp, "The Red Man's Burden," p. 752.

48. "Speech by Matthew K. Sniffen to the Lake Mohonk Conference," November 1910, copy filed with correspondence in IRA Papers.

49. *ARCIA* (1912): 5–6.

50. James McLaughlin, *My Friend the Indian*, p. 389; *CR*, 61–2, 6081.

51. Robert G. Valentine, "Making Good Indians," pp. 608, 611; for the text of the omnibus act, see 36 *U.S. Statutes* 855–63.

52. Chalmers G. Hill to Walter L. Fisher, May 27, 1911, Walter L. Fisher Papers.

53. McLaughlin, *My Friend the Indian*, pp. 403–4; McKenzie, *The Indian in Relation to the White*, pp. 47–49; Herbert Welsh, "IRA Circular," January 14, 1907, IRA Papers; Frederick H. Abbott to Walter L. Fisher, May

21, 1912, File 5–6, "Competent Indians," Central Classified Files, Office of the Secretary, RG 48, NA.

54. *CR*, 59–1, 3273; *CR*, 59–2, 2344.

55. "Indians as Wards," *Independent*, February 13, 1908, p. 381.

56. For a discussion of Owen's bill (S.6767, 62d Cong. 2d sess.), see Samuel Adams, first assistant secretary of interior, to Robert Gamble, June 1, 1912, Central Files: Legislation, File 1–64, Administrative General (62d Congress), RG 48; Myers's speech is in *CR*, 64–1, 2111–2, and the creation of the commission is described in *CR*, 63–1, 2038.

57. Franklin K. Lane to Scott Ferris, July 14, 1913, Entry 121, File 013, General Service, RG 75; Franklin K. Lane, "From the Warpath to the Plow," p. 87.

58. *Senate Document* no. 984, 63d Cong., 3d sess., p. 10; *CR*, 64–1, 7572; *CR*, 64–2, 2110.

59. *IRA AR* (1913): 52; *IRA AR* (1915): 4; Warren K. Moorehed, *The American Indian in the United States*, p. 434; Frederick H. Abbott to Robert LaFollette, June 17, 1915, LaFollette Papers.

60. *New York Times*, October 29, 1916, sec. v, 10.

61. This description of the ceremony is based on reports in the *Sioux City (Iowa) Tribune*, May 15, 1916, taken from the clippings in File 5–6, "Competent Indians," Central Classified Files, Office of the Secretary, RG 48, NA. The ceremony was also described in Harvey D. Jacobs, "Uncle Sam—The Great White Father," p. 701; "A Ritual of Citizenship," *Outlook*, May 24, 1916, pp. 161–62; and Pfaller, *James McLaughlin*, pp. 333–38.

62. *CR*, 64–2, 2112; Herbert Welsh to Cato Sells, March 23, 1917, Entry 121, General Service Files, File 020, RG 75, NA.

63. Cato Sells, "A Declaration of Policy in the Administration of Indian Affairs," April 17, 1917, reprinted in *ARCIA* (1917): 3–4; ibid., p. 5; Circular, dated April, 1917, copy in Richard H. Pratt Papers.

64. Samuel Brosius to Matthew Sniffen, April 17, 1917, IRA Papers; "A New Step in Our Indian Policy," *Outlook*, May 23, 1917, p. 136; Superintendent of Red Cliff, Wisconsin, Agency to Cato Sells, April 27, 1917, Entry 121, File 020, General Service, RG 75, NA.

65. The one-million-acre figure is from *ARCIA* (1918): 19; Sells, "The First Americans as Loyal Citizens," p. 524; ARCIA (1919): 8; see 40 *U.S. Statutes* 591 and 41 *U.S. Statutes* 9; ARCIA (1920): 169.

66. *ARCIA* (1920): 9; *CR*, 66–1, 258.

67. Theodore Roosevelt to Francis Leupp, September 4, 1907, Series 2, Roosevelt Papers. For a description of the aftermath of one "Last Arrow" ceremony, see Yankton Superintendent A. W. Leech to Franklin K. Lane, June 21, 1916, File 5–6, "Competent Indians," Central Classified Files, Office of the Secretary, RG 48, NA. After describing the large number of automobile purchases and land sales completed after the ceremony, the agent added, "I regret that I cannot furnish a more favorable report . . . but when the disposition of the Indian and the greed and activity of the white man is taken into consideration, it is no more than could have been expected."

68. *ARCIA* (1917): 26–29; Calvin H. Asbury to Malcom McDowell, secretary of the Board of Indian Commissioners, December 24, 1917, Entry 1386, Officials, 1915–18, RG 75, NA; *ARCIA* (1920): 23.

69. Owen Wilson, "Rescuing a People by an Irrigating Ditch," pp. 14815–17; *CR* 63–2, 10787.

70. *ANR*, Fort Hall (1920), sec. 4, 10; see *House Document* no. 387, 66th Cong., 2d sess., p. 10.

71. Cato Sells to Board of Indian Commissioners, March 16, 1914, Entry 121, File 339, General Service, RG 75, NA.

72. 41 *U.S. Statutes* 31–32. Treaty reservations could be mined under an 1891 law. For a description of the background to the Hayden bill, see Lawrence C. Kelly, *The Navajo Indians and Federal Indian Policy*, pp. 39–42.

73. *CR*, 65–3, 4940. Kelly describes the impact of this attitude on the Navajos in his *Navajo Indians and Federal Policy*, pp. 43–47 and chap. 4.

74. Carlson's *Indians, Bureaucrats and Land* provides striking confirmation of this view. Carlson shows that as the pace of allotment quickened, whites gained readier access to Native American resources. Self-sufficient Indian agriculture gave way to economic dependence and poverty. Carlson argues that this process proves the government failed to act as the guardian of the tribes. It is my contention that policy makers and bureaucrats *redefined* their role as guardians, rejecting the old objective (the Indian as yeoman farmer) and adopting a new one—the Indian as colonial subject.

Chapter 6

1. *ARCIA* (1895): 354; *ARCIA* (1896): 1016.

2. *ARCIA* (1895): 338–39.

3. *ARCIA* (1892): 55.

4. *ARCIA* (1899): 15.

5. *CR*, 55–2, 1008; *CR*, 57–2, 1427.

6. *CR*, 58–3, 1147.

7. *CR*, 57–2, 1426.

8. *CR*, 57–2, 1278; Lyman Abbott, "Our Indian Problem," p. 724.

9. Frank W. Blackmar, "Indian Education," pp. 814–15; Herbert Welsh, "Comment on Thomas Morgan's 'Indian Education,'" p. 178; Hollis Burke Frissell, "What is the Relation of the Indian of the Present Decade to the Indian of the Future?" reprinted in *ARCIA* (1900): 470; *ARCIA* (1898): 1096.

10. Frissell, "The Indian Problem," *Proc. NEA* (1901): 628–83, 692.

11. Calvin M. Woodward, "What Shall Be Taught in an Indian School?" *ARCIA* (1901): 471, 472, 473; Garland, "Indian Education," *Proc. NEA* (1903): 397–98.

12. Lummis, "Lame Dancing Masters," pp. 356–57; idem, "A New Indian Policy," *Land of Sunshine*, December, 1901, p. 464; John T. Bramhall, "Red, Black and Yellow," *Overland Monthly*, February, 1901, p. 723; "Indian Industrial Development," *Outlook*, January 12, 1901, p. 101; "Cutting Indians' Hair," *Harper's Weekly*, March 22, 1902, p. 357; Ella H. Cooper, "How to Educate the Indians," p. 454.

13. *ARCIA* (1901): 431. See also Reel's first annual report, *ARCIA* (1898): 334–49.

14. Commissioner of Indian Affairs, Circular #43, September 19, 1900, Entry #718, RG 75, NA; Estelle Reel to William A. Jones, August 20, 1904, Special Series A, Box 8, RG 75, NA.

15. See "Circulars Issued by the Education Division" (no. 85), November 6, 1902, Entry #718, RG 75, NA; ibid., (no. 48), February 18, 1901. For a fuller view of Jones's perspective, see *ARCIA* (1901): 1–5.

16. *ARCIA* (1901): 9, 426, 418–57.

17. George Bird Grinnell to Estelle Reel, April 14, 1902, Entry #173, RG 75, NA.

18. Thomas J. Morgan, "Indian Education," p. 173.

19. *ARCIA* (1903): 381; Samuel Brosius to Herbert Welsh, November 14, 1900, IRA Papers; *Proc. NEA* (1904): 983, 984.

20. *ARCIA* (1905): 1, 3; Leupp, "Indians and Their Education," *Proc. NEA* (1907): 71.

21. Leupp, *The Indian and His Problem*, p. 139; idem, "Back to Nature for the Indian," p. 336; *ARCIA* (1905): 8–9.

22. Charles B. Dyke, "Essential Features in the Education of the Child Races," *Proc. NEA* (1909): 929, 930, 932; Leupp, "Why Booker T. Washington Has Succeeded in His Life Work," p. 327. The role of racial "pessimism" in the development of industrial education is a central theme of Donald Spivey, *Schooling for the New Slavery*. For the impact of these ideas on the administration of the United States' colonies, see Glenn Anthony May, *Social Engineering in the Philippines*.

23. G. Stanley Hall, "How Far Are the Principles of Education along Indigenous Lines Applicable to American Indians?" p. 1163; Coffin, "Education of Backward Races," p. 46. It should be noted that Hall called for greater sensitivity to Indian traditions and respect for tribal lifeways. Coming before the emergence of the concept of cultural pluralism, however, his pleas were understood as recommendations for a lowering of governmental expectations.

24. *ARCIA* (1908): 24; Commissioner of Indian Affairs Circular #175, December 3, 1907, Entry 718, RG 75, NA.

25. *ARCIA* (1905): 3; *ARCIA* (1906): 407.

26. Marvin Lazerson, *Origins of the Urban School*, p. 245; "The Need for Practical Training for the Indians," *Journal of Education* 69 (March 18, 1909): 300.

27. *ARCIA* (1905): 5; Leupp, *The Indian and His Problem*, p. 156.

28. See *ARCIA* (1906): 9 (forty-nine schoolboys and three adults took home $1,672.56 for six weeks' work); C. W. Goodman to Charles Dagenett, September 7, 1908, Entry 121, General Service File, File #920, RG 75, NA. Goodman went on to say that Indians received $6–$20 per month while whites received $15–$40.

29. *ARCIA* (1906): 8, 15.

30. Herman Charles, secretary of the Imperial Valley Board of Trade, to Charles Dagenett, April 30, 1908, Entry 121, General Service File, File #920, RG 75, NA; F. E. Leupp to James R. Garfield, February 10, 1908, Series 1, Roosevelt Papers.

31. *ARCIA* (1907): 20.

32. School Circular Number 161 (July 1, 1907), Entry 718, RG 75, NA; Circular Number 216, (June 21, 1908), Entry 718, RG 75, NA; Leupp, "Back to Nature for the Indian," p. 337; F. E. Leupp to E. A. Morse, December 30, 1908, Entry 121, File 803 General Service, RG 75, NA; see action on H.R. 26916, 60th Cong., 2d sess. In February 1909, Congress eliminated the four boarding schools and authorized the construction of thirty new day schools.

33. *CR*, 60–1, 1707, 1712. For school attendance figures, see *ARCIA* (1905–10).

34. *ARCIA* (1906): 46; see introduction in Marvin Lazerson and W. Norton Grubb, eds., *American Education and Vocationalism*, especially p. 25.

35. *ARCIA* (1909): 4; *ARCIA* (1915): 7, 8.

36. *ARCIA* (1910): 14–15.

37. *ARCIA* (1916): 9.

38. Ibid., pp. 11–21, 22.

39. *ARCIA* (1910): 8; Robert G. Valentine to D. D. Wiley, December 18, 1909, Entry 121, General Service File #920, RG 75, NA; Valentine also increased the number of Indian employees of the Indian Office. See Diane T. Putney, "Robert Grosvenor Valentine," in Kvasnicka and Viola, eds., *Commissioners of Indian Affairs*, pp. 235–36.

40. *ARCIA* (1918): 36.

41. *ARCIA* (1909): 20, *ANR, Walker River (1911): 10; ANR*, Cheyenne and Arapaho (1910): 14.

42. Robert G. Valentine to W. W. Scott, August 8, 1911, Entry 121, File 803, Crow Agency, RG 75, NA; *ANR*, Crow (1913), "Schools."

43. See *ANR*, Fort Lapwai (1910), "Education," *ANR*, Fort Lapwai (1912), "Public Schools;" *ANR*, Yakima (1913) 3:2; "Response to Circular #612, March 14, 1912," from Bishop, California, Special Series A, RG 75, NA.

44. *ARCIA* (1914): 7; Carl Price to Cato Sells, January 9, 1916, and Edgar Meritt to Price, January 21, 1916, Entry 121, General Service File, File 803, RG 75, NA.

45. *ANR*, Uintah and Ouray (1915): 15; ibid., (1919): 15, ibid., (1920): 11.

46. Charles H. Asbury to Edgar Meritt, January 29, 1919, Entry 121, File 803, Crow Agency, RG 75, NA.

47. *ARCIA* (1919): 26.

48. *ARCIA* (1920): 11.

Chapter 7

1. *ARCIA* (1895): 249. The agent's fears were repeated in 1899; see *AR-CIA* (1899): 283.

2. William B. Hornblower, "The Legal Status of the Indians," *Reports of the Fourteenth Annual meeting of the American Bar Association* 14 (1891), p. 277; Board of Indian Commissioners quoted in *ARCIA* (1899): pt. ii, 236–37.

3. 30 *U.S.* 1 (1831). For a discussion of Marshall's philosophy, see Wilcomb E. Washburn, *Red Man's Land/White Man's Law*, pp. 59–74.

4. *U.S.* v. *Mullin*, 71 F. 685, (1895).

5. *Hitchcock* v. *U.S. ex rel Big Boy*, 22 *Appeals Cases, District of Columbia*, 284–85 (1904). For the development of the doctrine of federal jurisdiction in this area, see also *U.S.* v. *Gardner*, 133 F. 285 (1904); and *McKnight* v. *U.S.*, 130 F. 659 (1904).

6. *Tiger* v. *Western Investment Co.*, 221 *U.S.* 286 (1911).

7. *U.S.* v. *Fitzgerald*, 201 F. 296 (1912); *Heckman* v. *U.S.*, 224 *U.S.* 445 (1912), emphasis added.

8. Lyman Abbott, "The Rights of Man," *Outlook*, June 1901, p. 351.

9. *U.S.* v. *Rickert*, 188 *U.S.* 437, 442, 445 (1903).

10. *U.S.* v. *Thurston Co., Nebraska*, 143 F. 289, 292 (1906).

11. *U.S.* v. *Schock*, 187 F. 862 (1911); *Choate* v. *Trapp*, 224 *U.S.* 665 (1911); *Colman J. Ward et al* v. *Board of County Commissioners of Love County, Oklahoma*, 253, *U.S.* 17 (1920); *Indian Illumination Oil Co.* v. *State of Oklahoma*, 240 *U.S.* 522 (1916); *U.S.* v. *Pearson Co. Treasurer et al*, 231 F. 522 (1916); and *U.S.* v. *Board of County Commissioners of Osage Co., Oklahoma*, 251 *U.S.* 130, 133 (1919).

12. *Matter of Heff*, 197 U.S. 497, 499, 508 (1905).

13. *House Report* no. 1558, 59th Cong. 1st sess., pp. 2, 1.

14. *Senate Report* no. 1998, 59th Cong., 1st sess., pp. 3–4.

15. *CR*, 59–1, 4655.

16. *ARCIA* (1906): 128, 46; and see Samuel Brosius to Merrill Gates, October 30, 1908, IRA Papers.

17. *ANR*, Cheyenne and Arapaho, 1918, I, 2.

18. *Dick* v. *U.S.*, 208 *U.S.* 354 (1908); *U.S.* v. *Celestine*, 215 *U.S.* 278 (1909); and *U.S.* v. *Sutton*, 215 *U.S.* 291 (1909).

19. *Hallowell* v. *U.S.*, 221 *U.S.* 324 (1911).

20. *Mosier* v. *U.S.*, 198 *F.* 58, 59 (1912).

21. *U.S.* v. *Sandoval*, 231 *U.S.* 39, 45–46 (1913).

22. *U.S.* v. *Nice*, 241 *U.S.* 600 (1916), emphasis mine. The background of the *Nice* decision and its implications for subsequent litigation are discussed in David H. Getches, et al., *Cases and Materials on Federal Indian Law*, pp. 495–99.

23. 23 *U.S. Statutes*, 385 (1885); 24 *U.S. Statutes* 388–91, sec. 6 (1887); and see *U.S.* v. *Kiya*, 126 *F.* 879 (1903); and *State* v. *Howard*, 74 *Pac.* 382 (1903).

24. *In re Now—Ge-Zhuck*, 76 *P.* 880 (1904); *Report of the Twenty-Sixth Annual Meeting of the American Bar Association* 26 (1903): 498.

25. *ARCIA* (1898): 96–100 and *ARCIA* (1899): 130–31.

26. *ARCIA* (1902): 288.

27. *IRA AR* (1906): 46. Leupp's falling out with the IRA is described by Donald Parman, "Francis Ellington Leupp," in Kvasnicka and Viola, eds., *Commissioners of Indian Affairs*, pp. 224–30.

28. Samuel Brosius to Matthew Sniffen, June 15, 1908, IRA Papers; Francis Leupp to Charles C. Binney, November 11, 1908, IRA Papers. For a detailed description of the incident, see Parman, "The 'Big Stick' in Indian Affairs: The Bai-a-lil-le Incident in 1909," pp. 343–60.

29. Leupp to George Bird Grinnell, December 26, 1908, James R. Garfield Papers; see also the statement from the Boston Indian Citizenship Committee December 16, 1908, IRA Papers.

30. Theodore Roosevelt to John Davis Long, Edward Henry Clement, and John S. Lockwood, December 29, 1908, *Letters of Theodore Roosevelt* 6: 1449, 1450.

31. *Ex Parte Bi-a-lil-le et al.*, 100 *P.* 451 (1909). The Arizona court used a spelling of the Navajo leader's name that varies from the one adopted by subsequent commentators.

32. *215 U.S.* 290–91 (1909).

33. 232 *U.S.* 449, 450 (1913).

34. Response to Circular #612, March 14, 1912, from Fond du Lac, Wis., Special Series A, RG 75, NA; ibid., from Neah Bay. For a summary of the responses to Luddington's survey, see Appendix 3.

35. "Rough Draft of an Analysis of Answers Sent by Superintendents to Circular #612," March 14, 1912, Special Series A, RG 75, NA.

36. For voting statistics, see C. F. Hauke to Ruby Bans, March 2, 1919,

Entry 121, File 128, General Service, RG 75, NA; McKenzie, *The Indian in Relation to the White*, p. 35; *Cofield* v. *Farrell*, 134 *Pac.* 409 (1913).

37. For a brief description of the Supreme Court in these years, see Robert G. McCloskey, *The American Supreme Court* (Chicago: University of Chicago Press, 1960), chap. 5 and pp. 208–19; and C. Vann Woodward, *Origins of the New South*, chap. 12.

38. See Colorado Constitution of 1876, Art. 7, Sec. 1; Montana *Laws of 1913*, chap. 1; Nebraska Constitution of 1875; Art. 6, Sec. 1; Oregon Constitution, Art. 2, Sec. 2; South Dakota Constitution of 1889, Art. 7, Sec. 1; and Wyoming Constitution, Art. 6, Sec. 10. The Oklahoma law was struck down by the U.S. Supreme Court in 1915. For the Nebraska decision, see *State* v. *Norris*, 55 *N.W.*, 1086 (1893). For South Dakota statistics, see South Dakota Secretary of State, *Annual Report* (1910); U.S. Bureau of the Census, *Thirteenth Census of the U.S. Population*, Vol. 3 (Washington: Government Printing Office, 1913).

39. *Anderson* v. *Matthews*, 163 P. 905 (1917).

40. California Constitution of 1849, Art. 2, Sec. 1; Minnesota Constitution of 1857, Art. 7, Sec. 1; North Dakota Constitution of 1889, Art. 5, Sec. 121; Oklahoma Constitution of 1907, Art. 3, Sec. 1; and Wisconsin Constitution of 1848, Art. 3, Sec. 1. Oklahoma's reasoning in this instance was revealed in *Atwater* v. *Hassett*, 111 P. 802 (1910).

41. *ARCIA* (1896): 143; *Opsahl* v. *Johnson*, 163 *N.W.* 988 (1917).

42. Idaho Constitution of 1890, Art. 6, Sec. 3; New Mexico Constitution of 1911, Art. 7, Sec. 1; and Washington Constitution of 1889, Art. 6, Sec. 1. New Mexico allowed Pueblo Indians to vote, however. See *U.S.* v. *Ortez*, 1 *New Mexico Reports* 422; Arizona Constitution of 1912, Art. 7, Sec. 2; Nevada Constitution of 1864, Art. 2, Sec. 1; and Par. 11, Sec. 20–2–14, *Utah Code Annotated, 1953* (first adopted in 1898); Arizona Secretary of State, *Annual Report* (1912), and U.S. Bureau of Census, *Thirteenth Census of the U.S. Population*, II. Nevada's laws were clarified by two attorney general's opinions. The first (issued September 10, 1900) barred "half-breeds" from the polls, and the second, issued October 17, 1912, declared flatly that Indians, because they were not citizens, were not entitled to vote. Utah's restrictions on Indian voting were upheld by that state's Supreme Court in 1956. See *Allen* v. *Merrell*, 305 P 2nd. 490 (1956).

43. *Porter* v. *Hall*, 271 P. 419 (1928). For a discussion of the reversal of this decision in 1948, see Getches, et al., *Federal Indian Law*, pp. 520–21.

44. *Piper et al.* v. *Big Pine School District of Inyo County et al.*, 226 P. 929 (1924). While accepting the legality of separate schools for Indians, the court ordered Piper and the other plaintiffs to be admitted to the local white schools because the district did not provide separate facilities for Native Americans. See also *Crawford* v. *District School Board for District No. 7*, 137 P. 217 (1913) for the Oregon case; and *State* v. *Wolf*, 59 S.E. 40 (1907) for the North Carolina case. See 33 *U.S. Statutes* 619, Sec. 7; *Senate Report* no. 744, 58th Cong. 2d sess.; and the debates on the bill in *CR* 58–2, 3081–82.

45. See Arizona *Statutes* (1913), Sec. 3837; Nevada *Revised Statutes* (1912), Sec. 6515; North Carolina State Constitution, Art. 14, Sec. 8; and Oregon *Laws* (1920), Sec. 2163. For the tests of the Arizona and Oregon laws, see *In re Walker's Estate*, 46 P. 67 (1896), and *In re Pacquet's Estate*, 200 P. 911 (1921).

46. Chauncey Shafter Goodrich, "The Legal Status of the California Indian," pp. 176–77, 178, 178–79.

47. Neal Doyle Houghton, "The Legal Status of Indian Suffrage in the United States," pp. 520, 516.

Chapter 8

1. Walter M. Camp, "The Condition of Reservation Indians," typescript of a report submitted to Malcom McDowell, secretary of the Board of Indian Commissioners, June 8, 1920. Copy in Edward Ayer Collection, the Newberry Library.

2. Ibid., p. 3.

3. Ibid., pp. 6, 6–8, 13–14.

4. Ibid., pp. 5–6, 14.

5. The Brookings Institution, Institute for Government Research, *The Problem of Indian Administration*, pp. 199, 201, 357, 454.

6. For an anthropologist's view of the relationship between external pressure and cultural survival, see Edward H. Spicer, "Persistent Cultural Systems," *Science*, November 19, 1971, pp. 795–800. For a case study of this phenomenon, see Frederick E. Hoxie, "From Prison to Homeland: The Cheyenne River Indian Reservation before World War I," *South Dakota History* 10 (Winter 1979): 1–24.

Bibliography

The notes that follow should guide the reader through the bibliography. A simple strategy lies behind these long lists. For each aspect of the study I began with a central source or cluster of sources: governmental actions and attitudes were found first in the *Congressional Record* and the *Annual Reports* of the commissioners of Indian affairs; for scientific attitudes I consulted the principal professional journals (*American Anthropologist, American Journal of Sociology*); and for popular opinion, the articles and stories about Indians cited in *Poole's Index* and the *Readers' Guides* to magazines. Each basic source formed the center of a series of concentric circles. The *Congressional Record* led me to committee reports and transcripts of hearings. These in turn led to archival collections, contemporary commentaries, and the activities of lobbyists and reformers. In the process new circles were formed; they too generated concentric rings. Before long, the networks began to intersect. Policy overlapped with science, popular attitudes with political philosophy, "expert" opinion with bureaucratic practice. The story became more tangled—and more interesting. One hopes the study produced from such diverse sources is simple enough to be meaningful and complex enough to be true.

Those interested in further research should consult three excellent bibliographical sources that appeared during the course of my work: Francis Paul Prucha, *A Bibliographical Guide to the History of Indian-White Relations in the United States* (Chicago: University of Chicago Press, 1977); Imre Sutton, *Indian Land Tenure: Bibliographical Essays and a Guide to the Literature* (New York: Clearwater, 1975); and the Newberry Library Center for the History of the American Indian Bibliography Series, edited by Francis Jennings and published by Indiana University Press, Bloomington, Indiana. Finally, the National Archives has published a useful guide to their massive holding in the records of the Bureau of Indian Affairs: Edward E. Hill, *Preliminary Inventory of the Records of the Bureau of Indian Affairs* (Record Group 75), 2 vols. (Washington, D.C.: National Archives and Records Service, 1965).

Notes

1. *Archival Sources.* Material was consulted in the areas indicated within Record Group 75 and Record Group 48. Specific cases were traced through the "letters received" and "letters sent" areas, and special topics such as education or citizenship were pursued through the general service files. "Special Cases" contains material removed from the regular files for congressional inquiries or other purposes; it provided information on the implementation of allotment legislation and irrigation projects. For detailed descriptions of each heading, consult the Edward Hill inventory cited above. The National Anthropological Archives at the Smithsonian Institution contain both the Alice Fletcher papers and the best collection available of letters to and from John Wesley Powell.

The personal papers of persons involved in Indian affairs were extremely useful, particularly the often-used Henry Dawes papers, the Pratt papers, and the McGee papers. The Indian Rights Association papers revealed several points at which the activities of one group—reformers—intersected with those of politicians, scientists, and others.

2. *Government Documents.* The records of the debates on legislation affecting Indians for the years 1880 to 1920 were a fundamental resource for

the study. House and Senate documents and related reports were also inval-
uable. These records provided an illuminating picture of the intersection of
political, ideological, and scientific interests in Indian policy making. The
published reports of the Bureau of American Ethnology (particularly Powell's introductions to the *Annual Reports*), the Bureau of Education, and
the Office of Indian Affairs for the years 1880–1920 were also read systematically.

3. *Newspapers and Other Contemporary Publications*. The newspapers
listed were studied carefully for the crisis year of 1879–80, described in
Chapter 1. In addition, they constituted a useful measure of public reactions
to such important events as the passage of the Burke Act or the opening of
the Chicago world's fair.

Specialized publications were consulted for information on specific policy areas. Those listed were examined for the entire 1880–1920 period, except for the *Railroad Gazette*, which was used for the years immediately
surrounding the passage of the Dawes Severalty Act.

4. *Primary Sources*. Drawn from *Poole's* and the *Readers' Guide*, as well
as the holdings of the Boston Public, Widener, Langdell, Newberry, and
Goldfarb libraries and the Library of Congress, this section contains all contemporary materials consulted for the study. Unsigned editorials have been
included, alphabetized by title.

1. Archival Sources

American Philosophical Society, Philadelphia
    Franz Boas Papers (microfilm)
Beinecke Rare Book and Manuscript Library, Yale University
    Richard Henry Pratt Papers
Harvard University Archives
    Frederick Ward Putnam Papers
Houghton Library, Harvard University
    Barrows Family Papers
Library of Congress, Washington, D.C., Manuscripts Division
    Henry L. Dawes Papers
    Walter L. Fisher Papers
    James R. Garfield Papers

Joseph Hawley Papers
Robert M. LaFollette Papers
William John McGee Papers
Key Pittman Papers
Hugh L. Scott Papers
Theodore Roosevelt Presidential Papers (microfilm)
William Howard Taft Presidential Papers (microfilm)
Woodrow Wilson Presidential Papers (microfilm)
National Anthropological Archives, Smithsonian Institution,
Washington, D.C.
Alice Cunningham Fletcher Papers
John Wesley Powell Letterbook, 1897–1902
National Archives and Records Service, Washington, D.C.
Record Group 75, Records of the Bureau of Indian Affairs. (Both here and
in the note citations, entry numbers refer to listings in Hill's *Preliminary
Inventory*. The term *File* refers to the decimal classification used in Entry
121.)
Board of Indian Commissioners General Correspondence (Entry 1386)
Central Classified Files (Entry 121)
Letters Received by the Office of Indian Affairs (Entries 75, 79)
Letters Sent by the Office of Indian Affairs (Entries 80, 84)
Register of Centennial Correspondence (Entry 78)
Special Cases
Superintendents' Annual Narrative Reports (Entry 960)
Record Group 48, Records of the Department of Interior
Office of the Secretary of Interior, Central Classified Files
Pennsylvania Historical Society, Philadelphia
Indian Rights Association Papers
Rochester University Library
Lewis Henry Morgan Papers

2. Government Documents

Bureau of American Ethnology, Annual Reports
U.S. Bureau of Education, Circulars of Information, Annual Reports of the
Commissioner

U.S. Commissioner of Indian Affairs, Annual Reports
U.S. Congress
  Congressional Record
  House Documents
  House Reports
  Senate Documents
  Senate Reports

3. Newspapers and Other Contemporary Publications

Newspapers
  Alta California (San Francisco)
  Atlanta Constitution
  Boston Daily Advertiser
  Boston Evening Transcript
  Boston Post
  Chicago Tribune
  New Orleans Times-Picayune
  New York Times
  New York Tribune
  Philadelphia Bulletin
  St. Louis Post-Dispatch
  San Francisco Examiner
  Virginia City (Nevada) *Territorial Enterprise*
Other
  American Bar Association Annual Reports
  Journal of Education
  National Education Association Proceedings
  Railroad Gazette
  Red Man (newspaper for the Indian Industrial School, Carlisle, Pa.)

4. Primary Sources

Abbott, L. J. "The Race Question in the Forty-Sixth State." *Independent*,
  July 25, 1907, pp. 206–11.

Abbott, Lyman. "Our Indian Problem." *North American Review* 167 (December 1898): 719–29.

———. "The Approaching End of the Indian Problem." *Independent*, October 25, 1902, pp. 2586–87.

Armstrong, S. C. *The Indian Question.* Hampton, Va.: Hampton Normal School Steam Press, 1883.

Austin, Mary. *The Arrow Maker.* New York: Duffield and Co., 1911.

Baker, Frank. "The Ascent of Man." *Annual Report of the Board of Regents of the Smithsonian Institution, 1890.* Washington: Government Printing Office, 1891, pp. 447–466.

Baker, Ray Stannard. "The Day of the Run." *Century*, September 1903, pp. 643–55.

Bancroft, Hubert Howe. *The Book of the Fair.* Chicago: Bancroft, 1894.

Bandelier, Adolph. *The Delightmakers.* New York: Dodd Mead, 1890.

———. *Kin and Clan: An Address before the Historical Society of New Mexico.* Santa Fe, 1882.

Baxter Springs Board of Trade. *Memorial.* Baxter Springs, Kans., November 20, 1888.

Blackmar, Frank W. "The Socialization of the American Indian." *American Journal of Sociology* 34 (January 1929): 653–99.

———. "Indian Education." *Annals of the American Academy of Political and Social Science* 2 (May 1892): 813–37.

Bland, Thomas A. *A History of the Sioux Agreement: Some Facts Which Should Not Be Forgotten.* Washington, 1889.

———. *The Indian—What Shall We Do with Him?* Washington, D.C., 1887.

———. *The Indian Question.* Boston, 1880.

Blue Book of the Panama-Pacific International Exposition at San Francisco, 1915. San Francisco, 1915.

Boas, Franz. "Census of the North American Indians." *Publications of the American Economic Association*, n.s. 2 (March 1899): 49–53.

———. *The Ethnography of Franz Boas.* Ed. Ronald P. Rohner. Chicago: University of Chicago Press, 1969.

———. "The Half Blood Indian: An Anthropometric Study." *Popular Science Monthly*, October 1894, pp. 761–70.

———. *The Mind of Primitive Man.* New York: Macmillan, 1911.

———. "A Review of the Data for the Study of the Prehistoric Chronology of

America." *Proceedings of the American Association for the Advancement of Science*, 1887, pp. 283–301.

Brinton, Daniel Garrison. *The American Race: A Linguistic Classification and Ethnographic Description of the Native Tribes of North and South America*. New York: N.D.C. Hodges, 1891.

———. *The Basis of Social Relations: A Study in Ethnic Psychology*. Ed. Livingston Farrand. New York: G. P. Putnam's Sons, 1902.

———. *Races and Peoples: Lectures on the Science of Ethnography*. New York: N.D.C. Hodges, 1890.

Brookings Institution, Institute for Government Research. *The Problem of Indian Administration*. Baltimore: Johns Hopkins University Press, 1928.

Brosius, Samuel. "Turning the Indian Loose." *Case and Comment* 23 (February 1917): 739–41.

Bruce, Edward C. *The Century: Its Fruits and Its Festival*. Philadelphia: Lippincott, 1877.

Bryce, James. *The Relations of the Advanced and the Backward Races of Mankind*. Oxford: Clarendon Press, 1902.

Buchanan, Beverly. "A Tribute to the First American." *World Today*, January 1911, pp. 25–33.

Canfield, George F. "Carl Schurz on the Indian Problem." *Nation*, June 30, 1881, pp. 457–58.

———. "The Legal Position of the Indian." *American Law Review* 15 (January 1881): 21–37.

Carpenter, C. C. *Grand Rush for the Indian Territory*. Independence, Kans.: P. H. Tiernan, 1879.

Chapman, Arthur. "Indian Lands for the White Man." *World Today*, September 1905, pp. 980–83.

Chase, O. G. *The Neutral Strip, or No Man's Land: The Cimarron Territory*. Dodge City [?] Kans., 1886.

Coffin, Ernest W. "On the Education of Backward Races." *Pedogogical Seminary* 15 (March 1908): 1–62.

Collins, Mary C. *Practical Suggestions on Indian Affairs*. New York, n.d.

Cook, Joseph. *Frontier Savages, White and Red*. Philadelphia: Indian Rights Association, 1885.

Cook, W. A. "Vocational Training for the Indian." *Vocational Education* 2 (March 1913): 289–98.

Cooper, Ella H. "How to Educate the Indians." *Gunton's Magazine*, May 1902, pp. 452–55.

Crane, Leo. "A Man Ruined by an Idea." *Harper's Weekly*, June 26, 1900, p. 15.

Crook, George. "The Apache Problem." *Journal of the Military Service Institution of the United States* 7 (October 1886): 257–69.

———. *General George Crook: His Autobiography*. Ed. Martin F. Schmitt. Norman: University of Oklahoma Press, 1946.

———. *Letter from George Crook on Giving the Ballot to the Indians*. Philadelphia: Indian Rights Association, 1885.

Curtis, Edward S. *The North American Indian*. 20 vols. Cambridge, Mass.: University Press, 1907–30.

"Cutting Indians' Hair." *Harper's Weekly*, March 22, 1902, p. 357.

Dawes, Henry L. "Have We Failed with the Indian?" *Atlantic Monthly*, August 1899, pp. 280–85.

———. "The Present Crisis." *Lend a Hand* 11 (November 1893): 346–52.

———. "The Indian Territory." *Independent*, October 25, 1900, pp. 2561–65

Day, Sherman. "Civilizing the Indians of California." *Overland Monthly*, n.s., December 1883, pp. 575–81.

"Dealing with the Indians Individually." *Independent*, December 14, 1905, pp. 1419–20.

Decker, A. "Making the Warrior a Worker." *Munsey's Magazine*, October 1901, pp. 88–95.

Densmore, Francis. "Indian Education in Government Schools." *Overland Monthly*, November 1905, pp. 456–59.

Dewey, John. "Interpretation of Savage Mind." *Psychological Review* 9 (May 1902): 217–30.

Dewey, Mary E. *Historical Sketch of the Formation and Achievements of the Women's National Indian Association in the United States*. Philadelphia: Women's National Indian Association, 1900.

Dixon, Joseph K. "The Indians." *Case and Comment* 23 (February 1917): 712–16.

———. *The Vanishing Race: The Last Great Indian Council*. Garden City, N.Y.: Doubleday, 1913.

[Dodge, Richard I.] *A Living Issue*. Washington, D.C.: F. B. Mohun, 1882.

————. *Our Wild Indians: Thirty Years' Personal Experience among the Red Men of the Great West.* Hartford: A. D. Worthington and Co., 1882.

Dowd, Jerome. "Discussion of 'Leadership in Reform.'" *American Journal of Sociology* 16 (March 1911): 633–35.

Eastman, Elaine Goodale. "The Education of Indians." *Arena*, October 1900, pp. 412–14.

————. "Self-Teaching in the Indian Schools." *Educational Review* 1 (January 1891): 57–59.

Eells, Reverend Myron. *Justice to the Indian.* Portland, Oreg.: G. H. Himes, 1883.

Eggleston, Edward. *The Ultimate Solution of the American Negro Problem.* Boston, R. G. Badger, 1913.

Ellerbe, Rose L. "A School on a 'Ranchita.'" *Journal of Education* 53 (May 16, 1901): 313–14.

Farrand, Livingston. *Basis of American History: 1500–1900.* New York: Harper, 1904.

Fletcher, Alice Cunningham. "Indian Education and Civilization." *Senate Executive Document* no. 95, 48th Cong., 2d sess., ser. 2264.

————. "Preparation of the Indian for Citizenship." *Lend a Hand*, September 1892, pp. 190–98.

Flower, Elliott. "Law and the Indian." *Atlantic Monthly*, October 1910, pp. 488–90.

Flynn, Clinton R. "The Legal Status of the Indians in the United States," *Central Law Journal* 62 (May 25, 1906): 399–404.

Forbes-Lindsey, C. H. "Making Good Indians." *Harper's Weekly* 52 (October 31, 1908): 12–13.

————. "The North American Indian as a Laborer: His Value as a Worker and a Citizen." *Craftsman*, May 1908, pp. 146–57.

————. "Shaping the Future of the Indian." *World Today*, March 1907, pp. 290–92.

Francis, David R. *The Universal Exposition of 1904.* St. Louis: Louisiana Purchase Exposition, 1913.

Funsten, Rev. James B. "The Indian as a Worker." *Outlook*, December 9, 1905, pp. 875–78.

Garland, Hamlin. *The Book of the American Indian.* New York: Harper, 1923.

——. *Captain of the Gray Horse Troop.* New York: Harper, 1902.

——. *Hamlin Garland's Observations on the American Indian, 1895– 1905.* Comp. and ed. Lonnie E. Underhill and Daniel F. Littlefield, Jr. Tucson: University of Arizona Press, 1976.

——. "The Red Man as Material." *Booklover's Magazine,* August 1903, pp. 196–98.

——. "The Red Man's Present Needs." *North American Review* 174 (April 1902): 476–88.

——. "The Red Plowman." *Craftsman,* November 1907, pp. 180–82.

Garth, Thomas R. "White, Indian and Negro Work Curves." *Journal of Applied Psychology* 5 (March 1921): 14–25.

Gibbon, John. "Our Indian Question." *Journal of the Military Service Institution of the United States* 2 (1881): 101–20.

Giddings, Franklin H. "The Causes of Race Superiority." In *America's Race Problems.* Philadelphia, 1901.

——. *Democracy and Empire.* New York: Macmillan, 1901.

——. "A Social Marking System." *American Journal of Sociology* 15 (March 11, 1910): 721–40.

Gilman, Samuel C. *The Future Indian: A Brief Treatise on the Indian Question.* Indianapolis: Carlon and Hottenbeck, 1891.

Goodrich, Chauncey Shafter. "The Legal Status of the California Indian." *California Law Review* 14 (January 1926): 1–48.

Grafton, B. F. *Argument of B. F. Grafton.* Washington, 1879.

Grant, Madison. *The Conquest of a Continent.* New York: Scribner, 1933.

——. *The Passing of the Great Race.* 4th rev. ed. New York: Scribner, 1922.

Grinnell, George Bird. *Blackfoot Lodge Tales.* New York: Scribner, 1892.

——. *Held Up by the Senate.* Philadelphia: Indian Rights Association, 1896.

——. "The Indian on the Reservation." *Atlantic Monthly,* February 1899, pp. 255–67.

——. *The Indians of Today.* New York: H. S. Stone, 1900.

——. *The Passing of the Great West: Selected Papers of George Bird Grinnell.* Ed. John F. Rieger, New York: Winchester Press, 1972.

——. "Portraits of Indian Types." *Scribner's* 37 (March 1905): 259–73.

——. *The Punishment of the Stingy and Other Stories.* New York: Harper, 1901.

——. *The Story of the Indian*. New York: D. Appleton and Co., 1895.

——. "Tenure of Land Among the Indians." *American Anthropologist*, n.s. 9 (January–March 1907): 1–11.

——. *When Buffalo Ran*. New Haven: Yale University Press, 1920.

——. "The Wild Indian." *Atlantic Monthly*, January 1899, pp. 20–29.

Grinnell, George Bird, and Theodore Roosevelt, eds. *American Big Game Hunting*. New York: Forest and Stream Publishing, 1893.

——. *Hunting at High Altitudes*. New York: Harper, 1913.

Hall, G. Stanley. "How Far Are the Principles of Education Along Indigenous Lines Applicable to American Indians?" *National Education Association Journal of Proceedings and Addresses, 1908*, pp. 1161–64.

Hare, William Hobart. *An Address Delivered by William Hobart Hare, Missionary Bishop of South Dakota, in Calvary Cathedral, Sioux Falls, South Dakota, January 10, 1888*. Sioux Falls, 1888.

Harsha, William Justin. "Law for the Indian." *North American Review* 134 (March 1882): 272–92.

——. *Ploughed Under*. New York: Fords, Howard and Hulbert, 1881.

——. *A Timid Brave*. New York: Funk and Wagnalls, 1886.

Harvey, Charles M. "The Indian of Today and Tomorrow." *American Monthly Review of Reviews*, June 1906, pp. 696–705.

——. "The Last Race Rally of the Indians." *World's Work*, May 1904, pp. 4803–9.

——. "The Red Man's Last Roll Call." *Atlantic Monthly*, March 1906, pp. 323–30.

Hayes, Helen E. *A Teacher's Testimony*. New York, 1888.

Hewitt, Edgar L. "Ethnic Factors in Education." *American Anthropologist*, n.s. 7 (January–March 1905): 1–16.

Hibbitts, J. H. *Peace, Civilization and Citizenship: The Indian Problem*. Topeka, Kans.: G. W. Martin, 1877.

Higginson, Thomas W. *Contemporaries*. Boston: Houghton Mifflin, 1899.

Hodge, Frederick Webb, ed. *The Handbook of American Indians of North of Mexico*. 2 vols. Washington: Government Printing Office, 1907–10.

Hoffman, Frederick L. "Race Traits and Tendencies of the American Negro." *Publications of the American Economic Association* 11 (1896): 1–329.

Holmes, William Henry. "Biographical Memoir of L. H. Morgan, 1818–

1881." *National Academy of Science Biographical Memoirs* 6 (1909): 219–39.

———. "Classification and Arrangements of the Exhibits of an Anthropological Museum." *Annual Report of the U.S. National Museum*. Washington, D.C.: Goverment Printing Office, 1901.

———. "Sketch of the Origin, Development and Probable Destiny of the Races of Men." *American Anthropologist* 4 (July–September 1902): 369–91.

———. "Some Problems of the American Race." *American Anthropologist* 12 (April–June 1910): 149–82.

———. "World's Fair Congress of Anthropology." *American Anthropologist*, o.s. 6 (1893): 423–34.

Houghton, Neal Doyle. "The Legal Status of Indian Suffrage in the United States." *California Law Review* 19 (July 1931): 507–20.

———. "Wards of the United States—Arizona Applications: A Study of the Legal Status of the Indians." *University of Arizona Bulletin* 16 (July 1, 1945): 5–19.

Howard, Oliver Otis. *My Life and Experiences among Our Hostile Indians*. Hartford: A. D. Worthington, 1907.

Humphrey, Seth K. *The Indian Dispossessed*. Boston: Little, Brown, 1905.

———. *The Racial Prospect*. New York: Scribner, 1920.

Hutchinson, Dr. Woods. "The Strength of Races." *World's Work*, May 1908, pp. 10262–68.

"Indians as Wards." *Independent*, February 13, 1908, pp. 380–81.

"The Indian School Blunder." *Independent*, February 9, 1905, p. 333.

"The Indian Schools." *Independent*, April 12, 1906, pp. 883–84.

Jackson, A. P., and E. C. Cole. *Oklahoma!* Kansas City, Mo.: Ramsey, Millett and Hudson, 1885.

Jackson, Helen Hunt. "Wards of the United States Government." *Scribner's Monthly* 19 (March 1880): 775–82.

———. *A Century of Dishonor*. New York: Harper, 1881.

Jacobs, Harvey D. "Uncle Sam—The Great White Father." *Case and Comment* 23 (February 1917): 703–9.

James, Juliet. *Sculpture of the Exposition Palaces and Courts*. San Francisco: H. S. Crocker, 1915.

Johnson, Mrs. Ellen Wadsworth Terry. *Historical Sketch of the Connecticut*

Indian Association from 1881–1888. Hartford: Press of the Flower and Miller Co., 1888.

Keasbey, Lindley M. "Civology—A Suggestion." *Popular Science Monthly*, April 1907, pp. 365–71.

Kennan, George. "Have Reservation Indians Any Vested Rights?" *Outlook*, March 29, 1902, pp. 759–65.

———. "Indian Lands and Fair Play." *Outlook*, February 27, 1904, pp. 498–501.

Kroeber, Alfred L. "Eighteen Professions." *American Anthropologist* 17 (April–June 1915): 283–88.

———. "Inheritance by Magic." *American Anthropologist* 18 (January–March 1916): 19–40.

———. "Ishi, the Last Aborigine: The Effects of Civilization on a Genuine Survivor of Stone Age Barbarism." *World's Work*, July 1912, pp. 304–8.

———. "The Morals of an Uncivilized People." *American Anthropologist* 12 (July–September 1910): 437–47.

Kyle, James H. "How Shall the Indians Be Educated?" *North American Review* 159 (October 1894): 434–47.

Lane, Franklin K. "From the Warpath to the Plow." *National Geographic*, January 1915, pp. 73–87.

Leupp, Francis E. "Back to Nature for the Indian." *Charities and the Commons*, June 6, 1908, pp. 336–40.

———. "The Failure of the Educated American Indian." *Appleton's Booklover's Magazine*, May 1906, pp. 594–609.

———. "Four Strenuous Years." *Outlook*, June 5, 1909, pp. 328–33.

———. "A Fresh Phase of the Indian Problem." *Nation*, November 16, 1899, pp. 367–68.

———. *The Indian and His Problem*. New York: Scribner, 1910.

———. "Indian Lands: Their Administration with Reference to Present and Future Use." *Annals of the American Academy of Political and Social Science* 33 (1909): 620–30.

———. "The Indian Land Troubles and How to Solve Them." *American Monthly Review of Reviews*, October 1910, pp. 468–72.

———. *The Latest Phase of the Southern Ute Question: A Report*. Philadelphia: Indian Rights Association, 1895.

———. "The Red Man, Incorporated." *Collier's*, January 9, 1909, p. 20.

———. "The Red Man's Burden." *Hearst's Magazine*, May 1913, pp. 741–52.

———. "A Review of President Roosevelt's Administration." *Outlook*, February 6, 1909, pp. 298–307.

———. "Why Booker T. Washington Has Succeeded in His Life Work." *Outlook*, May 31, 1902, pp. 326–33.

Lowie, Robert. *Culture and Ethnology*. New York: D. C. McMurtrie, 1917.

———. *Primitive Society*. New York: Boni and Liveright, 1920.

———. "Reminiscences of Anthropological Currents in America Half a Century Ago." *American Anthropologist* 58 (December 1956): 995–1016.

Lummis, Charles F. *Bullying the Moqui*. Ed. Robert Easton and Mackenzie Brown. Prescott, Ariz.: Prescott College Press, 1968.

———. "Lame Dancing Masters: An Indian View of Government Schools." *Out West*, May 1900, pp. 356–58.

———. "My Brother's Keeper." *Out West*, August 1899, pp. 139–47; September 1899, pp. 207–13; October 1899, pp. 263–67; November 1899, pp. 333–35; December 1899, pp. 28–30; January 1900, pp. 90–94; February 1900, pp. 178–80.

McGee, William John. "Anthropology and Its Larger Problems." *Congress of Arts and Sciences: Universal Exposition, St. Louis, 1904*. Ed. Howard J. Rogers. Boston: Houghton Mifflin, 1905–7.

———. "Man's Place in Nature." *American Anthropologist*, n.s. 3 (January–March 1901): 1–13.

———. "The Science of Humanity." *Proceedings of the American Association for the Advancement of Science* (1897): 296–323.

———. "The Science of Humanity." *Proceedings of the American Association for the Advancement of Science* (1897): 296–323.

———. "Strange Races of Men." *World's Work*, August 1904, pp. 5185–88.

McKenzie, Fayette A. "Assimilation of the American Indian." *American Journal of Sociology* 19 (May 1914): 761–72.

———. "The American Indian of Today and Tomorrow." *Journal of Race Development* 3 (October 1912): 135–55.

———. *The Indian in Relation to the White Population of the United States*. Columbus, Ohio: Privately printed, 1908.

McLaughlin, James. *My Friend the Indian*. Boston: Houghton Mifflin, 1910.

McSpadden, J. Walter. *Famous Sculptors of America*. New York: Dodd, Mead, 1924.

Manypenny, George W. *Our Indian Wards*. Cincinnati: R. Clarke and Co., 1880.

Mason, Otis T. "Influence of Environment upon Human Industries and Arts." *Annual Report of the Board of Regents of the Smithsonian Institution, 1895*. Washington: Government Printing Office, 1896, pp. 639–65.

———. "Mind and Matter in Culture." *American Anthropologist* 10 (April–June 1908): 187–96.

———. "The Scope and Value of Anthropological Studies." *Proceedings of the American Association for the Advancement of Science*, 1883, pp. 367–83.

———. "Similarities in Culture." *American Anthropologist*, o.s. 8 (April 1895): 101–17.

———. "The Uncivilized Mind in the Presence of Higher Phases of Civilization." *Proceedings of the American Association for the Advancement of Science*, 1883, pp. 367–83.

Mayo-Smith, Richmond. "Assimilation of Nationalities in the United States." *Political Science Quarterly* 9 (December 1894): 649–70.

Meserve, Charles F. *A Tour of Observations among Indians and Indian Schools in Arizona, New Mexico, Oklahoma and Kansas*. Philadelphia: Indian Rights Association, 1894.

Miles, Nelson A. "The Indian Problem," *North American Review* 128 (March 1879): 304–14.

Miller, Joaquin. *Life amongst the Modocs*. London: R. Bentley, 1873.

———. *Shadows of Shasta.* Chicago: Jansen, McClurg and Co., 1881.

Monsen, Frederick. "The Destruction of Our Indians." *Craftsman*, March 1907, pp. 683–91.

Moon, Carl. "In Search of the Wild Indian." *Outing*, February 1917, pp. 533–45.

Moorehead, Warren K. *The American Indian in the United States; 1850–1914*. Andover, Mass.: Andover Press, 1914.

Morgan, Lewis Henry. *Ancient Society*. New York: Henry Holt and Co., 1877.

———. "Factory System for Indian Reservations." *Nation*, July 27, 1876, pp. 58–59.

———. *Houses and House Life of the American Aborigines*. Washington: Government Printing Office, 1881.

———. "The Hue and Cry Against the Indians." *Nation*, July 20, 1876, pp. 40–41.

———. *The Indian Journals of Lewis Henry Morgan, 1859–1862.* Ed. Leslie A. White. Ann Arbor: University of Michigan Press, 1959.

———. *League of the Ho-de-no-sau-nee or Iroquois.* Rochester: Sage and Brother, 1851.

———. "Lewis Henry Morgan's Journal of a Trip to Southwestern Colorado and New Mexico." Ed. Leslie White. *American Antiquity* 8 (July 1942): 1–26.

———. *Systems of Consanguinity and Affinity of the Human Family.* Smithsonian Contributions to Knowledge, vol. 17. Washington: Smithsonian Institution, 1871.

Morgan, Thomas J. "Indian Education." *Journal of Social Science* 40 (December 1902): 165–80.

National Indian Defense Association. *The Sioux Nation and the United States: A Brief History.* Washington: National Indian Defense Association, 1891.

"The Need for Practical Training for the Indians." *Journal of Education* 69 (March 18, 1909): 300.

Neuhaus, Eugen. *The Art of the Exposition.* San Francisco: P. Elder, 1915.

"A New Step in Our Indian Policy." *Outlook*, May 23, 1917, p. 136.

Newell, Alfred C. "The Philippine Peoples." *World's Work*, August 1904, pp. 5128–45.

Newlin, James W. *Proposed Indian Policy.* Philadelphia, 1881.

Oskison, John M. "In Governing the Indian, Use the Indian!" *Case and Comment* 23 (February 1917): 723–33.

Owen, G. W. *The Indian Question.* Ypsilanti, Mich., 1881.

Painter, Charles C. *Civilization by Removal!* Philadelphia: Indian Rights Association, 1889.

———. *The Dawes Land in Severalty Bill and Indian Emancipation.* Philadelphia: Indian Rights Association, 1887.

Painter, George S. "The Future of the American Negro." *American Anthropologist* 21 (October–December 1919): 410–20.

Palladino, Lawrence Benedict, S. J. *Indian and White in the Northwest, or a History of Catholicity in Montana.* Baltimore: J. Murphy and Co., 1894.

Pancoast, Henry S. *The Indian before the Law.* Philadelphia: Indian Rights Association, 1884.

Parker, Arthur C. "The Social Elements of the Indian Problem." *American Journal of Sociology* 22 (September 1916): 252–67.

Peabody, Elizabeth P. *The Piutes*. Cambridge, Mass.: J. Wilson and Son, 1887.

Pope, John. *The Indian Question*. Cincinnati, 1878.

Popenoe, Paul, and Roswell Hill Johnson. *Applied Eugenics*. New York: Macmillan, 1918.

Powell, John Wesley. "Competition as a Factor in Human Evolution." *American Anthropologist*, o.s. 1 (October 1888): 297–324.

———. "Darwin's Contributions to Philosophy." *Proceedings of the Biological Society of Washington*, 1882, pp. 60–71.

———. "Discourse on the Philosophy of the North American Indians." *Bulletin of the American Georgraphical Society of New York* 2 (1876–77): 46–62.

———. "From Barbarism to Civilization." *American Anthropologist*, o.s. 1 (April 1888): 97–123.

———. "From Savagery to Barbarism." *Transactions of the Anthropological Society of Washington* 3 (1885): 173–96.

———. "Human Evolution." *Transactions of the Anthropological Society of Washington* 2 (1883): 176–208.

———. *Introduction to the Study of Indian Languages*. Washington: Government Printing Office, 1877.

———. "The Non-Irrigable Lands of the Arid Region." *Century*, March 1890, pp. 766–76, 915–22.

———. "The Larger Import of Scientific Education." *Popular Science Monthly*, February 1885, pp. 452–56.

———. "The North American Indians." In *The United States of America: A Study of the American Commonwealth*, ed. Nathanial S. Shaler, 2 vols. New York: Appleton, 1894, 1:190–272.

———. "Outlines of Sociology." *Transactions of the Anthropological Society of Washington* 1 (1882): 106–29.

———. "Proper Training and the Future of the Indians." *Forum*, February 1895, pp. 638–52.

———. "Relation of Primitive Peoples to Environment." *Smithsonian Institution Annual Report*, 1895, pp. 625–37.

———. *Report on Lands of the Arid Region of the United States*. Washington: Government Printing Office, 1878.

————. *Selected Prose of John Wesley Powell.* Ed. George Crosette. Boston: D. R. Godine, 1970.

————. "Sketch of Lewis Henry Morgan." *Popular Science Monthly*, November 1880, pp. 114–21.

————. "Sociology, or the Science of Institutions." *American Anthropologist*, n.s. 1 (July 1899): 475–509; (October 1899): 695–745.

————. "The Three Methods of Evolution." *Bulletin of the Philosophical Society of Washington* 6 (1884): 27–52.

————. "Views of Major Powell on the Propriety of Transferring the Indian Bureau from the War Department to the Interior Department." *House Report* no. 240, 44th Cong., 1st sess., ser. 1708.

Pratt, Richard H. *Address by Captain Pratt before the National Convention of Charities and Correction at Denver, Colorado, June 28, 1892.* Denver, 1892.

————. *Battlefield and Classroom: Four Decades with the American Indian, 1867–1904.* Ed. Robert M. Utley. New Haven: Yale University Press, 1964.

————. *The Indian Industrial School at Carlisle, Pennsylvania.* Carlisle, Pa.: Hamilton Library Association, 1908.

Proceedings of the Convention to Consider the Opening of Indian Territory Held at Kansas City, Mo., February 8, 1888. Kansas City, Mo.: Press of Ramsey, Millet and Hudson, 1888.

Proctor, Edna Dean. *The Son of the Ancient People.* Boston: Houghton Mifflin, 1893.

Reeves, John T. "Probating the Indian Estates." *Case and Comment* 23 (February 1917): 727–29.

Remington, Frederic. *John Ermine of the Yellowstone.* New York: Macmillan, 1902.

Rhoads, Dr. James E. *The Indian Question in the Concrete.* Philadelphia: Women's National Indian Association, 1886.

————. *Our Next Duty to the Indian.* Philadelphia: Indian Rights Association, 1887.

Riggs, Alfred L. "Where Shall Our Indian Brothers Go to School?" *Journal of Education* 14 (September 29, 1881): 199–200.

Ripley, William Z. *The Races of Europe: A Sociological Study.* New York: D. Appleton, 1899.

Roe, Walter C. "The Mohonk Lodge: An Experiment in Indian Work." *Outlook*, May 18, 1901, pp. 176–78.

Rogers, Howard J., ed. *Congress of Arts and Sciences: Universal Exposition, St. Louis, 1904* 8 vols. Boston: Houghton Mifflin, 1905–7.

Roosevelt, Theodore. *Addresses and Papers of Theodore Roosevelt*. Ed. Willis Fletcher Johnson. New York: Sun Dial Classics, 1908.

———. *Addresses and Presidential Messages of Theodore Roosevelt, 1902–1904*. New York: G. P. Putnam's Sons, 1904.

———. *American Ideals and Other Essays, Social and Political*. New York: G. P. Putnam, 1902.

———. *Biological Analogies in History*. Oxford: Clarendon Press, 1910.

———. *A Book Lover's Holidays in the Open*. New York: Scribner, 1919.

———. *Letters of Theodore Roosevelt*. Ed. Elting E. Morison. 8 vols. Cambridge, Mass.: Harvard University Press, 1951–54.

———. *Report of Hon. Theodore Roosevelt Made to the U.S. Civil Service Commission, upon a Visit to Certain Indian Reservations and Indian Schools in South Dakota, Nebraska, and Kansas*. Philadelphia: Indian Rights Association, 1893.

Rowe, E. C. "547 White and 268 Indian Children Tested by the Binet-Simon Test." *Pedagogical Seminary* 21 (September 1914): 454–68.

Russell, Isaac Franklin. "The Indian before the Law." *Yale Law Journal* 18 (March 1909): 328–37.

Sanders, Helen Fitzgerald. "The Opening of the Flathead Reservation." *Overland Monthly*, August 1909, pp. 120–40.

———. "The Red Bond." *Overland Monthly*, August 1911, pp. 161–64.

———. *Trails through Western Woods*. London: Everett and Co., 1911.

———. *The White Quiver*. New York: Duffield and Co., 1913.

Schurz, Carl. "Carl Schurz on Indian Education." *Journal of Education* 13 (April 28, 1881): 283.

———. *Speeches, Correspondence and Political Papers of Carl Schurz*. Ed. Frederic Bancroft. 6 vols. New York: Putnam, 1913.

Seachrest, Effie. "James Earle Fraser." *American Magazine of Art* 8 (May 1917): 276–78.

Seely, O. C. *Oklahoma Illustrated: A Book of Practical Information*. Guthrie, Oklahoma Territory; Leader Printing, 1894.

Sells, Cato. "The First Americans as Loyal Citizens." *American Monthly Review of Reviews*, May 1918, pp. 523–24.

Simons, Sarah E. "Social Assimilation." *American Journal of Sociology* 6 (May 1901): 790–822; 7 (January 1902): 539–56.

Skiff, F. J., et al. "An Historical and Descriptive Account of the Field Columbian Museum." *Field Columbian Museum Publications* 1 (1895).

Smith, William Benjamin. *The Color Line: A Brief in Behalf of the Unborn.* New York: McClure, Phillips and Co.. 1905.

Stefansson, Vilhjalmar. "The Indian and Civilization." *Independent*, December 28, 1911, pp. 1434–38.

Stoddard, Theodore Lothrop. *The Rising Tide of Color against White World Supremacy.* New York: Scribner, 1920.

Stone, Alfred Holt. *Studies in the American Race Problem.* New York: Doubleday, Page and Co., 1908.

Strong, Josiah. *Our Country: Its Possible Future, and Its Present Crisis.* New York: American Home Missionary Society, 1885.

Suksdorf, Henry F. *Our Race Problems.* New York: Shakespeare Press, 1911.

Sumner, William Graham. "The Indians in 1887." *Forum*, May 1887, pp. 254–62.

Swanton, John R. "Some Anthropological Misconceptions." *American Anthropologist* 19 (October–December 1917): 459–70.

Taft, William Howard. *Present Day Problems.* New York: Dodd, Mead, 1908.

———. *Presidential Addresses and State Papers.* New York: Doubleday, Page and Co., 1910, vol. 1.

Tatum, Lawrie. *Our Red Brothers and the Peace Policy of President U.S. Grant.* Philadelphia: J. C. Winston and Co., 1899.

Thayer, James Bradley. "A People without Law." *Atlantic Monthly*, October–November 1891, pp. 540–51, 676–87.

———. "The Dawes Bill and the Indians." *Atlantic Monthly*, March 1888, pp. 315–22.

Thomas, William Isaac. "The Mind of Woman and the Lower Races." *American Journal of Sociology* 12 (January 1907): 435–69.

Tibbles, Thomas H. *Buckskin and Blanket Days.* Garden City, N.Y.: Doubleday, 1957.

———. *Hidden Power.* New York: G. W. Carleton, 1881.

———. *The Ponca Chiefs.* Boston: Lockwood, Brooks and Co., 1880.

———. *Western Men Defended.* Boston: Lockwood, Brooks and Co., 1880.

Tillinghast, Joseph A. "The Negro in Africa and America." *Publications of the American Economic Association*, 3d Series, 3 (May 1902): 401–638.

"A Trust Not Trustworthy." *Independent* 56 February 25, 1904, pp. 450–501.

Tydings, Thomas J. "Rights of Indians on Public Lands." *Case and Comment* 23 (February 1917): 743–47.

United States Bureau of Census. *Indian Population in the U.S. and Alaska, 1910*. Washington: Government Printing Office, 1915.

U.S. Bureau of Education. *Are the Indians Dying Out? Preliminary Observations Relating to Indian Civilization and Education*. Washington, D.C.: Government Printing Office, 1877.

Valentine, Robert G. "Making Good Indians." *Sunset*, June 1910, pp. 598–611.

Walker, Francis A. *The Indian Question*. Boston: J. R. Osgood and Co., 1874.

———, ed. *International Exhibition, 1876*. 9 vols. Washington: Government Printing Office, 1880–84.

Ward. Lester F. "Social Differentiation and Integration." *American Journal of Sociology* 8 (May 1903): 721–45.

———. "The Transmission of Culture by the Inheritance of Acquired Characteristics." *Forum*, May 1891, pp. 312–19.

Washington, Booker T. "Inferior and Superior Races." *North American Review* 201 (April 1915): 538–42.

Waterman, T. T. "The Subdivisions of the Human Race and Their Distribution." *American Anthropologist* 26 (October–December 1924): 474–90.

Welsh, Herbert. *Allotment of Lands: Defense of the Dawes Land in Severalty Bill*. Philadelphia: Indian Rights Association, 1887.

———. "Comment on Thomas Morgan's 'Indian Education.'" *Journal of Social Science* 40 (December 1902): 178.

———. *How to Bring the Indian to Citizenship*. Philadelphia: Indian Rights Association, 1892.

———. "The Indian Problem and What We Must Do to Solve It." *Wowapi*, November 7, 1883, pp. 8–9.

———. "The Meaning of the Dakota Outbreak." *Scribner's Magazine*, April 1891, pp. 439–52.

Williams, Talcott. "Was Primitive Man a Modern Savage?" *Annual Report of the Board of Regents of the Smithsonian Institution, 1896.* Washington: Government Printing Office, 1898.

Willsie, Honore. *Lydia of the Pines.* New York: Frederick A. Stokes, 1915.

———. *Still Jim.* New York: Frederick A. Stokes, 1917.

———. "We die! We Die! There Is No Hope!" *Everybody's Magazine,* March 1912, pp. 337–44.

Wilson, Owen. "Rescuing a People by an Irrigation Ditch." *World's Work,* September 1911, pp. 14815–17.

Wissler, Clark. *The American Indian.* New York: D. C. McMurtrie, 1917.

———. "The Psychological Aspects of the Culture-Environment Relation." *American Anthropologist* 14 (April–June 1912): 217–25.

Wister, Owen. *Red Men and White.* New York: Harper, 1895.

———. *Roosevelt: The Story of a Friendship, 1880–1919.* New York: Macmillan, 1930.

———. *The Virginian.* New York: Macmillan, 1902.

Wood, C. E. S. "Our Indian Question." *Journal of the Military Service Institution of the United States* 2 (1881): 101–20.

Woodward, Calvin M. "The Function of the Public School." *National Education Association Proceedings,* 1887, pp. 212–24.

Woodworth, R. S. "Racial Differences in Mental Traits." *Science* 31 (February 4, 1910): 171–86.

5. Secondary Sources—Books

Adams, Evelyn C. *American Indian Education: Government Schools and Economic Progress.* New York: King's Crown Press, 1946.

Allen, Robert L. *Reluctant Reformers.* Cambridge, Mass.: Harvard University Press, 1974.

Andrist, Ralph D. *The Long Death: The Last Days of the Plains Indians.* New York: Macmillan, 1964.

Athearn, Robert G. *William Tecumseh Sherman and the Settlement of the West.* Norman: University of Oklahoma Press, 1960.

Bailey, John W. *Pacifying the Plains: General Alfred Terry and the Decline of the Sioux, 1866–1890.* Westport, Conn.: Greenwood Press, 1979.

Bannister, Roger C., Jr. *Ray Stannard Baker: The Mind and Thought of a Progressive.* New Haven: Yale University Press, 1956.

Beale, Howard Kennedy. *Theodore Roosevelt and the Rise of America to World Power*. Baltimore: Johns Hopkins University Press, 1956.

Beatty, Donald R. *History of the Legal Status of the American Indian with Particular Reference to California*. Rand Research Associates Ethnic Studies Series. San Francisco: Rand E. Research Associates, 1974.

Beaver, R. Pierce. *Church, State and the American Indians: Two and a Half Centuries of Partnership in Missions Between Protestant Churches and Government*. St. Louis: Concordia Publishing, 1966.

Benson, Ramsey. *Hill Country: The Story of J. J. Hill and the Awakening West*. New York: Frederick A. Stockes Co., 1928.

Berkhofer, Robert F., Jr. *The White Man's Indian: Images of the American Indian from Columbus to the Present*. New York: Knopf, 1978.

Berry, Brewton. *Almost White*. New York: Macmillan, 1963.

———. *The Education of American Indians*. Washington: Government Printing Office, 1969.

Berthrong, Donald J. *The Cheyenne and Arapaho Ordeal: Reservation and Agency Life in the Indian Territory, 1875–1907*. Norman: University of Oklahoma Press, 1976.

Bremner, Robert Hamlett. *From the Depths: The Discovery of Poverty in the United States*. New York: New York University Press, 1956.

Brimlow, George Francis. *The Bannock Indian War of 1878*. Caldwell, Idaho: Caxton Printers, 1942.

Burg, David F. *Chicago's White City of 1893*. Lexington: University of Kentucky Press, 1976.

Burrow, J. W. *Evolution and Society*. Cambridge: Cambridge University Press, 1966.

Carlson, Leonard A. *Indians, Bureaucrats and Land: The Dawes Act and the Decline of Indian Farming*. Westport, Conn.: Greenwood Press, 1981.

Coan, Otis W., and Richard G. Lillard. *America in Fiction: an Annotated List of Novels that Interpret Aspects of Life in the United States*. 3d ed. Stanford: Stanford University Press, 1949.

Cohen, Felix S. *Handbook of Federal Indian Law*. University of New Mexico edition. Albuquerque: University of New Mexico Press, 1971.

Coletta, Paolo E. *The Presidency of William Howard Taft*. Lawrence, Kans.: Regents Press, 1973.

Chamberlin, J. E. *The Harrowing of Eden*. New York: Seabury, 1975.

Cremin, Lawrence. *The Transformation of the School.* New York: Knopf, 1961.

Danziger, Edmund J. *Indians and Bureaucrats: Administering the Reservation Policy During the Civil War.* Urbana: University of Illinois Press, 1974.

Darnell, Regna, ed. *Readings in the History of Anthropology.* New York: Harper and Row, 1974.

Darrah, William Culp. *Powell of the Colorado.* Princeton: Princeton University Press, 1951.

Debo, Angie. *The Rise and Fall of the Choctaw Republic.* Norman: University of Oklahoma Press, 1934.

Dippie, Brian W. *The Vanishing American: White Attitudes and U.S. Indian Policy.* Middletown, Conn.: Wesleyan University Press, 1982.

Drinnon, Richard. *Facing West: The Metaphysics of Indian Hating and Empire Building.* Minneapolis: University of Minnesota Press, 1980.

Dyer, Thomas G. *Theodore Roosevelt and the Idea of Race.* Baton Rouge: Louisiana State University Press, 1980.

Eastman, Elaine [Goodale]. *Pratt: The Red Man's Moses.* Norman: University of Oklahoma Press, 1935.

Eggan, Fred. "Lewis H. Morgan and the Future of the American Indian." In *The American Indian: Perspectives for the Study of Social Change.* Ed. Fred Eggan. Chicago: Aldine Publishing, 1966.

————. ed. *Social Anthropology of North American Tribes.* 4th ed. Chicago: University of Chicago Press, 1965.

Farb, Peter. *Man's Rise to Civilization: The Cultural Ascent of the Indians of North America.* 2d ed. New York: Dutton, 1978.

Fisher, Berenice M. *Industrial Education: American Ideals and Institutions.* Madison: University of Wisconsin Press, 1967.

Fothergill, Philip. *Historical Aspects of Organic Evolution.* New York: Philosophical Library, 1953.

Fredrickson, George M. *The Black Image in the White Mind.* New York: Harper and Row, 1971.

Friedman, Lawrence J. *The White Savage: Racial Fantasies in the Post Bellum South.* Englewood Cliffs, N.J.: Prentice Hall, 1970.

Fritz, Henry Eugene. *The Movement for Indian Assimilation, 1860–1890.* Philadelphia: University of Pennsylvania Press, 1963.

Frost, O. W. *Joaquin Miller.* New York: Twayne Publishers, 1967.

Furner, Mary O. *Advocacy and Objectivity: A Crisis in the Professionalization of American Social Science, 1865–1905*. Lexington: University of Kentucky Press, 1975.

Gehm, Katherine. *Sarah Winnemuca*. Phoenix: O'Sullivan Woodside, 1975.

Getches, David H., et al. *Cases and Materials on Federal Indian Law*. American Casebook Series. St. Paul: West Publishing, 1979.

Goetzmann, William H. *Exploration and Empire: The Explorer and the Scientist in the Winning of the American West*. New York: Knopf, 1966.

Goldman, Eric. *Charles J. Bonaparte, Patrician Reformer: His Earlier Career*. Johns Hopkins University Studies in Historical and Political Science, series 61, no. 2. Baltimore: Johns Hopkins University Press, 1943.

Goldschmidt, Walter, ed. *The Uses of Anthropology*. Washington, D.C.: American Anthropological Association, 1979.

Gordon, Dudley. *Charles F. Lummis: Crusader in Corduroy*. Los Angeles: Cultural Assets Press, 1972.

Gossett, Thomas F. *Race: The History of an Idea in America*. Dallas: Southern Methodist University Press, 1963.

Green, Norman Kidd. *Iron Eye's Family*. Lincoln, Nebr.: Johnson Publishing, 1969.

Haber, Samuel. *Efficiency and Uplift: Scientific Management in the Progressive Era, 1890–1910*. Chicago: University of Chicago Press, 1964.

Hagan, William T. *United States—Comanche Relations: The Reservation Years*. New Haven: Yale University Press, 1976.

Haller, John S. *Outcasts From Evolution: Scientific Attitudes of Racial Inferiority, 1859–1900*. Urbana: University of Illinois Press, 1971.

Halloway, Jean. *Hamlin Garland: A Biography*. Austin: University of Texas Press, 1960.

Handy, Robert T. *A Christian America: Protestant Hopes and Historical Realities*. New York: Oxford University Press, 1971.

Harbaugh, William. *Power and Responsibility: The Life and Times of Theodore Roosevelt*. New York: Farrar, Straus and Cudahy, 1961.

Harris, Marvin. *The Rise of Anthropological Theory*. New York: Crowell, 1968.

Hellman, Geoffrey. *Bankers, Bones and Beetles: The First Century of the American Museum of Natural History*. New York: Natural History Press, 1968.

Helm, June, ed. *Pioneers in American Anthropology*. Seattle: University of Washington Press, 1966.

Henry, Jeanette, ed. *The American Indian Reader: Anthropology*. San Francisco: Indian Historian Press, 1972.

Hertzberg, Hazel. *The Search for an American Indian Identity: Modern Pan-Indian Movements*. Syracuse: Syracuse University Press, 1971.

Higham, John. *Strangers in the Land: Patterns of American Nativism, 1860–1925*. 1955. Reprint. New York: Atheneum, 1970.

Hinsley, Curtis M., Jr. *Savages and Scientists: The Smithsonian Institution and the Development of American Anthropology, 1846–1910*. Washington, D.C.: Smithsonian Institution Press, 1981.

Holt, James. *Congressional Insurgents and the Party System, 1909–1916*. Cambridge, Mass.: Harvard University Press, 1967.

Hunt, Aurora. *Major General James Henry Carlton, 1814–1873; Western Frontier Dragoon*. Glendale, Calif.: Arthur H. Clark, 1958.

Jaher, Frederic Cople. *The Age of Industrialism in America: Essays in Social Structure and Cultural Values*. New York: Free Press, 1968.

Jones, Howard Mumford. *The Age of Energy: Varieties of American Experience, 1865–1915*. New York: Viking, 1971.

Judd, Neil M. *The Bureau of American Ethnology: A Partial History*. Norman: University of Oklahoma Press, 1967.

Katz, Michael B. *Class, Bureaucracy and the Schools: The Illusion of Educational Change in America*. New York: Praeger, 1971.

Keiser, Albert. *The Indian in American Literature*. New York: Oxford University Press, 1933.

Kelly, Lawrence C. *The Navajo Indians and Federal Indian Policy: 1900–1935*. Tucson: University of Arizona Press, 1968.

Kennedy Galleries. *James Earle Fraser: American Sculptor*. New York, 1969.

Kinney, J. P. *A Continent Lost—A Civilization Won*. Baltimore: Johns Hopkins University Press, 1937.

Kirby, Jack Temple. *Darkness at the Dawning: Race and Reform in the Progressive South*. Philadelphia: Lippincott, 1972.

Knight, Oliver. *Following the Indian Wars: The Story of the Newspaper Correspondents among the Indian Campaigns*. Norman: University Oklahoma Press, 1960.

Kvasnicka, Robert M., and Herman J. Viola, eds. *The Commissioners of Indian Affairs, 1824–1977*. Lincoln: University of Nebraska Press, 1979.

Laidlaw, Sally Jean. *Federal Indian Land Policy and the Fort Hall Indians.* Occasional Papers of the Idaho State College Museum, no. 3. Pocatello: Idaho State College, 1960.

Lamar, Howard. *Dakota Territory, 1861–1889: A Study of Frontier Politics.* New Haven: Yale University Press, 1956.

———. *The Far Southwest, 1846–1912; A Territorial History.* New Haven: Yale University Press, 1966.

Lazerson, Marvin. *Origins of the Urban School.* Cambridge, Mass.: Harvard University Press, 1971.

Lazerson, Marvin, and W. Norton Grubb, eds. *American Education and Vocationalism; A Documentary History, 1870–1970.* New York: Teacher's College Press, 1974.

Linderman, Gerald F. *The Mirror of War: American Society and the Spanish American War.* Ann Arbor: University of Michigan Press, 1974.

Link, Arthur S. *Wilson: The New Freedom.* Princeton: Princeton University Press, 1956.

Lubove, Roy. *The Professional Altruist: The Emergence of Social Work as a Career, 1880–1930.* Cambridge, Mass.: Harvard University Press, 1965.

McGee, Emma R. *The Life of W. J. McGee.* Farley, Iowa, 1915.

McNickle, D'Arcy. *Indian Man: The Life of Oliver La Farge.* Bloomington: Indiana University Press, 1971.

McSpadden, J. Walker. *Famous Sculptors of America.* New York: Dodd, Mead, 1924.

Mardock, Robert W. *The Reformers and the American Indian.* Columbia, Mo.: University of Missouri Press, 1971.

Mark, Joan. *Four Anthropologists: An American Science in Its Early Years.* New York: Neale Watson Academic Publications, 1981.

Marty, Martin E. *Righteous Empire: The Protestant Experience in America.* New York: Dial Press, 1970.

May, Glen Anthony. *Social Engineering in the Philippines: The Aims, Execution, and Impact of American Colonial Policy, 1900–1913.* Westport, Conn.: Greenwood Press, 1980.

May, Henry F. *The End of American Innocence.* New York: Knopf, 1959.

Meyer, Roy W. *History of the Santee Sioux: United States Indian Policy on Trial.* Lincoln: University of Nebraska Press, 1968.

Miner, H. Craig. *The Corporation and the Indian: Tribal Sovereignty and*

Industrial Civilization in Indian Territory, 1866–1907. Columbia: University of Missouri Press, 1976.

————. *The St. Louis-San Francisco Transcontinental Railroad: The 35th-Parallel Project, 1853–1890.* Lawrence: University Press of Kansas, 1972.

Mott, Frank Luther. *Golden Multitudes: The Story of Best Sellers in the United States.* New York: Macmillan, 1947.

Nash, Roderick, *Wilderness and the American Mind.* New Haven: Yale University Press, 1967.

Newby, I. A. *Jim Crow's Defense.* Baton Rouge: Louisiana State University Press, 1965.

Nohlen, Claude. *The Negro's Image in the South: The Anatomy of Supremacy.* Lexington: University of Kentucky Press, 1967.

Odell, Ruth. *Helen Hunt Jackson (H. H.).* New York: D. Appleton-Century, 1939.

Olson, James C. *Red Cloud and the Sioux Problem.* Lincoln: University of Nebraska Press, 1965.

Oswalt, Wendell H. *Other Peoples, Other Customs: World Ethnography and Its History.* New York: Holt, Rinehart and Winston, 1972.

Otis, D. S. *The Dawes Act and the Allotment of Indian Lands,* ed. Francis Paul Prucha. Norman: University of Oklahoma Press, 1973.

Parry, Ellwood. *The Image of the Indian and the Black Man in American Art, 1590–1900.* New York: G. Braziller, 1974.

Pearce, Roy Harvey. *Savagism and Civilization: A Study of the Indian and the American Mind.* Rev. ed. Baltimore: Johns Hopkins University Press, 1967.

Pfaller, Louis L. *James McLaughlin: The Man with an Indian Heart.* New York: Vantage Press, 1978.

Price, Monroe E. *Law and the American Indian: Readings, Notes and Cases.* Indianapolis: Bobbs-Merrill, 1973.

Priest, Loring Benson. *Uncle Sam's Stepchildren: The Reformation of United States Indian Policy, 1865–1887.* New Brunswick, N.J.: Rutgers University Press, 1942.

Prucha, Francis Paul. *American Indian Policy in Crisis: Christian Reformers and the Indian, 1865–1900.* Norman: University of Oklahoma Press, 1975.

————. *The Churches and the Indian Schools, 1888–1912.* Lincoln: University of Nebraska Press, 1979.

————, ed. *Americanizing the American Indian: Writings by 'Friends of the Indian,' 1865–1900*. Cambridge, Mass.: Harvard University Press, 1973.

Purcell, Edward A., Jr. *The Crisis of Democratic Theory: Scientific Naturalism and the Problem of Value*. Lexington: University of Kentucky Press, 1973.

Pyle, Joseph Gilpin. *The Life of James J. Hill*. 2 vols. New York: Doubleday Page, 1917.

Rahill, Peter A. *The Catholic Indian Missions and Grant's Peace Policy, 1870–1884*. Washington, D.C.: Catholic University of America Press, 1953.

Resek, Carl. *Lewis Henry Morgan: American Scholar*. Chicago: University of Chicago Press, 1960.

Rister, Carl Coke. *Land Hunger: David L. Payne and the Oklahoma Boomers*. Norman: University of Oklahoma Press, 1942.

Robbins, Roy M. *Our Landed Heritage: The Public Domain, 1776–1936*. Princeton: Princeton University Press, 1942.

Ross, Dorothy. *G. Stanley Hall: The Psychologist as Prophet*. Chicago: University of Chicago Press, 1972.

Schmeckebier, Laurence F. *The Office of Indian Affairs: Its History, Activities and Organization*. Baltimore: Johns Hopkins University Press, 1927.

Schmitt, Peter J. *Back to Nature: The Arcadian Myth in Urban America*. New York: Oxford University Press, 1969.

Service, Elman R. *Cultural Evolutionism: Theory in Practice*. New York: Holt, Rinehart and Winston, 1971.

Smith, Henry Nash. *Virgin Land: The American West as Symbol and Myth*. Cambridge, Mass.: Harvard University Press, 1950.

Smith, Jane, and Robert Kvasnicka, eds. *Indian-White Relations: A Persistent Paradox*. Washington: Howard University Press, 1976.

Solomon, Barbara Miller. *Ancestors and Immigrants: A Changing New England Tradition*. Cambridge: Harvard University Press, 1956.

Spivey, Donald. *Schooling for the New Slavery: Black Industrial Education, 1868–1915*. Westport, Conn.: Greenwood Press, 1978.

Sprague, Marshall. *Massacre: The Tragedy at White River*. Boston: Little Brown, 1957.

Stegner, Wallace. *Beyond the Hundredth Meridian: John Wesley Powell and the Second Opening of the West*. Boston: Houghton Mifflin, 1954.

Stern, Bernard J. *Lewis Henry Morgan: Social Evolutionist.* Chicago: University of Chicago Press, 1931.

Stewart, Omer C. *Ethnohistorical Bibliography of the Ute Indians of Colorado.* University of Colorado Studies Series in Anthropology, no. 18. Boulder: University of Colorado Press, 1971.

Stocking, George W., Jr. *Race, Culture and Evolution: Essays in the History of Anthropology.* New York: Free Press, 1968.

————, ed. *The Shaping of American Anthropology.* New York: Basic Books, 1974.

Stuart, Paul. *The Indian Office: Growth and Development of an American Institution, 1865–1900.* Ann Arbor: University of Michigan Research Press, 1979.

Sutton, Imre. *Indian Land Tenure: Bibliographical Essays and a Guide to the Literature.* New York: Clearwater Publishing, 1975.

Szasz, Margaret. *Education and the American Indian: The Road to Self-Determination, 1928–1973.* Albuquerque: University of New Mexico Press, 1974.

Textor, Lucy E., M. A. *Official Relations between the United States and the Sioux Indians.* Palo Alto: The University, 1896.

Thoreson, Timothy H., ed. *Toward a Science of Man: Essays in the History of Anthropology.* The Hague: Beresford Book Service, 1975.

Trefethen, James B. *Crusade for Wildlife: Highlights in Conservation Progress.* Harrisburg, Pa.: Stackpole, 1961.

Turner, Katharine C. *Red Man Calling on the Great White Father.* Norman: University of Oklahoma Press, 1951.

Washburn, Wilcomb E. *The Assault on Indian Tribalism: The General Allotment Law (Dawes Act) of 1887.* Philadelphia: Lippincott, 1975.

————. *Red Man's Land/White Man's Law: A Study of the Past and Present Status of the American Indian.* New York: Scribner, 1971.

Weigley, Russell F. *The American Way of War: A History of United States Military Strategy and Policy.* New York: Macmillan, 1973.

Weinstein, James. *The Corporate Ideal in the Liberal State, 1900–1918.* Boston: Beacon Press, 1968.

Welter, Rush. *Popular Education and Democratic Thought in America.* New York: Columbia University Press, 1962.

Weston, Rubin. *Racism in U.S. Imperialism: The Influence of Racial As-*

sumptions on American Foreign Policy, 1893–1946. Columbia: University of South Carolina Press, 1972.

White, G. Edward. *The Eastern Establishment and the Western Experience: The West of Frederic Remington, Theodore Roosevelt and Owen Wister.* New Haven: Yale University Press, 1968.

Wilson, Dorothy Clarke. *Bright Eyes: The Story of Susette La Flesche, an Omaha Indian.* New York: McGraw-Hill, 1974.

Wynes, Charles, ed. *The Negro in the South since 1865.* New York: Harper and Row, 1965.

Zolla, Elemire. *The Writer and the Shaman.* New York: Harcourt Brace Jovanovich, 1973.

6. *Secondary Sources—Articles*

Abrams, Richard M. "Woodrow Wilson and the Southern Congressmen, 1913–1916." *Journal of Southern History* 22 (November 1956): 417–37.

Ahern, Wilbert H. "Assimilationist Racism: The Case of the Friends of the Indian." *Journal of Ethnic Studies* 4 (Summer 1976): 23–34.

Allen, Howard W., Aage R. Clausen, and Jerome M. Clubb. "Political Reform and Negro Rights in the Senate, 1909–1915." *Journal of Southern History* 37 (May 1971): 191–212.

Beatty, Willard W. "The Federal Government and the Education of Indians and Eskimos." *Journal of Negro History* 7 (July 1938): 267–72.

Berens, John F. "Old Campaigners, New Realities: Indian Policy Reform in the Progressive Era, 1900–1912." *Mid-America* 59 (January 1977): 51–64.

Berthrong, Donald J. "Cattlemen on the Cheyenne-Arapaho Reservation." *Arizona and the West* 13 (Spring 1971): 5–32.

———. "White Neighbors Come among the Southern Cheyenne and Arapaho." *Kansas Quarterly* 3 (Fall 1971): 105–15.

Bloom, Paul. "Indian Paramount Rights to Water Use." *Rocky Mountain Mineral Law Review Proceedings* 16 (1969): 669–93.

Blumenthal, Henry. "Woodrow Wilson and the Race Question." *Journal of Negro History* 48 (January 1963): 1–21.

Chaput, Donald. "Generals, Indian Agents, Politicians: The Doolittle Survey of 1865." *Western Historical Quarterly* 3 (July 1972): 269–83.

Clark, J. Stanley. "Ponca Publicity." *Mississippi Valley Historical Review* 29 (March 1943): 495–516.

Clubb, Jerome M., and Howard W. Allen. "Party Loyalty in the Progressive Years: The Senate, 1909–1915." *Journal of Politics* 29 (August 1967): 567–84.

Coats, A. W. "American Scholarship Comes of Age: The Louisiana Purchase Exposition, 1904." *Journal of the History of Ideas* 22 (July–September 1961): 404–17.

Cohen, Sol. "The Industrial Education Movement, 1906–1917." *American Quarterly* 20 (Spring 1968): 95–110.

Critchlow, Donald T. "Lewis Meriam, Expertise, and Indian Reform." *Historian* 43 (May 1981): 325–44.

Cronin, Morton. "Currier and Ives: A Content Analysis." *American Quarterly* 4 (Winter 1952): 317–30.

Crow, Charles. "Indians and Blacks in White America." In *Four Centuries of Southern Indians*. Ed. Charles M. Hudson. Athens: University of Georgia Press, 1975.

Darnell, Regna. "The Professionalization of American Anthropology." *Social Science Information* 10 (April 1971): 83–103.

Davison, Kenneth E. "President Hayes and the Reform of American Indian Policy." *Ohio History* 82 (Summer–Autumn 1973): 205–14.

Davison, Stanley R. "Hopes and Fancies of the Early Reclamationists." In *The Montana Past: An Anthology*. Ed. Michael P. Malone and Richard B. Roeder. Missoula: University of Montana Press, 1969.

Deutsch, Herman J. "Indian and White in the Inland Empire: The Contest for the Land, 1880–1912." *Pacific Northwest Quarterly* 47 (April 1956): 44–51.

Dexter, Ralph W. "Putnam's Problems in Popularizing Anthropology." *American Scientist* 54 (September 1966): 315–32.

Ellis, Richard. "The Humanitarian Generals." *Western Historical Quarterly* 3 (April 1972): 169–79.

Englund, Donald R. "Indians, Intruders, and the Federal Government." *Journal of the West* 13 (April 1974): 97–105.

Ewing, Douglas. "The North American Indian in Forty Volumes." *Art in America* 60 (July 1972): 84–88.

Fear, Jacqueline M. "English versus the Vernacular: The Suppression of Indian Languages in Reservation Schools at the End of the Nineteenth Century." *Revue Francaise d'Etudes Americaines* 5 (April 1980): 13–24.

Fritz, Henry E. "George Manypenny and Our Indian Wards." *Kansas Quarterly* 3 (Fall 1971): 100–105.

———. "The Making of Grant's Peace Policy." *Chronicles of Oklahoma* 37 (Winter 1959–1960): 411–32.

Gates, Paul W. "The Homestead Law in an Incongruous Land System." *American Historical Review* 41 (July 1936): 652–81.

Haan, Richard L. "Another Example of Stereotypes on the Early American Frontier: The Imperialist Historians and the American Indian." *Ethnohistory* 20 (Spring 1973): 143–52.

Hagan, William T. "Civil Service Commissioner Theodore Roosevelt and the Indian Rights Association." *Pacific Historical Review* 44 (May 1975): 187–201.

———. "Private Property, the Indian's Door to Civilization." *Ethnohistory* 3 (Spring 1956): 125–37.

Haller, John S. "Race and the Concept of Progress in Nineteenth-Century American Ethnology." *American Anthropologist* 73 (June 1971): 710–24.

Hallowell, Irving A. "The Beginnings of Anthropology in America." In *Selected Papers from the American Anthropologist*. Ed. Frederica De Laguna. Evanston, Ill.: Row Peterson, 1960.

———. "The Backwash of the Frontier: The Impact of the Indian on American Culture." In *The Frontier Perspective*. Ed. Walker D. Wyman and Clifton B. Kroeber. Madison: University of Wisconsin Press, 1957.

Haney, James E. "Blacks and the Republican Nomination of 1908." *Ohio History* 84 (Autumn 1975): 207–21.

Hayes, James R. "Sociology and Racism: An Analysis of the First Era of American Sociology." *Phylon* 34 (December 1973): 330–41.

Hayter, Earl W. "The Ponca Removal." *North Dakota Historical Review* 6 (July 1932): 262–75.

Holford, David M. "The Subversion of the Indian Land Allotment System, 1887–1934." *Indian Historian* 8 (Spring 1975): 11–21.

Horsman, Reginald. "Scientific Racism and the American Indian in the Mid-Nineteenth Century." *American Quarterly* 27 (May 1975): 152–68.

Hough, Walter. "Alice Cunningham Fletcher." *American Anthropologist* 25 (April–June 1923): 254–58.

Johnson, Ronald M. "Schooling and the Savage: Andrew S. Draper and Indian Education." *Phylon* 35 (March 1974): 74–82.

Kaestle, Carl F. "Social Reform in the Urban School." *History of Education Quarterly* 12 (Summer 1972): 211–28.

Keller, Robert H., Jr. "American Indian Education: An Historical Context." *Journal of the West* 13 (April 1974): 75–82.

King, James T. "A Better Way: General George Crook and the Ponca Indians." *Nebraska History* 50 (Fall 1969): 239–57.

———. "General Crook: Indian Fighter and Humanitarian." *Arizona and the West* 9 (Winter 1967): 333–48.

Knepler, Abraham E. "Education in the Cherokee Nation." *Chronicles of Oklahoma* 21 (December 1943): 378–401.

La Flesche, Francis. "Alice C. Fletcher." *Science*, August 17, 1923, p. 115.

Lowie, Robert H. "Evolution in Cultural Anthropology: A Reply to Leslie White." *American Anthropologist* 48 (January–March 1946): 223–33.

Lurie, Nancy Oestreich. "The Lady from Boston and the Omaha Indians." *American West* 3 (Fall 1966): 31–33, 80–85.

Mardock, Robert W. "Irresolvable Enigma? Strange Concepts of the American Indian Since the Civil War." *Montana* 7 (January 1957): 36–47.

Meyer, Roy W. "Hamlin Garland and the American Indian." *Western American Literature* 2 (Summer 1967): 109–25.

Mintz, Sidney. *Afro-American Anthropology*. Foreword. Ed. Norman E. Whitten, Jr., and John F. Szwed. New York: Free Press, 1970.

Murphee, Idus L. "The Evolutionary Anthropologist: The Progress of Mankind. The Concepts of Progress and Culture in the Thought of John Lubbock, Edward B. Bylor and Lewis Henry Morgan." *Proceedings of the American Philosophical Society* 105 (June 1961): 265–300.

Nash, Roderick. "The American Cult of the Primitive," *American Quarterly* 18 (Fall 1966): 517–39.

Nichols, Roger L. "Printer's Ink and Red Skins: Western Newspapermen and the Indians." *Kansas Quarterly* 3 (Fall 1971): 82–88.

Pandey, Triloki Nath. "Anthropologists at Zuni." *Proceedings of the American Philosophical Society* 116 (August 1972): 321–28.

Parman, Donald L. "The 'Big Stick' in Indian Affairs: The Bai-a-lil-le Incident in 1909." *Arizona and the West* 20 (Winter 1978): 343–60.

Peterson, Robert L. "The Completion of the Northern Pacific Railroad System in Montana." In *The Montana Past: An Anthology*. Ed. Michael P. Malone and Richard B. Roeder. Missoula, Mont.: 1969.

Powers, Ramon. "Why the Northern Cheyenne Left Indian Territory in

1878: A Cultural Analysis." *Kansas Quarterly* 3 (Fall 1971): 72–81.

Prucha, Francis Paul. "Indian Policy Reform and American Protestantism." In *People of the Plains and of the Mountains*. Ed. Ray Billington. Westport, Conn.: Greenwood Press, 1973.

Quandt, Jean B. "Religion and Social Thought: The Secularization of Post-Millenialism." *American Quarterly* 25 (October 1973): 390–409.

Radin, Paul. "The Mind of Primitive Man." *New Republic* 98 (April 19, 1939): 300–303.

Roberts, Gary L. "Conditions of the Tribes, 1865: The Report of General McCook." *Montana*, December 1974, pp. 14–25.

Rogin, Michael Paul. "Liberal Society and the Indian Question." *Politics and Society* 1 (May 1971): 269–312.

Rubenstein, Bruce. "To Destroy a Culture: Indian Education in Michigan, 1855–1900." *Michigan History* 60 (Summer 1976): 137–60.

Schiener, Seth N. "President Theodore Roosevelt and the Negro, 1901–1908." *Journal of Negro History* 47 (July 1962): 169–82.

Shanas, Ethel. "The American Journal of Sociology through Fifty Years." *American Journal of Sociology* 50 (March 1950): 522–33.

Sievers, Harry J. "The Catholic Indian School Issue and the Presidential Election of 1892." *Catholic Historical Review* 38 (July 1952): 129–55.

Taber, Ronald W. "Sacagawea and the Suffragettes: An Interpretation of a Myth." *Pacific Northwest Quarterly* 28 (January 1967): 7–13.

Unrau, William. "The Civilian as Indian Agent: Villain or Victim?" *Western Historical Quarterly* 3 (October 1972): 405–20.

Utley, Robert. "The Celebrated Peace Policy of General Grant." *North Dakota History* 20 (July 1953): 121–42.

Voget, Fred W. "Progress, Science, History and Evolution in Eighteenth- and Nineteenth-Century Evolution." *Journal of the History of the Behavioral Sciences* 3 (April 1967): 132–55.

Waltmann, Henry G. "Circumstantial Reformer: President Grant and the Indian Problem." *Arizona and the West* 13 (Winter 1971): 323–42.

White, Leslie A. "Evolution in Cultural Anthropology: A Rejoinder." *American Anthropologist* 49 (July–September 1947): 400–411.

Willis, William S., Jr. "Anthropology and Negroes on the Southern Colonial Frontier." In *The Black Experience in America: Selected Essays*. Ed. James C. Curtis and Lewis L. Gould. Austin: University of Texas Press, 1970.

———. "Divide and Rule: Red, White and Black in the Southeast." *Journal of Negro History* 48 (July 1963): 157–76.

Williams, Walter L. "United States Indian Policy and the Debate over Philippine Annexation: Implications for the Origins of American Imperialism." *Journal of American History* 66 (March 1980): 810–31.

Wiebe, Robert H. "The Social Functions of Public Education." *American Quarterly* 21 (Summer 1969): 147–64.

Wish, Harvey. "Negro Education and the Progressive Movement." *Journal of Negro History* 49 (July 1964): 184–201.

7. Dissertations and Theses

Bannon, Helen Marie. "Reformers and the Indian Problem, 1878–1887 and 1922–1934." Ph.D. dissertation, Syracuse University, 1976.

Bieder, Robert E. "The American Indian and the Development of Anthropological Thought in America, 1780–1851." Ph.D. dissertation, University of Minnesota, 1972.

Burgess, Larry E. "The Lake Mohonk Conference on the Indian, 1883–1916." Ph.D. dissertation, Claremont Graduate School, 1972.

Cauthers, Janet Helen. "The North American Indian as Portrayed by American and Canadian Historians, 1830–1930." Ph.D. dissertation, University of Washington, 1974.

Clark, Ira G. "The Railroads and the Tribal Lands: Indian Territory, 1838–1890." Ph.D. dissertation, University of California, Berkeley, 1947.

Coen, Rena Neumann. "The Indian as the Noble Savage in Nineteenth-Century American Art." Ph.D. dissertation, University of Minnesota, 1969.

Darnell, Regna. "Daniel Garrison Brinton: An Intellectual Biography." M.A. thesis, University of Pennsylvania, 1967.

———. "The Development of American Anthropology, 1879–1920: From the Bureau of American Ethnology to Franz Boas." Ph.D. dissertation, University of Pennsylvania, 1969.

Fear, Jacqueline M. "American Indian Education: The Reservation Schools, 1870–1900." Ph.D. dissertation, University College, London, 1978.

Gilcreast, Everett Arthur. "Richard Henry Pratt and the American Indian Policy, 1877–1906." Ph.D. dissertation, Yale University, 1967.

Hazen, Don C. "The Awakening of Puno: Government Policy and the Indian Problem in Southern Peru, 1900–1955." Ph.D. dissertation, Yale University, 1974.

Hinsley, Curtis M., Jr. "The Development of a Profession: Anthropology in Washington, D.C., 1846–1903." Ph.D. dissertation, University of Wisconsin, 1976.

Keller, Robert H. "Protestant Churches and Grant's Peace Policy: A Study in Church State Relations." Ph.D. dissertation, University of Chicago Divinity School, 1967.

Layman, Martha E. "A History of the Board of Indian Commissioners and Its Relation to the Administration of Indian Affairs, 1869–1900." M.A. thesis, American University, 1951.

Nicklason, Fred H. "The Early Career of Henry L. Dawes." Ph.D. dissertation, Yale University, 1967.

Preston, Frederick William. "Red, White, Black and Blue: The Concept of Race in American Sociology: An Exploration in the Sociology of Knowledge." Ph.D. dissertation, Ohio State University, 1970.

Rieger, John F. "George Bird Grinnell and the Development of American Conservation, 1870–1901." Ph.D. dissertation, Northwestern University, 1970.

Stocking, George W., Jr. "American Social Scientists and Race Theory, 1890–1915." Ph.D. dissertation, University of Pennsylvania, 1960.

Trosper, Ronald L. "The Economic Impact of the Allotment Policy on the Flathead Indian Reservation." Ph.D. dissertation, Harvard University, 1975.

Walker-McNeil, Pearl Lee. "The Carlisle Indian School: A Study of Acculturation." Ph.D. dissertation, American University, 1979.

Waltmann, Henry George. "The Interior Department, War Department and Indian Policy, 1865–1887." Ph.D. dissertation, University of Nebraska, 1962.

Winer, Lilian Rosenbaum. "Federal Legislation on Indian Education, 1819–1970." Ph.D. dissertation, University of Maryland, 1972.

Wolfson, Harry. "The History of Indian Education under the Federal Government, 1871–1930." M.A. thesis, City University of New York, 1932.

Index

Abbott, Frederick, 179–80
Abbott, Lyman, 71, 73, 192, 217
Adams, Henry, 17, 90
Agency schools. *See* Schools
Agrarian reform and destruction of
  reservations, 49
Allen, John B., 149
Allison, William Boyd, 36
Allotment: acceleration in, 163; administration of, 80; bills, 70, 71,
  178; Burke Act, 165; and citizenship, 73–75, 211; Coke-Dawes
  proposal, 72, 73; congressional
  power over, 164; consent by
  tribes, 246; Curtis Act, 154;
  Dawes's views on, 71–72; debate
  over, 165; and education, 76–77;
  federal authority over uses,
  214–15, 222, 229; Fletcher's
  views on, 25–26; Garland's view
  of, 98; General Allotment Act,
  70, 77–78; guidelines for, 78–79;

and *Heff* decision, 220; inalienability of, 72; in Indian Territory, 153; under William Jones,
  152ff; leasing of, 79, 158–59,
  170–71, Lummis's and Grinnell's
  views on, 100–101; McKenzie's
  efforts, 133; of Omaha lands,
  26–27; pace of, 78, 284; presidential discretion over, 72–73;
  public debate over, 71; of Puyallup tribe, 148; sale of, 166, 251;
  and social scientists, 145; timetable for, 154
American Anthropological Association: and Boas, 141; founding of,
  23; McGee's address to, 118–19;
  mentioned, 139
American Association for the Advancement of Science, 119, 131
American Bar Association, 212;
  Committee on Indian Legislation,
  225

American Folklore Society, 139
American Missionary Association, 55
American Social Science Association, 197
American World's Fairs and public image, 85–86
Annuity payments, limitations on, 246
Anthropological Society of Washington, 16, 23, 130
Anthropologists: and assimilation campaign, 143–45; Boas's training of, 134; and Dawes, 33; and Indians, 16–17; and policy, 28–29; and race, 116–17
Anthropology: Boas's contributions to, 140–41; domination of by Powell and Bureau of Ethnology, 23; maturation as discipline, 16, 23; Morgan's influence on, 20; research, 22; and racial hierarchy, 142; and scientific method, 135; Wissler's influence on, 130
Anthropometry, 129
Apache reservation, mineral leases, 186
Arapaho: allotment, 153; irrigation projects, 169; property rights, 212; and public schools, 207
Armstrong, Samuel Chapman, 55–57
Army. *See* U.S. Army officers
Ashurst, Henry, 109, 181, 185–86
Assimilation: appeal of, 33, 39; changing meaning of, 173, 241; changes affecting, 115ff; cultural anthropologists' influence on, 143–44; education the basis for, 63; hostility to, 111–12; incongruity of in 1880s and '90s, 33; national values expressed in, 15, 241ff; phases of, x–xi; politi-

cal support for, 29; Powell's view of as goal of legislation, 24; racial formalists' view of, 129; as regional concern, 104; Roosevelt's views on, 105–6; scientific support for doubts about, 117; Sells's view of, 210
Atlanta Exposition, 86
Atkins, John, 61, 78–79, 167

Bai-a-lil-le case, 226–28
Baird, Spencer, 55
Baker, Ray Stannard, 95
Baldwin, James, 103
Bancroft, Hubert Howe, 88
Bandelier, Adolph, 21, 263
Bannock-Shoshone Reserve land cessions, 44, 46
Belford, James, 37
Beneficial use doctrine, 170–72
Big Boy, 215
Blackfoot Indians: irrigation projects, 170; land cessions, 44, 50–51; leases, 171
Black Hawk, 7, 102
Blackmar, Frank W., 134
Blair, Henry, 69
Blair bill, 69
Boarding schools: appropriations for, 248; deemphasis of, 206; elimination of, 202–3; expansion in West, 57; off-reservation, 53; opposition to, 61–62; popularity of, 60; proposed on reservations, 63; and Teller, 58; for Utes, 246. *See also* Education; Schools
Board of Indian Commissioners, 246
Boas, Franz: attack on racial formalism, 142; contributions to anthropology, 140–41; controversy surrounding, 141; culture concept, 117, 134ff; defense of McGee, 121; *The Mind of Primi-*